Logic for Illogical People

Introduction to

Sentential and Predicate Logic

By Don Adams

Copyright © 2019 Don Adams

All rights reserved.

ISBN: 9781521138403

CONTENTS

About the Author — i

Preface — ii

Read This Introduction — iv

How to Get an 'A' — vi

Chapter 1: The Basic Idea — Pg 8

Chapter 2: Translation — Pg 38

Chapter 3: Symbols — Pg 58

Chapter 4: Truth Tables — Pg 72

Chapter 5: Truth Tables (continued) — Pg 87

Chapter 6: Simple Derivations — Pg 100

Chapter 7: Derivations (continued) — Pg 120

Chapter 8: Predicates and Quantifiers — Pg 142

Chapter 9: Derivations with Quantifiers — Pg 162

What's Next? — Pg 175

Solutions to odd numbered problems — Pg 176

ABOUT THE AUTHOR

Don Adams received his Bachelor of Arts degree from Reed College with a major in philosophy. From there he went to Cornell University where he studied with Terence Irwin, Gail Fine and Norman Kretzmann. His Ph.D. dissertation was a comparative study of love and friendship in the moral theories of Socrates, Plato, Aristotle and Aquinas. He has taught logic and the history of European philosophy, especially ancient Greek philosophy, at about half a dozen colleges and universities across the USA. He is now Professor of Philosophy at Central Connecticut State University

PREFACE

In every logic course I have ever taught there have always been two kinds of students: (a) those who pick up logic very quickly and easily, and (b) the rest of us. There are many excellent logic textbooks for the first group, but I have yet to find a good logic textbook for the second group. This book is intended to fill the void.

The problem is that illogical people don't think badly, we just think differently. Logic has the beauty of simplicity, but that is the main reason why illogical people have trouble with it: life isn't simple. People who think logically are able to forget about the complexities of the real world, and focus in on the pristine simplicity of logic. People who think illogically are always attuned to complexity, to different ways of seeing things, and to how things actually work in real life, in their actual experience of this complex and messy world.

The trick, then, in teaching logic to illogical people, is to use our strengths as assets, rather than as obstacles. The easiest way to do this is to use examples where practical knowledge helps, rather than hinders understanding of logical rules. Logic textbooks all too often try to wean students away from relying on practical knowledge by using examples that don't make sense in real life. In this book I try to stick to "if, then" claims that are either simple definitions (e.g. "if Joe is a bachelor, then Joe is unmarried") or obvious causal chains (e.g. "if Joe drank the poison, then Joe died").

I should add at this point that writing style is also very important. Every other logic textbook I have used is written either in a terse, syntactically complex but logical style; or else is written informally, but rambles on and on. The former style is impenetrable and unhelpful to most students; the latter is readable but also unhelpful because it is hard for many students to figure out just what they are supposed to be focusing on. I have tried to keep my writing simple and to the point.

A simple writing style also requires avoiding the use of symbols whenever possible. This may sound odd in a book on symbolic logic, but it is extremely important. Students have enough difficulty dealing with the basic symbols; when they see the additional exotic symbols textbooks resort to in order to give general definitions (they call it a "metalanguage"), many feel that the mountain is just too steep for them to climb, and that they'll never be able to learn to think logically. These extra obstacles are unnecessary; in this book I give definitions in familiar English as often as possible.

Another way logic textbooks baffle and alienate students is to introduce complications and tricky problems too soon. We logic teachers have a strong tendency to teach to the best students in the class, and so we continually want to challenge the students who already think logically. Unfortunately this not only leaves many students out of the fun, but it often makes them feel frustrated. Just when they thought they were getting the hang of it, suddenly they are confronted with problems that seem impossible. A textbook should challenge students, but it should not make them feel like they can't ever learn the material.

This is a worry for all teachers: if you teach to the best students, you'll lose the rest of the class; and if you teach to the slower students, you'll bore the best students. Fortunately in logic there is a way out of this dilemma: the problem sets need to be graduated. Start with simple problems and work up to more difficult problems. All textbooks do this, of course, but they don't do it properly. Textbooks shy away from including very, very simple problems. I guess they feel like they are insulting the intelligence of logic students when they include very, very simple problems. But very, very simple problems are very, very helpful for three reasons.

First of all, they are important diagnostic tools for the instructor. When a student has read through the chapter, and has heard the teacher explain the material, the student should be able to do very simple problems. If a student is unable to do a very simple problem, then the teacher knows that the student has missed something fundamental, and needs to go back over the basics with that student. This helps to separate those students who don't get the basics from students who do get the basics but need help applying those basics to more complicated problems.

Second, illogical students are often a bit timid in the face of symbolic logic. Even if they understand the material and can do the problems, they sometimes freeze up when they are confronted with logic problems. Most students need confidence-builders; they need problems they can do, and do easily. Success is what education is all about. Once they see that they actually can do the problems, once they see that they do in fact understand the material, they are encouraged and can then move on to tackle the more complex problems without being held back by their own fears.

Third, the main goal of a logic course is to develop in students the ability to think logically. In order to do that, students need to get to the point where they can do logic problems "in their heads" without having to work them out slowly on paper. They need to get to the point where they can "just see" the logical solution to problems. In order to help this process along, it is important to all the students to be confronted with problems that, sooner or later, they can do in their heads.

PREFACE

There is one more important way in which this book steers a course between opposing dangers. On the one hand, logic textbooks that are written logically are all too often structured in such a way as to develop a complete logical system. Historically this is a remnant of when the so-called "logical positivists" wanted to perform a complete logical reconstruction of philosophy and natural science. While I think it is essential that philosophers know a complete system of symbolic logic, I also think that there is a place for a working knowledge of symbolic logic that is less than formally complete.

On the other hand, many logic textbooks avoid the detail and complexity of developing a complete system of logic by including too many different areas of logic. Many textbooks end up being a sort of grab bag of logical tools, both formal and informal. The sheer amount of material can seem to many students to be a constant reminder of how little they know, and this in turn is a constant discouragement. Students need to have a sense that the material is manageable. In addition, a narrow focus on symbolic logic is very helpful since, not only is symbolic logic the very core of all logical thought, but once students learn the basics of symbolic logic, they show remarkable facility for learning other logical skills. In steering a course between these two dangers, I have tried to select just those skills in symbolic logic that are essential and very useful.

I thank the following students, in alphabetical order, for their help: Ajay Adur, Brian Cassidy, Ed Chabot, Christopher Coe, Heather Eck, Ronald Gambardella, Lucy Inghilterra, Amy Lavorgna, Marco Marchesano, Heather Marr, Raymond Morse, Paul Rottenberg, Laura Sanchez, Vicki Sylvestro, and Byron Syphrett. Very special thanks go to the following students, whose hard work inspired me to begin work on this book: Niki Podaras, Eva Tarnawski, and Robin Kane. Finally, I would like to thank my TA John Soboslai for his indispensable help and support.

DON ADAMS

READ THIS INTRODUCTION

Every kind of muscle is strengthened by exercise. The brain is a kind of muscle. Therefore, the brain is strengthened by exercise.

That simple argument is the basic reason why I decided to write this book. Logic is to the brain what working out in a gym is to the body. Why do football players work on their biceps in isolation by doing curls in a weight room? Why do runners work on their quadriceps in isolation by doing leg presses in a weight room? If you want to be a good football player, shouldn't you just play football? If you want to be a good runner, shouldn't you just run?

Football players should play football, and runners should run, but doing those and other activities well requires a solid foundation of physical preparedness. It is too easy to let the big muscles compensate for the weak muscles, and so in order to get a full and well-rounded work out, you need to isolate the weak muscles and exercise them one at a time. That way, when you are actually playing football or competing in a track meet, you are far more prepared to do well, and to avoid injury.

The same is true with your brain muscle. It is too easy to rely on your mental strengths, and allow them to compensate for your weaker skills. Many people are avid readers, and are excellent at following complex plots involving many characters with complicated motivations. Other people have strong mechanical skills and can readily understand how things work. Other people have a very high "emotional intelligence" and are good at understanding how people are feeling. It is often easy to rely upon your intellectual strengths and fail to develop the abilities that are weaker. The ability to think logically is another intellectual skill, and sadly it is one that too many people fail to develop. If you want well-rounded mental development, you need to work on those skills that don't come naturally to you, and for a lot of people, that means working some logic problems.

It is by now a cliché criticism used by school students against learning certain subjects to ask, "When am I going to need to know this in real life?" Well, when is a football player every going to need to be able to do curls in a football game? When is a runner going to need to be able to do leg presses during a track meet? They don't do those exercises because they will be called upon to do them in their sport, or in their life. They do those exercises in order to prepare their bodies to perform their best.

The same is true with the brain. When in life are you going to need to know logic? There will probably never come a time when your boss requires that you work a problem in symbolic logic. You need to learn logic not because you will be called upon to work logic problems in your career or in your life, but because you need your brain to perform its best. Thinking logically is not the only way to think, but it is one important way to think, and mentally you can't perform your best unless you develop your brain-power fully. Learning logic is an ideal way to exercise your intellectual muscles.

But even more than that, how do you know that you will never be called upon to use symbolic logic in your life? Knowing logic is like knowing CPR: you may never actually have to use it, but then again you might. It is in fact possible that in a job interview you will be asked to solve an intellectual puzzle, as a test of your ability to think logically. You may be asked to defend a proposal that you make, and if you don't know how to structure an argument logically, you won't convince reasonable people that you are right; in fact, your failure to argue logically might convince them that you don't really know what you are talking about.

I had a student who was in a Shakespeare class the same semester he was in my logic class. He had to write six papers in the Shakespeare class, and on the first five of them he received a score of 5.5 out of 6 possible points. He couldn't break that barrier and get the full 6 points … until he used logic. His final paper was on Richard III and he decided to use a sub-derivation (Chapter 7). He formulated his argument logically, and he so impressed the instructor that he finally got a perfect score. The ability to reason logically can help you out in unexpected ways.

Finally, and to my mind most importantly, a developed ability to think logically is especially important in a democratic country. In a country that is ruled by an elite class, the rest of the people don't have to think because the rulers do all the thinking for them. But a democracy is only as intelligent as its citizens. If we the people are unable to think through problems logically, we cannot expect our government to make logical decisions.

Note on the Title of this book: When I first began developing this book I asked my students what I should call it, and they came up with the main title. I resisted, saying, "But you people aren't illogical." But they liked it, so the title stayed.

The rest of the title is there so that you can tell other logic teachers what you learned. "Sentential logic" is simply the logic of sentences, or logic applied to sentences. "Joe is a bachelor. If Joe is a bachelor, then Joe is unmarried. Therefore, Joe is unmarried." Those are complete sentences and together they form a logically valid argument. "Predicate logic" breaks sentences up into subjects and predicates (yes, just like in your English grammar classes). In

INTRODUCTION

the sentence, "Joe is a bachelor," predicate logic will break that up into two parts: Joe (the subject), and being a bachelor (the predicate). It turns out that the logical study of predicates is really quite fascinating. Predicate logic includes "quantifiers" (and so it includes "quantificational logic"). Quantifiers quantify, i.e. they answer the question "How many?" If someone in the room is a bachelor, that's a quantity. If we have collected a bunch of bachelors in a room to conduct a psychological study, then we might say that "everybody in the room is a bachelor." "All" and "some" are quantities, and so they are part of "quantificational logic."

Next, many books that cover sentential (or "propositional") logic say that they include "Sentential Calculus." It's the same with predicate logic (i.e. "Predicate Calculus"). I don't use the word "calculus" because usually when people include it, they mean that they are developing a complete axiomatic system of logic, and that's not what I'm doing in this book. In my experience, the development of logic as an axiomatic system is a more advanced exercise that should be reserved for an upper level mathematics or logic course. The details involved in completing a system of logic turn out to be too distracting to introductory students, and they just make things confusing. This is one of the many places where the difference between (a) those who pick up logic very quickly and easily, and (b) the rest of us, is extremely important. Treating logic as a "calculus," as a complete axiomatic system, makes things very clear for group (a), but group (b) just doesn't see the point of all the extra symbols and complications. Both sentential and predicate logic is really helpful to everybody – especially in a democracy – and so I think group (b) deserves a book that focuses in on the useful tools logic has to offer, without the all the technical bells and whistles.

Finally, this book covers only "first order" sentential and predicate logic: I cover the logic of sentences and the logic of predicates. A "second order" logic would cover the logic of the logic of sentences, and the logic of the logic of predicates. Second order logic is for logicians who want to study logic itself. It's really interesting, but it's more advanced. Oh, and yes, you can study "third order" logic, or "fourth order" logic, as far as you want to go. Knock yourself out.

DON ADAMS

HOW TO GET AN 'A'

In 1953 an expedition of over 400 people set off to climb to the top of Mt. Everest. They set up their base camp in March and waited patiently for two months, and when conditions would allow it, Edmund Percival Hillary and his sherpa Tenzing Norgay made it to the peak. They didn't try to do the entire climb all at once – if they'd done that, they would certainly have died in one way or another, e.g. freezing, oxygen deprivation, falling. Instead, they patiently took things one careful step at a time and in the end they managed to do something extraordinary.

Learning logic should be similar: trying to cram everything into your head at the last minute might work well for you in some classes, but odds are that it won't work in logic, you'll fail in one way or another. You need to take things one step at a time, and in the end you will accomplish something wonderful: you will be a smarter and more knowledgeable person (which, incidentally, also means that you'll probably have a good grade on your college transcript, and that you'll impress people in job interviews with the clarity of your thinking and your ability to express yourself logically).

When I talk with students about how they are doing in the class, they always say they are studying very hard. Students who get D's and F's as well as students who get B's and A's all say that they are studying very hard. The main difference is that what the A and B students mean by "studying very hard" is not the same as what the D and F students mean. I've noticed what I call three different levels of studying that are characteristic of students who achieve different levels of understanding.

How to earn a D or an F in logic. Most students who do poorly study only the night before an exam. Short-term memory is unreliable and it is not the same thing as actually learning something. I once heard that when he was about 10 years old, Albert Einstein was given a geometry textbook. Allegedly he read it in a couple of days and said, "That makes sense, what's next?" If you are genius, you can study like that. If you are not a genius, you need to try a different strategy.

Another way to earn a D or an F is to come to class without having read the material that will be covered. This way, when the teacher covers the material, you are hearing it for the first time and you'll be struggling to learn and remember it when the teacher is moving on to new material. You'll probably get confused and feel frustrated. That's no way to learn.

Finally, if you really want to make sure that you do poorly, when you finally do get around to the reading, make sure that there is a television on nearby, you have your earphones in and are listening to your favorite music, and be sure to have other people around talking. Many times I have heard students say that they study better when they have the tv on. The sad thing is that this might in fact be true: put these students in a quite room in the library without any distractions and they might be incapable of studying. Their attention spans might be so short that they have become incapable of concentrated study. Please don't become that mentally debilitated. Some background noise ("white noise") can be useful because we tend to tune that out and concentrate more on what we are trying to focus on; but telephone conversations, entertaining television programs, certain kinds of music and so on can make it harder for you to learn. Tune that stuff out and focus.

How to earn a C in logic. The first step towards getting a decent grade in logic is to develop the ability to study in a quiet place where you won't be disturbed. If you are used to distractions, this won't be easy for you. Start by setting yourself a goal of 5 minutes: go to the library, find a quiet area and read for 5 minutes without any music or any distractions at all. It doesn't have to be the library because sometimes background "white noise" can actually help you to concentrate, but find someplace where you won't be distracted or interrupted. The first few times you study like this you might not make any progress at all. You might read the same paragraph several times and it still might not make any sense to you. Keep at it, and gradually increase the amount of time that you can study this way. Distractions prevent your mind from focusing on just one thing; the only way to increase your ability to focus clearly on just one thing is to practice focusing clearly on just one thing. Do this and your brain power will increase significantly, not just in logic, but in every task where you use your brain.

The second step towards getting a decent grade is to go over the assigned reading before the material is covered in class. If there is a set of problems related to the material you are reading, do those problems. Make a note on anything you don't understand, have trouble with or have questions about. Write in your book to mark the place where you have your question and be sure to ask the teacher about it in class. You might highlight the important parts, e.g. the definitions, so that it is easy for you to find them again and drill yourself. And yes, that means you also need to go back over the material and drill yourself on it. For example, in chapter 1 I give you a definition of "premise." Highlight it, memorize it, close the book and repeat the definition, then open the book and check to make sure you got it right. Then, the most important part is to be sure that you can explain the idea in your own words. Memorization is good, it helps you learn, but you should also go beyond memorization by checking to see that you really understand the ideas. If you are not sure you accurately grasp the material - ask questions in class.

How to earn a B or an A in logic. The simplest way to give yourself a chance to learn the material well is to begin right away by making a set of flash cards that you can use to drill yourself on the basic concepts. You'll see that to learn logic, you need to memorize some definitions: write the word on one side of a card, and the definition with an example on the other side. Add new flash cards for each chapter, but don't forget to practice the cards you made for the previous chapter. Refresh your memory often.

Treat the problems at the ends of the chapters in the same way that you use your flash cards. Work the problems at the end of the chapter we are on, and then the next day, work them again. I begin each problem set with some extremely simple exercises. Make sure that you can do these problems, and that it is easy for you to do them. If you have trouble with any of the extremely simple problems, then you are missing something fundamental and you need to go back over the chapter to see what you missed, or else you need to go to your teacher and find out what the problem is. Remembering the solutions to problems you have already worked will help to embed the knowledge firmly in your mind, and this will make your brain much quicker to spot logical patterns, i.e. you will become more logical and quicker intellectually. Practice being successful and success will come more easily.

Next, don't simply work the problems that I've come up with: write your own. Come up with logic problems on your own and solve them. Be creative. The more you use your knowledge, the more firmly it will be planted in your mind and your memory.

The fourth strategy is something that works no matter what subject you are studying: connect what you are learning in logic with other things you are studying. I mentioned above a student who used sub-derivations that he learned in logic to help him write a paper on Shakespeare. While you are learning logic, make a habit of analyzing everything logically. Identify claims and organize reasoning into logical patterns, noticing when they are valid and when they are invalid. It is possible to go overboard with this, but believe me, in today's world, too much logic is not the worry!

Finally, in addition to everything I've mentioned, the best way to do well in logic is to get a partner to study with. A studying partner is not just someone you study next to; a studying partner is someone you tutor, and who tutors you. Start by asking simple questions. With your book open and your partner's book closed, ask your partner to define "premise." Correct your partner if she or he doesn't get it right; hold yourself and your partner to very high standards. Ask a few questions like this, and then change roles: have your partner ask you questions. You might work together on creating flash cards with important terms on one side and then definitions and examples on the reverse side. Take turns quizzing each other on the material in the reading before you get to class. Make up your own problems to give to your study partner, and do the problems that your partner makes up for you.

Results are definitely not guaranteed. If you want guaranteed success, then set very low goals. You have only one life, and your main guide through that life is your brain: develop a strong, agile brain and you will give yourself the best chance possible for a great life.

CHAPTER 1: THE BASIC IDEA

WARNING: learning logic is easy as long as you learn each step as it comes. Trust me; I've been teaching logic for many years now and right around mid-term it's easy to tell who has been keeping up and who has been letting things slide, thinking that they'll catch up later. The trouble is: the later things are easy to learn only if you already learned the early things—so if you don't learn the early things right away, it will be extremely difficult to learn the later things. Just keep up with logic and you'll find it easy.

FRIENDLY TIP: learning logic is like learning a new language. There are new vocabulary words for you to learn. Memorize them. I'm serious. It's a good idea to make your own flash cards: put the new word or phrase on one side and its definition plus an example on the other side. When you are standing in line somewhere, take the cards out and practice. You are exercising your brain, and making your work in the long run much easier.

THE BIG IDEA: a course in logic is strength and agility training for your mind. A course in logic is not job training; you are not learning facts or skills that you will use in your future career—*although employers do occasionally ask job applicants to solve logic problems to see if they can think logically*. Many people have great physical strength and agility, but they find it difficult to focus mentally on a line of reasoning for more than just one or two steps, and they have a hard time understanding conceptual distinctions. Logic trains your mind to develop your focus and your attention span. Many of the examples you will see in this book are unrealistic—again, that's because this isn't job training, it is strength and agility training for your mind.

Section 1: Evaluating Arguments.
Many people think in stereotypes. It's a very lazy way to think and you make lots of errors thinking that way. For example, a common misconception is that only boys play video games. In fact, lots of girls play video games too. In fact, people of all ages enjoy video games. Even if the only people that you've seen playing video games have been boys, it does not follow logically that only boys play video games. Personal experience is subjective and very limited, so you can't make a safe generalization simply based on your own personal experience.

"Hasty generalization" or "faulty generalization" is an error in reasoning, so it is illogical. A logical thinking will easily spot the error, and will avoid falling victim to it. To think logically is to take a bit of reasoning, understand how it works, and say whether it is good or bad. Reasoning is to a logical person what a car is to an auto-mechanic. Give an auto-mechanic a car and she or he knows exactly what to look for to see what condition the car is in. Give a bit of reasoning to someone who thinks logically, and she or he knows exactly what to look for to see what condition it is in. Good auto-mechanics can easily spot problems in cars, and logical thinkers can easily spot flaws in reasoning.

At the very heart of reasoning is the argument. Now when you see the word "argument," don't automatically think of angry people yelling at one another. "Argument" comes from the Latin word *arguere* pronounced are-GOO-uh-ray which means "to show," "to make known" or "to prove." For example, suppose on the way home from soccer practice your bike gets a flat tire and you have to walk the rest of the way. Your parents may want to know why you are late. If you tell them about the flat tire and they don't believe you, you can prove it to them by showing them the flat tire. By providing a reasonable explanation for your lateness, you have given your parents a logical argument, and you have avoided having a screaming-and-yelling-argument. Logical arguments can be very helpful in many situations. An "argument" in the screaming-and-yelling sense is an illogical fight. That is often what happens when people stop thinking logically and start reacting emotionally.

Now don't get me wrong. I'm not putting down emotions or the honest display of feelings. That is an extremely important part of living a human life. It is just that sometimes it is also helpful to be able to "argue" logically, to think things through with a clear head and a calm heart. For example, look at the hasty generalization I started with.

1. The first person I saw playing a video game was a boy.
2. The second person I saw playing a video game was a boy.
3. So, all people who play video games are boys.

Obviously that is very poor reasoning: you can't just go from "some" to "all." Or how about this?

1. Most pigs like to have their bellies rubbed.
2. Arnold is a pig.
3. So, Arnold likes to have his belly rubbed.

That is also poor reasoning: you can't just go from "most" to "all." Arnold might be one of the few pigs who does not like to have his belly rubbed, so don't just walk up to him and start rubbing his belly.

The things I've numbered 1 and 2 in both of those arguments are called "premises" and the thing that comes after the "So" is called the "conclusion." The premises can be called the "support" or "evidence" for the conclusion; but whatever you call them, the premises are the things you give when you are trying to give the reasons why you believe something, or when you are trying to justify some claim you have made, or (like my example of the boss and the copy machine) when you are trying to explain the reasons why you have made some decision. Here are the definitions.

A ***premise*** is a claim that is used as a reason for thinking that another claim (the conclusion) is true.

A ***conclusion*** is a claim that has been given reasons (the premises) for thinking that it is true.

Arguments are made of premises and conclusions. But premises and conclusions all have to be statements or claims. So arguments are made of statements or claims. A question, for example, cannot be a premise or a conclusion. "Who is that? Is that Arnold?" Those are questions, and so cannot be premises or conclusions. A command also cannot be a premise or a conclusion. "Don't let Arnold in here! Go close that door." These are commands which tell someone to do something. They cannot be premises or conclusions. When you are identifying premises and conclusions, just skip over questions and commands, and look only at the statements.

A **claim** (or **statement**) is a verbal description of a state of affairs that is true if things are the way it describes them, and is false if things are not the way it describes them.

A **question** is a request for information.

A **command** is an order that something be done.

Now look back at the argument about Arnold the pig. Premise 1 uses the word "most." That gives us *some reason* to think that this pig, Arnold, likes to have his belly rubbed, but it isn't a *conclusive reason*. For all we know, Arnold might be one of the few pigs who gets irritated when people rub his belly. To some extent we are "jumping to conclusions" when we go from "most pigs like it" to "Arnold likes it." If the argument isn't absolutely 100% sure, then it isn't strong enough to justify the conclusion fully.

If you understand why these arguments are bad, then you can understand why good arguments are good. Here is a good argument.

1. All pigs like to have their bellies rubbed.
2. Arnold is a pig.
3. So, Arnold likes to have his belly rubbed.

Here's another good argument—this one isn't about pigs at all.

1. If Joe drank the poison, then Joe died.
2. Joe drank the poison.
3. So, Joe died.

Think about what makes these two arguments good. Switching from "most" to "all" closes a loophole: "most" allows for some exceptions, and Arnold could, for all we know, be one of the exceptions. But if we knew that literally *all* pigs like to have their bellies rubbed—100% of them—then given that Arnold is a pig, it follows logically that Arnold likes to have his belly rubbed. Something similar is true in the second argument: if the first premise is in fact true—if Joe really did die if he drank the poison—and if it turns out that he did in fact drink the poison, then there's no escaping the conclusion: Joe died.

But now take just one more logical step here. Compare those two arguments with these.

1. All unicorns like butterflies.
2. Sparkle is a unicorn.
3. So, Sparkle likes butterflies.

Here's another good argument—this one isn't about pigs at all.

1. If Joe lives on the sun, then Joe can withstand very high temperatures.
2. Joe lives on the sun.
3. So, Joe can withstand very high temperatures.

I admit right away that both of these arguments are silly and unrealistic. Unicorns aren't real and people can't live on the sun. These arguments are not *realistic*, but they are *logical*. The difference is very important. Logic applies to reality, but it covers so much more—that is part of the power of logic. If you can think logically, then you can think outside the box. Logic gives you the mental power to conceive of logical alternatives that are not currently real. Many employers highly value employees who are able to think outside the box, but still think logically. The ability to conceive of things that are logical but not currently real is necessary for innovation. If you learn logic, you might help to develop new products or services that are a tremendous advance over what we currently have.

Compare those previous four arguments. You should be able to see some similarities. You should be able to look past the actual content of the arguments to see the *argument patterns*. Just to make sure that you see the *argument patterns*, consider this argument.

1. All cats are mammals.
2. Bubba is a cat.
3. So, Bubba is a mammal.

And compare this next argument to the one's you've seen above.

1. If Joe successfully registered for his classes, then Joe got is PIN.
2. Joe successfully registered for his classes.
3. So, Joe got his PIN.

These arguments are realistic. Bubba is one of my cats, and because all cats really are mammals, my cat Bubba is a mammal. In the second argument, in order to register for classes you have to enter your personal identification number (PIN) before the system will allow you to register—so you know that if someone successfully registered, they had to have gotten their PIN. But ignore the content for a moment and just focus on the *patterns*. Look at all three pairs of arguments. The first member of each pair works like this:

1. All A's are B's.
2. This is an A.
3. So, this is a B.

The second member of each pair works like this:

1. If A, then B.
2. A.
3. So, B.

The thing to notice about these patterns is that no matter what you put in for A and B, these are inevitably going to be good arguments. Even if you put silly and unrealistic things in for A or B, the argument pattern will still be good in a particular way: *if the premises are true, then the conclusion also has to be true*. In other words, all arguments that follow either of these patterns are *valid arguments*.

A **valid argument** is a pattern of reasoning in which any situation that makes the premise or premises true, also necessarily makes the conclusion true.

An **invalid argument** is a pattern of reasoning in which there is a possible situation that makes the premise or premises true, but also makes the conclusion false.

Notice that these definitions apply even in silly or unrealistic situations, like my argument about Sparkle the unicorn. Obviously there is no situation that makes the claim "Sparkle is a unicorn" true—unicorns aren't real. However, validity isn't about the actual truth of the premises; validity is only about the connection between the premises and the conclusion: could there be a situation that make both of the premises true, but also made the conclusion false? If the answer to that question is "no," then the argument is *valid*. Could there possibly be a situation in which "all unicorns like butterflies" is true, and "Sparkle is a unicorn" is also true, but "Sparkle likes butterflies" is false? No. Even if you hypothetically imagine a world in which there are unicorns, any such world where literally *all* unicorns like butterflies, and in which Sparkle is one of those unicorns, is necessarily a world in which "Sparkle likes butterflies" is also true.

Another way to put this point is to use a phrase that logicians often use when describing valid argument patters. We often say that valid inferences are "*truth-preserving*." A valid argument pattern can never lead you from true premises to a false conclusion: valid arguments never lead you astray. Of course, it's also true that "garbage in, garbage out." If you put false premises into a valid argument pattern (e.g. "Sparkle is a unicorn"), then you'll get a false conclusion (e.g. "Sparkle likes butterflies"). But the point that logicians focus on is that valid argument patterns will never lead you from true premises to a false conclusion.

"*Most A's are B's, and this is an A, so this is a B*" is not a truth-preserving argument pattern. "Most" can get you into trouble: you can put all true premises into this argument pattern and still come up with a false conclusion. This is an invalid argument pattern: invalid arguments can lead you astray—they can lead you from truth into error.

CHAPTER 1: THE BASIC IDEA

Validity is very powerful. If you can give a valid argument for your view, then you have a rock solid connection between your premises and your conclusion. You can be absolutely sure that as long as you can get someone to accept your premises, then they also have to be persuaded that your conclusion is true. If they accept your premises but reject your conclusion, they are being illogical or irrational.

A student of mine gave me an excellent example to use here. This really happened to him, but I'll change their names. So let's call the two people "Bob" and "Carl." Bob and Carl share a dorm room; Carl has a car (that's why I called him "Carl"). During the semester, Bob finished driver training and got his driver's license. Carl then said to Bob, "I'll let you borrow my car if it's an emergency." A few weeks later there was an emergency. It wasn't a medical emergency or anything like that, but it was an emergency, so Bob asked if he could borrow Carl's car. Carl said, "no." Bob was surprised. "But you said I could borrow your car in an emergency," said Bob. "Yes, that's right," replied Carl. Bob was very confused, but he was in my class so he laid things out clearly and logically:

1. If there is an emergency, then Bob can borrow Carl's car.
2. There is an emergency.
So 3. Bob can borrow Carl's car.

Bob asked Carl, "you accept premise 1, don't you?" Carl said "yes." "And you also agree that premise 2 is true, right?" Again Carl said "yes." "So you agree that I can borrow your car, right?" "No," said Carl. At this point, Bob just broke into laughter.

Carl was clearly being illogical. Bob had given a perfectly valid argument, and Carl accepted the premises but rejected the conclusion. That is about as illogical as you can get. If Carl had rejected one of the premises, he would not have been illogical. He might, for example, say that when he offered Bob his car, he meant only in cases of medical emergencies. That would make premise 2 false because the emergency was not medical. But Carl didn't do that. Carl accepted that both the premises were true, so because the argument is perfectly valid, when Carl refuses to accept the conclusion, it shows that he's just not being rational here. Clearly he was reacting emotionally, he was worried about Bob driving his car, and his emotions defeated his reason.

It is important to emphasize the difference between these two different reactions Carl might have. Usually when two people disagree and one person gives a reason for their view, the other responds, "no, you are wrong." Carl could have done this with premise 2 of the argument above. Carl could have said, "no, premise 2 is false because I didn't mean that you could borrow my car for any emergency, I only meant that you could borrow it in case of a medical emergency." That is reasonable. But if he accepts that both premises are true, then the validity of the argument forces him into the conclusion, and if he doesn't go along, he's just being irrational.

Go back to the example about the copy machine at the beginning of this chapter. Your boss comes in and announces this new policy about what you have to do in order to use the copy machine. You ask "Why?" and the boss says, "It will save us money." Is that good reasoning? Put it in the form of an argument and see. Here it is.

1. This new policy will save us money.
2. So, we must adopt this new policy.

Maybe that sounds pretty convincing to you right off the top of your head, but remember, you are trying to think logically about arguments now. Does this argument really make logical sense? Ask yourself whether or not it is a valid argument. Is there a possible situation that would make the premise true, but the conclusion false? Is it ever possible that a policy would save us money, but it would be false to say that we must adopt it? Does the premise rule out all possibility of the conclusion being false? If the policy saves the company some money, would that all by itself entail with 100% certainty that we should adopt the policy? Hypothetically, would you be irrational if you accepted that the premise was true, but rejected the conclusion? With Arnold, I imagined a situation in which the premises were true, but the conclusion was false. I pointed out that although most pigs like to have their bellies rubbed, Arnold could possibly be one of the few pigs who doesn't like to have his belly rubbed. To see if this argument is valid, we have to do the same sort of thing. See if you can imagine a situation in which the premise is true, but the conclusion is false.

Assume for now that the first premise is true; assume that the new policy really will save money. Does it automatically, necessarily, and with 100% certainty follow that we ought to adopt that policy? Is saving money all by itself, automatically a reason for doing something? Is saving money the only thing a good office manager is concerned with? What about productivity and efficiency? What if you need to make some copies of a document to give to a client, but the boss's secretary happens to be out of the office, and the desk drawer is locked so you can't get the key to the copy machine? This new policy could make the office very inefficient and less productive, even if it does save money *in the short run*. That could very well make it a bad policy that should be avoided. So this argument is invalid: the conclusion could possibly be false even if the premise is true.

Of course you might also reject the premise as false. If you can't make the copy to give to the client, the client may take her business elsewhere and you'll lose money. The money you save in preventing people from making copies they don't need may not make up for the money you lose because clients get tired of waiting for the copies they do need. You can always question the truth of the premises.

But notice that you may also question the validity of the argument. Even if you agree that the premise is true, the argument may still fail to prove the conclusion, because the argument may be invalid. People all too often fail to check their arguments for validity, but this is an extremely important step. To check for validity, think hypothetically: "Let's suppose your premises are true, we still need to find out if those premises make your conclusion 100% necessary." If someone's argument is invalid then you can say, "I can accept all your premises but still reject your conclusion because your premises don't entail your conclusion, you have insufficient proof for your view." If their argument is valid and you accept their premises, then you would be just as irrational as Carl to reject their conclusion. However, if their argument is invalid, then even if you do accept their premises you can still reject their conclusion without being at all irrational.

This is the first step in thinking logically. Your first task is always to figure out whether or not the argument is a valid argument. The first stumbling block to thinking logically is that people have a tendency to react to the premises rather than thinking about the argument as a whole. When someone reaches a conclusion you think is false, or a conclusion you don't like, you probably will have a knee-jerk reaction to just say "no" to the conclusion or to the premises. Learn to fight this tendency. If you give in to this tendency you'll probably get locked into a childish, "no it's not true," "yes, it is true," "no, it's not true," "yes, it is true" sort of fight. That kind of fight is unproductive. To avoid this, just remember: validity first.

The best way to get good at something is to practice. So if you want to get good at spotting valid arguments, you need to see lots of arguments and practice identifying which are valid and which are invalid. I end this section with a few simple examples.

Invalid Argument:
1. Arnold is a pig.
2. Most pigs like to have their bellies rubbed.
3. Arnold likes to have his belly rubbed.

Valid Argument:
1. Arnold is a pig.
2. All pigs like to have their bellies rubbed.
3. So, Arnold likes to have his belly rubbed.

These arguments are almost identical. Only two words separate them: "most" and "all." The invalid argument makes a claim about most pigs, but the valid argument makes a claim about all pigs. That makes the difference between being invalid and being valid. The invalid argument does not rule out all possibility of the conclusion being false. If we hypothetically assume that the premises are true, just assume that Arnold is a pig and that most pigs like to have their bellies rubbed, there is still a possibility that Arnold does not like to have his belly rubbed: he might possibly be one of those few pigs who don't like to have their bellies rubbed.

The valid argument, however, closes off this possibility. The valid argument seals the deal and leaves no possibility of error. If we hypothetically grant that Arnold is a pig, and that all pigs like to have their bellies rubbed, then we can't avoid drawing the conclusion that Arnold likes to have his belly rubbed. The connection between the premises and the conclusion is one of rational inevitability. Just to make the point absolutely clear, compare the following two arguments.

Invalid Argument:
1. Arnold is a pig.
2. 99% of pigs like to have their bellies rubbed.
3. So, Arnold likes to have his belly rubbed.

Valid Argument:
1. Arnold is a pig.
2. 100% of pigs like to have their bellies rubbed.
3. So, Arnold likes to have his belly rubbed.

Again, the invalid argument leaves a little bit of room for error, just 1%. The valid argument leaves absolutely no room for error. With 100% certainty, if those two premises are true, then the conclusion would also have to be true. Validity is a matter of closing off absolutely all possibility for error.

CHAPTER 1: THE BASIC IDEA

Section 2: Some Basic Logical Vocabulary.

Logicians approach the analysis of reason very scientifically: they break everything down into their basic components and then study the various ways those components can be combined. This is the part where learning logic is like learning medicine. Before you can perform surgery on someone, you need to memorize human anatomy. If you are supposed to cut a "ligament" but instead you cut an "artery," your patient is in big trouble. You have already learned the difference between a "premise" and a "conclusion," and you've also learned the differences between claims, questions and commands. Remember that only claims can be premises or conclusions because only claims can be true or false. Logicians express this by saying that only claims can have a "truth value." Usually logicians say that there are only two "truth values," i.e. true and false. So we can say that only claims have truth values, and that is why only claims can be premises or conclusions.

Note for more advanced students: in chapter 4 I will point out that I am assuming a "two-valued" logic in which there are only two truth-values, i.e. true and false. In other systems of logic that allow more than just two truth-values, then a claim doesn't have to be either true or false, it could have a third truth-value if your system of logic allows for other values besides true and false.

In logic, we are interested only in claims. On rare occasions someone can use a question or a command to state a claim, but that's a really tricky matter of interpretation, so I'll usually stay away from that in this book. But be aware that people can state claims in all kinds of ways, and sometimes you have be very careful when you interpret what they say.

Claims are the basic building blocks of logic. You can compare building a logical argument out of claims to building a house out of bricks: put them in the correct order and you get something really solid; but if you put them in a bad order, then it will all come crumbling down. If you want your basic building blocks to function effectively, then you need to put them together properly. Mortar helps bricks to function properly in building walls for houses. Nails, screws and glue help wood to function properly if you are a carpenter. And, of course, if you are doing mathematics, you have a number of basic functions like addition, subtraction, multiplication and division.

Or think about a doctor. A surgeon performs operations on people to make them healthy. In a way, you could say the same thing about the carpenter: the carpenter performs "operations" on wood, glue, nails, screws, saws and so on to build a bookcase or a table. Logicians also perform "operations," and to do that, we use our own specific "operators."

"And" is a logical operator. The logical operator "and" puts two claims together to form a more complex claim. In English, the word "and" is called a "conjunction" because it joins or "conjoins" two things together. So a "conjunction" or "conjunctive claim" is a claim made up of simpler claims, and the conjunction says that both of the simpler claims are true.

A ***conjunction*** is a complex claim composed of two simpler claims which states that the two simpler claims it is composed of (the conjuncts) are both true.

This is pretty obvious, and in fact all the things I'm going to say in this section are pretty obvious and easy. The only trouble is that you need to learn the vocabulary logicians use to talk about these things. There is a standard vocabulary to make it easy to identify exactly what you are talking about, so you just have to memorize the words and definitions I give you (yes, it's time to start making flash cards). Memorize the words "conjunction" and "conjunct," and memorize the definition.

Now that you know "conjunction," you should know about its partner "disjunction." Compare conjunction and disjunction with addition and subtraction in math. By addition and subtraction you can put the same numbers together to yield different results: $7 + 5 = 12$, but $7 - 5 = 2$. In logic, conjunction and disjunction put claims together in different ways, and they yield different results. Roughly, a CON-junction adds two things together; a DIS-junction separates them as alternatives.

To understand disjunction, think of a scenario where a parent offers a child two routes to a reward. For example, "If you get an 'A' in math this semester, or you get an 'A' in English, then we'll take you to *The Wizarding World of Harry Potter* this summer." That is an *either...or* proposition: you need to get *either* an 'A' in math, *or* an 'A' in English to get your trip to *The Wizarding World of Harry Potter* this summer. Either one or the other will do the trick. That's the difference between disjunction and conjunction. If they had said, "If you get an 'A' in math this semester, AND you get an 'A' in English, then we'll take you to *The Wizarding World of Harry Potter* this summer," then your job would be tougher. But if it is a disjunction, you only need one 'A'. In an "either...or" situation, you only need one of the two; you don't absolutely have to have both.

A ***disjunction*** is a complex claim composed of two simpler claims which states that at least one of the two simpler claims it is composed of (the disjuncts) is true.

According to logicians, when someone states a *dis*-junction, they are telling you that at least one of the two smaller claims is true. The problem is with the "at least one" part of this definition. What if both of the two smaller claims are true?

Think about the parent's offer to the child again. If the kid gets an 'A' in math, then she gets to go to *The Wizarding World of Harry Potter* this summer. If she gets an 'A' in English, she also gets to go. What if she gets an 'A' in BOTH math AND English? Does she get to go? Of course she does! In fact, if she gets an 'A' in both, she should also get to buy a wand at Ollivander's Wand Shop. "Either…or" means one, or the other, *or both*. Logicians say that disjunction is "inclusive" because it includes all *three* possibilities: one, *or* the other, *or* both.

Unfortunately there is a problem here: this inclusive possibility creates an ambiguity, and logicians hate ambiguity. "If you are wearing jeans or a t-shirt, please step to the back of the room" is clearly *inclusive*: "one or the other" *includes* the third possibility that you are wearing both jeans and a t-shirt. But there are exclusive cases of disjunction: when a coin lands either heads or tails, it can't lad both head and tails. In order to be clear about this, logicians speak of the "*inclusive disjunction*" and the "*exclusive disjunction*" (I'll give you the definitions soon).

Another good example of the "inclusive disjunction" is the standard claim about oil changes for cars. People say that you should change your oil every 3,000 miles or every 3 months, whichever comes first. What happens if you reach 3,000 miles in exactly 3 months? It could happen. "Either 3,000 miles or 3 months is the oil-change interval" means that you should change your oil after driving 3,000 miles, or you should change your oil after driving for 3 months, or you should change your oil after both driving 3,000 miles and driving for 3 months.

Or how about at the grocery store when they ask you, "Paper or plastic?" What if you want some things in paper bags, but other things in plastic bags? Or what if you want a paper bag put inside a plastic bag? The question "paper or plastic?" doesn't rule out any of those options: you can have paper or plastic or both.

I'll give you one more example, because I have found that many students have trouble with the "inclusive disjunction." Consider the following exchange.

Server: Good day, sir. Would like coffee or tea?
Al: Coffee, please.
Server: And you madam? Coffee or tea?
Betty: I'll have tea, thank you.
Server: And you, sir? Will it be coffee or tea for you?
Carl: Both.
Server: Excuse me?
Carl: Both. You asked if I would like coffee or tea, and I'd like one of each. Is that ok?
Server: Certainly, sir. It's just that I don't usually get that answer.

This won't work all the time. There are situations where you get a coupon for a drink that will allow you to get either coffee or tea but not both: this is an *exclusive* offer. But if you are not in that kind of situation, if no one has explicitly ruled out the option of getting both, then "either … or …" includes the possibility of both: "coffee or tea" is an *inclusive* offer.

As I said, logicians hate ambiguity, so they have developed a way of handling this situation. If you are in a situation where either one or the other or both could be true, then you use the "inclusive-or." If you are in a situation where either one or the other but not both could be true, then you use the "exclusive-or." Logicians write the "inclusive-or" as "OR," and they write the "exclusive-or" as "XOR," where the "X" helps to remind you that this is "eXclusive." So remember, whenever you see plain, ordinary "or," you are in an inclusive situation where one of the alternatives or both of the alternatives might be true. If you see "XOR," then you are in an exclusive situation, only one of the two alternatives can be true, not both of them.

The **inclusive disjunction** ("OR") is a complex claim composed of two simpler claims, and it states that either one or the other or both of the two simpler claims is true.

The **exclusive disjunction** ("XOR") is a complex claim composed of two simpler claims, and it states that either one or the other but not both of the two simpler claims is true.

For the rest of this book I am going to follow this practice. Whenever you see "or," I mean the inclusive disjunction. "Jane did it or Joe did it" means that at least one of them, but perhaps both of them, did it. "Jane did it XOR Joe did it" means that exactly one of them, not both of them, did it. Notice that logicians use all capital letters for "XOR," they don't use "XOR." Don't forget: for the rest of this book, "or" is inclusive.

If you had any trouble with disjunction, then you'll be happy with the next vocabulary word, since this one is very easy: negation. Compare "the book is on the table" with "the book is not on the table." When you negate a claim, you are saying that the claim is not true, you are saying that the claim is false. Here's the definition.

A **negation** is a complex claim which states that the claim being negated is false.

The only tiny problem here is in calling a negation a "complex claim." As far as complex claims go, the negation is the least complex. A conjunction conjoins two complete claims; a disjunction disjoins two complete claims. A negation doesn't do that, it simply denies a claim. Nevertheless, because the negation performs a significant logical operation on a claim, we have to class a negation as a complex claim.

For now there is only one more logical "operator" for you to master. Look back over the arguments I've given in this chapter so far and you'll see a kind of sentence repeated again and again. This sentence structure I've repeated is not conjunction, disjunction or negation, it is called a "conditional." Remember these?

If Arnold is a pig, then Arnold likes to have his belly rubbed.
If Smooshy is a cat, then Smooshy likes to have her belly rubbed.
If the Sun is a star, then the Sun is hot.
If Socrates is human, then Socrates is mortal.

All of these are "conditional" claims because they make one thing conditional on another. The first one says that on the condition that Arnold is a pig, then he likes to have his belly rubbed. The second one says that Smooshy likes to have her belly rubbed on the condition that Smooshy is a cat. The third one says that if the sun satisfies the condition of being a star, then it is hot. The fourth one says that Socrates' mortality is conditional on his being human.

A conditional claim is a complex claim that involves two simpler claims, just like conjunction and disjunction. The big difference is that with conjunction and disjunction, the order doesn't really matter. "Cake and ice cream" is just as good as "ice cream and cake." "Coffee or tea" gives you exactly the same options as "tea or coffee." Which comes first and which comes second doesn't matter from a logical point of view. But with conditional claims, which one comes first makes a huge difference. "If you cut the blue wire, then the bomb explodes" makes sense, but "If the bomb explodes, then you cut the blue wire" doesn't. With conditional claims, you have to be very careful about which comes first and which comes second, and so logicians have names for the first part, the "if …" part, and also for the "then …" part.

Much of the vocabulary of modern logicians derives from the Latin terminology of medieval logicians. In Latin, "*ante*" means "before" and "*cedere*" means "go." So in Latin if you want to say that one thing "goes in front of" something else, you say "ante *cedere*." This Latin phrase has been turned into the English word "antecedent." The "if" part of an "if, then" claim is called the "antecedent" because the "if" part is supposed to go before the "then" part. Of course that means the "then" part is supposed to follow the "if" part. In Latin you use the verb "*consequi*" to say that one thing follows behind another, and this also has been turned into an English word: "consequent." Here are the definitions:

A **conditional claim** is a complex claim composed of two simpler claims which states that if one simpler claim (the antecedent) is true, then another simpler claim (the consequent) is also true.

An **antecedent** is the "if …" part of a conditional claim, it is the condition for the truth of another claim (the consequent).

A **consequent** is the "then …" part of a conditional claim, it is the consequence which is said to follow if another claim (the antecedent) is true.

"Socrates is human" is a simple claim, and "if Socrates is human, then Socrates is mortal" is a complex claim. The antecedent of that conditional is "Socrates is human" and the consequent of that conditional claim is "Socrates is mortal."

Before we can return to analyzing arguments, there is just one last contrast to draw. This one is easy because we have been using it all along. Distinguish between simple claims and complex claims. A conditional claim is a complex claim that is composed of two simpler claims. All the examples we've seen so far are composed not only of two simpler claims, they have been composed of two simple claims. Roughly, a complex claim can be broken down into simpler claims, but a simple claim cannot be broken down any further into simpler claims. Here's an example of breaking down a complex claim into simple claims.

Complex Conditional Claim: If you smoke, then your growth will be stunted.
Simple Antecedent Claim: you smoke
Simple Consequent Claim: your growth will be stunted.

The simple claims can't be broken down any further into simpler claims. "You smoke" can be broken down into "You" and "smoke," but individually those are both just words. The word "You" does not state a claim; the same is true for the word "smoke." The command "Smoke!" (e.g. "Smoke 'em if you got 'em!") is not a claim at all, since it is an imperative. Notice that this makes a negation a complex claim.

Complex Negated Claim: Joe is not guilty. (It is not the case that Joe is guilty)
Simple Claim: Joe is guilty.

You can take out the negation and you still have a claim, so the negation is a complex claim. Here are the definitions:

A **simple claim** is a claim that does not contain any logical operators.
A **complex claim** is a claim that contains at least one logical operator.

For now you know only four logical operators: conjunction, disjunction, conditional and negation. If a claim contains at least one of these, then it is a complex claim, otherwise it is a simple claim.

In the past, some students have had difficulty with this distinction, so I want to say just a little more about it so that you are clear. Compare the following three claims.

The Civil War was fought over slavery.
Plants photosynthesize sunlight into food.
The coin toss was heads or the coin toss was tails.

All three of these are claims because each one can be true or false, but the first two claims are logically simple, while the third claim is logically complex. This probably sounds weird because when you first read them, you may have thought that the first claim was complicated, and you probably thought that the third claim was too obvious for anyone to say out loud. The Civil War was a huge event involving lots of people; yes, slavery is an important part of the story, but there are others parts to the story also, and if you want a full grasp of what caused the Civil War you are going to have to study quite a complicated history. The causes of the Civil War were complex. Logicians look past all that complicated history and just look at logical form: as far as the logic of the claim goes, it is perfectly simple: it does not contain an "if…, then…," it does not contain a conjunction, a disjunction or a logical negation. It contains no logical "operator" and so although it is *historically complex*, it is *logically simple*.

We can say the same thing about the second claim. If you've studied plant biology then you know that photosynthesis is a very complex process; there is nothing simple about the bio-chemistry involved in photosynthesis. We can say that the second claim is biologically complex, but still it is logically simple. All it does is state a claim with no logical complexity to it whatsoever; it is not a conditional claim, it is not a conjunction, a disjunction or a negation.

There is nothing particularly difficult about the third claim. Most people have tossed a coin, or played a sport where a coin toss was used to decide who was up first or which team got the ball first or something like that. We all know that a coin has two sides and that it is highly unlikely that a coin will end up on its side, so obviously either it will be heads or it will be tails. What could be simpler? Actually, the answer to that question is obvious: "the coin toss was heads" is logically simpler, and so is "the coin toss was tails." The one word that makes this a logically complex claim is that little word "or." This claim is a disjunction, and so it is logically complex: it contains two disjuncts. It is not a complicated claim, but it is logically complex.

You can think of the terminology I've just covered as a kind of dissection of arguments. Like you might dissect a frog in biology class, we've just dissected the parts of arguments down to their components. Arguments have premises and conclusions, but premises and conclusions all have to be claims, and you know there are two kinds of claims: complex and simple. You also know that for now there are only four kinds of complex claims: conjunctions, disjunctions, conditionals and negations. You can break complex claims down into simple claims, and that's as far as the dissection goes. The most basic parts in logic are the claims.

The next step is to put these basic kinds of simple and complex claims together to form arguments, and evaluate the different kinds of arguments. But before I do that, I should pause to point out something very important. In a way, the terminology you learned in this section is just a means to an end. In order to evaluate reasoning, in order to perform a logical analysis, you need to know the basic tools of the trade. Carpenters distinguish between "rip saws" and "cross-cut saws." If you are not a carpenter, you might think this distinction is stupid because they are all just saws. You might think that memorizing the difference between a "rip saw" and a "cross-cut saw" is a pointless exercise or mere busy work. But for carpenters, this distinction is very important. If you try to use a rip saw when you should use a cross-cut saw, you'll get into a lot of trouble, you might waste a lot of time and money, and you might ruin the project you are working on. The same is true for any trade. Each discipline has its own terminology, and in order to do the job well, you have to put in the time to learn the basics accurately. The same is true with logic.

The incredible thing about logic, however, is that logic is the very basis of rational thought – every kind of rational thought! When you study carpentry, you might not learn anything you can use outside of carpentry. But when you learn

CHAPTER 1: THE BASIC IDEA

logic, you develop your intellectual acuity, strength and stamina, and you can apply this to absolutely any discipline that involves rational thought. By memorizing the distinctions I drew in Section 2, you have already enhanced your intellectual acuity. You can see things that others cannot because you can separate conjuncts, disjuncts, antecedents and consequents, and you can easily notice when a claim has logical complexity. Even if you don't become a logician and never use this material professionally to earn money, your intellect itself has been improved, so you will be better equipped to perform any job that involves mental effort.

Section 3: Reiteration, Conjunction Introduction and Elimination.

A valid argument is a pattern of reasoning in which any situation that makes the premise or premises true, also necessarily makes the conclusion true. Valid arguments are truth-preserving: they cannot possibly lead you from true premises to false conclusions. They can lead you from false premises to false conclusions, but they will never lead from true premises to false conclusions. Valid arguments are a sort of "gold standard" for logic, and so logicians study them and try to discover all of them. The basic patterns aren't very difficult—some are really, painfully obvious, like this:

1. Joe died.
2. So, Joe died.

Obviously if premise 1 is true, then there's no way that the conclusion is false because the conclusion just repeats or reiterates the premise. If you are looking for argument patterns in which a true premise couldn't possibly lead you to a false conclusion, this is it—and it's called reiteration.

Reiteration is a valid argument pattern in which the conclusion repeats the premise exactly.

Why would you ever repeat or reiterate a premise? Well, in fact, reiteration is sometimes very useful because some arguments are long and people forget things that came earlier. But again, remember that logic isn't about job training; I'm not teaching you about reiteration because you are going to have to use it in your job to satisfy your boss or to earn money. I'm teaching you reiteration so that you understand how logic works, and to develop your ability to think logically. What you should notice that that no argument pattern more clearly fits the definition of a valid argument than reiteration: in reiteration, there is no way at all for a true premise to lead to a false conclusion: if a claim is true, then that claim is true.

The second pattern I want to show you is almost as obvious as reiteration. Remember that a conjunction is a complex claim that says both of the simpler claims it is composed of are true. How could a conjunction be the conclusion of a valid argument? What premises could possibly let you know for 100% certain that both of the conjuncts were true? Obviously each of the two premises has to assert that one of the conjuncts is true, like this.

1. Joe stole from the mob.
2. Joe is informing the police about the mob's illegal activities.
3. So Joe stole from the mob, and Joe is informing the police about the mob's illegal activities.

Here's an argument that follows the same pattern (although this argument is more boring).

1. I left my ID card in my wallet.
2. I left my wallet at home.
3. So I left my wallet at home, and I left my ID card in my wallet.

Both of these arguments fit the pattern called "conjunction introduction."

Conjunction Introduction: a valid argument pattern in which two premises are conjoined in the conclusion.

Notice that this definition doesn't say anything about the order in which the two premises are conjoined in the conclusion. The conclusion is simply the conjunction of the two premises—order doesn't matter. Obviously this is going to be valid anytime you do it, regardless of what claims the premises state.

1	A
2	B
3	So, A and B

1	A
2	B
3	So, B and A

1	B
2	A
3	So, B and A

1	B
2	A
3	So, A and B

Clearly this pattern could not possibly lead from true premises to a false conclusion because the conclusion doesn't add anything that wasn't already asserted in the premises.

Please keep in mind that you can combine conjuncts in either order, and that the order of the premises doesn't really matter as long as you keep the premises before the conclusion. This is the "Rule of Order."

Rule of Order: the order of the premises doesn't matter as long as:
(1) each line is numbered in order beginning with "1," and
(2) the conclusion comes last.

The Rule of Order holds true for all argument patterns. Always keep the premises before the conclusion, but other than that, the premises can come in any order you like.

Now that you've seen conjunction introduction, you should see it's partner: conjunction elimination. You should be able to figure this out simply by understanding the definition of a valid argument pattern: a valid argument cannot possibly lead from true premises to a false conclusion, so what if instead of concluding with a conjunction, you started with a premise that is a conjunction?

1	A and B
2	So, A

1	A and B
2	So, B

1	B and A
2	So, B

1	B and A
2	So, A

Think about it: could any of those conclusions be false if the premise is true? No, because the premise already asserts that the conclusion is true.

Conjunction Elimination: a valid argument pattern in which
(a) a premise is a conjunction, and
(b) the conclusion affirms one of the two conjuncts in the conjunctive premise.

If it is true to say that "Al is here and Betty is here," then it is true to say that "Al is here," and, of course, it is also true to say that "Betty is here." Conjunction elimination is very much like reiteration—it cannot possibly lead from a true premise to a false conclusion: it is a truth-preserving inference, i.e. it is a valid argument.

So now think about the last two argument patterns you just learned: conjunction introduction and conjunction elimination. Logicians try to think systematically about logic, and there is a system to the laws that they recognize. The basic system is define introduction and elimination rules for each logical operator. *Introduction*: under what circumstances is it logical to *introduce a conjunction*? What premises would logically entail a conjunction as a conclusion? Obviously you need two premises, and each premise has to state one or the other of the two conjuncts. *Elimination*: under what circumstances is it logical to *eliminate a conjunction*? If you begin by asserting a conjunction, what necessarily truth-preserving conclusion could you draw? Obviously you could assert either of the two conjuncts. To be systematic about this, we are going to have to study the introduction and elimination rules for each and every one of the logical operators that we recognize: conjunction, disjunction, conditional, negation.

	Conjunction	Disjunction	Conditional	Negation
Introduction	1. A 2. B 3. So, A and B			
Elimination	1. A and B 2. So, A			

Please notice that for conjunction introduction and elimination I've given two *schematic examples*. Those aren't definitions, they are just ways to remind you of the sort of thing that counts as conjunction introduction and elimination. You should remember the rule of order, and you should remember that after a conjunction you may assert either of the two conjuncts (*conjunction elimination*), and that after asserting both of the conjuncts separately, you may conjoin them together in the conclusion in either order (*conjunction introduction*). We've already seen the two conjunction rules. Now let's see some of the others.

Note for more advanced students: logic textbooks often give schematic definitions of inference rules. I don't do that in this book, I only give schematic examples. In order to give schematic definitions, I would have to talk about logical rules, but in talking about those rules I could not use those rules. I would have to invent a separate language for referring to logical rules. Such a language is called a "meta-language." Most logic textbooks use a meta-language. I avoid it. Logic is complicated enough without adding a meta-language.

Section 4: Valid Disjunctive and Conditional Argument Patterns.

Now we need to see *disjunction introduction* and *disjunction elimination*, plus *conditional introduction* and *conditional elimination*. Actually, conditional introduction is more complicated, so I'll wait for later chapters to explain this.

Already in this chapter we've seen many examples of conditional elimination. Think about it. *Conjunction* elimination begins by asserting a conjunction, and then it concludes by eliminating that conjunction and simply asserting one of the two conjuncts. *Conditional* elimination is going to work in basically the same way: it begins by asserting a conditional connection between two simpler claims—the antecedent and the consequent—and it concludes by eliminating the conditional and asserting one of the two simpler claims. How can you do this logically? How can you make 100% certain that conditional elimination cannot possibly lead from true premises to a false conclusion? Here's an example.

1. If Alice registered for classes, then Alice got her PIN.
2. Alice registered for classes.
3. So, Alice got her PIN.

This should be pretty obvious. It looks even more obvious when you put it schematically.

1. If A, then B.
2. A.
3. So, B.

Sometimes people say that in line 3 we "discharge" the conditional. The conditional tells us that if a certain condition is satisfied, then another condition is also satisfied—so if we find that the first condition is satisfied, we can do exactly what the conditional claim tells us: we can go ahead and assert that the second condition—the consequent—is also satisfied.

Logicians like to keep track of, and log, absolutely every step. This is, in fact, one of the main reasons why it is important for you to study logic: logical thinking is methodical and precise. Many people are haphazard in vague thinkers; you can get away with that kind of sloppy thinking in many situations, but sometimes being methodical and precise can be extremely valuable. Many employers are very eager to hire people who can think methodically and precisely, so you would do well to develop these abilities in yourself. To be methodical and precise, logicians keep track of every single line in an argument. Here are simple examples for each argument pattern we know.

| 1 | Alice registered for classes. | Premise |
| 2 | So, Alice registered for classes. | From 1, valid by reiteration |

1	Alice got her PIN.	Premise
2	Bert got his PIN.	Premise
3	So, Alice got her PIN and Bert got his PIN.	From 1,2 valid by conjunction introduction

| 1 | Alice is on campus and Bert is on campus. | Premise |
| 2 | So Bert is on campus. | From 1, valid by conjunction elimination |

1	If Alice is on campus, then Alice has a class.	Premise
2	Alice is on campus.	Premise
3	So, Alice has a class.	From 1,2 valid by modus ponens

Notice that every premise must be marked as a premise, and every conclusion has to be explained with three pieces of information: (1) which premise or premises is it derived from, (2) is it a valid or an invalid inference, and (3) what is the name (if any) of the pattern of reasoning that it follows. Notice also that the fourth argument above is not called "conditional elimination," it is called "modus ponens." Actually, that is a shortened version of its traditional Latin name, which is "*modus ponendo ponens*," which means "the method of putting by putting." Here's my definition.

Modus Ponens: a valid argument pattern in which
(a) one premise is a conditional claim,
(b) the other premise affirms the antecedent of the conditional claim, and
(c) the conclusion affirms the consequent of the conditional claim.

I suppose that the medieval logicians who called this "modus ponens" thought of it this way: if you have a conditional claim, then if you "put" down the antecedent as true, then you can also "put" down the consequent as true.

We don't call modus ponens "conditional elimination" partly because its traditional name is "modus ponens," but also because there is a different form of "conditional elimination" that is just as important. Instead of the method of putting by putting, the companion to modus ponens is the method of taking by taking, i.e. *modus tollendo tollens*, or as it is more usually called: modus tollens. Compare these two together.

1	If Joe drank the poison, then Joe died.	Premise
2	Joe drank the poison.	Premise
3	Joe died.	From 1,2 valid by modus ponens

1	If Joe drank the poison, then Joe died.	Premise
2	Joe did not die.	Premise
3	Joe did not drink the poison.	From 1,2 valid by modus tollens

A conditional claim can be "eliminated" or "discharged" in two different ways. A conditional claim asserts a conditional or hypothetical connection between two simpler claims: it asserts that if the antecedent is true, then the consequent is also true. So, if you know that the antecedent is true, then you also know that the consequent is true. But this works the other way as well: if the consequent is not true, then the antecedent cannot be true either, because if the antecedent were true, then the conclusion would also be true, but it isn't! Here's the definition.

Modus Tollens: a valid argument pattern in which
(a) one premise is a conditional claim,
(b) the other premise denies the consequent of the conditional claim, and
(c) the conclusion denies the antecedent of the conditional claim.

Don't be confused by modus tollens. Assuming that the poison really will kill Joe if he drinks it, then if we find out that he's not dead, then we know he didn't drink the poison—if he had drunk the poison, then he would have died, but he didn't die, so he cannot have drunk the poison…*yet*. If he's still alive, we've still got a chance to save him if we can get to his apartment and pour the poison down the sink before he has a chance to drink it!

Now that you've seen modus tollens—which is a form of conditional elimination—let's compare it with an argument pattern that students often confuse it with: disjunction elimination. Please don't get confused: modus tollens applies only when you have a conditional claim; disjunction elimination applies only when you have a disjunction

1	Either Alice rushed home or Bert rushed home.	Premise
2	Bert did not rush home.	Premise
3	So Alice rushed home.	From 1,2 valid by disjunction elimination

Suppose Alice and Bert are brother and sister, and suppose they both just got a text message that there is an emergency at home so at least one of them has to get there as soon as possible. Hopefully both of them will go and handle the situation together, but let's make sure we are dealing with a disjunction: either one of them can handle the situation alone (although both together might be better). If we are sure that at least one of the two of them made it home, and then we find out that it wasn't Bert, we can deduce that it was Alice. Here's the definition.

Disjunction Elimination: a valid argument pattern in which
(a) one premise is a disjunction,
(b) the other premise denies one of the two disjuncts, and
(c) the conclusion affirms the other of the two disjuncts.

In general: if you can boil a situation down to only two alternatives, and then you can rule out one of those two alternatives, you can be sure that the other alternative must be true. If it's either A or B, and it's not B, then it must be A. It's only logical.

That leaves only one more basic valid argument pattern to learn in this opening chapter: disjunction introduction. Remember that conjunction introduction starts with two premises and the conclusion simply conjoins the two of them. If you know that A is true, and you also know that B is true, then you know that A and B are both true. You start without the conjunction so that you can *introduce* it in the conclusion: that's why it is conjunction *introduction*. It's going to be similar for disjunction introduction: you start without the disjunction so that you can *introduce* it, that's why it's called disjunction *introduction*. Here are two examples.

1	Alice is home.	Premise
2	So, either Alice is home or Bert is home.	From 1, valid by disjunction introduction

1	I have an apple.	Premise
2	So either I have an apple or I have a banana.	From 1, valid by disjunction introduction

CHAPTER 1: THE BASIC IDEA

Remember what we are doing: we are doing a methodical and precise survey of basic valid argument patterns. We want to understand how it is *valid* to introduce a disjunction. What kind of premise could you assert such that if it is true, then a disjunction is also necessarily true? Answer: one of the two disjuncts.

Students never like this argument, which is why I save it for last. Why would you ever do this? When are you ever going to just add on a disjunct to a claim that you already know for sure? Actually, I have heard people use this inference when they are playing with their children. For example:

1. I brought you a bag of peanuts.
2. So, either I brought you a bag of peanuts, or I brought you an elephant.

This is just a silly joke, but in fact it is valid, and you need to understand that it is valid. Any situation that makes one disjunct true automatically makes the disjunction true…and it doesn't matter what the other disjunct is! If you don't understand why this inference is valid, then you don't understand validity. But by now I think that you do understand validity, so I think that you do understand why disjunction introduction is valid.

Here's another example of disjunction introduction. In 2009 the old game show "Let's Make A Deal" was revived. In this show, the host offers to make various deals with audience members. For example, the host may have an assistant bring a box out, and then offer an audience member either $50 or the contents of the box, not both. The audience member can take the $50 and the deal is over. Alternatively, the audience member can gamble that the box contains something worth more than $50, say "no" to the cash and instead get whatever is inside the box. Sometimes the host will give silly "clues" regarding the contents of the box to tantalize them into thinking about what they might possibly get if they give up the cash and go for the box. Suppose that in a specific case, the host knows that inside the box is a very expensive Cartier watch. The host can't ever lie to an audience member, but what he can do is use disjunction introduction.

1. The box contains an expensive Cartier watch worth hundreds of dollars.
2. So either the box contains an expensive Cartier watch worth hundreds of dollars, or the box contains a rubber duck worth less than a dollar.

The host knows that premise 1 is true, and wants to tease the audience member without saying anything false or being illogical, and so the host states the conclusion to the audience member, keeping the premise to himself for the time being. Does premise 2 follow validly from premise 1? Of course it does. If the host knows that the box really does contain a Cartier watch, then he knows that either it contains a Cartier watch or else it contains a rubber duck. Remember the logic of disjunction: a disjunction is a complex claim composed of two simpler claims which states that at least one of the two simpler claims it is composed of (the disjuncts) is true. If the host knows that one disjunct is true, then the host knows that at least one of the two disjuncts is true.

So now you know 7 basic valid argument patterns: reiteration, conjunction introduction, conjunction elimination, disjunction introduction, disjunction elimination, modus ponens, and modus tollens. We can keep track of all this in the table I gave you above.

	Conjunction	Disjunction	Conditional	Negation
Introduction	1. A 2. B 3. So, A and B	1. A 2. So A or B	?	?
Elimination	1. A and B 2. So, A	1. A or B 2. Not-B 3. So A	1. If A, then B 2. A 3. So, B 1. If A, then B 2. Not-B 3. So, not-A	?

The three question marks indicate argument patterns that depend upon a more complicated kind of reasoning. We'll see these valid patterns later.

Section 5: Two Invalid Argument Patterns.

If you understand how valid arguments work, then you can figure out, and you should be able to recognize, invalid argument patterns. The real trouble is that so many people fall for these arguments and think they are valid. See if you can figure out why this is invalid before I explain it.

1. If Joe drank the poison, then Joe died.
2. Joe died.
3. So, Joe drank the poison.

This looks a lot like some arguments we've already seen, but we have not seen an argument exactly like this before. As before, let's just assume that the premises are true. Remember, when you are thinking about validity, you are only considering whether there is any possible situation that could make the premises true but the conclusion false. So let's imagine a situation that makes the premise true: Joe actually did die, and the poison was in fact enough to kill him if he drank it. Can there possibly be a situation in which those are both facts, but in which Joe did *not* actually drink the poison? Joe died, and the poison was enough to kill him if he drank it. Isn't it obvious that he drank it? Otherwise, how else could he have died? Well, think about it: there are other ways to die besides drinking poison. If the mob wants Joe dead so badly that they planted poison in his apartment, then maybe they had a backup plan. It is *possible*, and so this argument pattern is invalid. Maybe he did drink the poison and maybe that's why he died; it certainly is reasonable, given these premises. But "reasonable" isn't enough for validity.

Remember the argument about how "most pigs like to have their bellies rubbed"? If that's true, then it is reasonable to think that Arnold the pig likes to have his belly rubbed, but this inference is not valid—it is possible for the conclusion to be false even if the premise is true.

An invalid argument is often called a "fallacy," and an invalid inference is often called a "fallacious inference." A fallacy does not necessarily have a false conclusion, but it is possible for the conclusion to be false even if the premises are true. You cannot automatically assume that the conclusion is true even if the premises are all true. With an invalid argument pattern people sometimes say that you are "jumping to a conclusion." That's what we have in the case of Joe and the poison. If you are a police detective and you see (a) Joe lying dead in his apartment, and (b) a glass that you know has a very strong poison in it, you should not immediately jump to the conclusion that he died from drinking the poison. You need more facts before you can draw that conclusion. The name of this particular fallacy is "the fallacy of affirming the consequent." Here's the definition.

Fallacy of Affirming the Consequent: an invalid argument pattern in which
(a) one premise is a conditional claim,
(b) the other premise affirms the consequent of the conditional claim, and
(c) the conclusion affirms the antecedent of the conditional claim.

Here's another simple example.

1	If Leticia scored 95 on the exam, then Leticia got an A.	Premise
2	Leticia got an A.	Premise
3	So, Leticia scored 95 on the exam.	From 1,2 invalid by Fallacy of affirming the consequent

Just because Leticia got an A on the exam it doesn't automatically follow that her score was 95. If she had gotten a 96 or a 94 she would have gotten an A. Again, you are jumping to a conclusion if you assume she scored 95 simply because you know she got an A.

You can keep this clear in your mind by looking at it schematically, and comparing it with the valid modus ponens. Compare these two.

Modus Ponens—Valid	
1	If A then B	Premise-conditional claim
2	A	Premise-affirm antecedent
3	So, B	Conclusion-affirm consequent

Fallacy of Affirming the Consequent—Invalid	
1	If A then B	Premise- conditional claim
2	B	Premise-affirm consequent
3	So A	Conclusion-affirm antecedent

In the valid modus ponens, you go from antecedent to consequent, just like the conditional claim says. But in the invalid fallacy of affirming the consequent you go backwards: from the consequent you infer the antecedent, and that is not what the conditional claim says.

The other fallacy you should learn right away is another argument that lots of my students don't like. Lots of students think that this is a perfectly valid argument and don't see why it's considered a fallacy. Here's an example.

1. They only put models or celebrities on the cover of *Cosmopolitan*.
2. There's a celebrity on this month's cover of *Cosmopolitan*.
3. So this month's cover of *Cosmopolitan* does not have a model on it.

CHAPTER 1: THE BASIC IDEA

I'm not 100% sure that premise 1 is actually true, but let's suppose it is. Let's imagine only situations in which both of those premises are true. Is it possible for the conclusion to be false if both of those premises are true? Just because it's a celebrity on the cover, couldn't that person also be a model? Aren't some people both models and celebrities? Sure. You are jumping to an unwarranted conclusion if you draw this inference. Here's the definition.

Fallacy of Affirming a Disjunct: an invalid argument pattern in which
(a) one premise is a disjunction,
(b) the other premise affirms one of the two disjuncts, and
(c) the conclusion denies the other disjunct.

Remember that in logic, the default disjunction is the *inclusive disjunction* which means that one or the other or both of the disjuncts are true. If you affirm one of the two disjuncts, you can't jump to the conclusion that the other is false. Consider another example.

1	Either Tom broke the lamp, or Sue broke the lamp.	Premise
2	Tom broke the lamp.	Premise
So 3	Sue did not break the lamp.	From 1,2 invalid by fallacy of affirming a disjunct

If Tom and Sue were the only people in the room when the lamp was broken, then one of them had to have broken the lamp, or both of them together broke it. If Tom confesses, but doesn't want to get Sue in trouble, we might know that Tom broke the lamp, but it would be illogical automatically to assume that Sue wasn't also involved. If there are two options and you find out that one of them is true, you can't automatically infer that the other one is false. That rests on the false assumption that you can't have both options true at the same time. But you can't just assume that.

Now, if you think about it, you can probably come up with situations where it is pretty clear that both options cannot be true at the same time. Here is one.

1	The coin landed heads, or the coin landed tails.	Premise
2	The coin landed heads.	Premise
So 3	The coin did not land tails.	From 1,2 ???

This might look valid to you, but it's not. Because it uses "or" and not "XOR" in premise 1, you must call this argument *invalid by fallacy of affirming a disjunct*. The reason is that in logic, you are not allowed to make any assumptions that are not explicitly stated, and if you think that the "or" in this argument is exclusive it is because you are assuming that the coin being used is a standard coin. How do you know for sure that the coin is a standard coin? There are two-headed coins in existence, and there are two-tailed coins in existence. Some people use them as jokes or as a way to cheat. Who knows, there might be a coin where the "heads" side is also "tails" side: maybe the figure is a horse that shows both its head and its tail.

When you are doing logic, you are not allowed to take for granted anything other than the definitions of the logical operators involved. "Or" is always inclusive. So if you want this last argument to be valid, you have to state it this way:

1. The coin landed heads XOR the coin landed tails.
2. The coin landed heads.
3. So, the coin did not land tails.

Now it is absolutely clear that this argument is valid. We are not making any extra assumptions about what kind of coin we are dealing with: premise 1 states that we are dealing with a coin that has heads on one side and not tails, and on the other side it has tails and not heads. So if the coin landed heads, necessarily we know that it did not land tails.

The unfortunate result is that we have two disjunctions. If we use both, you'll have to learn (1) "or introduction", (2) "or elimination," (3) "XOR introduction" and (4) "XOR elimination." Ask yourself, "Do I want to have to memorize four rules or two?" I've taught this course many times, and every time I give students the option of learning just two rules instead of four, they always opt for just two.

Section 6: The Last of the Basics.
So far I have been focusing on the difference between valid and invalid arguments. That is the primary focus of logical analysis. But there is a larger issue that is even more important. Logicians tend to fall into the trap of focusing too narrowly on validity and logical patterns, they often lose sight of the larger forest because they are focusing on the minute details of each tree. The larger and more important issue is the truth.

With validity, we just take the premises for granted and look to see whether or not the conclusion necessarily follows from the premises. Given the premises, is there any way for the conclusion to be false? But remember that I've repeatedly mentioned that in logic we shouldn't make assumptions. Unless something is explicitly stated, you can't take it for granted, you can't assume that it is true. But shouldn't the rule against making assumptions apply to the premises also? Why should we assume that the premises are true just because someone wrote them down? Shouldn't we, at some point, call the premises into question?

Yes, of course we should. When we do, we have moved on from considering the validity of the argument to considering whether or not it is "sound."

Sound: an argument which is valid and whose premises are all true.

Notice that this is a conjunction. In order to be sound, an argument must satisfy both conditions: (a) it must be valid, and (b) it must also have all of its premises be true. That means there are two different ways in which an argument can fail to be sound, i.e. there are two different ways in which an argument can be unsound.

Unsound: an argument which is either invalid, or has a false premise.

Notice that this is of course the inclusive disjunction. An argument which is both invalid and has a false premise is unsound. Also notice that even one false premise will do the trick. If all the premises are false, then the argument is unsound, but even one false premise will do. And also notice that every fallacy is automatically unsound because it is invalid.

So an argument can be valid or invalid, sound or unsound. If you put these together, it looks as if there are four possibilities:

Valid and Sound
Valid but Unsound
Invalid but Sound
Invalid and Unsound

Start with the possibility that an argument can be both valid and sound. Here is a simple example.

1	If Socrates was married, then Socrates was a husband.	Premise
2	Socrates was married.	Premise
3	So, Socrates was a husband.	From 1,2, valid by modus ponens

This is a fairly simple case of modus ponens, and both of the premises are true. The first premise is true by definition of what it means to be married, and what it means to be a husband. The second premise is true because it is an historical fact. Socrates had a wife named Xanthippe. This argument proves conclusively that Socrates was in fact a husband. Because it is modus ponens we know that it is valid, which means that if the premises are true, the conclusion must also be true: a valid inference is truth-preserving, i.e. if you put in all true premises, then you are guaranteed to get a true conclusion out of it. Furthermore, our knowledge of what it is to be married, and what it is to be a husband tells us that premise 1 is true; and our historical research has shown us that premise 2 is true. Hence we have discovered that the conclusion is a fact.

That was an example of an argument that is simultaneously valid and sound. It is possible for an argument to be valid but unsound. Here is an example of that.

1	If Socrates died a bachelor, then Socrates died unmarried.	Premise
2	Socrates died a bachelor.	Premise
3	So, Socrates died unmarried.	From 1,2, valid by modus ponens

This is a perfectly valid argument because it is another clear example of modus ponens. However, as I just told you, Socrates was actually married. Premise 1 is true, but premise 2 is false. It only takes one false premise to make the entire argument unsound, in spite of the fact that it is perfectly valid. Here is how you would analyze this argument.

1	If Socrates was a bachelor, then Socrates was an unmarried man.	Premise
2	Socrates was a bachelor.	Premise
3	So, Socrates was an unmarried man.	From 1,2, valid by modus ponens

Valid, but unsound because although premise 1 is true, premise 2 is false

Notice what is written in italics after the conclusion. That is what you do to analyze the logic of an argument. If you wanted to take one further step, then you would add on an explanation of why premise 2 is false. In this case, you could cite a history book that authoritatively records Socrates' marital status when he died (he was married at the time); or you could cite the historical evidence we use to prove that he was married.

So now you have seen an example of an argument that is valid and sound, and example of an argument that is valid but unsound. Here is an example of an argument that is invalid and whose premises are false.

1	If Socrates was Persian, then Plato was Persian.	Premise
2	Plato was Persian.	Premise
3	So, Socrates was Persian.	From 1,2, invalid by fallacy of affirming the consequent

Invalid and both premises are false; unsound argument.

This argument is unsound for two different reasons. First, it is invalid, it commits the fallacy of affirming the consequent. In order to be sound, an argument must be valid; since this argument is invalid it is automatically unsound. But furthermore, both of the premises are false. In order to be sound, all the premises have to be true, and so the false premises automatically make this an unsound argument. As far as arguments go, this one is about as bad as it gets.

Now look back at the four possibilities. We have seen examples of three different types of argument:

Valid and Sound
Valid but Unsound
Invalid and Unsound

Is there a fourth possibility? Could an argument be invalid, but sound? Think about it. Go back to the definition; what does it mean to say that it is sound? For an argument to be sound, all of its premises must be true, and it must also be valid. By definition, if an argument is not valid, then it cannot be sound. Cross out the lower left box because no argument can be sound but invalid. However, put checks in the other boxes because it is perfectly possible for an argument to be valid and sound, valid but unsound, or invalid and unsound.

I'd like to conclude this chapter by going all the way back to the beginning. At the start of this chapter I said that logic is the art of evaluating reasoning. The primary focus of this evaluation is determining the difference between an invalid argument and a valid one. But now you have seen that there is a larger and more important issue, i.e. the issue of soundness and truth. With this larger issue in mind, there are basically three degrees of evaluation in arguments. Let me go over them from worst to best.

The worst possible argument is one that is invalid (and so automatically unsound), and has all false premises. Anyone who gives you an argument that bad has got a lot of work to do. It's back to the drawing board for them. They probably should just give up, and admit that they are wrong and you are right.

Next come the arguments that are invalid but have one true premise. If someone gives you an argument like this, it means that they are on to something. This is very useful, because it gives you some common ground with them. If you don't want to be harsh and judgmental, you might focus on the one true premise and point out that you agree with them on that premise. The difference of opinion between you two comes in the other premise, and also with the validity of the argument. It is always helpful if you can find some way of saying something positive about another person's argument, because if you just focus on your negative criticism, they may very well get hostile, and you two will stop "arguing" in the logical sense, and you will start "arguing" in the emotional sense. That won't help either of you.

Next comes the argument that has all true premises, but is invalid. This might be like the first argument about Arnold the pig. Maybe most pigs do like to have their bellies rubbed, and maybe Arnold too likes to have his belly rubbed, it is just that the argument doesn't prove it beyond the shadow of a doubt. The argument isn't 100% sure, there is still some room for possible doubt. Of course there may be only a little room for doubt. Consider this:

1	Arnold is a pig.	Premise
2	999 out of 1000 pigs studied liked to have their bellies rubbed.	Premise
So 3	Arnold likes to have his belly rubbed.	From 1,2, invalid

That is a better argument, but it is still not 100% sure, so it is still invalid. Of course, sometimes 99% sure is close enough for practical purposes, even though strictly speaking the argument is invalid. But in order to think logically, you always have to notice when an argument is anything less than 100% absolutely sure. The reason is that if it is not perfectly valid, then there is always the chance, even if it is only a very slim chance, that you are wrong, and that you need to keep on looking in order to be sure that you've found the truth. Or think of it this way: if someone gives you an argument that you know is not valid, that immediately gives you a reason for thinking of alternative explanations. They might be wrong, and so you should spend a little time, at least, thinking about alternatives to their position.

Next come the valid arguments. If an argument is valid, you really have to wake up and pay close attention. If the argument is valid, that means the conclusion cannot possibly be false when the premises are true. In other words, if the premises are true, the conclusion must be true; if you accept the premises, you are forced to accept the conclusion, even if you don't want to! This is the power of logic. Consider this argument.

1	If there is motion now, then there exists a First Mover, which is God.	Premise
2	There is motion now.	Premise
So 3	There exists a First Mover, which is God.	From 1,2, valid by modus ponens

This is a valid argument, which means that if those two premises are true, then the conclusion has to be true also. In other words, if those two premises are both true, then this proves that God really does exist! Many people have been convinced by logic that God exists, and have become very devout believers as a result. The universe couldn't just start itself, could it? Something had to begin it all, and that has to be God, doesn't it? Of course you have to consider the opposite side as well. Many people have been convinced by logic that God does not exist.

1	If the world contains evil, then God does not exist.	Premise
2	The world contains evil.	Premise
So 3	God does not exist.	From 1,2 valid by modus ponens

If there was such a powerful, all-knowing and benevolent deity watching over the world, then why is there so much injustice and crime, and why are there such horrible diseases that strike newborn children? How can God just sit back and allow innocent children, for example, to suffer at the hands of wicked people or painful diseases that God could easily prevent? According to this argument, God wouldn't. If God really existed, God wouldn't stand for that. A loving God would help the weak and defenseless instead of letting them be mistreated by bad people and by very bad diseases. But since the defenseless are clearly not protected in far too many cases, there clearly is no benevolent God watching out for them, according to this argument. Not long after 9/11/01 when terrorists destroyed the twin towers of the World Trade Center in New York City, there were newspaper stories of people across the country having crises of faith: how could God allow such evil? This argument has convinced many people that there is no God, and they have lost their faith. Logic can have a very powerful effect in a person's life.

So a valid argument is something to pay close attention to. Even if it has a false premise, the structure is good, and so it might be salvaged. If you can figure out a way to modify the false premise to make it true, then you might be able to turn an argument which is valid but unsound into the best kind of argument there is: valid and sound.

Sound arguments are the cream of the crop. Ideally, when you are giving reasons for your belief, or your policy or theory or whatever, you want to have a sound argument. This is what is usually called proof. A proof is a beautiful thing. You can defend your claim decisively when you have proof, but much more importantly, when you have a proof that some claim is actually true, then you have one of the finest things a human being is capable of: *knowledge of the truth*.

This point, however, is the limit of the usefulness of pure logic. Pure logic is usually not very helpful in determining which premises are true and which are false. In order to do this, you usually have to go out and check your facts. This can be very time consuming, and very often you may not know where to go to find out. But there is one simple key to solving these problems: education. The more you educate yourself, the easier it will be for you to check on the truth of premises. Logic builds you a solid base from which you can go on to learn almost anything you set your mind to.

In closing this chapter, I'd just like to make one final point. Thinking logically is not about winning an argument, it is about the sincere pursuit of the truth. If you just want to win, then you should learn techniques of debate and you should be willing to use false premises and invalid inferences in order to score points against your opponent. But when you think logically, you can't think of the person you disagree with as an opponent, you have to think of them as someone who has an alternative perspective that you might learn from. In approaching an issue logically, you have to look at things from different sides and make a reasoned judgment and be willing to admit when you are wrong. You have to see things from the point of view of the other person, and imagine how they might defend what they are saying. An important impediment to logical thinking is failing to put yourself in the other person's shoes to figure out why they think what they think, what premises and what argument patterns they might use to prove that they are right and you are wrong. People all too often think strategically about how to put their own view in the best light, and how to put someone else down. To think logically, you must try to stop thinking strategically. Logic isn't a game you are trying to win, and it isn't a weapon you are trying to use against people. Logic is a tool whose proper use is in helping you discover the truth, helping you understand the truth, and helping you communicate the truth clearly to others.

CHAPTER 1: THE BASIC IDEA

Chapter Conclusion

That's an overview of what it is to think logically. Always remember the very first step in approaching an argument logically is to think of it hypothetically. Ask yourself, "Hypothetically, if the premises were true, would the conclusion have to be true also? Memorize the basic argument patterns, and as you do that, your mind will begin to develop its logic-muscles and you will be able to think more clearly and more logically.

Basic Vocabulary to memorize:

A **premise** is a claim that is used as a reason for thinking that another claim (the conclusion) is true.

A **conclusion** is a claim that has been given reasons (the premises) for thinking that it is true.

A **valid argument** is a pattern of reasoning in which any situation that makes the premise or premises true, also necessarily makes the conclusion true.

An **invalid argument** is a pattern of reasoning in which there is a possible situation that makes the premise or premises true, but also makes the conclusion false.

A **claim** is a verbal description of a state of affairs that is true if things are the way it describes them, and is false if things are not the way it describes them.

A **question** is a request for information.

A **command** is an order that something be done.

A **conjunction** is a complex claim composed of two simpler claims which states that the two simpler claims it is composed of (the conjuncts) are both true.

A **disjunction** is a complex claim composed of two simpler claims which states that at least one of the two simpler claims it is composed of (the disjuncts) is true.

The **inclusive disjunction** is a complex claim composed of two simpler claims, and it states that either one or the other or both of the two simpler claims is true.

The **exclusive disjunction** is a complex claim composed of two simpler claims, and it states that either one or the other but not both of the two simpler claims is true.

The **default disjunction** in logic is the inclusive disjunction.

A **negation** is a complex claim which states that the claim being negated is false.

A **conditional claim** is a complex claim composed of two simpler claims which states that if one simpler claim (the antecedent) is true, then another simpler claim (the consequent) is also true.

An **antecedent** is a claim that is the condition in a conditional claim, it's truth is claimed to be the condition for the truth of another claim (the consequent); in an "if …, then …" conditional claim, the antecedent is properly placed in the "if" position.

A **consequent** is a claim whose truth is claimed to be conditional on the truth of another claim (the antecedent); in an "if …, then …" conditional claim, the consequent is properly placed in the "then" position.

A **simple claim** is a claim that does not contain any logical operators.

A **complex claim** is a claim that contains at least one logical operator.

Rule of Order. The order of the premises doesn't matter as long as:
(1) each line is numbered in order beginning with "1," and
(2) the conclusion comes last.

A **sound argument** is an argument which is valid and whose premises are all true.

An **unsound argument** is an argument which is either invalid, or has a false premise.

Valid Argument Patterns:

Reiteration is a valid argument pattern in which the conclusion repeats the premise exactly.

Conjunction Elimination: a valid argument pattern in which
(a) a premise is a conjunction, and
(b) the conclusion affirms one of the two conjuncts in the conjunctive premise.

Conjunction Introduction: a valid argument pattern in which two premises are conjoined in the conclusion.

Modus Ponens: a valid argument pattern in which
(a) one premise is a conditional claim,
(b) the other premise affirms the antecedent of the conditional claim, and
(c) the conclusion affirms the consequent of the conditional claim.

Modus Tollens: a valid argument pattern in which
(a) one premise is a conditional claim,
(b) the other premise denies the consequent of the conditional claim, and
(c) the conclusion denies the antecedent of the conditional claim.

Disjunction Elimination: a valid argument pattern in which
(a) one premise is a disjunction,
(b) the other premise denies one of the two disjuncts, and
(c) the conclusion affirms the other disjunct.
Disjunction Introduction: a valid argument pattern in which
(a) the premise is a claim, and
(b) the conclusion is a disjunction, with the premise as one of the two disjuncts.

Invalid Argument Patterns:
Fallacy of Affirming the Consequent: an invalid argument pattern in which
(a) one premise is a conditional claim,
(b) the other premise affirms the consequent of the conditional claim, and
(c) the conclusion affirms the antecedent of the conditional claim.
Fallacy of Affirming a Disjunct: an invalid argument pattern in which
(a) one premise is a disjunction,
(b) the other premise affirms one of the two disjuncts, and
(c) the conclusion denies the other disjunct.

Exercises for Chapter 1

Note: I begin the exercises for each chapter with a section of extremely simple problems. I do this for two reasons. First, extremely simple problems serve a diagnostic purpose: if you cannot do these problems, and do them easily, then you simply need to go back to the chapter and learn what you overlooked. Second, one of the biggest hurdles students face in learning logic is simply a lack of confidence. Many students tell themselves that logic is hard and that they can't learn it, so they give up when they find a problem difficult to work. By working problems, and working them easily, not only do you help solidify your grasp on the material, you also build confidence. As you proceed to the more challenging problems, you might want to back track every once in a while and re-work the extremely simple problems just to remind yourself that you do know the material, and that you can succeed!

Exercise 1.1: Identifying Claims. Each of the following sentences is a claim, a question or a command. You know that arguments require claims, so you need to be able to spot a claim. Properly label each of the following.

Sample Problems:	*Correct Solutions:*
The book is on the table.	CLAIM
Is the book on the table?	QUESTION
Put the book on the table.	COMMAND

1. The plate is on the table.
2. Set the table, please.
3. Did you put the forks on the proper side of the plates?
4. Do we need more water glasses?
5. The centerpiece is lovely.

6. Greed is bad.
7. Greed is wrong.
8. The death penalty is legal in many U.S. states.
9. Is capital punishment morally acceptable?
10. Kill him! Kill him! Kill him!

Exercise 1.2: Identifying Kinds of Claims. The logic of arguments is derived from the logic of claims. If you don't notice the types of claims you are dealing with, you will probably misunderstand the logic of your argument.

Sample Problems:	*Correct Solutions:*
The book is on the table.	SIMPLE CLAIM
Al is home or Bo is home	DISJUNCTION (inclusive)
Al is home and Bo is home	CONJUNCTION
If Al is home, then Bo is home	CONDITIONAL

1. The plate is on the table.
2. Either the plate is on the table, or the plate is on the floor.
3. Half of the plate is on the table, and the other half of the plate is on the floor.
4. If you put the plate on the table, then you ought to put the glass on the table.
5. The centerpiece is lovely.

6. If Al registered for classes, then Al paid his library fees.
7. Al had to have gotten his pin if he successfully registered for courses.
8. Al registered for courses only if he got his PIN before registering.
9. Al registered or he's taking a semester off.
10. Al paid his library fees but he did not get his PIN.

11. The American Civil War began when the Confederate artillery bombarded Union soldiers all day long at Fort Sumter, South Carolina on April 12, 1861.
12. You have only two alternatives: surrender or die.
13. Your first alternative is to surrender; your second alternative is to die.
14. First you are going to surrender, and after that you are going to die.
15. We will let you live only on the condition that you surrender peacefully and come out with your hands up.

Exercise 1.3: Identifying Argument Patterns. Assess each argument for validity.

	Sample Problem:	Correct Solution:
1	Harry is a horse.	Premise
2	If Harry is a horse, then Harry is a mammal.	Premise
3	So, Harry is a mammal.	From 1,2, valid by modus ponens

Problem 1:
1. If Socrates is human, then Socrates is mortal.
2. Socrates is human.
3. So, Socrates is mortal.

Problem 2:
1. Sally is a mustang.
2. If Sally is a mustang, then Sally should slow down.
3. So, Sally should slow down.

Problem 3:
1. If we've got everything down to a science, then we know everything.
2. We've got everything down to a science.
3. So, we know everything.

Problem 4:
1. If my opinions are like kittens, then I can just give them away.
2. My opinions are like kittens.
3. So, I can just give them away.

Problem 5:
1. Socrates is human.
2. If Socrates is human, then Socrates is mortal.
3. So, Socrates is mortal.

Problem 6:
1. Socrates is mortal.
2. If Socrates is human, then Socrates is mortal.
3. So, Socrates is human.

Problem 7:
1. Socrates is mortal.
2. Socrates is human or Socrates is mortal.
3. So, Socrates is not human.

Problem 8:
1. Socrates is human.
2. Socrates is human or Socrates is mortal.
3. So, Socrates is not mortal.

Problem 9:
1. Dogs are smart.
2. Dogs are obedient.
3. So, dogs are smart and dogs are obedient.

Problem 10:
1. Dogs are smart and dogs are obedient.
2. So, dogs are obedient.

Problem 11:
1. Dogs are obedient.
2. If dogs are smart, then dogs are obedient.
3. So, dogs are smart.

Problem 12:
1. If dogs are obedient, then dogs are smart.
2. Dogs are smart.
3. So, dogs are obedient.

Problem 13:
1. If dogs are obedient, then dogs are smart.
2. Dogs are obedient.
3. So, dogs are smart.

Problem 14:
1. If dogs are smart, then dogs are obedient.
2. Dogs are not obedient.
3. So, dogs are not smart.

Problem 15:
1. If apples are fruit, then apples are sweet.
2. Apples are fruit.
3. So, apples are sweet.

Problem 16:
1. If bones are brittle, then bones can break.
2. Bones cannot break.
3. So, bones are not brittle.

Problem 17:
1. Either bones are brittle, or bones are durable.
2. Bones are not durable.
3. So, bones are brittle

Problem 18:
1. Rabbits are soft.
2. Rabbits are cute.
3. So, rabbits are soft and rabbits are cute.

Problem 19:
1. Rabbits are soft and rabbits are cute.
2. So, rabbits are cute.

CHAPTER 1: THE BASIC IDEA

Problem 20:
1. Cars are fast or cars are dangerous.
2. Cars are dangerous.
3. So, cars are not fast.

Problem 21:
1. Cars are fast.
2. If cars are red, then cars are fast.
3. So, cars are red.

Problem 22:
1. Charity is a virtue.
2. So, either charity is a virtue, or hope is a virtue.

Problem 23:
1. If justice is a virtue, then cheating is a vice.
2. Cheating is not a vice.
3. So, justice is not a virtue.

Problem 24:
1. Courage is a virtue.
2. Temperance is a virtue.
3. So, temperance is a virtue and courage is a virtue.

Problem 25:
1. Either hope is a virtue, or pride is a virtue.
2. Pride is not a virtue.
3. So, hope is a virtue.

Problem 26:
1. Prudence is a virtue.
2. Patience is a virtue.
3. So, patience is a virtue and prudence is a virtue.

Problem 27:
1. If faith is a virtue, then we must seek truth.
2. Faith is a virtue.
3. So, we must seek truth.

Problem 28:
1. If hope is a virtue, then despair is a vice.
2. Hope is a virtue.
3. So, despair is a vice.

Problem 29:
1. Either vengeance is a vice, or justice is a vice.
2. Justice is a not vice.
3. So, vengeance is a vice.

Problem 30:
1. Cats are mammals and dogs are mammals.
2. So, dogs are mammals.

Problem 31:
1. Cats are mammals.
2. So, cats are mammals or dogs are mammals.

Problem 32:
1. Rats are mammals, and shrews are mammals.
2. So, shrews are mammals.

Problem 33:
1. Rats have teeth.
2. So, either rats have teeth or dogs have teeth.

Problem 34:
1. If Pikas are lagomorphs, then hares are furry.
2. Hares are furry.
3. So, pikas are lagomorphs.

Problem 35:
1. Either rats are rodents or rats are carnivores.
2. Rats are not rodents.
3. So, rats are carnivores.

Problem 36:
1. Either mice are rodents or skunks are rodents.
2. Skunks are not rodents.
3. So, mice are rodents.

Problem 37:
1. Marmots are closely related to squirrels.
2. So, marmots are closely related to squirrels or marmots are closely related to snakes.

Problem 38:
1. If cats eat rats, then rats eat flies.
2. Cats eat rats.
3. So, rats eat flies.

Problem 39:
1. If bugs are crunchy, then cats eat bugs.
2. Cats eat bugs.
3. So, bugs are crunchy.

Problem 40:
1. Cats do not eat flies.
So 2. Cats do not eat flies or cats do eat flies.

Exercise 1.3: Slightly Trickier Arguments.

Problem 1:
1. If cats are not amphibians, then dogs are not amphibians.
2. Cats are not amphibians.
3. So, dogs are not amphibians.

Problem 2:
1. Cats are not amphibians and dogs are not amphibians.
2. So, dogs are not amphibians.

Problem 3:
1. If each being is what it is composed of, then you can't step into the same river twice.
2. Each being is what it is composed of.
3. So, you can't step into the same river twice.

Problem 4:
1. Evil does not exist.
2. So, God does not exist or evil does not exist.

Problem 5:
1. Either God exists or evil does not exist.
2. God exists.
So 3. Evil does not exist.

CHAPTER 1: THE BASIC IDEA

Practice Exam for Chapter 1
Note: the actual exam may contain more problems in each section

Part I: Definitions. Define the following terms (10 pts each).
Problem 1: conclusion.
Problem 2: valid.
Problem 3: sound.

Part II: Arguments. Fully assess the following arguments for validity (10 pts each).

Problem 4:
1. If Joe is a bachelor, then Joe is unmarried.
2. Joe is a bachelor.
3. So, Joe is unmarried.

Problem 5:
1. If Joe is a bachelor, then Joe is unmarried.
2. Joe is unmarried.
3. So, Joe is a bachelor.

Problem 6:
1. Joe is unmarried.
2. Joe is male.
3. So, Joe is unmarried and Joe is male.

Problem 7:
1. Joe is unmarried and Joe is male.
2. So, Joe is unmarried.

Problem 8:
1. Joe is male or Joe is female.
2. Joe is not female.
3. So, Joe is male.

Problem 9:
1. Joe is male.
2. So, Joe is male or Joe is female.

Problem 10:
1. Joe is male or Joe is female.
2. Joe is male.
3. So, Joe is not female.

Sample Answers for Practice Exam

Note: this exam would earn only a C-, find the errors – including spelling errors.

Problem 1: the conclusion of an argument is a sentence that you are led to from other claims. An example of a conclusion would be to say that Joe is a bachelor.

Problem 2: an argument is valid when you accept the premises and then have to accept the conclusions. You are illogical if you reject a valid argument.

Problem 3:

Definition: a sound argument is an argument that satisfies both of the following conditions: (1) it is valid, and (2) all of its premises are true.

Explanation: a sound argument is a proof that a particular claim (the conclusion) is in fact true. A sound argument relies on true claims as premises, and then validly infers the conclusion. In a valid argument, the premises entail the conclusion, so in a sound argument the fact that the premises are true means that the conclusion must also be true. In order to be sound, the premises of an argument do not have to be proven or even known to be true, they simply have to be true.

Example:
Premise 1: Socrates was a husband.
Premise 2: If Socrates was a husband, then Socrates was male.
Conclusion: Socrates was male.

This argument satisfies both conditions for being sound. (1) It is valid because it is an instance of modus ponens. (2) Both of its two premises are true. Premise 1 is a known historical fact, and premise 2 is true by definition, since a husband is a married male.

Problem 4:
1. Premise.
2. Premise.
So 3. modus ponens.

Problem 5:
1. Premise.
2. Premise.
So 3. From 1,2 invalid by fallacy of affirming the consequent.

Problem 6:
1. Premise.
2. Premise.
So 3. From 1,2 valid by conjunction introduction.

Problem 7:
1. Premise.
So2. From 1, valid by conjunction elimination.

Problem 8:
1. Premise.
2. Premise.
So 3. From 1,2 valid by disjunction elimination.

Problem 9:
1. Premise.
So2. From 1, valid by disjunction introduction.

Problem 10:
1. Premise.
2. Premise.
So 3. From 1,2 invalid by fallacy of affirming a disjunct.

Analysis of Sample Answers for Practice Exam

Problem 1: this answer earns only 2 points.

First, the answer is only vaguely correct, and so it begins with only a grade of C, i.e. 70% credit (7 out of 10 points). It is only vaguely correct because it uses the vague metaphor of "led to" in order to explain the connection between the premises and the conclusion of an argument.

Second, 1 point is deducted because the answer says that a conclusion must be a sentence, not that a conclusion must be a claim. "The cat is on the mat" and "The mat is what the cat is on" are two different sentences, but they state exactly the same claim. The conclusion of an argument is not a sentence, but the claim stated by the sentence.

Third, 1 point is deducted because the answer fails to give a clear example of a conclusion. "Joe is a bachelor" is not a conclusion until some reason is given for thinking that Joe is in fact a bachelor.

Finally, 3 points are deducted for misspelling the word "argument."

Problem 2: this answer earns only 5 points.

First, the answer is only vaguely correct and it makes a false claim, so it begins with only a grade of D, i.e. 60% credit (6 out of 10 points). It is only vaguely correct because it uses the vague phrase "have to" in order to explain connection between the premises and the conclusion of a valid argument. It makes the false claim that you have to accept the premises in order for an argument to be valid. The second sentence uses the word "illogical," but never explains what is meant.

Second, 1 point is deducted because it fails to include a clear example.

Third, the word "argument" is misspelled in exactly the same way it was misspelled in the first answer. I do not deduct additional points in such cases, but if the word were misspelled in a different way, then 3 points would be deducted.

Problem 3: this answer earns 10 points. This is a model answer.

Problem 4: this answer earns only 5 points.

First, the argument is modus ponens, so the answer starts out with all 10 points.

Second, 2 points are deducted for failing to indicate the premises that give reason for thinking that the conclusion is true. This is not a big problem in short arguments, but it is a severe problem in longer arguments, so it is important to get in the habit of always citing the premises that allegedly give reason for thinking that the conclusion is true.

Third, 3 points are deducted for failing to state that the argument is valid. The single most important issue when evaluating reasoning is whether or not the reasoning pattern is valid.

Problems 5-10: each answer earns 10 points. These are model answers.

Total Points Earned = 72 = C-

CHAPTER 2: TRANSLATION

Chapter 1 introduced you to the heart of logic: argument patterns. Logic is primarily about seeing the difference between a valid argument pattern and an invalid argument pattern. I tried to make things easy in that chapter by sticking to fairly short, clear arguments. Unfortunately, in life the arguments you come across will not always be short and clear. In this chapter, I will introduce you to some tools you can use to help you deal with longer arguments.

Section 1: Longer Arguments.

So far I have shown you arguments with two premises and then the conclusion, and you've learned to spot the pattern which the argument follows. Here is a simple example.

1	If Socrates is Greek, then Socrates is human.	Premise
2	Socrates is Greek.	Premise
∴ 3	Socrates is human.	From 1,2 valid by modus ponens

Notice that the symbol ∴ simply indicates the conclusion. Instead of saying "so," you may now use the symbol which indicates the conclusion. The simplest way in which you can have longer arguments is by adding extra steps onto an argument, like this.

1	If Socrates is Greek, then Socrates is human.	Premise
2	Socrates is Greek.	Premise
∴ 3	Socrates is human.	From 1,2 valid by modus ponens
4	If Socrates is human, then Socrates is mortal.	Premise
∴ 5	Socrates is mortal.	From 3,4 valid by modus ponens

Notice that step 4 is just a premise, and so you label it as just another premise. Also notice that the justification for the conclusion at step 5 is just plain modus ponens. You don't have to cite anything other than the two premises that are used to draw the conclusion at step 5. Treat these longer arguments as if they are separate blocks that you can take apart and put back together again.

But also notice that there is something odd about these longer arguments. Steps 1 through 3 form a simple argument, steps 1 and 2 are the premises, and step 3 is the conclusion. You know that step 3 is the conclusion because it has those three dots in front of it. This is all familiar to you from Chapter 1. But now look at the second part of the argument. Step 5 is a conclusion, which follows from steps 3 and 4. That means steps 3 and 4 are the *premises*, which entail the conclusion in step 5. Think about it: step 3 is the *conclusion* of 1-3, but step 3 is a *premise* in 3-5. Step 3 is both a conclusion (of 1-3) and a premise (of 3-5). In longer arguments, this happens all the time. Step 3 is called a "sub-conclusion," and step 5 is the "main conclusion."

A ***sub-conclusion*** is a conclusion that is also used as a premise for a further conclusion, it is not a final conclusion.
A ***main conclusion*** is a conclusion that is not also used as a premise for a further conclusion, it is a final conclusion.

An argument can have as many sub-conclusions as you want, but it can only have one main conclusion. Every argument has to have one main conclusion: the whole point of an argument is its main conclusion. So if you are confronted with a longer argument, begin by looking for the main conclusion; that way you know the point of the whole argument.

In fact, the main conclusion is so important, that the argument which gives you the main conclusion is called the main argument. The arguments which give you the sub-conclusions are called the sub-arguments.

A ***sub-argument*** is an argument for a sub-conclusion.
A ***main argument*** is an argument for a main conclusion.

Here is another longer argument.

1	Either Socrates is Greek, or Socrates is Persian.	Premise
2	Socrates is not Persian.	Premise
∴ 3	Socrates is Greek.	From 1,2 valid by disjunction elimination
4	If Socrates is Greek, then Socrates is human.	Premise
∴ 5	Socrates is human.	From 3,4 valid by modus ponens
6	If Socrates is human, then Socrates is mortal.	Premise
∴ 7	Socrates is mortal.	From 5,6 valid by modus ponens

CHAPTER 2: TRANSLATION

In this long argument, 1-3 is the first sub-argument, and 3 is the first sub-conclusion. 3-5 is the second sub-argument, and 5 is the second sub-conclusion. Finally, 5-7 is the main argument, and 7 is the main conclusion. Step 7 tells you what the whole argument is really all about. Everything that comes before, is all organized around proving the truth of the main conclusion.

Notice also that the first sub-argument (1-3) is valid by disjunctive argument, but the second sub-argument (3-5) and the main argument (5-7) are both modus ponens. A long argument can have any combination of patterns in its sub-arguments. In fact, a long argument can contain sub-arguments that are invalid. Here is an example.

1	If dogs eat cats, then cats eat rats.	Premise
2	If cats eat rats, then rats eat flies.	Premise
∴ 3	If dogs eat cats, then rats eat flies.	From 1,2 valid by chain argument
4	Rats eat flies.	Premise
∴ 5	Dogs eat cats.	From 3,4 invalid by fallacy of affirming the consequent

The sub-argument (1-3) is valid, but the main argument (3-5) is invalid. But now ask yourself this question: is the argument as a whole valid or invalid? If you have a long argument, and you know that part of it is valid, but part of it is invalid, what is your judgment of the argument as a whole? Answer: the argument is invalid. If any part of the argument is invalid, then the entire argument is invalid. Of course, parts of the argument can be valid, but as a whole, the argument fails to prove the conclusion, and so the argument as a whole is not valid.

This can be very helpful. If you have a long complex argument for an important conclusion, but you find out that some of your sub-arguments are invalid, what you can do is focus just on the invalid sub-arguments and try to fix them. You don't have to trash the entire thing. This also helps if you disagree with someone else. You can point out to them that you agree with them on part of their argument. You can point out that there is some common ground between the two of you. Part of the argument is valid, you just disagree with the invalid part. This does, of course, make the argument as a whole invalid, but you don't disagree with them totally.

Section 2: Affirming and Denying.

Logicians often talk of "affirming" or "denying" (or "negating") claims. Essentially this is just a way to refer to saying "yes, I agree" or "no, I don't agree." So if someone says, "you owe me $50" and you *affirm* their claim, then you might say, "yea, yea, yea, I know, quit bugging me, I owe you $50, so I'll pay you your $50!" However, if you *deny* their claim, you might say, "What?! No way! I do *not* owe you $50!"

To be a bit more precise, if you affirm the claim "you owe me $50," then you are *affirming an affirmation*, because the original claim (i.e. "you owe me $50") is itself an affirmative statement, it is an affirmation. "You don't owe me anything" is a "negative" statement, or a "denial" because it negates or denies the claim that you owe something. It is possible to *affirm this denial* by saying, "That's right: I don't owe you anything." There are four possibilities here. You can:

Affirm an affirmation,
Affirm a denial,
Deny an affirmation, or
Deny a denial.

Here are simple examples.

Original Affirmation	*Affirm the Affirmation*	*Deny the Affirmation*
Joe drinks	Joe drinks	Joe does not drink

Original Denial	*Affirm the Denial*	*Deny the Denial*
Joe does not drink	Joe does not drink	Joe does not not drink (Joe does drink, or Joe drinks)

To affirm a claim is simply to repeat it exactly. To deny a claim is to add a negation. However, since a denial is already a negation, when you deny a negation you are asserting a *double negation*. Probably you don't have any trouble with the "Law of Double Negation," but I'll introduce it explicitly in Section 4 below.

Section 3: Three More Argument Patterns.

As you practice, you will find that longer and more complex arguments are easier and easier to analyze. This indicates that the logic-muscles of your brain are getting stronger and more agile. You are developing your intellectual powers.

1	If Leticia scored 95, then Leticia got an A.	Premise
2	Leticia got an A.	Premise
∴ 3	Leticia scored 95.	From 1,2, invalid by fallacy of affirming the consequent

Probably that argument was no trouble for you. Even if both of those premises are true, the conclusion could still be false: Leticia could have gotten her A because she scored 96 on the exam. Compare that fallacy with this argument.

1	If Leticia scored 95, then Leticia got an A.	Premise
2	Leticia did not get an A.	Premise
∴ 3	Leticia did not score 95.	From 1,2 ???

If you accepted those premises, would you have to accept the conclusion also? Yes, absolutely. 95 is an A (from premise 1), but we know she didn't get an A (from premise 2) and so there is no way she scored 95. Think of it this way: hypothetically, if she had scored 95, then she would have gotten an A, but premise 2 tells us that she did not get an A, and so didn't score 95 … because if she had scored 95, she would have gotten an A, but she didn't get an A, so she didn't score 95 … because if she had, she would have gotten an A, but she didn't. You can go on like this for a long time if you want. This logic is air-tight and inescapable: it's an example of *modus tollens*.

Now you know three argument patterns that involve a conditional claim: (1) modus ponens and (2) modus tollens are valid, while (3) the fallacy of affirming the consequent is invalid. There is a fourth you need to know, and if you think about it, this fourth completes a pattern that you might be able to figure out in advance. Here is an example.

1	If Leticia scored 95, then Leticia got an A.	Premise
2	Leticia did not score 95.	Premise
∴ 3	Leticia did not get an A.	From 1,2 ???

Think about this argument and see if you can determine whether it valid. If Leticia scored 95, then she got an A; but she did not score 95. Does that necessarily mean that she did not get an A? Does that necessarily follow with 100% certainty? Would the truth of the premises rule out all possibility of the conclusion being false? There must be no possible way for the conclusion to be false when the premises are true. Do we have that with this argument? Just because Leticia did not score 95, does that automatically mean there is no way she could have gotten an A? Is there any other way to get an A than to score 95? Sure, how about if she scored 94 or 96? Even if she did not score 95 on the exam, she could still have gotten an A. So even if both of the premises are true, the conclusion could still be false. This argument is invalid and it is an example of the fallacy of denying the antecedent.

Fallacy of Denying the Antecedent: an invalid argument pattern in which
   (a) one premise is a conditional claim,
   (b) the other premise denies the antecedent of the conditional claim, and
   (c) the conclusion denies the consequent of the conditional claim.

Remember that a conditional claim sets up a condition and a result: if you satisfy the condition, then the result will follow. Modus ponens is valid because it sets up a conditional claim, affirms the antecedent and then affirms the consequent: if you satisfy the antecedent, then you get the result; but you do satisfy the antecedent, so you get the result. With the fallacy of denying the antecedent, you don't satisfy the antecedent. What follows? There is no way of knowing for sure. The conditional tells you what happens if you *do* satisfy the antecedent, it doesn't tell you what happens if you *do not* satisfy the antecedent.

Consider another example.

1	If you press the red button, then the bomb explodes.	Premise
2	You do not press the red button.	Premise
∴ 3	The bomb does not explode.	From 1,2 invalid by the fallacy of denying the antecedent

Is that valid? No. It is another example of the fallacy of denying the antecedent. Just because we know what happens if we do press the red button, it doesn't automatically follow that we know what happens if we do not press the red button. You are jumping to a conclusion if you make that assumption, and in this case it is an assumption that could cost you your life. A member of the bomb squad can't afford to go around making lots of assumptions. When your life depends on it, don't assume that you are safe without considering whether there are dangers you haven't thought about yet. The bomber might have designed the bomb with some kind of back-up plan in mind. For example, if no one presses the red button within one hour, then the bomb will go off automatically. You can't risk making the assumption that the bomber designed only one way for the bomb to go off. If you have figured out enough about the bomb to know that if you press the red button, then you will detonate the bomb, you have some helpful information. But don't assume that tells you what will happen if you don't press the red button.

So when you deny the antecedent, you are getting yourself into logical trouble. What about when you deny the consequent?

1	If you press the red button, then the bomb explodes.	Premise
2	The bomb does not explode.	Premise
∴ 3	You do not press the red button.	From 1,2 valid by modus tollens

Suppose that pressing the red button really will set the bomb off. Now suppose that the bomb doesn't go off. Does it follow that you didn't press the red button? Yes, absolutely. If you had pressed the red button, the bomb would have gone off; it didn't go off, so you must not have pressed the red button because if you had pressed the button it would have gone off, but it didn't. This logic is inescapable; it is 100% solid with absolutely no room for doubt at all. The premises necessarily entail the conclusion with 100% certainty.

Using the bomb example, let's contrast all four of the argument patterns that involve the use of a conditional premise.

The Modus Ponens Version:

1	If you press the red button, then the bomb explodes.	Premise
2	You press the red button.	Premise
∴ 3	The bomb explodes.	From 1,2, valid by modus ponens

The Modus Tollens Version:

1	If you press the red button, then the bomb explodes.	Premise
2	The bomb does not explode.	Premise
∴ 3	You do not press the red button.	From 1,2 valid by modus tollens

The Fallacy of Affirming the Consequent Version:

1	If you press the red button, then the bomb explodes.	Premise
2	The bomb explodes.	Premise
∴ 3	You press the red button.	From 1,2, invalid by fallacy of affirming the consequent

The Fallacy of Denying the Antecedent Version:

1	If you press the red button, then the bomb explodes.	Premise
2	You do not press the red button.	Premise
∴ 3	The bomb does not explode.	From 1,2, invalid by fallacy of denying the antecedent

All four arguments have the same first premise so you can compare them easily. Based on that conditional claim, modus ponens affirms the antecedent and concludes by affirming the consequent: that is valid. Modus tollens denies the consequent and concludes by denying the antecedent: that too is valid. The fallacy of affirming the consequent affirms the consequent and then concludes by affirming the antecedent: this reverses modus ponens and is invalid. The fallacy of denying the antecedent denies the antecedent and then concludes by denying the consequent: this reverses modus tollens and is invalid. Look for patterns like this. Logic is filled with patterns.

Next, here is a new argument pattern that has conditional claims.

1	If you land the Johnson account, then you get a raise.	Premise
2	If you get a raise, then you'll be able to afford a new car.	Premise
∴ 3	If you land the Johnson account, then you can afford a new car.	From 1,2 ???

It's not hard to see that this argument is valid. Landing the Johnson account gets you the raise, and getting the raise will give you enough money to afford a new car. So landing the account will give you enough money to afford a new car. One thing leads to another, and that second thing leads to a third thing: a leads to b and b leads to c, so a leads to c. Obviously, if a gets you to b, and b gets you to c, then a gets you to c (through b). Because this argument pattern works like links on a chain, it is called a "chain argument."

Chain Argument: a valid argument pattern in which
(1) there are exactly two premises,
(2) the premises and the conclusion are conditional claims,
(3) the consequent of one premise is identical to the antecedent of the other premise, and
(4) the antecedent of the conclusion is identical to antecedent of the premise whose consequent is shared, and the consequent of the conclusion is identical to the consequent of the premise whose antecedent is shared.

Although it takes longer to define this argument pattern than any other, it's really pretty simple. Keep in mind the links on the chain analogy, and it should be easy to spot a chain argument.

1	If you land the Johnson account, then you get a raise.	Premise
2	If you get a raise, then you'll be able to afford a new car.	Premise
∴ 3	If you land the Johnson account, then you can afford a new car.	From 1,2 valid by chain argument

The fallacy associated with the chain argument pattern also relies on two conditional premises, but it fails to follow the proper order.

1	If you land the Johnson account, then you get a raise.	Premise
2	If you get a raise, then you can afford a new car.	Premise
∴ 3	If you can afford a new car, then you land the Johnson account.	From 1,2 ???

This argument takes the links of the chain and goes backwards. Landing the Johnson account leads to the raise, and the raise leads to being able to afford a new car, and so being able to afford the new car must mean that you landed the Johnson account, right? How else would you have been able to afford a new car? Answer: lots of ways. Just as there are lots of different ways that you can get a raise, there are lots of ways that you can afford a new car. Maybe the new car dealership is having a phenomenal sale, or perhaps you won the lottery, or perhaps you inherited a lot of money, and so on. This argument is invalid, it is called the "Fallacy of Reversing the Chain."

Fallacy of Reversing the Chain: an invalid argument pattern in which
(1) there are exactly two premises,
(2) the premises and the conclusion are conditional claims,
(3) the consequent of one premise is identical to the antecedent of the other premise, and
(4) the antecedent of the conclusion is identical to the consequent of the premise whose antecedent is shared, and the consequent of the conclusion is identical to the antecedent of the premise whose consequent is shared.

Like the definition of chain argument, this definition is very long and hard to follow. Don't worry about that, because the basic idea is very simple. Think of it like this:

a → b → c so a → c Chain Argument, valid
a → b → c so c → a Fallacy of Reversing a Chain, invalid

The chain argument follows logically from a to b to c. The Fallacy of Reversing a Chain makes a very huge assumption, i.e. that this chain is the only way to get to c. The assumption is that since a leads to b, and b leads to c, if we have c, we must have gotten it through a and b. But that is a very big assumption. There may be very many other ways to get c. Don't jump to conclusions; keep your mind open to alternative possibilities.

Section 4: Negations.

Another complication to deal with in arguments is denial or negation. I touched on this in Section 2 when I talked about Buridan teaching in Paris but not in London, but now it's time to be a little more formal about it. A negation is a denial, it is saying "no," so an affirmation is an acceptance, it is saying "yes." If Joe gives a long, complicated explanation of something and I simply want to agree with him, I might say, "Yes, affirmative, just exactly what he said, that's right." To affirm something is just to repeat it. So to deny something, to negate it, to contradict it, to say exactly the opposite. Here is the definition. Recall the definition from the previous chapter.

A **negation** is a complex claim which states that the claim being negated is false.

If I completely disagree with what Joe said, then I might reply, "No, negative, just exactly the opposite of what Joe said, he's wrong." If Joe says that Socrates is mortal, and I agree, then I can simply repeat what he said, "yes, Socrates is mortal." If Joe says that Socrates is mortal, and I disagree, then I can simply put a "not" in what Joe said, "no, Socrates is not mortal."

Initial Claim: Socrates is mortal.
Affirmation: Socrates is mortal.
Negation: Socrates is not mortal.

This list shows how to affirm or deny an initial claim that is itself simply an affirmation. The initial claim just claims that Socrates is mortal, there is no negation, no denial in the claim. But what if your initial claim *does* have a negation in it? What if Joe says that Socrates is *not* mortal, and I want to agree with him? What do I say? In general, to affirm something is just to repeat it exactly, so if Joe says that Socrates is not mortal, and I want to affirm what he says, then I have to say the same thing; I have to say that Socrates is not mortal. If I want to deny what Joe says, then I have to contradict Joe. In general, we contradict someone by putting a "not" into what they said. So If Joe says that Socrates is *not* mortal, and I want to deny what he says, then I have to say that Socrates is not not mortal. When you deny a negation, you have a double negation.

Initial Claim: Socrates is not mortal.
Affirmation: Socrates is not mortal.
Negation: Socrates is not not mortal.

The negation of an initial claim which is already a negation results in a double negation, or a double negative. In logic, a double negative cancels itself out. So in logic, "Socrates is not not mortal" means that Socrates *is* mortal.

Initial Claim: Socrates is not mortal.
Affirmation: Socrates is not mortal.
Negation (one version): Socrates is not not mortal.
Negation (another version): Socrates is mortal.

In logic, this is called the "Law of Double Negation."

Law of Double Negation: a claim and its double negation are logically equivalent.

I will explain below what it means to say that two claims are "logically equivalent," but for now, the basic idea should be clear: two claims are "logically equivalent" when they mean the same thing, you can substitute one for the other without any change in meaning. In logic, if you end up with a double negative, like "Socrates is not not mortal," you can simplify things by changing it to "Socrates is mortal" and you are not changing the meaning of the claim, just the logical form. In fact, in logic you can go the other way too if you want: from "Socrates is mortal" you can change to "Socrates is not not mortal." People don't usually do that, but logically speaking, it is perfectly reasonable.

Of course, this is not always true in ordinary English. For example, "He don't know nothing" is a double negative, but the double negative is used for emphasis: it means that he knows nothing. In logic, that double negative would cancel itself out, and so "He don't know nothing" would mean that he does know something. Remember this: in formal logic, a double negative always cancels itself out and means a positive.

In Chapter 1 I used very few negations. You've seen negations in disjunction elimination, modus tollens, and the fallacy of denying the antecedent. But since affirmation is just repeating something you agree with, and negation is simply denying something you disagree with, you can have negations in any argument pattern. Here is a modus ponens argument which includes negations.

1	If Socrates is not human, then Socrates is not mortal.	Premise
2	Socrates is not human.	Premise
∴ 3	Socrates is not mortal.	From 1,2 valid by modus ponens

This argument is just modus ponens because one premise is a conditional claim, the other premise agrees with or affirms the antecedent of the conditional claim, and then the conclusion agrees with or affirms the consequent of the conditional claim. Look again at premise 2. Premise 2 *affirms* the antecedent of the conditional claim in spite of the fact that it has a "not" in it. Since the antecedent of the conditional claim has a "not" in it, the affirmation has a "not" in it. To affirm something is just to agree with it; so if you agree that Socrates is *not* human, then your *affirmation* has to be "Socrates is *not* human." That one little word "not" is extremely important, and so you have to keep careful track of it. Consider this argument.

1	If Socrates is not married, then Socrates is not a husband.	Premise
2	Socrates is not a husband.	Premise
∴ 3	Socrates is not married.	From 1,2 invalid by fallacy of affirming the consequent

If you just look at the second premise and the conclusion, then you might think that this argument is valid by modus tollens, because modus tollens denies the consequent of a conditional, and then concludes by denying the antecedent of the conditional. But you have to look at what the conditional is before you know what affirming or denying the antecedent and consequent will look like. Although premise 2 has a "not" in it, it is *affirming* the consequent, because it is just repeating the consequent. So here are two simple guidelines for situations where you mix affirmation and negation (affirming and denying).

To negate an affirmation, use a negation (e.g. "not").
To affirm a negation, use a negation (e.g. "not").

What happens when you don't mix negation and affirmation? What happens when you affirm an affirmation, or negate a negation? The first is easy: to affirm that Socrates is married, just say "Socrates is married." You don't need to use "not" when you affirm an affirmation. What happens when you negate a negation? Consider this argument. If someone says that Socrates is not human and you disagree, you want to deny what they said, then you can use a double negation and say, "No, you are wrong, Socrates is not not human." But you could also use the Law of Double Negation and just say, "No, you are wrong, Socrates *is* human."

To affirm an affirmation, do not use a negation.
To deny a negation, do not use a negation (or use a double negation).

I'm always uncomfortable at this point because when you deny a negation by using an affirmation, you are skipping a logical step. Strictly speaking, the progression should go like this:

Original Claim: Socrates is not mortal.
Denial of Claim: Socrates is not not mortal.
Double Negation Elimination: Socrates is mortal.

I'm letting you skip the step where you add the "not" in and then take out the double negation.

Original Claim: Socrates is not mortal.
Denial of Claim: Socrates is mortal.

But, I have found through experience that people are not very likely to make mistakes when they work this way, and it turns out to be much easier for students to make progress when I allow them to do this. So although I'm uncomfortable allowing you to skip any logical step, I'll let you skip this one. You will make me feel better if every once in a while you stick in the double negation step, just to show me that you understand it is really a step in the argument. So both of the following are acceptable.

Version that skips the double negation:

1	If Socrates is not married, then Socrates is not a husband.	Premise
2	Socrates is a husband.	Premise
∴ 3	Socrates is married.	From 1,2, valid by modus tollens

Version that includes the double negation step:

1	If Socrates is not married, then Socrates is not a husband.	Premise
2	Socrates is not not a husband.	Premise
∴ 3	Socrates is not not married.	From 1,2, valid by modus tollens
∴ 4	Socrates is married.	From 3, valid by the Law of Double Negation

Let me take you slowly through another example.

1	If Socrates is not mortal, then Socrates is not human.	Premise
2	Socrates is human.	Premise
∴ 3	Socrates is mortal.	From 1,2 ???

Does this fit any argument pattern that you know? It is not modus ponens, because in modus ponens, you affirm the antecedent of the conditional premise. This argument doesn't do that. The second premise seems to be affirming something having to do with the consequent of the conditional claim, so is this the fallacy of affirming the consequent? No, because to affirm the consequent, you have to repeat it exactly, and premise 2 does not repeat the consequent exactly. What exactly is the difference between premise 2 and the consequent of the conditional? The difference is that the consequence of the conditional says that Socrates is *not* human, while premise 2 says that Socrates *is* human. Those are opposites. To say that Socrates *is* human is the same as saying that he is *not* not human. Double negation cancels itself out, and so "Socrates is human" is the denial of "Socrates is not human."

So premise 2 of that last argument is the negation or denial of the consequent of the conditional claim. What about the conclusion? If you say that Socrates *is* mortal, then you are denying the claim that Socrates is not mortal, you are saying that Socrates is *not* not mortal. "Socrates is mortal" is the *denial* of "Socrates is not mortal." So that argument has a conditional premise, the other premise denies the consequent of the conditional claim and the conclusion denies the antecedent of the conditional claim. That is modus tollens. Here are four arguments, and all of them are valid by modus tollens.

First Version:

1	If Plato is human, then Plato is mortal.	Premise
2	Plato is not mortal.	Premise
∴ 3	Plato is not human.	From *1,2 valid by modus tollens*

Second Version:

1	If Plato is human, then Plato is not mortal.	Premise
2	Plato is mortal.	Premise
∴ 3	Plato is not human.	From *1,2 valid by modus tollens*

Third Version:

1	If Plato is not human, then Plato is mortal.	Premise
2	Plato is not mortal.	Premise
∴ 3	Plato is human.	From *1,2 valid by modus tollens*

Fourth Version:

1	If Plato is not human, then Plato is not mortal.	Premise
2	Plato is mortal.	Premise
∴ 3	Plato is not not human.	From *1,2 valid by modus tollens*

Notice that the last argument concludes with a double negation. Probably you have been taught to avoid double negation, and that is a good rule of thumb in ordinary English. However, in logic, a double negation is no problem at all. You may leave a double negation alone, or you may use the law of double negation to eliminate it.

There is a very important reason why you can do this with the Law of Double Negation: it is not an *inference pattern*, it is a *logical equivalence*. An inference pattern is a way of arguing from one set of claims (the premises) to another claim (the conclusion). A valid argument says that hypothetically, if the premises turn out to be true, then the conclusion must also be true. A logical equivalence is different. The connection between two claims which are logically equivalent is much closer: two logically equivalent claims *mean exactly the same thing*. Two logically equivalent claims say the same thing in different words. "Socrates is not not human" and "Socrates is human" mean exactly the same thing in logic.

One important result of the fact that logically equivalent claims mean the same thing is that they are *intersubstitutable*, i.e. one can be substituted for the other. Here are two simple examples.

First Version:

1	It is not true that Socrates is not married.	Premise
∴ 2	Socrates is married.	From 1, valid by the law of double negation

Second Version:

1	Socrates is married.	Premise
∴ 2	It is not true that Socrates is not married.	From 1, valid by the law of double negation

Using the law of Double Negation, you may substitute a double negation for an affirmation, or an affirmation for a double negation. In fact, if you wanted, you could even add a double negation onto a negation, like this.

1	Socrates is not married.	Premise
∴ 2	Socrates is not not not married.	From 1 valid by the law of double negation

People don't usually do this but it is permitted by the laws of logic. You may add in or take out double negations, but you may not add in or take out quadruple negations, you have to take it step by step, like this.

1	Socrates is not not not not married.	Premise
∴ 2	Socrates is not not married.	From 1, valid by law of double negation
∴ 3	Socrates is married.	From 2, valid by law of double negation

You can add negations in pairs, just as you can take them out in pairs. This is a very important principle, because very often in logic you end up negating negations, and things will be much easier for you if you can easily spot, and handle these double negations.

Even more important is the fact that you can alter parts of complex claims using laws of logical equivalence. For example, consider this argument.

1	If Socrates is not not married, then Socrates is a husband.	Premise
∴ 2	If Socrates is married, then Socrates is a husband.	From 1, valid by law of double negation
3	Socrates is married.	Premise
∴ 4	Socrates is a husband.	From 2,3 valid by modus ponens

The first premise is a conditional claim whose antecedent is a double negation. Because the Law of Double Negation is a law of logical equivalence, and not an inference pattern, it may be used on the antecedent of the conditional claim to simplify it. You may not do this with inference patterns. Here is an example of an invalid argument which uses an inference pattern as if it were a law of logical equivalence.

1	If Socrates is male and Socrates is unmarried, then Socrates is a bachelor.	Premise
∴ 2	If Socrates is male, then Socrates is a bachelor.	From 1, **invalid**, improper use of conjunction elimination
3	Socrates is male.	Premise
∴ 4	Socrates is a bachelor.	From 2,3 valid by modus ponens

This argument is invalid because it uses conjunction elimination as if it were a law of logical equivalence. You may change

If Socrates is not not married, then Socrates is a husband

to

If Socrates is married, then Socrates is a husband

because in making that change you have not altered the meaning of the claim. They are two different ways of saying the same thing. But you may *not* change

If Socrates is male and Socrates is unmarried, then Socrates is a bachelor

to

If Socrates is male, then Socrates is a bachelor

because these two claims say two very different things. This improper use of conjunction elimination changes the meaning of the claim. So again, remember that you may use laws of logical equivalence inside complex claims, but you may not use inference patterns inside complex claims. Laws of logical equivalence give you laws for changing one claim into a different claim which means the same thing, while inference patterns give you rules for inferring one claim from other claims which mean very different things.

At this point, some people get frustrated with logic: why would anybody in their right mind ever do a quadruple negation? "Not, not, not, not" changes to "not, not" which cancels itself out, so why bother? The honest, simple, and most important answer to this question is: it's the truth. The study of logic is perhaps the most basic of all the sciences: to study logic is to study the most fundamental principles of human thought. So the principle of double negation is interesting in itself as a deep fact about logic.

On top of that, it is an excellent form of mental gymnastics: practice two, three, four and more negations simply to focus your attention and to keep your logical skills limber and robust. And who knows? There actually are occasions where double and triple negations come up in real life, e.g. in computer programming, in law, in mapping out procedures for complex tasks, and so on.

Section 5: The Principle of Charity.

Logic requires precision. Unfortunately for logicians, ordinary spoken and written languages are often very imprecise. Not only do people make mistakes, but often people skip over things they take for granted. These can lead to very dramatic problems in logic, but let's begin with a simple, easily fixed problem. Consider the following argument.

1	If Socrates is human, then Socrates is mortal.	Premise
2	Socrats is human.	Premise
∴ 3	Socrates is mortal.	From 1,2 ???

Notice that in the second premise, Socrates' name is spelled "Socrats." That is a simple misspelling that can happen to anyone. If you assume that words spelled differently mean different things, then you have to say that this argument is invalid. To be modus ponens, that premise would have to affirm the antecedent of the conditional claim, and to do that it would have to say that "Socrates" is human. But it doesn't say that, it only says that "Socrats" is human. So the argument is invalid.

In calling that last argument invalid I am using what I call the "Principle of Absolute Pickiness." This is a principle you can use when you interpret arguments.

Principle of Absolute Pickiness: Attribute to an author the argument that most exactly fits what the author wrote.

This is the principle I have been using so far. You might think of it as "the e-mail principle," because you know that in typing an e-mail address, if you get even one letter wrong, your mail will not be delivered to the person you want. Everything must match with absolute precision. If the argument says "Socrats," then we use "Socrats" in our assessment of the argument. I call this being "picky" because if someone actually wrote this argument, you would know that when the author wrote "Socrats" they had simply misspelled "Socrates." No matter what the cause, it is perfectly obvious that they meant to write "Socrates." You are being very picky if you stick to what they actually happened to *write*, instead of what you know they really *meant*.

Using the principle of absolute pickiness all the time is like being a lawyer who is always looking for a loophole in the law to win their case on a technicality rather than trying to make sure the trial is fair and that justice is done. If you are out for logical fairness, and you want to do justice to the arguments you consider, then you have to be a bit more charitable. An alternative to the principle of absolute pickiness is the principle of charity.

Principle of Charity: Attribute to an author the best argument that is compatible with what the author wrote.

This principle tries to balance faithfulness to what the author actually wrote, with fairness to what the author clearly intended to say.

If you use the principle of charity, you have to re-write the original argument. Start with the argument you are given, and make whatever changes are required to pass the principle of absolute pickiness, and justify the changes you make. Here's an example.

Original Argument

1	If Socrates is human, then Socrates is mortal.
2	Socrats is human.
∴ 3	Socrates is mortal.

Revised Argument

1	If Socrates is human, then Socrates is mortal.	Premise
2	Socrates is human.	Premise; "Socrats" means "Socrates"
∴ 3	Socrates is mortal.	From 1,2 valid by modus ponens

This is a simple and pretty obvious change to make. There are other changes you can make that are perfectly reasonable and charitable. Consider this example.

Original Argument

1	If Socrates is human, he's mortal.
2	He's human.
∴ 3	Socrates is mortal.

Revised Argument

1	If Socrates is human, then Socrates is mortal.	Premise; "he" refers to Socrates, the consequent of a conditional is introduced by "then"
2	Socrates is human.	Premise; "he" refers to Socrates
∴ 3	Socrates is mortal.	From 1,2 valid by modus ponens

In this example there are a few changes. Most obviously I've replaced the "he" with "Socrates" since that is obviously what the author means. Notice also that in the original version premise 1 leaves out the "then" in the conditional claim. When you revise the argument to put it in perfect form, you need to make sure that everything is stated perfectly, all the way down to including the "then" in a conditional claim.

You may have to make some pretty substantial changes to an argument. For example, usually people don't even bother to number their premises. Very often you have to number the premises and put them in the proper order. Here is an example.

Original Argument
If Socrates is human, then he's mortal. But Socrates is human. So Socrates is mortal.

Revised Argument

1	If Socrates is human, then Socrates is mortal.	Premise; "he" refers to Socrates
2	Socrates is human.	Premise
∴ 3	Socrates is mortal.	From 1,2 valid by modus ponens

This is a much more radical revision of the argument, but it is still faithful to what the author intended. Because these kinds of revisions are very often needed, and because they can sometimes be tricky, I'll give you a few tips to help make things easier.

The first and most important tip on making these kinds of revisions is to *find the conclusion first*. The conclusion is the most important part of an argument: it's the whole point of making the argument. Usually it is easy to find the conclusion because it has a "conclusion indicator" in front of it, like "so" or "therefore" or "hence" (there are many other conclusion indicators in the English language, so be on the lookout for them). Here is another example of translating an argument from ordinary language into logic.

Original Argument
If Socrates is human, he's mortal. But he is human. That's how we know that Socrates was mortal.

Revised Argument

1	If Socrates is human, then Socrates is mortal.	Premise; "he" refers to Socrates; "then" is required for a consequent
2	Socrates is human.	Premise; "he" refers to Socrates
∴ 3	Socrates is mortal.	From 1,2 valid by modus ponens; "That's how we know" indicates the conclusion

Compare this original argument with the previous original argument. They are different in a number of ways. But if you think about them, really they are making exactly the same argument. Notice also that the conclusion doesn't have one of the "conclusion indicator" words that I just mentioned. You don't have to have an explicit conclusion indicator to know that you've got the conclusion. The conclusion is the thing that someone is trying to prove, and so anything the author says to let you know what is supposed to be proven by the argument indicates the conclusion of the argument.

There is another very important trick you have to notice while we are on the topic of finding the conclusion of the argument first. Think about this example.

Original Argument
We know that Socrates is mortal because he is human, and of course if he's human, then he's mortal.

Revised Argument

1	If Socrates is human, then Socrates is mortal.	Premise; "he" refers to Socrates
2	Socrates is human.	Premise; "he" refers to Socrates; and "because" indicates a premise
∴ 3	Socrates is mortal.	From 1,2 valid by modus ponens; "We know that" indicates the conclusion

Compare this original argument with the previous two original arguments. Logically speaking, it is really saying exactly the same thing as the other arguments: it is a simple modus ponens argument. But notice that it is worded very differently. The main differences are that the conclusion comes first, and the whole argument is in one sentence. You need to get used to seeing the conclusion first, because authors very often state their conclusion first. This is a courtesy to the reader; it is nice to let your reader know what it is you are trying to prove, so that your reader sees your point right away. Why are you talking about Socrates being human? Because you are proving that Socrates is mortal. You should also get used to seeing an entire argument in one paragraph. Short, simple arguments very often occur in one sentence. It is your job to take the sentence apart, piece by piece, to analyze its logic. Again remember, first of all you need to *find the conclusion*.

The second most important tip on revising arguments is that once you have found the conclusion, *look for logical operators*. A logical operator is a conditional, a disjunction, a conjunction, a negation (and other things which we will see later in this book). For example, look back at the last original argument. At the very end you see "if he's human, then he's mortal." Right away you know that is a conditional claim, and so you are going to make that one of your premises. So there are two important tips for you to remember when you translate arguments into logic.

1. Find the conclusion.
2. Find all logical operators.

If you start out by following these two tips, you will be in a very good position to understand the logic of an argument. To understand the third tip, I'll translate the next argument using only the two tips I just mentioned.

Original Argument
If Socrates were a monkey, he'd be mortal. But he's not mortal, because he's not a monkey.

Revised Argument (first two stages)

1	If Socrates is a monkey, then Socrates is mortal.	Premise
2	?	Premise
∴ 3	Socrates is not mortal.	From 1,2 ???

I started by finding the conclusion. In this case, the conclusion was in the middle of the argument. I knew that because of the word "because." Whenever someone says x because y, you know that y is a reason (a premise) and x is a conclusion. In the case of "he's not mortal" *because* "he's not a monkey," what comes after the "because" is the premise, and what comes before the "because" is the conclusion.

After finding the conclusion, I had to look for logical operators. The one that jumped right out at me was the "if" in the very first sentence. It doesn't have a "then" following it, but that didn't fool me. Whenever you have an "if" you need to put it in standard form with a "then" (there are many other ways to state a conditional claim in the English language, and we'll see more of them in the next chapter). Also, notice that I changed the "if Socrates *were* a monkey" to "if Socrates *is* a monkey." As long as you are not changing the meaning of what the author is trying to say, you should try to standardize the language as much as possible, and try to put it into the simple present tense using "is." If, in your judgment, the actual wording of the original is essential to its meaning, then be faithful to what the author actually said. But in general, try to standardize the language.

At this point we have most of the argument figured out. We have the conclusion, and we have a premise. Before we go back to the original argument to see if there is another premise, take a moment to look at the revised argument as I have it. One premise is a conditional claim, and what is the conclusion? The conclusion *denies the consequent* of the conditional claim. Look back in chapter 1 at the list of argument patterns that you know. Look to see which of the argument patterns has a conditional claim, and a conclusion which denies the consequent of the conditional claim. You will find only one argument pattern that fits: the fallacy of denying the antecedent. Before you finish looking at the argument, you should already suspect that this argument is invalid because it commits the fallacy of denying the antecedent.

In other words, when you are translating arguments from ordinary language into logic, you should make it as easy for yourself as possible, and treat it as if it is a simple multiple-choice problem. Look at all the patterns you know, and assume that the argument in front of you fits one of those patterns. From my own years of experience with arguments, I can tell you that most of the arguments you encounter in the world will fit one of those patterns. Of course, you have to be on your guard for that small percentage of arguments that doesn't fit those patterns, but always start out by looking to see if it fits one of the patterns you do know, and usually you will quickly find the answer.

In fact, I'm going to make your job even easier. The principle of charity tells you to attribute to an author the *best* argument that is compatible with the words the author actually used. Start out by looking for a match between what the author actually said, and the *valid* argument patterns. That narrows things down even further for you. In this case, the argument does not have an "either ..., or ..." and so it can't be a disjunctive argument. That narrows things down for us. Next, look to see if it could be a chain argument. In order for it to be a chain argument, it has to have two "if ..., then ..." claims. So go back to the original argument, look at what we've left out, and see if what we've left out is an "if ..., then ..." claim. We've done the first sentence (that's premise 1 of the revised argument), and we've done what comes before the "because" (that's the conclusion of the revised argument). All that's left is what comes after the "because" in the second sentence (that is a reason, or a premise, because of the word "because"). What comes after the word "because" in the original argument is this: "he's not a monkey." That is not an "if ..., then ..." claim, and so we know that this argument is not a chain argument.

You should continue the process of elimination. Go through all the valid argument patterns you learned in chapter 1, and see if this fits any of them. The two it comes closest to are modus ponens and modus tollens. But now look again at the first premise of the argument we have so far.

1. If Socrates is a monkey, then Socrates is mortal.   Premise

What would the second premise have to be if this argument were going to be a modus ponens? What would it have to be if it were modus tollens? Compare that to what we actually have. In a modus ponens, you have a conditional premise, and then the other premise *affirms the antecedent* of the conditional claim; in a modus tollens, you have a conditional premise, and then the other premise *denies the consequent* of the conditional claim. Compare these with what we actually have after the "because" in the original version of the argument:

Modus ponens premise 2: Socrates is a monkey.
Modus tollens premise 2: Socrates is not mortal.
Actual premise 2: Socrates is not a monkey.

The actual second premise doesn't fit the pattern of modus ponens, but it doesn't fit the pattern of modus tollens either. If we can rule out all the other valid patterns, then we have to start looking for invalid argument patterns for it to fit. If we can't find even an invalid argument pattern for it to fit, then we can just say it is "invalid" without specifying any reason or pattern for it at all.

But in fact, it isn't hard at this point to see what invalid argument pattern it does fit: the fallacy of denying the antecedent. Here is our finished translation of the argument.

Revised Argument (first two stages)

1	If Socrates is a monkey, then Socrates is mortal.	Premise
2	Socrates is not a monkey.	Premise
∴ 3	Socrates is not mortal.	From 1,2 invalid by fallacy of denying the antecedent

Sometimes it will be very easy to spot which pattern an argument fits, and the more you practice, the easier it will be for you to spot argument patterns. But in order to get good at this, you need to make things easy on yourself by making translation a simple multiple-choice problem. You know the patterns, just look to see which pattern the actual argument fits. Also, remember that the principle of charity says that you should look first to see if the argument fits one of the valid argument patterns. Give the author the benefit of the doubt if the argument really could reasonably be interpreted as a valid argument. When you are translating from arguments in ordinary language, use the principle of charity; but when you are working with arguments in strict logical format, only then should you use the principle of absolute pickiness.

Section 6: Enthymemes.

There is a time to be precise, and a time to give someone the benefit of the doubt. When you are dealing with arguments in ordinary language, you need to be a bit charitable; but when you are dealing with formal logic, you need to be absolutely picky and stick to the rules precisely. For example, here's an argument that seems perfectly reasonable:

1	Socrates is human.	Premise
So 2	Socrates is mortal.	From 1, ???

Obviously, all humans are mortal; usually this "goes without saying." But logic requires that you actually say these things that usually go without saying. You need to take that previous argument and re-write it like this:

1	Socrates is human.	Premise
2	If Socrates is human, then Socrates is mortal.	Premise; hidden premise
∴ 3	Socrates is mortal.	From 1,2 valid by modus ponens

What is happening in the original argument is that the second premise is so obvious that you are saying it in your head, silently, and just writing down the end result. The Greek word for "in" is *en*, and one of the Greek words for the mind is *thymos*, so when you skip a step because you did it silently "in your head," the argument is called an "enthymeme."

An **enthymeme** is an argument with at least one hidden premise.

The hidden premise of an enthymeme can also be called a missing premise or a suppressed premise. Strictly speaking, every enthymeme is invalid, but like the previous argument, if you add in the step that was skipped, then the argument is valid. Here is another enthymeme.

1	Socrates is a bachelor.	Premise
∴ 2	Socrates is unmarried.	From 1 ???

Is this a valid argument? Could the conclusion be false when the premise is true? If Socrates is a bachelor, is there any way he could possibly be married? The correct response is to say this: it depends upon what you mean by "bachelor." If by "bachelor" you mean "unmarried man," then Socrates can't be married if he is a bachelor. But if you mean something different by "bachelor," then maybe the argument is invalid.

But this is silly. What else could "bachelor" mean except "unmarried man"? Everyone knows what the word "bachelor" means, right? Normally, yes. But notice that we are making an assumption here. We are assuming that when the argument uses the word "bachelor" it means "unmarried man." That's not much of an assumption, but it is an assumption. Hidden assumptions very often have a way of creating unnecessary confusion, and so it is a good idea to state all of your assumptions explicitly. Time and time again when two people disagree about something, and can't seem to resolve their disagreement, it is because one of them is making an assumption that the other person doesn't accept. If you learn now to state your assumptions, no matter how obvious you think they are, it will help you immensely.

In other words, that last argument is *invalid*. Why? Because it is an enthymeme; it is relying upon a hidden assumption about what the author means by "bachelor." There is one weird possibility for the premise to be true when the conclusion is false, i.e. if the author of the argument has some other definition of "bachelor" in mind. If you wanted to fix the argument to make it valid, you would do this.

1	Socrates is a bachelor.	Premise
2	If Socrates is a bachelor, then Socrates is unmarried.	Premise; hidden premise
∴ 3	Socrates is unmarried.	From 1,2 valid by modus ponens

In this case, assuming that "bachelor" means "unmarried man" is a very obvious assumption, but you still have to state it explicitly. It is a perfectly reasonable assumption, but it is an assumption, and so it has to be stated, you can't hide it. Don't get me wrong: it is ok to make assumptions. Sometimes we can't do without making assumptions. But you always have to make your assumptions explicit.

This also holds for longer arguments which have obvious sub-conclusions. Consider this simple example.

1	If you land the Johnson account, then you get a raise.	Premise
2	If you get a raise, then you can afford a new car.	Premise
∴ 3	If you land the Johnson account, then you can afford a new car.	From 1,2 valid by chain argument

What if you extend the chain even further, like this?

1	If you land the Johnson account, then you get a raise.	Premise
2	If you get a raise, then you can afford a new car.	Premise
3	If you can afford a new car, then you can sell your old car.	Premise
∴ 4	If you land the Johnson account, then you can sell your old car.	From 1-3 ???

Is that a valid chain argument? No, it's not. A chain argument can only be two premises long. Chain arguments take just two steps and then stop. If you want to continue the chain, then you have to stop and sum up with a sub-conclusion, and then add your extra premises on like this.

1	If you land the Johnson account, then you get a raise.	Premise
2	If you get a raise, then you can afford a new car.	Premise
∴ 3	If you land the Johnson account, then you can afford a new car.	From 1,2 valid by chain argument; hidden assumption
4	If you can afford a new car, then you can sell your old car.	Premise
∴ 5	If you land the Johnson account, then you can sell your old car.	From 3,4 valid by chain argument

Chapter Conclusion.

From this chapter you see again the importance of memorizing the different argument patterns. If you know the patterns by sight, you won't be confused when you see them stacked on top of one another in longer arguments, and you won't be fooled by negations, or enthymemes.

Basic Vocabulary to Memorize:

A **sub-conclusion** is a conclusion that is also used as a premise for a further conclusion, it is not a final conclusion.

A **main conclusion** is a conclusion that is not also used as a premise for a further conclusion, it is a final conclusion.

A **sub-argument** is an argument for a sub-conclusion.

A **main argument** is an argument for a main conclusion.

Law of Double Negation: a claim and its double negation are logically equivalent.

An **enthymeme** is an argument with at least one hidden premise.

Principle of Absolute Pickiness: attribute to an author the argument that most exactly fits what the author wrote.

Principle of Charity: Attribute to an author the best argument that is compatible with the words the author actually used.

Tips on Translating Arguments:

1. Find the conclusion.
2. Find all logical operators.
3. Try to match the argument first to a valid pattern, then to an invalid pattern.

Argument Patterns:

Fallacy of Denying the Antecedent: an invalid argument pattern in which
(a) one premise is a conditional claim,
(b) the other premise denies the antecedent of the conditional claim, and
(c) the conclusion denies the consequent of the conditional claim.

Chain Argument: a valid argument pattern in which
(1) there are exactly two premises,
(2) the premises and the conclusion are conditional claims,
(3) the consequent of one premise is identical to the antecedent of the other premise, and
(4) the antecedent of the conclusion is identical to the antecedent of the premise whose consequent is shared, and the consequent of the conclusion is identical to the consequent of the premise whose antecedent is shared.

Fallacy of Reversing the Chain: an invalid argument pattern in which
(1) there are exactly two premises,
(2) the premises and the conclusion are conditional claims,
(3) the consequent of one premise is identical to the antecedent of the other premise, and
(4) the antecedent of the conclusion is identical to the consequent of the premise whose antecedent is shared, and the consequent of the conclusion is identical to the antecedent of the premise whose consequent is shared.

Exercises for Chapter 2
Reminder: "or" is always inclusive; unless it is spelled "XOR," interpret "or" as the inclusive disjunction.
Exercise 2.1: Longer Arguments. *Fully assess the following arguments for validity*

Sample Problem:

1	If Socrates is not Greek, then Socrates does not speak Greek.
2	Socrates speaks Greek.
∴ 3	Socrates is Greek.
4	If Socrates is Greek, then Socrates is philosophical.
∴ 5	Socrates is philosophical.

Solution:

1	If Socrates is not Greek, then Socrates does not speak Greek.	Premise
2	Socrates speaks Greek.	Premise
∴ 3	Socrates is Greek.	From 1,2 valid by modus tollens
4	If Socrates is Greek, then Socrates is philosophical.	Premise
∴ 5	Socrates is philosophical.	From 3,4 valid by modus ponens

Problem 1
1. Socrates speaks Greek.
2. If Socrates speaks Greek, then Socrates is Greek.
∴ 3. Socrates is Greek.
4. If Socrates is Greek, then Socrates is human.
∴ 5. Socrates is human.

Problem 2
1. Socrates speaks Greek, or Socrates speaks Babylonian.
2. Socrates does not speak Babylonian.
∴ 3. Socrates speaks Greek.
4. If Socrates speaks Greek, then Socrates is Greek.
∴ 5. Socrates is Greek.

Problem 3
1. If Socrates is Persian, then Socrates speaks Babylonian.
2. If Socrates speaks Babylonian, then Socrates speaks Assyrian.
∴ 3. If Socrates is Persian, then Socrates speaks Assyrian.
4. If Socrates speaks Assyrian, then Socrates is a polyglot.
∴ 5. If Socrates is a polyglot, then Socrates is Persian.

Problem 4
1. If Socrates is Greek, then Socrates is a philosopher.
2. Socrates is Greek.
∴ 3. Socrates is a philosopher.
4. Either Socrates is Athenian, or Socrates is not a philosopher.
∴ 5. Socrates is Athenian.

Problem 5
1. Socrates is Athenian.
2. If Socrates is a philosopher, then Socrates is Athenian.
∴ 3. Socrates is a philosopher.
4. Either Socrates is a politician, or Socrates is a philosopher.
∴ 5. Socrates is not a politician.
6. If Socrates is powerful, then Socrates is a politician.
∴ 7. Socrates is not powerful.
∴ 8. Socrates is a philosopher and Socrates is not powerful.

Exercise 2.2: Translation. *Fully assess the following arguments for validity.*

Sample Problem:
Socrates is human. If Socrates is human, then he is mortal. So he's mortal.

Solution:

1	Socrates is human.	Premise
2	If Socrates is human, then Socrates is mortal.	Premise
∴ 3	Socrates is mortal.	From 1,2 valid by modus ponens

1. Socrates is Greek. If Socrates is Greek, then Socrates speaks Greek. So Socrates speaks Greek.
2. Socrates is old. If Socrates is old, then Socrates has white hair. So Socrates has white hair.
3. Socrates is not Persian. Either Socrates is Greek, or Socrates is Persian. So Socrates is Greek.
4. If Socrates is human, then Socrates is mortal. Socrates is not mortal. So Socrates is not human.
5. Horses are pretty. If horses are pretty, then ponies are pretty. So ponies are pretty.

6. Ponies are pretty because horses are pretty, and because if horses are pretty, then ponies are pretty.
7. If horses are pretty, then ponies are pretty. But ponies are not pretty. So horses are not pretty.
8. If horses are pretty, then ponies are pretty. That's why ponies are pretty, because horses are pretty.
9. If horses are pretty, then ponies are pretty. But horses are not pretty, so ponies are not pretty.
10. Harry is a horse, and if he's a horse, then he wears army boots. So Harry wears army boots.

11. Andy is not a horse. But if he were a horse, then he would be pretty. So Andy is not pretty.
12. If Harry's a horse, he has an odd number of toes. But he's got an odd number of toes. So he's a horse.
13. Andy is a horse, and he wears shoes. So he's a horse.
14. Andy wears army boots. So either he is a pink elephant, or he wears army boots.
15. Sally is a zebra. That's how I know that Sally has been cloned; because if she is a zebra, she's been cloned.

16. Either Sally is equine, or she's a zebra. But she's a zebra, so she's not equine.
17. Betty is a zebra, and if so, then she's got an odd number of toes. So Betty has an odd number of toes.
18. Actually Betty has an even number of toes, because she's a zebra, and as everybody knows, if you're a zebra, you've got an even number of toes.
19. Sally is a zebra, and hence she's either a cow or a zebra.
20. If Tommy is a tapir, then he must have an even number of toes. I know that because if he's a tapir, then he's a relative of the rhino family, and if he's a relative of the rhino family, then he's got an even number of toes.

21. Carl is one of them toe-tappin' tapirs. And another thing; Carl is one heck of a snappy dresser. So he's both a snappy dresser and a toe-tappin' tapir.
22. If Socrates is not Greek, then I'm a monkey's uncle. But I'm not a monkey's uncle. So Socrates is Greek.
23. If you keep spinning like that, you are just going to toss your cookies. You know that, don't you? And if you stay on that ride, then you are going to keep spinning and spinning. So if you toss your cookies, then you must have stayed

on that ride far too long.

24. Tommy is a tapir. All tapirs are related to rhinos. So Tommy is related to rhinos.

25 Did you know that if you're a tapir you've got an odd number of toes? You didn't know that? Well, it's true. Isn't that interesting? Anyway, the zoo just bought this tapir named Tommy – Tommy the tapir, isn't that funny? Where was I? Oh yes, I remember (I've got to stop getting side-tracked like this). Anyway, I guess Tommy must have an odd number of toes.

Exercise 2.3: Translation of Longer Arguments*. Translate each of the following arguments into a logical form (using the principle of charity), and then evaluate the argument (using the principle of absolute pickiness). Be sure to mark all hidden assumptions in enthymemes.*

Sample Problem:
Rabbits are cute because they are furry. And if they are cute, then Robin is sure to want one.
So I'm sure that Robin is going to want a rabbit.

Solution:

1	*Rabbits are furry.*	*Premise*
2	*If rabbits are furry, then rabbits are cute.*	*Premise; hidden assumption*
∴ 3	*Rabbits are cute.*	*From 1,2 valid by modus ponens*
4	*If rabbits are cute, then Robin will want a rabbit.*	*Premise*
∴ 5	*Robin will want a rabbit.*	*From 3,4 valid by modus ponens*

1. Socrates is a philosopher. If Socrates is a philosopher, then Socrates is human. So Socrates is human. If Socrates is human, then Socrates is mortal. So Socrates is mortal.

2. If Socrates is a philosopher, then Socrates is human. Socrates is a philosopher. But if Socrates is human, then he is mortal. So Socrates is mortal.

3. Either Socrates is Persian, or he is Greek. He's not Greek. So he must be Persian. But if he is Persian, then he must speak Babylonian. So Socrates speaks Babylonian.

4. If Socrates is a philosopher, then he's not a politician. But he is a politician. So he must not be a philosopher. But if he is not a philosopher, then not an intellectual. So Socrates is not an intellectual.

5. If Socrates is not from Persia, then he must be Egyptian. So he must be from Persia, because he's not Egyptian. So we know that Socrates speaks Persian.

6. Because avarice is a vice, charging interest on loans is immoral. But if charging interest on loans is immoral, then banking is immoral. So banking is immoral.

7. If you are too picky about how your food is prepared, then you suffer from a kind of gluttony. Joe does not suffer from gluttony, and that's why he isn't too picky about how his food is prepared. But either he or his brother is too picky about how his food is prepared. So it must be Joe's brother.

8. Wrath is an excessive desire for revenge, but an excessive desire for revenge is a vice. So wrath is a vice. But that means that wrath is a sin.

9. Sloth is a vice. So wrath is a vice, or sloth is a vice. But we know that wrath is a vice. So sloth is not a vice.

10. Eddie gets upset when other people benefit. If he weren't envious, then he wouldn't get upset when other people benefit. Hence, Eddie is envious. But if he is envious, then he is sinful. It follows that Eddie is sinful.

11. Andy wants to be celebrated for something completely unworthy. So Andy suffers from the vice of vainglory. If he did not suffer from the vice of vainglory, then he would not be so unhappy. So Andy is unhappy.

12. If justice is a virtue, then we ought to care about the welfare of others. We ought to care about the welfare of others, and so justice is a true virtue. But if justice is a virtue, then so is honesty. So honesty is a virtue.

13. If patience is a virtue, then so is courage. But if courage is a virtue, then we should never fear death more than dishonor. And of course if we should never fear death more than dishonor, then we must never give up hope. So if patience is a virtue, then we must never give up hope.

14. If temperance is not a virtue, then it is not wrong to get drunk before an exam. But it is wrong to get drunk before an exam. The conclusion is obvious. But either temperance is not a virtue or drunkenness is not a virtue. It follows that drunkenness is not a virtue.

15. Prudence and circumspection are both virtues. Obviously, then, circumspection is a virtue. But so is foresight. So prudence and foresight are both virtues.

Exercise 2.4: More Arguments. *Fully assess the validity of the following arguments.*

Sample Problem:
Apples are either fruit or vegetables. But they are not vegetables. Furthermore, if they are fruit, then they are sweet; and if they are sweet, then they'd be good in a pie. So apples would make a great pie.

Solution:

1	Either apples are fruit, or apples are vegetables.	Premise
2	Apples are not vegetables.	Premise
∴ 3	Apples are fruit.	From 1,2 valid by disjunction elimination; hidden assumption
4	If apples are fruit, then apples are sweet.	Premise
∴ 5	Apples are sweet.	From 3,4 valid by modus ponens; hidden assumption
6	If apples are sweet, then apples would make a great pie.	Premise
∴ 7	Apples would make a great pie.	From 5,6 valid by modus ponens

1. Cats are mammals and dogs are mammals. But if dogs are mammals, then so are wolves. So wolves are.

2. Rats and shrews are mammals. But either shrews are not mammals, or possums are not. This shows that possums are not mammals.

3. Weasels are rodents or carnivores. But if they were rodents, then their incisor teeth would grow continuously throughout their lives. They don't, so weasels must be carnivores.

4. Both voles and lemmings are closely related to gerbils, so I know that voles are closely related to gerbils. This means that either moles or voles are closely related to gerbils.

5. Raccoons are closely related either to beavers or to bears. If they are closely related to beavers, then they have incisors that keep growing through life. But they don't, so they aren't. Hence, raccoons are closely related to bears.

6. Either squirrels or skunks are rodents. But skunks lack specialized incisors, and possess highly developed canines. That makes them carnivores. So they aren't rodents, so squirrels are rodents.

7. If there were no marsupials outside of Australia, then no animals in South America would have a marsupium. But if no animals in South America had a marsupium, then there would be no opossums in South America. But there are opossums in South America. Hence there are marsupials outside of Australia.

8. Shrews and moles both look a lot like voles. So either moles look like voles, or shrews look like rats.

9. Justice demands equality of exchange, and if that is so, then charging interest on a monetary loan is unjust. And if charging interest on a monetary loan is unjust, then the whole credit card racket is corrupt. But if the whole credit card racket is corrupt, then the whole banking system is corrupt. Therefore, the entire system of banks is fundamentally immoral.

10. If war is always contrary to peace, then war is always wrong. And if war is always wrong, then a massive defense budget is equally wrong, and our fiscal policy is based on the wrong priorities. Obviously, then, the fiscal policy of the United States is wrong.

11. If there were a God, then there would exist a power of infinite goodness in the universe. But if the universe contained an infinite good, there would be no evil. But evil clearly exists in the world. So there is no God.

12. Every observable fact can be accounted for scientifically, without positing the existence of a divine being. But if that is true, then there is no scientific basis for belief in God. If God did exist, there would be a scientific basis for belief in God. Hence, there is no God.

13. It is a scientific fact that motion exists. But if there were no First Mover who began all motion, then motion would not exist. So there must be a First Mover. If there is a First Mover, then God exists. So God exists.

14. The human heart grows naturally for the purpose of pumping blood. If so, then a natural organ has a purpose; and if a natural organ has a purpose, then either all purposes are conscious, or there is an intelligent designer who assigns purposes to natural organs. Not all purposes are conscious, so there exists a God who created the world according to an intelligent plan.

15. God could possibly exist. Hence, God's existence is not impossible. Hence, God's existence is necessary. Hence, God actually exists.

CHAPTER 3: SYMBOLS

Now it is time to begin learning a system of symbolic logic. There is an extremely important reason why you need to learn to use symbolic notation when you analyze the logic of arguments: living languages are illogical. From a logical point of view, the English language, and in fact every language actually spoken by human beings, is a complete mess. The only way to capture the pristine beauty of logic is to invent an artificial set of symbols that are very far removed from any spoken tongue.

Actually, you can turn this truth around and say that from the point of view of human language and human life, symbolic logic is hopelessly limited. A purely logical language has no room in it for poetry, for metaphor, for playful ambiguity or jokes. Illogical human languages can express the heights of religious illumination and the depths of human despair. Consider this sentence: "If King David murdered Uriah the Hittite, and took his widow, Bathsheba, to be his own wife, then the wrath of God will fall mightily upon him." A logician looks at that sentence and sees only this: "**If** *blah blah blah*, **and** *blah blah blah*, **then** *blah blah blah*.*"* If you were in a literature class or if this were a line from a poem, you might tend to read it in exactly the opposite way: *"blah* King David **murdered** Uriah the Hittite, *blah* took his widow **Bathsheba**, to be his own **wife**, *blah* the **wrath of God** will fall mightily upon him." Logicians abstract from the content of a claim and look only at the bare, logical operators. The dry, barren system of logical notation may be ideal for computers, but not for human beings.

However I don't see the artificial language of symbolic logic as being at odds with or in tension with the natural language that we learn to speak and write as we grow up. In human life there is room for both. There is a time for playful ambiguity, and there is a time for clarity and precision. As a living human being who will face many different situations, you owe it to yourself to develop all of your abilities, so that you can determine when to use the cold clarity of logic, and when not to. If you don't develop your ability to think logically, you deprive yourself of that choice, and leave part of yourself undeveloped.

Section 1: The Symbols.

In order to approach the precision of logic, you need to memorize a few basic symbols, and how to do simple translations between them and English. Here are the main symbols you need to know right now.

→ (arrow) = If ..., then ... (conditional claim)
& (ampersand) = and (conjunction)
v (wedge) = or (disjunction)
~ (tilde) = not (negation)

For example, instead of

Socrates is Greek and Socrates is a philosopher

now you can write

Socrates is Greek & Socrates is a philosopher.

Instead of

If Socrates is human, then Socrates is mortal

now you can write

Socrates is human → Socrates is mortal.

Whenever you find a conditional, just put the arrow in the sentence in place of the "if ..., then ..." Whenever you find a conjunction, just put the ampersand in the sentence in place of the "and."

But that's just the first step. In symbolic logic we try to boil everything down to its logical essence; we try to get to the bare bones of the logic of the argument, we try to look past the actual English language argument to see the underlying logical structure. In symbolic logic we don't care about the nuances, the metaphors, the poetry of the language used to express an argument. So we do away with everything. To a living, breathing person, the sentence "If Socrates is human, then Socrates is mortal" brings to mind thoughts of our own mortality, thoughts of the possibility of an after-life, thoughts of God and so on. To a logician, this sentence is nothing more than a conditional claim – that's it.

In order to abstract from the actual content of what it said, and to focus just on the fundamental logical structure of the claim, logicians substitute letters for claims. For example, we might substitute the letter H for the claim that Socrates is human (guess why I picked H), and we might substitute the letter M for the claim that Socrates is mortal (guess why I picked M). We do that in this way:

H = Socrates is human
M = Socrates is mortal

This is called an *index*. It tells you what the English words are being replaced by, so you can keep track of where you are. So here is a translation of an argument from English into symbolic logic.

1. If Socrates is human, then Socrates is mortal.
2. Socrates is human.
∴ 3. Socrates is mortal.
H = Socrates is human
M = Socrates is mortal

1	H → M	Premise
2	H	Premise
∴ 3	M	From *1,2 valid by modus ponens*

That's all there is to it (for now). Here is another example.
1. Either Socrates is Greek, or Socrates is Persian.
2. Socrates is not Persian.
∴ 3. Socrates is Greek.
G = Socrates is Greek
P = Socrates is Persian

1	G v P	Premise
2	~P	Premise
∴ 3	G	From *1,2 valid by disjunction elimination*

Of course you remember that the wedge is the *inclusive* disjunction. If you want to use the *exclusive* disjunction, you must use a different symbol (feel free to make up your own symbol for exclusive disjunction).

One thing it is important for you to realize right away is that when you do your index, *you must use capital letters*. There will be more symbols for you to learn later, and we will need to use both lower and upper case letters, and things will get impossibly confusing if you don't keep capitals and lower case letters separate. When you are assigning letters for whole claims, like "Socrates is Greek," you must use a capital letter.

Another thing you have to realize right away is that when you make up your index, *you may not abbreviate*. You have to write the whole thing out, whatever the capital letter stands for. Do not let a capital letter stand for anything less than a complete claim.

Finally, when you do your index it is extremely important that you obey the following rule: *never include a logical negation in the index*. Let a positive stand for a positive, and let a negation stand for a negation. For example, consider the following modus tollens argument.

1. If Joe drank the poison, then Joe died.
2. Joe did not die.
∴ 3. Joe did not drink the poison.
P = Joe drank the poison
D = Joe died

1	P → D	Premise
2	~D	Premise
∴ 3	~P	From *1,2 valid by modus tollens*

Notice that I let P stand for the claim that Joe *did* drink the poison. That is what I mean when I say to let a positive stand for a positive. That way, when we have ~D in premise 2, that means Joe did *not* die. That is what I mean when I say to let a negative stand for a negative. I really don't want you even to think about doing this any other way, and so I'm not going to show you what it would look like if you violate this rule. Just take my word for it, if you violate this rule, you will, sooner or later, get confused in double or triple negations, and you will get an argument completely wrong. So let positives be positives, and let negations be negations; it's not just a rule, it's a good idea.

But I do need to clarify the rule just a bit more. When I say to let negations be negations, the only thing I am referring to is *logical negation*, i.e. ~ (tilde). Never include a *logical negation* in your index. For example, consider this argument.

1. If the meter has a negative reading, then the device is not working properly.
2. The meter has a negative reading.
∴ 3. The device is not working properly.
M = the meter has a negative reading
D = the device is working properly

1	M → ~D	Premise
2	M	Premise
∴ 3	~D	From *1,2 valid by modus ponens*

This is exactly right. Can you see why this obeys the rule that you should never include a logical negation in the index? How can I say that, when the index clearly has the word "negative" in it? Isn't the word "negative" a negation? Answer: no, because it is not a *logical* negation. M stands for the claim that the meter *does* have a negative reading. That is logically positive. That way ~M will stand for the claim that the meter does *not* have a negative reading. D stands for the claim that the device *is* working properly, and that way ~D will stand for the claim that the device *is not* working properly. This is exactly the way it should be. Let me give you one more example.

1. If the dial reads zero, then the tank is empty.
2. The tank is not empty.
∴ 3. The dial does not read zero.
D = the dial reads zero
T = the tank is empty

1	D → T	Premise
2	~T	Premise
∴ 3	~D	From *1,2 valid by modus tollens*

Again, positive D stands for the logically positive claim that the dial *does* read zero, so that ~D will stand for the logically negative claim that the dial does *not* read zero. Logically positive T stands for the claim that the tank *is* empty, and so ~T will stand for the logically negative claim that the tank is *not* empty. Always let a logical positive be a logical positive, and always let a logical negation be a logical negation.

Section 2: Translation.

In chapter 2 you learned the difference between the principle of absolute pickiness and the principle of charity. You use the principle of charity when you translate from ordinary language into logic, and you use the principle of absolute pickiness on arguments in logical form. You also saw that in the process of translation, you very often have to re-word things, and say them more concisely: you have to trim the fat. Here is a simple example.

Socrates was a human being. Furthermore, as is obvious, if Socrates was a human being, then he had to be mortal. Therefore, Socrates was mortal.

There are a few extra words in this argument, but it is pretty easy to see that from a logical point of view, all the author is trying to say is this:

1. Socrates was human.
2. If Socrates was human, then Socrates was mortal.
∴ 3. Socrates was mortal.
H = Socrates was human
M = Socrates was mortal.

1	H	Premise
2	H → M	Premise
∴ 3	M	From *1,2 valid by modus ponens*

I have just boiled down that paragraph to a very simple and short string of logical symbols. I've left out the personal style the author used, but I've gotten to the logical heart of the argument. Every time you translate from one language into another, you lose something in the translation. That is clearly true when we translate from English into symbolic logic. But in spite of the fact that we lose all the flavor of the author's original wording, what we gain is a precise and clear view of the basic logical structure of the author's argument. Here is another example.

They put so much poison in his coffee cup, I'm sure that if Joe drank it, he died. But wait! What's that? Are you sure? Joe drank the poison? Oh no! That's it for Joe! He must be dead!

1. If Joe drank the poison, then Joe is dead.
2. Joe drank the poison.
∴ 3. Joe is dead.
P = Joe drank the poison
D = Joe is dead

1	P → D	Premise
2	P	Premise
∴ 3	D	From *1,2 valid by modus ponens*

Here you see I've left out a whole lot of words. The exclamation points indicate that there is a lot of emotion in the author of the original argument, and all of that has been taken out. All that is left is just the bare logical structure.

The question, then, is, "How do you know what words to use and what words to throw out?" The answer is simple: *use all the words that are logically relevant*. To do that, use the tips on translating arguments from chapter 2:

1. Find the conclusion.
2. Find all logical operators (e.g. "and," "or," "if ..., then ...").
3. Try to match the argument first to a valid pattern, then to an invalid pattern.

From tip 3, you should remind yourself that translation from ordinary logic into English is a multiple-choice problem. Most of the arguments you come across will fit the patterns you already know. Your job is simply to use the principle of charity to find the best match.

There are many different ways for an author to indicate a conclusion. "So" is the one that I've used most, because it is so short. But there are many other ways as well. Here are a few.

Therefore ...
So ...
Hence ...
and so I conclude that ...
Consequently ...
that is why ...
we know that ...
this means that ...

Those words, and words like them, often (but not always) indicate that the author is giving you the conclusion of the argument.

Another thing to remember about finding the conclusions of arguments: authors very often *begin* the argument by stating the conclusion. This is actually very kind of authors, when they do it. They come right out and tell you what they are going to argue for, and then they give the argument. Of course, you know that when you put their argument into symbolic form, you have to put the conclusion last. Here's an example.

Socrates was mortal. How do I know that? I'll tell you. First of all, after extensive research I was able to discover that Socrates was in fact a human being. I won't go into all the details here, but suffice it to say that Socrates' humanity is beyond all doubt now. But of course, as we all know, if he was human, then he had to be mortal. There you have it.

1. Socrates was human.
2. If Socrates was human, then Socrates was mortal.
∴ 3. Socrates was mortal.
H = Socrates was human
M = Socrates was mortal

1	H	Premise
2	H → M	Premise
∴ 3	M	From *1,2 valid by modus ponens*

Notice that I have strayed very far from the author's original words. That's ok, because it is pretty clear, once you understand what the author is saying, that the basic logic is just a modus ponens argument.

One important thing you need to do when you are translating arguments from English into symbolic logic is to learn to recognize the different types of claims you can encounter: conditionals, conjunctions, disjunctions and negations. Negations are the easiest because they always include some form of "not" or "no." Disjunctions are probably the next easiest, because they almost always include "or." Another way to indicate a disjunction is to use the word "alternatively" or something like that. Here's an example.

There are only two alternatives: (a) Socrates was Greek, (b) Socrates was Persian. We have been able to rule out the second option. It follows that Socrates was Greek.

1. Either Socrates was Greek, or Socrates was Persian.
2. Socrates was not Persian.
∴ 3. Socrates was Greek.
G = Socrates was Greek
P = Socrates was Persian

1	G v P	Premise
2	~P	Premise
∴ 3	G	From *1,2 valid by disjunction elimination*

The words "it follows that" indicate the conclusion, and that's where I began. Next, I interpreted the two "alternatives" as an "either ..., or ..." and then the whole argument fell into place.

Conditional claims can be very tricky. The problem is that the English language has so many different ways of stating a conditional connection between two claims. The smallest deviation from the standard "if x, then y" is to say "if x, y" and just leave out the "then." You can say, "If Socrates is human, he's mortal." That is a conditional claim, and it will be translated by the arrow. A conditional claim can also be made using "when" or "whenever." You can say that "When Joe drinks the poison, then he dies" or "Whenever Joe drinks that poison, he dies." Both of these are simple conditional claims and will be translated by the arrow.

It is also possible in English to put the consequent before the antecedent. For example, you can say "Joe dies, if he drinks the poison." When you put this in a logical form, you have to flip it around the right way and put the antecedent first, and the consequent second. Consider this index:

D = Joe dies
P = Joe drinks the poison

If you stick to the author's original word order, then you might begin your translation like this: D, if P. But that doesn't make any sense. That is not English, and it is not symbolic logic. Remember that you are translating from one language into another, and you need to respect the rules of both languages. In English, you can put the antecedent of a conditional either before or after the consequent, but in symbolic logic the antecedent must come first. You must flip the conditional around the correct way, and use the proper symbol: P → D.

There is another extremely important way to make a conditional claim in English. You can use the word "sufficient" or "enough." For example, you can say "this poison is enough to kill Joe" or "this poison is sufficient to kill Joe." To make the logic of this claim clear, we need to turn it into a conditional claim. Roughly, "this poison is sufficient to kill Joe" is like saying "If this poison, then Joe is killed," but that doesn't make any sense. The antecedent and the consequent of a conditional claim must also be claims, and "this poison" is just a phrase, not a claim. Obviously this poison isn't going to kill Joe unless he ingests it somehow, e.g. by drinking it. So probably the best way to go is to use the following index:

P = Joe drinks this poison
D = Joe dies

It is reasonable to interpret "this poison is sufficient to kill Joe" to mean "If Joe drinks this poison, then Joe dies." So we can put this into symbols, given the index above, in the following way: P → D.

Notice that the "sufficient condition" ends up as the antecedent of the conditional. Remember this: *the sufficient condition is the antecedent of the conditional.* Anytime one thing is a "sufficient condition" for another thing, you are going to have a conditional claim, and the sufficient condition will end up as the antecedent of the conditional claim. Try this one: "a sufficient condition for passing the class is passing all the exams." Notice that "passing all the exams" comes at the end of the sentence, but it is the "sufficient condition." Ask yourself, according to this sentence, exactly what is the sufficient condition for passing the class? Answer: passing all the exams. Since we have a sufficient condition, we must translate it as a conditional claim, which means we must have an antecedent claim and a consequent claim, and the sufficient condition must be the antecedent claim. Since this sufficient condition clearly applies to any student, probably the best way to go is the following:

E = a student passes all the exams
C = a student passes the class

Since passing the exams is the sufficient condition, it must be the antecedent of the conditional and the other claim must be the consequent, so we end up with: E → C.

The partner to the "sufficient condition" is the "necessary condition." You can probably guess that if the sufficient condition is the antecedent of the conditional claim, then the necessary condition is the consequent of the conditional claim. That guess is exactly right. If drinking the poison truly is sufficient for Joe's death, then Joe's death is a "necessary condition" for Joe's drinking of the poison. If passing all the exams is truly a sufficient condition for passing the class, then passing the class is necessary if you pass all the exams. Compare the two conditional claims we have:

P → D
E → C

P is sufficient for D and D is necessary for P; E is sufficient for C and C is necessary for E. The antecedent is always the sufficient condition for the consequent, and the consequent is always the necessary condition for the antecedent.

Consider one more example: "To copy that document, you first have to make sure that the copy machine is turned on." What is the sufficient condition, and what is the necessary condition? Here it is easier to figure out the necessary condition first: obviously the copy machine has to be turned on if you are going to use it to make a copy. Having the machine turned on is necessary for making a copy. That gives us our index:

T = the copy machine is turned on
C = the document can be copied
C → T

Since the necessary condition is that the copy machine is turned on, we have to make that the consequent of the conditional claim, so the other claim has to be the antecedent. But once you see that, you know what the sufficient condition is: the fact that the document can be copied is sufficient for knowing that the copy machine is turned on. If the machine weren't turned on, then the document could not be copied; but since the document can be copied, that must mean that the copy machine is turned on.

To finish this section, I want to collect a bunch of sentences that are all a bit different, but could all be translated as a simple conditional:

H = Socrates is human
M = Socrates is mortal
H → M

All of the following sentences can be translated in this way:

If Socrates is human, then Socrates is mortal.
If Socrates is human, Socrates is mortal.
When Socrates is human, he is mortal.
Socrates is human, and so he is mortal.
Socrates is mortal, if he is human.
Being human is sufficient for Socrates's being mortal.
If Socrates is human, then necessarily he is mortal.
If Socrates is human, necessarily he is mortal.
Necessarily Socrates is mortal, if he is human.
Whoever is human is mortal.
All humans are mortal.
Being human is a sufficient condition for being mortal.
Being mortal is a necessary condition for being human.

Now I'll give you one more way of making a conditional claim. I saved this one for last because it drives most beginning students in logic crazy. Another way to say "If Socrates is human, then Socrates is mortal" is to say "Socrates is human *only if* he is mortal." The problem is obvious. Logically speaking there is a huge difference between "if" and "only if," but in English the two expressions are almost identical. You have to watch out for this. The following two sentences are logically identical:

If Socrates is human, then Socrates is mortal.
Socrates is human only if Socrates is mortal.

Just memorize this phrase, and remember that what comes before the "only if" is the antecedent and what comes after the "only if" is the consequent.

Section 3: The Bi-conditional.

Now that you know more about conditional claims, it is time to see a very special kind of conditional claim. Think about conditional claims that are true by definition. For example, here are two ways of saying the same thing.

If Socrates is a bachelor, then he is an unmarried man.
Being a bachelor is a sufficient condition for Socrates's being an unmarried man.

The special thing about definitions, however, is that you can turn them around. Definitions take you in circles. Being a bachelor is sufficient for being an unmarried man, but being an unmarried man is sufficient for being a bachelor. Definitions work both ways. The antecedent is sufficient for the consequent, but the consequent is also sufficient for the antecedent. But now think along these lines one step further. Let me use capital letters to make the next point.

If Socrates is a bachelor, then Socrates is an unmarried man
B = Socrates is a bachelor
M = Socrates is an unmarried man
B is sufficient for M (B → M)
M is sufficient for B (M → B)

Now remember that when the antecedent is sufficient for the consequent, then the consequent is necessary for the antecedent. In other words,

If B is sufficient for M, then M is necessary for B.
If M is sufficient for B, then B is necessary for M.

If being a bachelor is sufficient for being an unmarried man, then being an unmarried man is necessary for being a bachelor. Also, if being an unmarried man is sufficient for being a bachelor, then being a bachelor is necessary for being an unmarried man. Definitions take you in circles.

Now look at those last two sentences together. If you look through them you will see that they say B is *both necessary and sufficient* for M, and that M is *both necessary and sufficient* for B. This is peculiar to definitions. The definition and the term being defined are both necessary and sufficient conditions for each other. In other words, because this is true by definition, then if B, then M; and if M, then B. This is called a *bi-conditional*. It is a conditional claim that goes in both directions. Here is the definition.

A *bi-conditional* is a complex claim composed of two simpler claims which states that if one claim (the first condition) is true, then another claim (the second condition) is also true; and that if the second condition is true, then the first condition is also true.

This is so important that logicians usually have a special symbol to identify it. Here is the symbol I will use.

↔ (double arrow)=if and only if (bi-conditional claim)

Notice the translation I've given you for the double arrow. Remember that the "if" indicates that what comes next is the antecedent of the conditional, but the "only if" indicates that what comes next is the consequent of the conditional. So when you say "if and only if" you are saying that what comes next is both antecedent and consequent; in other words, you have a bi-conditional claim.

To help you understand the logic of bi-conditional claims, think of it in relation to other claims you already understand, and use Venn diagrams. For example, start with a simple conjunction: "Joe is married and Joe is a man." Here is how we might diagram the **CONJUNCTION**:

I put "Joe" in the shaded area because he is BOTH a man AND a married person: Joe goes in the intersection of the two boxes because we are dealing with a conjunction of both groups. This looks very different from the diagram for an **INCLUSIVE DISJUNCTION**:

If we say, "Either Joe is golfer, or Joe is a basketball player (or both)," then the entire diagram is shaded. The inclusive disjunction allows for any possibility: Joe might be a golfer who doesn't play basketball, or he might be a basketball player who doesn't play golf, or he might be a golfer and a basketball player. "Either one, or the other, or both" is completely inclusive. The diagram for the **EXCLUSIVE DISJUNCTION** looks different:

If we say, "Either Joe is a golfer XOR Joe is a basketball player (but not both)," then everything is shaded except where the two boxes intersect one another. Joe might be a golfer, but if he is, then he is not also a basketball player because we are in an exclusive situation: if he is a golfer, then he is exclusively a golfer and not also a basketball player. The same is true if he turns out to be a basketball player: we can't put him in the middle because our claim is an "XOR:" the claim says that he is one, or the other, but not both.

The diagram is going to look a lot different when we switch to the conditional and the bi-conditional. First, start by giving a diagram for a **CONDITIONAL** claim.

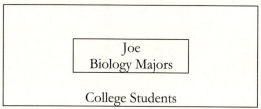

"If Joe is a biology major, then Joe is a college student." Here we have to put Joe inside a box that is inside another box. The conditional claim assumes that every biology major is a college student, then we put Joe inside the "Biology Majors" box, and then put that box inside the "College Students" box. Obviously there is room outside the box because it is possible to be a college student without being a biology major, you can be a chemistry major, a history major ... or even a philosophy major! The only thing the conditional claim is making sure is that if Joe fits inside the "Biology Majors" box, then there is no way he can fall outside of the "College Students" box: if he is inside the "Biology Majors" box, then he must also be inside the "College Students" box. Finally, we get to the **BI-CONDITIONAL** diagram:

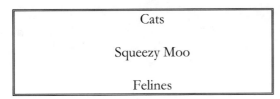

"Squeezy Moo is a cat if and only if Squeezy Moo is a feline." Here the two boxes completely overlap. If Squeezy Moo is inside the "Cats" box, then he is in the "Felines" box; and if he is in the "Felines" box then he is in the "Cats" box. Why? Because "Cats" and "Felines" are just two different names for the same group of animals.

Finally, now that you understand bi-conditionals, you have another rule of inference. Here is how "bi-conditional elimination" works. Consider the following argument.

1. Socrates is a bachelor if and only if Socrates is an unmarried man.
2. Socrates is an unmarried man.
∴ 3. Socrates is a bachelor.

B = Socrates is a bachelor
M = Socrates is an unmarried man

1	B ↔ M	Premise
2	M	Premise
∴ 3	B	From *1,2 valid by bi-conditional elimination*

Bi-conditional Elimination: a valid argument pattern in which
(a) one premise is a bi-conditional,
(b) the other premise affirms one of the two conditions, and
(c) the conclusion affirms the other of the two conditions.

Of course since a bi-conditional works both ways, you can eliminate the bi-conditional by affirming either of the two conditions. There is a bi-conditional introduction, but it's too complicated to give you right now.

Notice that bi-conditional elimination involves affirming one condition to conclude that the other condition must be satisfied as well. This makes it like modus ponens. Is there is a modus tollens version of bi-conditional elimination?

1. Socrates is a bachelor if and only if Socrates is an unmarried man.
2. Socrates is not an unmarried man.
∴ 3. Socrates is not a bachelor.

B = Socrates is a bachelor
M = Socrates is an unmarried man

1	B ↔ M	Premise
2	~M	Premise
∴ 3	~B	From *1,2 ???*

Think this through. Is it valid? If so, what should the rule be called? And is there a chain argument version of bi-conditional elimination. What if you link two bi-conditionals together?

1. The morning star is a planet if and only if Venus is a planet.
2. Venus is a planet if and only if the evening star is a planet.
∴ 3. The morning star is a planet if and only if the evening star is a planet.

M = the morning star is a planet
V = Venus is a planet
E = the evening star is a planet

1	M ↔ V	Premise
2	V ↔ E	Premise
∴ 3	M ↔ E	From *1,2 ???*

Think this through? Is this valid? If so, what should the rule be called? If it is valid, how would you prove that it is valid?

Chapter Conclusion.
In a way, this chapter was where we really began logic. The study of logic is the study of the abstract principles of reasoning, and in order to study the principles of reasoning in the abstract, we need to stop using real life arguments in the English language, and focus on abstract symbol manipulation.

Things to memorize from this Chapter:
→ (arrow) = If ..., then ... (conditional claim)
& (ampersand) = and (conjunction)
v (wedge) = or (disjunction)
~ (tilde) = not (negation)
↔ (double arrow) = ... if and only if ... (bi-conditional claim)

A ***bi-conditional*** is a complex claim composed of two simpler claims which states that if one claim (the first condition) is true, then another claim (the second condition) is also true; and that if the second condition is true, then the first condition is also true.

Bi-conditional Elimination: a valid argument pattern in which
(a) one premise is a bi-conditional,
(b) the other premise affirms one of the two conditions, and
(c) the conclusion affirms the other of the two conditions.

Exercises for Chapter 3.

Exercise 3.1: Using Symbols. *Translate each of the following English sentences into symbolic logic, and translate each of the following symbolic claims into English. Use the indices provided.*

Example 1
Problem. Either Toby is a cat or Spanky is a cat.
Solution. T v S

Example 2
Problem. T → S
Solution. If Toby is a cat, then Spanky is a cat.

Index for problems 1-10:
T = Toby is a cat
S = Spanky is a cat
M = Magnificat is a cat
F = Fafnir is a cat

1. Toby is a cat and Spanky is a cat.
2. Toby is a cat and Magnificat is a cat.
3. Either Toby is a cat, or Fafnir is a cat.
4. Either Toby is a cat or Magnificat is not a cat.
5. If Toby is not a cat, then Spanky is not a cat.

6. If Toby is a cat, then Magnificat is a cat.
7. Either Magnificat is a cat or Toby is not a cat.
8. If Toby is a cat, then Spanky is not a cat.
9. Spanky is a cat if and only if Magnificat is not a cat.
10. Fafnir is a cat if and only if Toby is a cat.

Index for problems 11-20
A = Alice is a dog
S = Sidney is a dog
W = Winston is a dog
M = Micmac is a dog
11. A & S
12. M & W
13. A v S
14. S v ~M

15. A → S
16. ~A → W
17. ~M
18. A & ~S
19. W ↔ ~M
20. A ↔ ~S

Exercise 3.2: Symbolizing Arguments. *Translate and evaluate the following arguments.*

Example 1
Problem
G = Socrates is Greek
P = Socrates is Persian

1	G v P	Premise
2	~P	Premise
∴ 3	G	From *1,2 valid by disjunction elimination*

Solution: (the evaluation is already done for you)
1. Either Socrates is Greek or he is Persian.
2. Socrates is not Persian.
∴ 3. Socrates is Greek.

Example 2
Problem
1. Socrates is human.
2. If Socrates is human, then he is mortal.
∴ 3. Socrates is mortal.
Solution
H = Socrates is human
M = Socrates is mortal

1	H	Premise
2	H → M	Premise
∴ 3	M	From *1,2 valid by modus ponens*

Index for Problems 1-6:
H = Socrates is human
M = Socrates is mortal
C = Socrates is a cat

Problem 1

1	H → M	Premise
2	H	Premise
∴ 3	M	From *1,2 valid by modus ponens*

Problem 2

1	H → M	Premise
2	M	Premise
∴ 3	H	From *1,2 invalid by fallacy of affirming the consequent*

Problem 3

1	H v C	Premise
2	~C	Premise
∴ 3	H	From *1,2 valid by disjunction elimination*

Problem 4

1	H	Premise
2	M	Premise
∴ 3	H & M	From *1,2 valid by conjunction introduction*

Problem 5

1	H → M	Premise
2	~M	Premise
∴ 3	~H	From *1,2 valid by modus tollens*

Problem 6

1	H	Premise
∴ 2	H v C1-2	From *1 valid by disjunction introduction*

Problem 7
1. Either Socrates is Egyptian or he is Greek.
2. Socrates is not Egyptian.
∴ 3. Socrates is Greek.

Problem 8
1. Socrates is Greek.
∴ 2. Either Socrates is Greek, or he is Persian.

Problem 9
1. Socrates is Greek and he is a philosopher.
∴ 2. Socrates is Greek.

Problem 10
1. If Socrates is Greek, then he's literate.
2. Socrates is not literate.
∴ 3. Socrates is not Greek.

Problem 11
1. If Toby is a cat, then Spanky is a cat.
2. Spanky is a cat.
∴ 3. Toby is a cat.

Problem 12
1. If Toby is a cat, then Spanky is a cat.
2. Toby is not a cat.
∴ 3. Spanky is not a cat.

Problem 13
1. Either Toby is a cat, or Spanky is a cat.
2. Spanky is not a cat.
∴ 3. Toby is a cat.

Problem 14
1. Toby is a cat.
∴ 2. Either Toby is a cat, or Spanky is a cat.

Exercise 3.3: Assorted Arguments. *Translate and evaluate the following arguments.*
Example 1
Problem: If Socrates is Greek, then he is human. But if he is human, then he is mortal. So if Socrates is Greek, then he is mortal.
Solution
1. If Socrates is Greek, then Socrates is human.
2. If Socrates is human, then Socrates is mortal.
∴ 3. If Socrates is Greek, then Socrates is mortal.
G = Socrates is Greek
H = Socrates is human
M = Socrates is mortal.

1	$G \to H$	Premise
2	$H \to M$	Premise
∴ 3	$G \to M$	From 1,2 valid by chain argument

Example 2
Problem: Joe is cruisin' for a bruisin'. He keeps asking that guy for money, and whenever he does that, he gets a bruisin'.
Solution
1. Joe keeps asking that guy for money.
2. If Joe keeps asking that guy for money, then Joe will get beaten.
∴ 3. Joe will get beaten.
J = Joe keeps asking that guy for money
B = Joe will get beaten.

1	J	Premise
2	$J \to B$	Premise
∴ 3	B	From 1,2 valid by modus ponens

1. Socrates is human. But being human is a sufficient condition for being mortal. Consequently, Socrates is mortal.

2. Being mortal is a necessary condition for being human. And furthermore, since Socrates is human, it follows that he must also be mortal.

3. Big Al is picking up a pizza, or else he's out getting beer. Oh, wait a minute! We've got plenty of beer, so he can't be out getting more. I guess that means he must be getting a pizza.

4. Joe has been working really, really hard. On top of that, he's been studying really, really hard. So I guess that Joe has been really hitting those books and studying.

5. I'll love you only if you plow me an acre of land between the salt water and the sea sand. But you couldn't possibly do that. So I guess that means I won't ever love you.

6. I'll love you if you plow me an acre of land between the salt water and the sea sand. But you couldn't possibly do that. So I guess that means I won't ever love you.

7. When Alice gets home, she'll be tired. But whenever she's tired, she always takes a nap. So when Alice gets home, I bet she'll take a nap.

8. Joe is a priest if and only if he's taken his vows. He is a real priest. So I guess that means he's taken his vows.

9. Miranda bakes brownies. Miranda is a Rudolph Valentino fan. So she's a brownie-baking-Valentino fan.

10. If you spent more time studying for your classes, you'd probably get better grades. Furthermore, if you quit drinking so much, you'd be able to spend more time studying. So if you knock off all that drinking, you'll probably get better grades.

11. Dr. Morbius will not succeed because a necessary condition for his success is that Robbie the robot keeps a clear head. But there's no way that Robbie is going to be able to keep a clear head, what with Dr. Morbius' subconscious running amok like that.

Exercise 3.4: Previous Arguments. *Translate and evaluate the arguments in Exercise 2.2, Exercise 2.3 and Exercise 2.4.*

Exercise 3.5: Alternative Language. *In Sections 2 and 3 of this chapter some new ways of indicating conclusions, conditionals and bi-conditionals were introduced. These exercises give you some practice with them. Use the "principle of charity."*

Example 1
Problem: All living things are precious. But it is wrong to take the life of any living thing if and only if all living things are precious. This means that it is wrong to take the life of any living thing.
Solution
1. All living things are precious.
2. It is wrong to take the life of any living thing if and only if all living things are precious.
∴ 3. It is wrong to take the life of any living thing.
P = all living things are precious
L = It is wrong to take the life of any living thing

1	P	Premise
2	L ↔ P	Premise
∴ 3	L	From 1,2 valid by bi-conditional elimination

Example 2
Problem: Dumb animals and plants are devoid of the life of reason. That is why it is not wrong to kill animals or plants, because being devoid of reason is a sufficient condition for being something that it is not wrong to kill.
Solution
1. Animals and plants are devoid of the life of reason.
2. If animals and plants are devoid of the life of reason, then it is not wrong to kill animals or plants.
∴ 3. It is not wrong to kill animals or plants.
A = animals and plants are devoid of the life of reason
K = it is wrong to kill animals or plants

1	A	Premise
2	A → ~K	Premise
∴ 3	~K	From 1,2 valid by modus ponens

1. If Al kills a plant to feed it to an animal, then Al uses the plant for its natural purpose. But whenever Al uses a plant for its natural purpose, then Al does not do anything wrong. And so, whenever Al kills a plant to feed it to an animal, Al isn't doing anything wrong.

2. Betty eats a lamb only if the lamb was killed for food. Furthermore, killing a lamb for food is sufficient for acting within the moral law. Hence, when Betty eats lamb, she is acting within the moral law.

3. Animals are not tools, but being a tool is a necessary condition for being something that it's ok to kill. Hence it's not ok to kill animals.

4. Whoever is capable of repentance does not deserve to be killed. Candy does not deserve to be killed, and so I conclude that Candy is definitely capable of repentance.

5. Doug does not act with charity towards Enid if he kills her. But executing her is sufficient for killing her. Consequently, if Doug executes Enid, then he is not acting with charity. But failing to act with charity is a sufficient condition for acting immorally. That is why executing someone is wrong.

6. By definition, Frank sins if and only if he departs from the order of reason. But departing from the order of reason is sufficient for becoming just like a dumb animal, which is a sufficient condition for being something that it's ok to kill. Frank is a sinner, and that is how we know that it is ok to kill Frank.

7. Jesus forbade uprooting the weed in order to spare the wheat (Matthew 13:29-30). This necessarily means that it is wrong to kill the wicked when the good might be killed with them. Hence, capital punishment is wrong.

8. The wicked are to society what an infection is to the body. That analogy is sufficient to entail a dilemma: either we cut out the infection, or we allow the entire body to be destroyed. But obviously we must not allow the body to be destroyed, which is why we must cut out the infection. Hence, capital punishment is right.

9. If it is morally permissible to excise an infection, then necessarily it is morally permissible to commit a lesser evil in order to avoid a greater evil. But suicide can be morally permissible, if we may choose the lesser of two evils. That is how we know that under certain circumstances, suicide is not immoral.

10. All suicide is murder, and all murder is wrong, so all suicide is wrong.

CHAPTER 4: TRUTH TABLES

Now it is time to dive into symbolic logic. Back in Chapter 1, just after defining validity, I said that as long as you reason validly, you will never be lead astray. Validity is an infallible guide in reasoning. Valid reasoning always leads from truth to more truth. Valid reasoning is "truth-preserving." This is really the point of logic: we want to discover how to think in such a way that we aren't lead astray. Truth tables are simple and effective means to demonstrate and discover valid patterns of reasoning. Their strength is in their simplicity. Unfortunately their simplicity limits their usefulness when it comes to long or complex arguments, so later we'll have to learn other methods for demonstrating and discovering valid patterns of reasoning. But the truth table is the best introduction to the study of symbolic logic.

Section 1: Truth Table for a Conditional Claim.

A valid argument is an argument whose conclusion cannot be false if the premises are true. Remember that this is a hypothetical claim: hypothetically, if the premises are true, then the conclusion also has to be true. Hypothetical claims can be tricky because they aren't real, they aren't solid, you can't set them on the table and look at them closely in good light. They exist only in your imagination. In order to make sure you don't get mixed up when you are thinking about hypothetical claims, it is useful to keep track of all the different possibilities by writing them down in a clear chart. That is what a truth table does: it gives you a precise format for keeping track of all the different possibilities.

Let's start with a simple example. Flip a coin and it will land either heads or tails. Well, I suppose it could land on it's side, but what are the odds of that happening? I'm not sure, but let's keep things simple and just assume that with a normal coin, there's a 50-50 chance that the coin will land heads, and a 50-50 chance that it will land tails. If you bet $1 on a coin toss, you have a 50% chance of winning and a 50% chance of losing. We could put this down in a table:

	Coin Toss
First Possibility	Heads
Second Possibility	Tails

If you are going to bet on heads, then we could also put the table this way:

	Heads?
First Possibility	True
Second Possibility	False

Again, let's just assume that there are only these two choices and that if it doesn't land heads then it lands tails. So far this is very simple.

But what if you wanted to make it more interesting and toss two coins? Can you figure out the different possibilities? This one's not too hard: you only have two possibilities for each of the two coins, so you have four possibilities. Both could land heads, both could land tails, or one could land heads and the other tails. We can put this into a table like this:

	Coin #1	Coin #2
	Heads?	Heads?
First Possibility	True	True
Second Possibility	True	False
Third Possibility	False	True
Fourth Possibility	False	False

There are four possibilities, so if you place a bet on any of them, you have a 1-in-4 (or 25% chance) of winning. Those are not great odds. The more possibilities there are, the lower the odds of winning if you bet on only one of the possibilities. We could do this with three coins, four, or any number of coins. But this is not a course in gambling, it is a course in logic, and I'm using this only as an example of logically laying out all the different possibilities. What we really need to do is see how this applies to claims in arguments.

Let's begin with a simple example. Consider the following argument.

1	H → M	Premise
2	H	Premise
∴ 3	M	From *1,2 valid by modus ponens*

You know that this argument is valid, even though you have no idea what the letters stand for. That is the power of argument *patterns*: any argument fitting the pattern is automatically valid, regardless of content. H might be true, but it might be false; M might be true, but it might be false. There is no way for you to know if this argument is sound.

Now let me ask you this: What does premise 1 say? In a way, you can't answer that question, because you don't know what the letters stand for. Nevertheless, you know that it is a conditional claim, and so you can say something about what it means: it is a complex claim which states that if one claim (the antecedent) is true, then another claim (the consequent) is also true.

Remember that claims are the things that are able to be either true or false. Premise 1 says that if H is true, then M is also true. It doesn't tell us anything about what would happen if H is false, but it does tell us what happens if H is true: in that case, M is also true. To put this same thing in other words, premise 1 is ruling out the possibility that H is true while at the same time M is false.

What we are doing here is thinking hypothetically, since you don't know what H and M actually say. We don't know whether the premises are *actually* true, so we can say that we don't know about the *actuality* of the situation. However, we can know a lot about the *possibilities* of the situation. In order to keep us from getting lost, we need a systematic way to keep track of the different possibilities. Here they are in a list:

First Possibility: H is true and at the same time M is true. (Both are true)
Second Possibility: H is true but at the same time M is false. (One is true, one is false)
Third Possibility: H is false but at the same time M is true. (One is false, one is true)
Fourth Possibility: H is false, and at the same time M is false. (Both are false)

Truth tables are handy ways of collecting just this sort of information. Since we have two different claims (H and M), we need two different columns. Since there are four different possibilities, each column needs to have four rows. Finally, we'll let "T" stand for "true" and we'll let "F" stand for "false." Here is a truth table which collects the information I just put in the list above.

	H	M
First Possibility	T	T
Second Possibility	T	F
Third Possibility	F	T
Fourth Possibility	F	F

At the top we have the two different capital letters we are dealing with, and then under them are the four different possibilities that I listed above. In the first possibility, both are true, in the second possibility the first is true but the second is false, in the third possibility the first one is false and the second one is true, and in the fourth possibility they are both false. This covers all the possibilities. You can't know which of the four possibilities is actual until you finish examining the soundness of the argument. But remember that we are just looking at validity, so all we have to think about are the different possibilities.

Now that we have the different possibilities laid out in a clear table, think back to premise 1 of the argument I started this section with. Premise 1 is a conditional claim, and it says that if H is true, then M is also true. In other words, premise 1 is ruling out the possibility that H is true while at the same time M is false. Out of these four possibilities, premise 1 is ruling out the second. Premise 1 is saying that the second possibility can't happen.

Again, it is important to remember that premise 1 isn't taking any stand on what happens if H turns out to be false. Premise 1 is neutral on that question. But it is definitely ruling out the second possibility, i.e. that the antecedent is true while the consequent is false. Consider the example of your boss promising you a raise. Your boss says, "If you do a good job on this project, then you will get a raise." The boss isn't saying what will happen if you don't do a good job on the project, or if you fail to complete the project at all. Maybe you'll get fired, maybe nothing will happen. We don't know because your boss hasn't said anything about that. All your boss has said is that if you do a good job, you will get the raise. The only thing your boss is ruling out is the situation where you do a good job, and you never get the raise. Suppose that happened. You do a good job, the boss explicitly tells you that you did a good job, but you never get the raise. You have legitimate grounds for complaint. You can go back to your boss and say, "You told me that if I did a good job, I'd get a raise. You then told me that I did do a good job. It follows logically that I will get the raise. That is what you told me." You are being perfectly logical here, and if your boss is also logical, and wasn't lying to you just to motivate you, then you will get your raise. Logic can pay off!

In order to represent this information in the truth table, we need to add a new column to the right of the two letters we have so far. We need to add a column to keep track of the various possibilities for the conditional claim. The truth table now looks like this:

CHAPTER 4: TRUTH TABLES

H	M	H → M
T	T	T
T	F	F
F	T	T
F	F	T

In order to read what the truth table means, take it one row at a time. In the first case, where H and M are both true, the truth-value of H → M is T, i.e. true. This means that if it turns out that the antecedent and consequent are both true, then the conditional claim is true. For example, if you did a good job on the project, and you did get the raise you were promised, then what your boss said was true: "if you do a good job on the project, then you will get a raise." In the second line, that is where the conditional claim is false. That is the line where you did do a good job on the project, but you didn't get the raise you were promised. In that case, the conditional claim is false. That is the case where your boss broke the promise or lied to you: you were told that if you did a good job you'd get a raise, but even after you did a good job you didn't get the raise. In that case the conditional claim is false.

What about the last two lines? As I mentioned before, the conditional claim only talks about what would happen if the antecedent is true. The conditional claim doesn't say anything about what would happen if the antecedent is false. Why, then, do I say that the conditional is true when the antecedent is false?

Think of it this way. Suppose your boss promises you a raise if you did a good job on the project. Is your boss lying to you with no intention of giving you a raise no matter how well you do? Unfortunately there are bosses out there who would do such a thing, but employees usually complain about them so much that either they clean up their act or they get fired. In general, when it comes to promises we use a principle of charity and assume that people are innocent until proven guilty. Assume that when someone promises you something, they mean what they say. Of course there are certain individuals whom you may have learned to distrust, but that shouldn't sour you on all promises. Assume promises are innocent until proven guilty. Take people at their word until they prove themselves to be unreliable.

Consider another example. A friend once told me about a friend of his who had two kids, and one day the older brother was bothering the younger brother. The mom stopped him a few times, but he just kept on bothering his younger brother, so she finally said, "if you bother your little brother one more time, then I will through you out of this window!" Sure enough, he bothered his younger brother one more time, and sure enough she picked him up and threw him out the window. There was a deep, soft snow bank just outside the window, so the kid wasn't hurt at all, but he learned his lesson. The next time she said to him, "If you don't stop that, I'll xyz," he stopped what he was doing immediately. In terms of logic, he was processing the truth of his mom's conditional claim: the conditional claim is true, even when the antecedent is false because now he knows that if the antecedent is true, then the consequent will be true also, and he doesn't want that to happen when there's no snow outside the window!

Let me explain this one more way, because this is an important point, and lots of people have trouble with it. This time I'll use some computer terminology, the default value of a claim is T, true. In truth tables, assume a claim is true (T) unless it can be proven false (F). So in the last two rows of the truth table above, the conditional claim is true (T). In the fourth case, you did not do a good job and you did not get a raise. That is probably what you expected. Your boss said that if you did a good job, then you'd get a raise; when you failed to do a good job, what did you expect?

The problem case is the third. In that case you failed to do a good job, but you got the raise anyway. What's up with that? Your boss told you that you would get a raise if you did a good job, and you ended up getting the raise even without doing a good job. Something funny is going on here, but stay focused on the question at hand. If you end up getting the raise in spite of the fact that you didn't do a good job on the project, does that prove your boss was lying, or that your boss's promise was false? Not at all. Your raise is certainly unexpected, but it doesn't prove that what your boss said was false. If you had done a good job, then you would have gotten the raise for doing such a good job. Perhaps you ended up getting the raise anyway because of seniority; perhaps you had worked there for a certain number of months, and there is a company policy of giving raises at various intervals in order to secure employee loyalty.

If you still think it is odd to say that your boss's promise is true when you got the raise in spite of the fact that you failed to do a good job on the project, then you are making an unfair assumption. When your boss said, "If you do a good job on the project, then you'll get a raise" you are making the assumption that the boss meant, "The *only* way you can possibly get a raise is if you do a good job on this project." But that is an assumption on your part; your boss never said that. In logic as in law, you have to be careful about not making extra assumptions.

Now back to the truth table for conditional claims. The moral of the story is that the only time a conditional claim is false is when the antecedent is true but the consequent is false. In three out of four possible cases, a conditional claim is true.

Notice one important thing about truth tables before we look at more of them. The arrow which represents a conditional claim is often called a "truth-functional operator." It connects two simpler claims into a more complex claim in such a way that the truth value (i.e. true or false) of the complex claim is completely determined by, or "is a function of" the truth values of the simpler claims. That is just a fancy way of saying that the truth value of P → Q depends upon the truth values of the P and the Q. P → Q is true in every case except when the P is true but the Q is simultaneously false.

Section 2: More Truth Tables.

Next consider disjunctive claims. Here is the truth table for a disjunction. I'll use different letters from now on, since I don't have any particular argument in mind. (I'm going to use "P" and "Q" just because those are the traditional dummy-letters that logicians use).

P	Q	P v Q
T	T	T
T	F	T
F	T	T
F	F	F

A disjunction is true when either one of the disjuncts is true, or when both are true. Remember that this is the *inclusive* disjunction, which means that one or the other or both of the disjuncts can be true. The only time a disjunction is false is when both of the disjuncts are false. If you tell me that either Carl or Betty is home, and I go there and find out that neither one of them is home, then what you said was false. You were wrong. But if I find Carl there, or if I find Betty there, or if I find them both there, then what you said was true. The case is very different with a conjunction.

P	Q	P & Q
T	T	T
T	F	F
F	T	F
F	F	F

A conjunction is false in every situation except where both of the conjuncts are true. If you tell me that both Carl and Betty are at home, and it turns out that only Carl is at home, then what you said was false.

The truth table for negation is a lot shorter. With a negation, we have only one letter, and then we negate it. Here is the truth table for a negation.

P	~P
T	F
F	T

When P is true, then ~P is false; and when P is false, then ~P is true. That's what "not" means. If it is true to say that Carl is home, then it is false to say that Carl is not home. If it is false to say that Carl is home, then it is true to say that Carl is not home. What part of "not" don't you understand?

Finally, we have to do the truth table for the bi-conditional. Think this one through. With the conditional claim we used the example of your boss promising you a raise if you did a good job on the project. Let's use the same example, but make it a bi-conditional instead of just a conditional. Now your boss says to you that you will get a raise *if and only if* you do a good job on the project. Doing a good job on the project will get you a raise, and it is the only way you can get a raise. Your boss is telling you, in effect, that there are no automatic promotions if you have been there for a certain length of time, and there is no other unforseen possibility of your getting a raise outside of doing a good job on the project. So if you do a good job, you expect a raise, and if you don't do a good job, you will expect not to get a raise.

P	Q	P ↔ Q
T	T	T
T	F	F
F	T	F
F	F	T

Think of the first and the fourth cases. In the first case, you do a good job on the project and you get a raise. In that case, what your boss said was true. Your boss said that doing a good job on the project would get you a raise (and that it was the only way to get a raise). In the fourth case, you don't do a good job on the project, and you don't get a raise. In that case what your boss said was true. Your boss said that the only way you would get a raise is by doing a good job on the project, and you didn't do that. So there is no way you could get the raise. When you end up not getting the raise, that shows you that what your boss said was true.

In the second case, you do a good job, but don't get the raise. That is the obvious case where you have good grounds for complaint. Your boss clearly told you doing a good job on the project would get you a raise, you did a good job, but didn't get the raise. In the third case, you failed to do a good job, but you got the raise anyway. You didn't expect that, because your boss explicitly said that doing a good job on the project was the only way for you to get a raise. Clearly it wasn't the only way for you to get a raise, because you failed to do a good job on the project, but you got the raise anyway. Your boss was just wrong, what your boss said was false, because doing a good job on the project was not the only way for you to get a raise.

Section 3: Parentheses.

So far I've given you examples without a lot of complications. Next I would like to do a truth table for a more complex claim. Suppose your boss doesn't just give you one condition for getting a raise; suppose there are two conditions.

If you stop coming in late, and you start treating the clients politely, then you get a raise.
L = You stop coming in late
P = You start treating the clients politely
R = You get a raise
(L & P) → R

Before I get to the truth table for this argument, I need to talk about the parentheses. Compare these two claims:
(L & P) → R
L & (P → R)

Except for the parentheses, they have exactly the same string of symbols in exactly the same order: they start with L, then an ampersand, then a P, then an arrow, and finally an R. But because the parentheses are located in different positions, the two claims are extremely different. Here is how you would translate them.

(L & P) → R: If you both stop coming in late and also start treating the clients politely, then you get a raise.
L & (P → R): You do stop coming in late, and if you start treating the clients politely then you get a raise.

These say two very different things. The second one says that you do stop coming in late, but the first one does not say that. The first one says only that *hypothetically, if you did* stop coming in late, and you also (again hypothetically) started treating the clients politely, then something would happen, i.e. you'd get a raise. This makes your raise conditional upon two different things. The second claim makes your raise conditional upon only on one thing, i.e. that you start to treat the clients more politely. The second one also happens to claim that in fact you do stop coming in late, but that is not a part of the conditional claim.

The proper way to identify the difference between these two claims is to say that the *main logical operator* of the first claim is the arrow, while the *main logical operator* of the second claim is the ampersand. In other words, the first claim is a conditional claim, while the second claim is a conjunction. Of course, the first claim is a complex conditional, and the second one is a complex conjunction, but fundamentally they are different.

Now, this isn't always a big deal. For example, suppose you have a complex conjunction which is just a string of different claims all conjoined.

1. Socrates is human, mortal and Greek.
∴ 2. Socrates is Greek.

H = Socrates is human
M = Socrates is mortal
G = Socrates is Greek

1	(H & M) & G	Premise
∴ 2	G	From 1 valid by conjunction elimination

With premise 1 here, there are different ways you could group the claims together, and when it gets right down to it, the differences don't really matter. For example, here are some different groupings, and how they would be translated.

(H & M) & G: Socrates is both human and mortal, and in addition he is Greek.
H & (M & G): Socrates is human, and in addition he is both mortal and Greek.

Obviously these two are really saying the same thing, i.e. that three different things are all true of Socrates. The difference doesn't really matter...

...*nevertheless you must put the parentheses in!* You cannot have more than one logical operator in a claim without having parentheses to tell you which is the *main logical operator*. Without parentheses, the claim would look like this:

WRONG!!! NEVER DO THIS!!! H & M & G

That might look ok to you, and in reality it makes perfect sense, but don't ever do it when you are trying to think logically and carefully about a claim. Logically speaking, this claim is ambiguous because it is not clear which ampersand is supposed to be the main logical operator. You always have to make it absolutely clear which logical operator is the main one. The same thing holds for disjunctive claims. Consider this:

H v (M v G)
(H v M) v G

These claims are just giving three alternatives, and so for practical purposes the difference between them doesn't really matter. But when you are doing symbolic logic, the parentheses are extremely important: you have to make it clear which wedge is the main logical operator.

The time when parentheses become most important of all is when you have a negation somewhere in your claim. It is extremely important to know if your boss is telling you that you DO get a raise, or that you DO NOT get a raise. That one little word "not" makes a huge difference, so you have to be extremely careful about parentheses when you have a negation. Compare these two claims.

~H → G
~ (H → G)

The main logical operator of the first claim is the arrow, the main logical operator of the second claim is the tilde. The first claim is a conditional claim; the second claim is a negation. That makes a huge difference. The first claim says that if Socrates is not human, then he is Greek (which doesn't really make any sense). The second claim says that it is NOT true to say that if Socrates is human, then he is Greek (which does make sense, since Socrates could be Persian or Egyptian if he is human).

Notice that in a way the first claim violates the rule that you cannot have more than one logical operator without parentheses. The tilde is a logical operator: it negates whatever is immediately to its right. If the H is immediately to the right of the tilde, then the H is being negated; if a left parenthesis is immediately to the right of the tilde, then whatever is inside the parentheses is being negated.

If you start playing fast and loose with parentheses, very soon you will make a tragic error and get an argument completely wrong. Take parentheses just as seriously as you take negations, even when you are just dealing with a list of conjuncts or disjuncts.

There is a very practical consequence of the requirement that you take parentheses very seriously. Go back to my conjunctive argument about Socrates being human, mortal and Greek. Here is how I did it above.

1	(H & M) & G	Premise
∴ 2	G	From *1 valid by conjunction elimination*

That works just fine. But suppose I had done the parentheses differently. Suppose that I had interpreted the list of conjuncts in this way:

H & (M & G)

Would the argument still work in the same way? Would it still be a two step argument that works by conjunction elimination? Answer: no. It turns into a three step argument with a sub-conclusion:

1	H & (M & G)	Premise
∴ 2	M & G	From *1 valid by conjunction elimination*
∴ 3	G	From *2 valid by conjunction elimination*

You can't just reach into something that is inside parentheses and take it out. Think about it. In premise 1, the main logical operator is the first ampersand, the one that is *outside* the parentheses. This means that premise 1 is a conjunction of *two claims*, one of which is H and the other of which is complex. Premise 1 is not a conjunction of three claims, it is only a conjunction of two claims; it just so happens that one of the conjuncts is itself complex and contains a conjunction. The rule of conjunction elimination permits you to take out only one of the two conjuncts. In premise 1, G is not one of the two conjuncts, so you can't take it out. You have to break the claim apart piece by piece. Be patient, take your time, do things methodically and logically. It is precisely when you start skipping logical steps that you make your worst mistakes.

So far, complex claims are not very difficult. It does get a bit tougher when you start negating complex claims. In later chapters we will see the different things that can happen when a complex claim is negated, but for now you should know a short-cut to dealing with negated complex claims.

In symbolic logic, negating a complex claim is simple. Just put a tilde in front of whatever you want to negate. If you want to negate

(H & (Q v R))

just write

~(H & (Q v R))

But suppose you have to negate the following claim:

Joe and Sally won't be going to the party.

Part of the complexity here is that you don't know if Joe and Sally are a couple. You don't know if they were thinking of going together, or if they are just two separate people who were invited. In cases like this, always assume that you are dealing with a simple conjunction of two distinct claims. In this case, we will have

Joe won't be going to the party and Sally won't be going to the party

The short-cut I want to give you is the phrase "it is not the case that." You can translate the previous claim this way

It is not the case that Joe and Sally will be going to the party.

When you have complex claims to negate, just remember the phrase "it is not the case that," and simply stick it on the front of the claim, and you are guaranteed of not making a mistake.

Before we get back to truth tables, there is one danger to warn you about. When you translate from English into logic, you have to be careful that you are not fooled by words that seem like logical operators. The most frequent one is the word "and." The word "and" is not always used to conjoin two distinct claims. The "and" in "Rock and Roll" is not really a logical operator. "Rock and Roll" music is not something that results from the combination of some "Rock" with some "Roll." So to translate the claim, "I like Rock and Roll music" you would simply do this:

R = I like rock and roll music.

You would not have two separate letters for "I like rock" and for "I like roll music." Logically, that is simply not how this claim works. The same can be said for the candy M & M's. The "&" is not a logical conjunction.

But there are tricky cases. For example, what would you do with the claim "John works for Smith and Wesson?" The corporation "Smith and Wesson" is in fact named after two people who worked together. Mr. Smith and Mr. Wesson combined and formed a corporation. Would you have two separate letters; one for "John works for Smith" and a different letter for "John works for Wesson?" No, you wouldn't, because "Smith and Wesson" is not functioning as a conjunction of two individuals, it is functioning as a proper noun, i.e. as the name of a single corporation. The same is true of law firms. John works for the law firm "Dewy, Cheatum & Howe" should not be broken down into three distinct claims, because "Dewy, Cheatum & Howe" is functioning as the name of a single corporate entity. There is also a mixed drink called a "Fine and Dandy" which is a mixture of gin, triple sec and lemon juice. But "Fine and Dandy" is not a conjunction of some "Fine" plus some "Dandy." It is a proper noun, used as the name of a mixed drink. So you would translate "Joe wants a Fine and Dandy" with a single letter, not with a conjunction of two letters.

The trickiest cases are ones that could go either way, depending upon the context. "Soup and crackers" or "soup and salad" could both be interpreted as conjunctions. "Joe ordered soup and salad" could be translated this way:

O = Joe ordered soup
A = Joe ordered salad

But "soup and salad" might be the name of a single menu item which includes several components, e.g. crackers for the soup and croutons for the salad might also be included in the meal. Especially if the restaurant does not permit any substitutions or alterations to menu items, you might take "soup and salad" as a proper name for a single item, and so you might translate "Joe ordered the soup and salad" with a single letter, like this.

S = Joe ordered the soup-and-salad

The hyphens make it clear that you interpret "soup and salad" as a single menu item, and not as a logical conjunction. It might be that Joe only wants the soup, but he has to order the "soup and salad" because the restaurant has restrictions about ordering off the menu.

Section 4: Complex Truth Tables

Now back to truth tables. Above I said that I would show you how to do the truth table for the following complex claim: (L & P) → R. The first thing to do is always to ask yourself, "What is the main logical operator?" Answer: the arrow. This claim is a conditional. It happens to have a complex antecedent, but when you boil it down it is really just a conditional claim. You already know how to do the truth table for a conditional claim: the conditional is true in every case except where the antecedent is true and the consequent is simultaneously false. So we need to figure out when the antecedent is true and the consequent is simultaneously false. How do we do that when the antecedent is complex? Answer: start with its components and build it back up. Here is where you might start.

L	P	L & P
T	T	T
T	F	F
F	T	F
F	F	F

So far this is right, but now we have a huge problem: how do we get R into it? Answer: you can't. This truth table works only when you have two simple claims. Think about it. When you have two simple claims, there are only four possibilities: both are true, both are false, the first is true while the second is false, the first is false while the second is true. When you have three simple claims, the number of possibilities increases; here they are.

L	P	R
T	T	T
T	T	F
T	F	T
T	F	F
F	T	T
F	T	F
F	F	T
F	F	F

Look at the pattern here. You should be able now to figure out how to start a truth table with four basic, simple claims. You should be able to figure out how to start a truth table with five, six or seven basic, simple claims. But rest assured, I won't ask you to go that far.

Now, back to our complex claim. We have established that the main logical operator is the arrow. The claim is a conditional claim, which is false only when the antecedent is true but the consequent is simultaneously false. So we need to find out when the antecedent is true. So make a column in the truth table for the antecedent.

L	P	R	L & P
T	T	T	T
T	T	F	T
T	F	T	F
T	F	F	F
F	T	T	F
F	T	F	F
F	F	T	F
F	F	F	F

The only two places where both L and P are simultaneously true are the first two lines of the truth table. In every other case at least one of the two is false, and so the conjunction is false in all those cases. Now that we've done that, we are ready to complete the truth table. We know when the antecedent is true, so we just check the two lines where the antecedent is true, and we see if in any of those cases the consequent, i.e. R, is false. Sure enough, in the second situation, R is false. That is the only place where the conditional is false. In every other case the conditional claim is true. So here is the complete truth table.

L	P	R	L & P	(L & P) → R
T	T	T	T	T
T	T	F	T	F
T	F	T	F	T
T	F	F	F	T
F	T	T	F	T
F	T	F	F	T
F	F	T	F	T
F	F	F	F	T

In the second case, L and P are both true, but R is false. That means that in the second case, the antecedent of the conditional is true but the consequent is false. You did stop coming in late and you did start treating the clients more politely, but your boss still didn't give you the raise. That is the only case in which your boss lied to you, and you have legitimate grounds for complaint.

You need to do a lot of truth tables to get the hang of them. Let me give you one more example. Consider the following complex claim.

If Socrates is human, then either he is Greek or Persian.
H = Socrates is human
G = Socrates is Greek
P = Socrates is Persian
H → (G v P)

What is the main logical operator? Answer: the arrow. This is a complex conditional claim. The antecedent is H, and the consequent is a disjunction. What are the truth-conditions for a conditional claim? A conditional claim is always true, except when the antecedent is true while the consequent is simultaneously false. So we are going to have to find out when the consequent is false. So we are going to have to have a column in our truth table for the consequent, so that we can see when the consequent is false. In order to do that, we need to have columns in our truth table for G and P, because those are the simple claims that the disjunction is made of. Here is the complete truth table.

H	G	P	G v P	H → (G v P)
T	T	T	T	T
T	T	F	T	T
T	F	T	T	T
T	F	F	F	F
F	T	T	T	T
F	T	F	T	T
F	F	T	T	T
F	F	F	F	T

The claim that G v P is true whenever either G or P is true; it is false only when both G and P are false. So the disjunction is false only in the fourth and eighth cases. It is true in every other case. That is the consequent of the conditional. You know that a conditional claim is automatically true except where the antecedent is true and the consequent is false. This gives you a short cut. If the antecedent is false, then the conditional is automatically true. So look at the column for the antecedent. In all of the last four cases, the antecedent is false, and that automatically makes the conditional true. So you can write four T's in the last four cases under the conditional claim. In the first four cases, the antecedent is true, and so if the consequent is false in any of those situations, the conditional is false. So look at the column for the consequent, and you see that it is false in only the fourth case. So it is only in the fourth case where we have the antecedent true while the consequent is false. So that is the only row where we write "F" under the conditional claim.

Section 5: True and False?

Notice that I keep using the distinction between "true and false." I don't say "true and not-true." There's an interesting reason for that.

Think again about the example I used at the beginning of this chapter: the coin flip. We assume that a coin is either going to land heads or it will land tails, and we assume that this is an "exclusive disjunction" (XOR). But isn't it possible for the coin to land on its edge? Maybe it is extremely improbable for that to happen, but it is theoretically possible. So maybe we should say that there are three options: heads, tails and edge (neither heads nor tails). What about truth-values? Could there be a third truth value?

Some logicians think that we should recognize a third truth-value. For example, suppose I just flipped a coin and it landed heads. In that case, we can say that "the coin landed heads" is true, and "the coin landed tails is "false." But what about the next flip of the coin? I haven't flipped it yet, but I'm ready to flip it. In this case, where I have not flipped the coin yet, what do we say about the claim that "the coin will land heads"? Can we say that it is true? No, because it hasn't landed yet. Can we say that this claim is false? No, for exactly the same reason: I haven't flipped it yet. Maybe we should say that before we flip the coin, the claim "the coin will land heads" is not true, but it is also not false: maybe we should say that this claim is "neutral." Maybe we need a third truth value: neither true, nor false, but neutral.

If you understand truth tables, then you should be able to figure out how to do truth tables for three truth-values instead of just two. Here's a start.

A	B
T	T
T	N
T	F
N	T
N	N
N	F
F	T
F	N
F	F

In a three-valued logic system, there are nine possibilities for two claims. This is going to make even simple truth tables much more complicated. Here's just one example.

A	B	A & B
T	T	T
T	N	F
T	F	F
N	T	F
N	N	F
N	F	F
F	T	F
F	N	F
F	F	F

In a two-valued logic system, the truth table for conjunction is only four rows long. In a three-valued logic, the truth table for conjunction is nine rows long. You can imagine how quickly these truth tables are going to get really complicated. So you should be grateful that in this book, I am sticking with just a two-valued system.

Actually, that three-valued truth table for conjunction is only one possibility. It assumes that a conjunction states that both conjuncts are true. It is possible for someone to think that a conjunction is not that stringent: maybe you think that a conjunction is only saying that both of the conjuncts are not false. You might think that if one or both of the conjuncts are neutral, then the conjunction is true. There are some interesting possibilities you might explore here if you think about it.

So one lesson you should learn is that "false" and "not true" do not mean the same thing. In a three-valued logic, "not true" includes both "false" and "neutral." "Not true" is ambiguous, so if you want to be precise and avoid ambiguity, then you should just say "false" when you mean to say that something is false. Avoid saying "not true" unless you really do want to allow for the possibility of both "false" or "neutral."

And just in case you are interested: yes, there are even more complex systems of logic. Some logicians think that truth is much more complicated than even a three-valued system can handle. For example, have you ever seen a bald man? Do you think that "Al is bald" is either just true or false? If you've seen bald men, then you know that there are many degrees of baldness: there is "slightly balding," there are people with "bald spots," there are people who are "really bald," and then there are the total "cue ball" kinds of baldness with the shiny head and all. Maybe in some cases we should accept that there are degrees of truth: maybe we should say that a truth value of 1.0 means "totally true," a truth value of 0.0 means "totally false," a truth value of 0.5 means "neutral, neither true nor false," a truth value of 0.7 means "close to being true," a truth value of 0.3 means "close to being false." Can you imagine doing a truth-table in a multi-valued logic? I leave it to you to figure out how that might go.

Chapter Conclusion.

In this chapter we began serious abstract symbol manipulation. Now you can see clearly that logic does not focus on the soundness of arguments, but only on validity. From now on our emphasis will be on using letters and symbols, and very often we won't have any index to tell us what the letters mean. They could mean anything at all, and it wouldn't affect what we are doing. We are studying the abstract principles of reasoning.

Oh, and by the way, the formula for figuring out how many rows you will need for your truth table is x^y where x = the number of values each item may have, and y = the number of items. In the case of logic, an "item" is a simple claim, and it can have only two values (T or F). So a truth table with only one claim will have 2^1 rows, i.e. 2 rows: T and F. A truth table with two claims will have 2^2 rows, i.e. four rows. A truth table with four claims will have 2^4 rows, i.e. 16 rows, but again, I won't ask you to do truth tables that long.

Things to memorize from this Chapter:

P	Q	P → Q
T	T	T
T	F	F
F	T	T
F	F	T

P	Q	P v Q
T	T	T
T	F	T
F	T	T
F	F	F

P	Q	P & Q
T	T	T
T	F	F
F	T	F
F	F	F

P	Q	P ↔ Q
T	T	T
T	F	F
F	T	F
F	F	T

P	~P
T	F
F	T

Exercises for Chapter 4
Exercise 4.1: Complex Claims. *Translate and evaluate the following arguments.*

Example 1
Problem:
If Socrates was a Greek philosopher, then he was probably pretty famous. But he was Greek, and he was a philosopher. So he must have been pretty famous.

Solution:
1. If Socrates is Greek and a philosopher, then he's probably pretty famous.
2. Socrates is Greek and a philosopher.
∴ 3. Socrates is probably pretty famous.
G = Socrates was Greek
P = Socrates was a philosopher
F = Socrates was famous

1	(G & P) → F	Premise
2	G & P	Premise
∴ 3	F	From 1,2 valid by modus ponens

Example 2
Problem:
If you don't stop that right now, then you will be punished, or else I'll go insane. Oh, that's it! You are not stopping it and so you have to bear the consequences!

Solution:
1. If you don't stop, then either you will be punished or I'll go insane.
2. You don't stop.
∴ 3. Either you will be punished, or I'll go insane.
S = You stop
P = You will be punished
I = I will go insane

1	~S → (P v I)	Premise
2	~S	Premise
∴ 3	P v I	From 1,2 valid by modus ponens

   1. If apples are fruit and carrots are vegetables, then roses are flowers. But apples are fruit, and carrots are vegetables. So roses are flowers.

   2. If John goes to the party and Al also goes to the party, then Bert goes to the party. But John and Al go to the party. Hence, Bert's going.

   3. John, Al and Bert are going to the party. Consequently Bert is going to the party.

   4. If Sally goes to the party, then Rupert is sure to show up. But I know for a fact that Sally is not going to the party because she's got better things to do with her time than go to silly parties. So Rupert won't be going to the party.

   5. Either John and Sally are going to the party, or else Maybelline will go to the party. But Maybelline won't be going. So John and Sally will.

   6. If Rupert and Ethel go to the party, then Franchesca will babysit for Edna. But if Franchesca babysits for Edna, then Edna and Herschel can go to the party. So if Rupert and Ethel go, then Edna and Herschel go.

   7. If I have the salad for lunch and I don't pig out, then I can have a piece of cake for dessert. But there's no way that I can have the salad for lunch and not pig out. So I guess that dessert's out of the question.

   8. Sex and drugs and rock and roll can each cause major problems. So drugs can cause major problems.

   9. Either you can have the alphabet soup and the crackers, or else you can have the grilled cheese with slaw. Oops! I take that back. We're all out of the soup and crackers. So you'll have to settle for the grilled cheese and slaw.

   10. Soup and salad leads to cookies for dessert. But you do have the soup and the salad. I guess you'll be getting cookies pretty soon!

   11. That's some mighty fancy shootin' there! So either you're doing some fancy shootin' or else you are cheating and we'll tar and feather you.

12. Casey let the first and the second pitches go by. That means he'll swing at the next one. So get ready for a mighty swing.

13. If Boston wins, and New York either ties or loses, then Cleveland has a chance. But Cleveland doesn't have a chance. You know what follows.

Exercise 4.2: Truth Tables. *Do a truth table for each of the following claims.*

Example 1
Problem: P & Q
Solution:

P	Q	P & Q
T	T	T
T	F	F
F	T	F
F	F	F

Example 2
Problem: P → Q
Solution:

P	Q	P → Q
T	T	T
T	F	F
F	T	T
F	F	T

1. A → B
2. A & B
3. A v B
4. A ↔ B
5. ~A

6. A → ~B
7. A & ~B
8. A v ~B
9. A ↔ ~B
10. ~(A → B)

11. ~(A & B)
12. ~(A v B)
13. ~(A ↔ B)
14. ~~A
15. ~~~~A

16. ~A → B
17. ~A & B
18. ~A v B
19. ~A ↔ B
20. ~A → ~B

21. ~A & ~B
22. ~A v ~B
23. ~A ↔ ~B
24. ~(~A → B)
25. ~(~A & B)

26. ~(~A v B)
27. ~(~A ↔ B)
28. ~(~A → ~B)

29. ~(~A & ~B)
30. ~(~A v ~B)

31. ~(~A ↔ ~B)
32. ~(A → ~B)
33. ~(A & ~B)
34. ~(A v ~B)
35. ~(A ↔ ~B)

36. (A & B) → C
37. (A & B) & C
38. (A & B) v C
39. (A & B) ↔ C
40. A & (B → C)

41. A & (B & C)
42. A & (B v C)
43. A & (B ↔ C)
44. (A → B) → C
45. (A → B) & C

46. (A → B) v C
47. (A → B) ↔ C
48. A → (B → C)
49. A → (B & C)
50. A → (B v C)

51. A → (B ↔ C)
52. (A v B) → C
53. (A v B) & C
54. (A v B) v C
55. (A v B) ↔ C

56. A v (B → C)
57. A v (B & C)
58. A v (B v C)
59. A v (B ↔ C)
60. (A ↔ B) → C

61. (A ↔ B) & C
62. (A ↔ B) v C
63. (A ↔ B) ↔ C
64. A ↔ (B → C)
65. A ↔ (B & C)

66. A ↔ (B v C)
67. A ↔ (B ↔ C)
68. (A & B) → ~C
69. ~(A & B) → C
70. ~(A & B) → C

CHAPTER 5: TRUTH TABLES (CONTINUED)

Arguments are made up of premises and conclusions. Premises and conclusions are made up of claims. Claims are the basic building blocks of symbolic logic. We saw in the last chapter that truth tables for claims are relatively simple. Each letter can be true or false. When you put letters together using the logical operators (e.g. the ampersand or the wedge), the truth table gets more complex. Now that we are going to be putting the claims together to form entire arguments, the truth tables are going to get even more complex.

Section 1: Truth Tables and Truth Conditions.

Now that you understand and can construct truth tables, it is time to see how useful they are. Actually, you've already seen the central use of truth tables: they can clarify the meaning of a claim. For example, by use of the truth table, you can clearly portray the fact that a conditional claim is false in only one case: when the antecedent is true and the consequent is simultaneously false. A conditional claim is true in every other circumstance.

P	Q	P → Q
T	T	T
T	F	F
F	T	T
F	F	T

The way logicians explain this is to say that *truth tables specify the truth conditions for a claim*. Once you know the truth conditions for a claim, it is much easier to figure out how you would verify or refute (or "falsify") a claim. For example, when you have a conditional claim, you know that if the antecedent is false, you don't have to worry about the truth of the claim as a whole: when the antecedent is false, you haven't given the conditional a fair test, and so out of charity you should accept that the claim is true (innocent until proven guilty). The truth table can tell you what circumstances will make the claim true and what circumstances will make a claim false.

But there are other things truth tables can do for you. I'll start with one that is simple and striking. Consider the following truth table.

P	~P	P & ~P
T	F	F
F	T	F

P has two possible truth values: T or F. But when P is true, ~P is false and vice versa. What happens when someone claims both P and ~P? Answer: what they say is necessarily false! There is no way in which the claim P & ~P can be true. This is called a contradiction.

A **contradiction** is a complex claim that is false simply because of its logical form regardless of the truth values of its component claims

A contradiction can also be called a self-contradiction since the claim contradicts itself. A contradiction can also be called a *logical falsehood*, or can be said to be *logically false*, because what makes it false is simply its logical form. It is not facts that we discover about the world which show us that it is false. Pure logic itself shows us that a contradiction cannot possibly be true. A contradiction can also be called a *truth-functional falsehood*, or can be said to be *truth-functionally false*, because it is false on every possible truth-value assignment in the truth table.

Now compare that last truth table with the following one:

P	~P	P v ~P
T	F	T
F	T	T

When you change the ampersand to a wedge, that changes everything. Now it is absolutely impossible for the claim to be false. This is sometimes called a "tautology." It is an expression which cannot possibly be false; it is true in every circumstance.

A **tautology** is a complex claim that is true simply because of its logical form regardless of the truth values of its component claims

A tautology can also be called a *logical truth*, or can be said to be *logically true*, because what makes it true is simply its logical form. It is not facts that we discover about the world which show us that it is true. In addition, a tautology can be called a *truth-functional truth*, or can be said to be *truth-functionally true*, because it is true on every possible truth-value assignment in the truth table.

I'll return to the idea of "tautology" later, but I need to point out something right away. You might first respond to the difference between contradiction and tautology as if it were a difference between bad and good: contradictions are bad things because they are always false, while tautologies are good things because they are always true. But that's not a helpful way to think about them. You should think of them as being equally bad, and for almost the same reason.

Compare a tautology with a conditional. "If you do a good job on the project, then you get a raise." You know exactly what conditions will make that claim true and exactly what conditions will make it false. By making that claim, your boss is ruling out the possibility that you do all that hard work to do a good job on the project, but then you don't get rewarded for all your hard work with a raise. But what if you boss said, "Either you get a raise or you don't get a raise." What are the truth conditions of that claim? Answer: it is always true. What is your boss trying to rule out with that claim? Answer: absolutely nothing. No matter what happens, what your boss said is true. In other words, there is no real content to what you boss said. Your boss isn't really saying anything. Tautologies are empty, they don't say anything because there is no way to focus in on the situations that would make it true *as opposed to the situations that would make it false*. There are no situations that would make it false. It is precisely in that difference that the content of most claims lie. Claims that actually say something would be made true by certain circumstances and would be made false by different circumstances. It is by understanding the differences between those circumstances that we understand exactly what the claim is ruling in and exactly what the claim is ruling out, i.e. it is how we know what the claim means.

Now think about a contradiction. Suppose your boss says to you, "You will get a raise and you will not get a raise." What the heck does that mean? Answer: nothing! Again, there is no difference between what would make that claim true and what would make it false, because it is always false. There is no way to focus on the situations *that would make it true as opposed to* the situations that would make it false, because there are no situations that would make it true. So contradictions are just as empty, just as meaningless as tautologies.

This is a very important point. Unscrupulous people often try to confuse you by subtle uses of contradictions and tautologies. For example, cult leaders often use tautologies to support their claims to magical or divine power: "Pray with me now and you will be healed, or your faith is too weak." This is a subtle way of saying, "Either you will be healed, or you will not be healed." You cannot possibly refute someone who makes that sort of claim because their claim has no content. They haven't really said anything. They might point out that you cannot refute them, but that is not a sign that they are right; it is just a sign that they are speaking in empty tautologies. Beware of claims that are irrefutable! Claims that cannot be refuted may be empty tautologies.

Unscrupulous people also rely on contradictions. Contradictions can sound very profound. "In death there is life," "God is infinite but finite," or after asking you to reach for your checkbook, "In poverty there is wealth." Strictly speaking, all of those claims are empty and meaningless. They don't say anything at all. However, if you think about them, you might be able to turn them into claims that actually do mean something. For example, "in physical death there is spiritual life." That is a claim that actually has meaning; it has conditions that will make it true as well as conditions that will make it false (unfortunately we would have to die in order to find out if it is possible for the antecedent to be true while the consequent is false). The problem is that often people don't take the time to think about contradictory claims. They just sound really profound, and so you assume the person who said it is really deep. Don't fall for that trick! Think through the contradiction to see if there is any content to it. Once an unscrupulous cult leader gets his hooks into you, you are in serious danger.

Next, just to be complete, if a claim is not a tautology and it is not a contradiction, then it is indeterminate. It could possibly be true and it could possibly be false.

A ***logically indeterminate*** claim can be true or false

As with contradictions and tautologies, logically indeterminate claims can be said to be *truth-functionally indeterminate*, because they are true on some truth-value assignments, but false on others.

Section 2: Consistency, Equivalence, and Contraposition.

There are a couple more concepts that are related to contradiction, tautology and logical indeterminacy. So far we have looked at concepts that deal with just one claim. Truth tables an also be used to compare two or more claims. Consider this truth table.

CHAPTER 5: TRUTH TABLES (CONTINUED)

P	Q	P & Q	P v Q
T	T	T	T
T	F	F	T
F	T	F	T
F	F	F	F

Focus on the last two columns: P & Q compared with P v Q. In the first case, where P and Q are each true, P & Q is true, and so is P v Q. In the last case, both are false, and in the middle two cases one is false while the other is true. The two complex claims P & Q and P v Q can both be false, they can both be true or one can be false while the other is true. Sometimes this is useful information. The fact that two claims can possibly both be true at the same time tells you that the two claims are logically consistent.

Two claims are *logically consistent* when they can both be true simultaneously

If someone claims P & Q, and then later claims P v Q, they are not being inconsistent. They are saying something a little different from what they said before, but logically speaking, they are not being inconsistent: both of their different claims could be simultaneously true.

Compare that with the following truth table.

P	Q	P & Q	P v Q	~(P v Q)
T	T	T	T	F
T	F	F	T	F
F	T	F	T	F
F	F	F	F	T

Suppose someone claims P & Q, and then later claims ~(P v Q). Look down the truth table and compare the truth values of both claims. In the first case, P & Q is true but ~(P v Q) is false, in the last case it is the reverse, and in the middle two cases both claims are false. In other words, it is logically impossible for both claims to be true simultaneously. That tells you that in this case, the person who made both of those claims is not being consistent.

Logical consistency could be called *truth-functional consistency* because of the truth-value assignments of the claims involved. Truth-functionally consistent claims have truth-value assignments in which both are simultaneously true in at least one case.

Next, remember that a claim which is true in every case is called a "tautology." The word "tautology" comes from the Greek word *tautologia* which means "to say the same thing." You can use truth tables to detect when claims that look different are actually saying the same thing. Here is an interesting example.

P	Q	~P	P → Q	~P v Q
T	T	F	T	T
T	F	F	F	F
F	T	T	T	T
F	F	T	T	T

Here I've worked out the truth table for a conditional and a disjunction. Compare the truth values for the conditional and the disjunction: the values are exactly the same in all four cases. These two claims have exactly the same truth conditions, and since truth conditions tell you the meaning of a claim, these two claims have exactly the same meaning. That is really surprising, because one of the claims is an "if ..., then ..." while the other is an "either ..., or ..." How can these two mean exactly the same thing?

Think about it. If P is true, then Q is also true. If you do a good job on the project, then you get a raise. This tells us what happens if you do a good job, but it doesn't tell us what happens if you don't do a good job. So if you don't do a good job, then all bets are off. We haven't really given the conditional claim a fair test, and so we will count it as automatically true because of the Principle of Charity: innocent until proven guilty. That takes care of one alternative: if you don't do a good job on the project, then all bets are off and the conditional claim is automatically true. The other alternative is that you actually do a good job on the project, and in that case, the conditional claim says that you get a raise. So you have two options here: either you don't do a good job on the project (~P), or else you do a good job and end up by getting a raise (Q). Either ~P or Q. The conditional and the disjunction are really saying the exact same thing. Logicians say that these two claims are *logically equivalent*, or are *truth-functionally equivalent*.

85

Two claims are ***logically equivalent*** when they have the same logical content in the sense that their truth values are the same in all possible cases

When someone tells you, "if this, then that" in essence they are telling you exactly the same thing as if they had said, "either not this, or that." I will use the triple bar symbol (≡) to indicate logical equivalence.

P → Q ≡ ~P v Q

By using truth tables, you can discover many more logical equivalences. Some of them are not very interesting. For example, P & Q is logically equivalent to Q & P. Here is the proof.

P	Q	P & Q	Q & P
T	T	T	T
T	F	F	F
F	T	F	F
F	F	F	F

I express this logical equivalence this way:

P & Q ≡ Q & P

Here is the proof of a more interesting logical equivalence.

P	~P	~~P
T	F	T
F	T	F

P ≡ ~~P

This proves that P and ~~P are logically equivalent. In chapter 2 I introduced "The Law of Double Negation." Now we have a truth-table proof of the law. Another way to think of it is that the two negations cancel each other out. This law is especially useful because it applies even to components of complex claims. Look at this truth table.

P	Q	~Q	~~Q	P → Q	P → ~~Q
T	T	F	T	T	T
T	F	T	F	F	F
F	T	F	T	T	T
F	F	T	F	T	T

Since Q and ~~Q are logically equivalent, substituting one for the other doesn't make any difference in the truth table.
    Logical equivalences are not always obvious. Here is a very important logical equivalence, but it may not ever have actually occurred to you before.

P	Q	~P	~Q	P → Q	~Q → ~P
T	T	F	F	T	T
T	F	F	T	F	F
F	T	T	F	T	T
F	F	T	T	T	T

P → Q ≡ ~Q → ~P

You probably never realized that P → Q is logically equivalent to ~Q → ~P. This is sometimes called "The Law of Transposition" or "The Law of Contraposition." I prefer the latter name. ~Q → ~P is the "contrapositive" of P → Q.
    Next, one conditional claim is the ***contrapositive*** of another if and only if the antecedent of the first is the negation of the consequent of the second, and the consequent of the first is the negation of the antecedent of the second.

Law of Contraposition: a conditional claim and its contrapositive are logically equivalent

Think about it using examples.

If Socrates is human, then Socrates is mortal.
   is logically equivalent to
If Socrates is not mortal, then Socrates is not human.

If you do a good job on this project, then you get a raise.
   is logically equivalent to
If you do not get a raise, then you did not do a good job on the project.

If Joe drank the poison, then Joe died.
   is logically equivalent to
If Joe didn't die, then Joe didn't drink the poison.

If this sounds familiar, it is because this is closely related to modus tollens. Modus tollens is a valid form of argument because of the Law of Contraposition.

There are many more logical equivalences (in fact, there is an infinite number of logical equivalences), but I'll end with two related examples. These are among the most important, helpful, and surprising examples. Here is the first example.

P	Q	~P	~Q	P & Q	~(P & Q)	~P v ~Q
T	T	F	F	T	F	F
T	F	F	T	F	T	T
F	T	T	F	F	T	T
F	F	T	T	F	T	T

The negation of a conjunction is the same as the disjunction of negations. For example, suppose your boss tells you that there isn't enough money to give you and your co-worker both raises.

P = You get a raise
Q = Your co-worker gets a raise
~(P & Q) = It is not the case that both you and your co-worker get raises
~P v ~Q = Either you don't get a raise, or your co-worker doesn't get a raise

In other words, if you can't both get raises, then at least one of you is not going to get a raise, either you won't get a raise, or your co-worker won't get a raise. Of course, your boss could still decide not to give anyone a raise. After all, if you are both equally deserving, it would be unfair to give one of you a raise without giving the other a raise also. When ~P and ~Q are both true, then ~P v ~Q is true. When neither of you gets a raise, your boss's claim was true: you didn't *both* get raises, because *neither* of you got a raise.

As I said, this is only one half of an important pair of logical equivalences. That is what happens when you negate a conjunction. The other half shows what happens when you negate a disjunction.

P	Q	~P	~Q	P v Q	~(P v Q)	~P & ~Q
T	T	F	F	T	F	F
T	F	F	T	T	F	F
F	T	T	F	T	F	F
F	F	T	T	F	T	T

The negation of a disjunction is the same as the conjunction of negations. For example, suppose your boss says, "Neither of you two gets a raise." That is the same thing as saying, "You do not get a raise, and your co-worker also does not get a raise." By the way, this also shows you how to translate the word "neither" into symbolic logic. "Neither" is the negation of a disjunction, or it is the conjunction of negations. "Neither of you gets a raise" can be translated in either of these ways because the two expressions are logically equivalent. It is entirely up to you which of these two ways you translate a "neither ..., nor ..." claim.

Together these two logical equivalences are called DeMorgan's Laws, after the logician who was the first to present a formal, symbolic proof of them.

~(P & Q) ≡ ~P v ~Q
~(P v Q) ≡ ~P & ~Q

DeMorgan's Laws: (a) the negation of a conjunction is logically equivalent to the negations of the two conjuncts disjoined, (b) the negation of a disjunction is logically equivalent to the negations of the two disjuncts conjoined.

Here is a very simple example of how useful logical equivalences can be. Look at the following argument.

1	~(P v Q)	Premise
∴ 2	~P & ~Q	From *1 valid by DeMorgan's Laws*
∴ 3	~Q	From *2 valid by conjunction elimination*

In an argument, you can always substitute one claim for another, as long as the two are logically equivalent. Of course you need to cite the name of the logical equivalence, and the line number of the claim for which you are making the substitution. Using this substitution, you can see that from ~(P v Q) it validly follows that ~Q. Without DeMorgan's Laws, this would be very difficult to prove.

Section 3: Truth Tables and Validity.

Now it is time to look again at arguments. Truth tables can be used to determine the validity of arguments. In order to see how, start by considering this truth table.

P	Q	P & Q	(P & Q) → P
T	T	T	T
T	F	F	T
F	T	F	T
F	F	F	T

P & Q is true in every circumstance where both P is true and Q is true, but that happens only in the first situation. It is false everywhere else. But in the fourth column, (P & Q) is the antecedent of the conditional, and you know that a conditional is true whenever the antecedent is false (because of the principle of charity). That automatically makes the conditional claim true in the last three cases. It is also true in the first situation because there the antecedent is true, and the consequent P is also true. So that means (P & Q) → P is true in every circumstance, and that makes it a tautology. But does it look familiar to you? Doesn't it remind you of a valid argument pattern? Remember this:

1	P & Q	Premise
∴ 2	P	From *1 valid by conjunction elimination*

That truth table is the truth table for the rule "conjunction elimination." Now look at this truth table.

P	Q	P v Q	P → (P v Q)
T	T	T	T
T	F	T	T
F	T	T	T
F	F	F	T

P v Q is true whenever P is true or Q is true, or both are simultaneously true, and that is so in the first three cases. It is false only in the fourth case where both P and Q are false. But that is the consequent of the conditional in the fourth column, and a conditional is false only when the antecedent is true while the consequent is false. That means if the consequent is true, the conditional is automatically true. So everywhere the consequent is false, the conditional is true, and that happens in the first three cases. In the fourth and final case, the antecedent of the conditional is false, and so the conditional is automatically true (because of the principle of charity). That means the conditional in column four is true in every circumstance, and that makes it a tautology. But does it look familiar to you? Doesn't it remind you of a valid argument pattern? Remember this:

1	P	Premise
∴ 2	P v Q	From *1 valid by disjunction introduction*

That last truth table is the truth table for the rule "disjunction introduction." Get it?

Truth tables can be used to determine the validity of any argument at all! All you have to do is slap an arrow in between the premises and the conclusion, work out the truth table, and if you get all T's, then the argument is valid. If you get even one F, then the argument is invalid. Why does this work? Remember the definition of a valid argument. A valid argument is one whose conclusion cannot possibly be false when the premises are true. That is just like a conditional claim, right? A conditional is false when the antecedent is true but the consequent is false. An argument is invalid when the premises can be true while the conclusion is false. That means an argument is valid when it never leads from true premises to a false conclusion, you can never have a situation where the premises are true but the conclusion is false. That is what is so useful about knowing and using valid arguments. When an argument is valid you know that it will not lead you astray; valid arguments are "truth-preserving."

But of course this means that when you turn a valid argument into a conditional claim with the premises as the antecedent and the conclusion as the consequent, you get a tautology! In a way, every valid argument is empty. I was just complaining about empty tautologies and contradictions, and now it turns out that the very heart of logic, i.e. the valid argument, is an empty tautology! What does that say about symbolic logic?

What it says about logic, is that symbolic logic can only take you so far. Logic ensures consistency, and that is all. Logic tells you that if you start out with true premises, then your conclusions are guaranteed to be true as well. But with logic as with computers: garbage in, garbage out. If you start with a false premise, your conclusion may be false as well. Checking the validity of an argument is important, but always remember that there is the next step of checking the truth of the premises. Logic is important, but it does have its limitations.

But so far I've just done the arguments that have only one premise. It is not quite as easy to do truth tables for arguments with more than one premise. Here is the truth table for modus ponens.

P	Q	P → Q	P & (P → Q)	[P & (P → Q)] → Q
T	T	T	T	T
T	F	F	F	T
F	T	T	F	T
F	F	T	F	T

Notice that modus ponens (column five) is always true. It cannot ever happen that the premises are true while the conclusion is false. If you turn modus ponens into a conditional claim, with the conjunction of the premises as the antecedent and the conclusion as the consequent, you get a tautology. Let me talk you through this one. First of all, remember how modus ponens works.

1	P	Premise
2	P → Q	Premise
∴ 3	Q	From *1,2 valid by modus ponens*

You have two premises that lead to the conclusion. The only basic claims you have are P and Q, so you need to start your truth table with P and Q. Next, you need to make sure that you have a column for your first premise, and that you have a separate column for your second premise. With modus ponens, one premise is just P, and we already have a column for that, i.e. column one. Next, you need a column for the second premise. After that, you need a column for the conjunction of the premises. This is extremely important. Put an ampersand in between the premises, and work out the truth conditions for the *conjunction of the premises*. Finally, put an arrow in between the conjunction of the premises and the conclusion of the argument. Work out the truth values, and if you get all T's, the argument is valid.

The truth table for modus tollens is even more difficult. I'll work it out just below, but first, let me show you modus tollens again, so you can see what is happening in the truth table.

1	P → Q	Premise
2	~Q	Premise
∴ 3	~P	From *1,2 valid by modus tollens*

Now here is the truth table.

P	Q	~P	~Q	P → Q	(P → Q) & ~Q	[(P → Q) & ~Q] → ~P
T	T	F	F	T	F	T
T	F	F	T	F	F	T
F	T	T	F	T	F	T
F	F	T	T	T	T	T

Just as you expected, the final column is all T's; modus tollens is valid, if you turn modus tollens into a conditional claim with the conjunction of the premises as the antecedent and the conclusion as the consequent, you get a tautology. Now I'll talk you through this one.

First, we have only two basic claims in modus tollens, so we start with a column for P and a column for Q. Whenever I have a negation of a basic claim, I like to do both of the negations immediately after the positive versions of the claims. You don't have to, but I find it helps me to keep track of where I am. With modus tollens we have both a ~P and a ~Q, so I have both of those columns next. After that, you need to have columns for both of the premises. One of the premises is just the negation of the consequent, and we already have a column for that. The other premise is the conditional claim, and so we need a column for that. Next, you are ready to do the column for the conjunction of the premises. Put both of the premises together with an ampersand. You are checking to see what happens if all the premises are simultaneously true. If you want to check for validity, you want to know whether the conclusion could be false *when all the premises are true*. So you need a column to identify the situations when all the premises are true. Since a conjunction is true only when both of the conjuncts are simultaneously true, we get a T only in the fourth case. Finally, put an arrow in between the conjunction of the premises and the conclusion. The conditional is automatically true when the antecedent is false, and if you look at the sixth column, you'll see that the antecedent is false in all of the first three situations. That means the conditional in the seventh and final column is true in all of the first three situations. In the final case, both the antecedent and the consequent are true, and that makes the conditional claim true, which means the conditional is true in every situation which makes it a tautology. Modus tollens is a valid argument pattern.

Theoretically, you could verify or discover the validity of any argument pattern at all using truth tables. How many are there? An infinite number. Of course, once you get into argument patterns that have more than two or three basic claims, or argument patterns that have more than two or three premises, the truth tables are going to be huge. Computer programs could be used to determine the validity of these larger arguments. However, there is a more efficient way to determine validity: derivations. That is the subject we will take up in the next chapter.

Here are step-by-step instructions for using a truth table to determine the validity of an inference.

Step #1: create a column for each of the simple claims
Step #2: create a column for each of the negated simple claims (if any)
Step #3: make sure that you have a column in the truth table for each premise
Step #4: make sure that you have a column in the truth table for the conclusion
Step #5: make sure that the final column of the truth table is a conditional claim where the antecedent is the conjunction of the premises and the consequent is the conclusion of the argument

- If the final column is all T's, then the argument is valid
- If the final column has even one F, then the argument is invalid

Chapter Conclusion

The primary point of this chapter was to give you a purely mechanical way to prove the validity of any argument. Truth tables are very useful, but in addition, they give you a clear and detailed understanding of what it means to think about language logically. In order to think logically, you must think *truth-functionally*. When you think about claims that involve truth-functional operators, you have to think about truth conditions; and specifically, you need to think about what conditions would have to be satisfied in order for the claim as a whole to be true, and what conditions would have to be satisfied in order for the claim as a whole to be false. By doing this, you grasp with complete precision exactly what the claim is ruling in and exactly what the claim is ruling out. You grasp the logical content of a claim only by thinking about the claim truth-functionally.

Unfortunately, although truth tables can in theory be used to evaluate any claim at all, they are very bulky to use. For claims or arguments that involve more than three simple claims, or for arguments that have complex premises, or more than just two premises, truth tables are just too much trouble. We need to develop another method for analyzing the validity of inferences. That method is the method of derivations or proofs, and it is the subject of the next chapter.

Things to memorize from this Chapter:

A **contradiction** is a complex claim that is false simply because of its logical form regardless of the truth values of its component claims

A **tautology** is a complex claim that is true simply because of its logical form regardless of the truth values of its component claims

A **logically indeterminate** claim can be true or false

Two claims are **logically equivalent** when they have the same logical content in the sense that their truth values are the same in all possible cases

Two claims are **logically consistent** when they can both be true simultaneously

One conditional claim is the **contrapositive** of another when the antecedent of the first is the negation of the consequent of the second, and the consequent of the first is the negation of the antecedent of the second.

Law of Double Negation: a claim and its double negation are logically equivalent.

Law of Contraposition: a conditional claim and its contrapositive are logically equivalent

DeMorgan's Laws: (a) the negation of a conjunction is logically equivalent to the negations of the two conjuncts disjoined, (b) the negation of a disjunction is logically equivalent to the negations of the two disjuncts conjoined.

Exercises for Chapter 5

Exercise 5.1: Truth Conditions. Use truth tables to determine which of the following are tautologies, which are contradictions, and which are logically indeterminate.

Example 1
Problem: A & ~A
Solution: Contradiction

A	~A	A & ~A
T	F	F
F	T	F

Example 2
Problem: A v ~A
Solution: Tautology

A	~A	A v ~A
T	F	T
F	T	T

1. P → P
2. P → ~P
3. ~P → P
4. ~P → ~p
5. ~(P → P)

6. P & P
7. P & ~P
8. ~P & P
9. P & ~P
10. ~(P & P)

11. P v P
12. P v ~P
13. ~P v P
14. ~P v ~P
15. ~(P v P)

16. P ↔ P
17. P ↔ ~P
18. ~P ↔ P
19. ~P ↔ ~P
20. ~(P ↔ P)

21. ~~P → P
22. P → ~~P
23. ~~P & P
24. P & ~~P
25. ~~P v P

26. P v ~~P
27. ~~P ↔ P
28. P ↔ ~~P
29. ~~(P & P)
30. ~~(P v P)

31. ~~(P → P)
32. ~~(P ↔ P)
33. Q → (P → Q)

34. R → (P → Q)
35. P → [(P → Q) → Q]

36. (P → Q) → (~Q → ~P)
37. (P → ~Q) → (Q → ~P)
38. (~P → Q) → (~Q → P)
39. (~P → ~Q) → (Q → P)
40. P → (~P → Q)

41. ~P → (P → Q)
42. (~P → P) → P
43. (P & Q) v R
44. (P v ~R) → Q
45. (P → Q) & R

46. (P & Q) → (Q & P)
47. (P & Q) → (~Q & ~P)
48. (P & ~P) → Q
49. (P & ~P) & Q
50. (P & ~P) v Q

51. (P & ~P) ↔ Q
52. ~P → (P & Q)
53. ~P → ~(P & Q)
54. P → (P v P)
55. ~Q → (P & Q)

56. ~Q → ~(P & Q)
57. (P → Q) v (Q → P)
58. (P & Q) → (~P v ~Q)
59. (P & Q) → ~(~P v ~Q)
60. (P v Q) → (~P & ~Q)

61. (P v Q) → ~(~P & ~Q)
62. (P → Q) → (Q → P)
63. (P & ~Q) → (P → Q)
64. (P & ~Q) → ~(P → Q)
65. (~P & Q) → (P → Q)

66. (~P & Q) → ~(P → Q)
67. [P → (Q → R)] → [Q → (P → R)]
68. [(P → Q) → Q] → [(Q → P) → P]
69. [(P v Q) → (P & Q)] → [(Q v P) → (Q & P)]
70. [(P → Q) v (Q → P)] → [(P & Q) v ~(P & Q)]

71. (A & B) → C
72. A v (B → C)
73. A → (B & ~C)
74. A ↔ (D ↔ B)
75. (~A & C) v ~B

76. (E ↔ ~G) → (G v ~H)
77. (H → ~J) ↔ (K & ~H)
78. (L & M) v (M ↔ O)
79. (P v Q) & (~Q v R)
80. (R ↔ S) → (~S ↔ ~T)

CHAPTER 5: TRUTH TABLES (CONTINUED)

Exercise 5.2: Logical Consistency and Logical Equivalence. *Use truth tables to determine which of the following pairs of claims are logically consistent with one another, and which are logically equivalent to one another.*

Example 1
Problem: A & B; ~B v ~A
Solution: Not logically consistent (circle every pair of truth values in the final two columns to show that the claims are never both T; not logically equivalent (circle one pair of truth values in the final two columns to show that they claims do not have exactly the same truth values)

A	B	~A	~B	A & B	~B v ~A
T	T	F	F	T	F
T	F	F	T	F	T
F	T	T	F	F	T
F	F	T	T	F	T

Example 2
Problem: P → Q; P & Q
Solution: logically consistent (circle the two T's side-by-side in the final two columns to show that it is possible for both claims to be true simultaneously; not logically equivalent (circle a T and an F side-by-side in the final two columns to show that the two claims do not have the same truth values in all circumstances)

P	Q	P → Q	P & Q
T	T	T	T
T	F	F	F
F	T	T	F
F	F	T	F

1. A & B; A v B
2. A → B; A ↔ B
3. A & B; A → B
4. A v B; A ↔ B
5. A ↔ B; A & B
6. A & ~B; ~A v ~B
7. ~A → B; A ↔ ~B
8. A & ~B; ~A → B
9. ~A v B; A ↔ ~B
10. ~A ↔ ~B; A & B
11. (A & B) → (A v B); A v ~A
12. (A & ~B) → (~A v ~B); A & ~A
13. (A v ~B) ↔ (~B v A); A ↔ B
14. (A → B) → (~B → ~A); A → ~B
15. (A ↔ B) ↔ (~B ↔ ~A); ~A → B
16. C → ~D; ~~D → ~C; ~C ↔ ~D
17. ~(E v G); ~E & ~G
18. ~(~H & J); H v ~J
19. K & (L & M); (K & L) & M
20. (N ↔ ~P) ↔ ~Q; N ↔ (~P ↔ ~Q)

Exercise 5.3: Validity. *Use truth tables to determine which of the following are valid.*

Example Problem:
1. P
2. P → Q
∴ 3. Q

Example Solution: Valid

P	Q	P → Q	P & (P → Q)	[P & (P → Q)] → Q
T	T	T	T	T
T	F	F	F	T
F	T	T	F	T
F	F	T	F	T

Problem 1:
1. A → B
2. A
∴ 3. B

Problem 2:
1. A → B
2. B
∴ 3. A

Problem 3:
1. A → B
2. ~A
∴ 3. ~B

Problem 4:
1. A → B
2. ~B
∴ 3. ~A

Problem 5:
1. A → B
2. ~A
∴ 3. B

Problem 6:
1. A → B
2. ~B
∴ 3. A

Problem 7:
1. A
2. B
∴ 3. A & B

Problem 8:
1. A & B
∴ 2. A

Problem 9:
1. A
∴ 2. A v B

Problem 10:
1. A
∴ 2. A v (B ↔ A)

Problem 11:
1. P v Q
2. P
∴ 3. Q

Problem 12:
1. P v Q
2. P
∴ 3. ~Q

Problem 13:
1. P v Q
2. ~P
∴ 3. Q

Practice Exam for Chapters 1-5
Note: the actual exam may have more problems in each section
Part I: Definitions. *Define the following (10 pts each).*
1. Tautology
2. Unsound

Part II: Translations. *Fully assess the following for validity (10 pts each).*
3. Socrates will die because he's human, and humanity is sufficient for mortality.

Part III: Truth Tables. *Complete truth tables for the following (10 pts each).*
4. P v Q
5. (P & Q); (Q & P)
6. Prove the validity of Chain Argument using a truth table

Sample Answers for Practice Exam

Note: the answer to problem 1 is poor; the other answers are model answers

Problem 1: a tautology is a claim that is always true

Analysis: $E = mc^2$ might always be true, but it is not a tautology; the concept of a tautology is not a concept of how long something is true, it is a concept of what kind of claim it is. If $E = mc^2$ is true, then it is true because of the way the cosmos works. A tautology is true because of its logical form no matter what the cosmos is like.

Problem 2:

Definition: an unsound argument is an argument that is either invalid or has a false premise

Explanation: an unsound argument tries but fails to prove that its conclusion is true. There are two ways in which a proof can fail: (1) one or more of the reasons (premises) it relies on to prove the truth of the conclusion are actually false, or (2) the reasons given for the truth of the conclusion do not in fact validly entail that the conclusion is true. An argument does not have to have both of these problems in order to be unsound. An argument can have all true premises, but if it is invalid, it will be unsound. Also, even if the argument is valid, if it has even one false premise then the entire argument is automatically unsound.

Example:
Premise 1: Socrates was a husband.
Premise 2: If Socrates was a husband, then Socrates had children.
Conclusion: Socrates had children.

This argument satisfies one condition for being sound: it has a false premise, i.e. premise 2. It is false to claim that Socrates had children just because he was a husband. The conclusion of the argument is true, in fact Socrates did have children, but he had children because his wife gave birth. It is true that most husbands do have children, but not all husbands have children. The argument is valid; if both premises were in fact true, then the conclusion would have to be true also, and would be proven true by the argument, but validity is not enough for soundness. One false premise makes a valid argument unsound.

Problem 3: this argument is an enthymeme, i.e. it has a hidden assumption

1	Socrates is human.	Premise
2	If Socrates is human, then Socrates is mortal.	*Hidden Premise; the universal claim is applied to Socrates, and since his being human is the sufficient condition, this must be the antecedent*
∴ 3	Socrates is mortal.	From 1,2 valid by modus ponens; the idea of dying is the same as the idea of being mortal

H = Socrates is human
M = Socrates is mortal

1	H	Premise
2	H → M	Premise
∴ 3	M	From *1,2 valid by modus ponens*

Problem 4:

P	Q	P v Q
T	T	T
T	F	T
F	T	T
F	F	F

Note: circle the T and the F in the bottom right corner of the table and say that this shows the claim is "logically indeterminate"

Problem 5:

P	Q	P & Q	Q & P
T	T	T	T
T	F	F	F
F	T	F	F
F	F	F	F

Note: circle the pairs of truth values in the two columns on the right and say that this shows the two claims are "logically equivalent"

Problem 6:

P	Q	R	P → Q	Q → R	P → R	(P → Q) & (Q → R)	(P → Q) & (Q → R) → (P → R)
T	T	T	T	T	T	T	T
T	T	F	T	F	F	F	T
T	F	T	F	T	T	F	T
T	F	F	F	T	F	F	T
F	T	T	T	T	T	T	T
F	T	F	T	F	T	F	T
F	F	T	T	T	T	T	T
F	F	F	T	T	T	T	T

Note: circle the entire column of T's on the right and say that this shows that Chain Argument is valid

CHAPTER 6: SIMPLE DERIVATIONS

In theory, you could use truth tables to discover or prove the validity or invalidity of any argument at all. So truth tables give you all that you need to evaluate the logic of any argument at all. The only problem is that truth tables are bulky. In practice it is hard to use them for very complex arguments. So we need another way of determining the validity of an argument. In this chapter we will develop a method of "proof" or "derivations."

Section 1: Introduction to Derivations.

Most people reserve the word "proof" for a sound argument, an argument which shows conclusively that some claim is actually true. In a real proof, the premises are actually true, and the argument is valid, and so the conclusion must also be true. A somewhat weaker word is "derivation." You can say that in a valid argument, the conclusion is "derived" from the premises in that it necessarily follows from the premises. Very often it is difficult to know for sure whether all the premises of an argument are true. Before you go to all the trouble to check on whether the premises are true, you might want to see if the argument is valid first. After all, if the argument is invalid, then even if the premises are true, the conclusion could still be false. So if the conclusion is validly derived from the premises, then you've learned something significant, even if that doesn't yet tell you whether the conclusion is in fact true.

Actually, you have already seen some derivations, and you already know how to do simple derivations. Here is one that you already know.

1	P	Premise
2	P → Q	Premise
∴ 3	Q	From *1,2 valid by modus ponens*

A derivation is just an argument. You have premises, from which can be derived various things by various rules. Now that you are familiar with arguments, you may begin to abbreviate certain things. But be careful with your abbreviations, there are still rules to follow. First, you may now abbreviate "Premise" with just "P." Next, with valid inferences, all you need to do is cite the rule it follows. If it follows a valid rule, then it follows that it is a valid inference. Also, there are certain abbreviations that go with the various valid inference patterns. Modus ponens, for example, may be abbreviated "MP." Finally, although you may still put in the three dots to indicate a conclusion, they are not necessary. So here is how you may now do the above problem.

1	P	P
2	P → Q	P
3	Q	1,2 MP

Here are examples of eight different valid rules, and the abbreviations you must learn for each. Notice that seven of them are rules you first learned in chapter 1. Bi-conditional elimination is a new, but very simple, rule.

Conjunction Elimination (CE)

1	P & Q	P
2	P	1 CE

Disjunction Elimination (DE)

1	P v Q	P
2	~Q	P
3	P	1,2 DE

Modus Tollens (MT)

1	P → Q	P
2	~Q	P
3	~P	1,2 MT

Chain Argument (CA)

1	P → Q	P
2	Q → R	P
3	P → R	1,2 CA

Reiteration (R)

1	P	P
2	P	1 R

Conjunction Introduction (CI)

1	P	P
2	Q	P
3	P & Q	1,2 CI

Disjunction Introduction (DI)

1	P	P
2	P v Q	1 DI

Modus Ponens (MP)

1	P → Q	P
2	P	P
3	Q	1,2 MP

Bi-conditional Elimination (BCoE)

1	P ↔ Q	P
2	P	P
3	Q	1,2 BCoE

Notice that with disjunction and conjunction there is both an elimination and an introduction rule. With a conditional you just have two elimination rules, modus ponens and modus tollens. Later there will be a conditional introduction rule, but we don't have the necessary machinery to introduce the rule now.

You also know several invalid argument patterns. Here they are with their usual abbreviations.

Fallacy of Affirming the Consequent (FAC)

1	P → Q	P
2	Q	P
3	P	1,2 invalid by FAC

Fallacy of Affirming a Disjunct (FAD)

1	P v Q	P
2	Q	P
3	~P	1,2 invalid by FAD

Fallacy of Denying the Antecedent (FDA)

1	P → Q	P
2	~P	P
3	~Q	1,2 invalid by FDA

Fallacy of Reversing a Chain (FRC)

1	P → Q	P
2	Q → R	P
3	R → P	1,2 invalid by FRC

With the valid argument patterns, you no longer have to say "valid by." But with invalid argument patterns you do have to specify that they are invalid. Notice also that premises will always be marked with a simple "P" while inferences will have a line number and the abbreviation for a rule. This means that inferences will always be visibly marked in the proof, and this, in turn, means that we no longer need to use the word "so" or the three dots "∴" to indicate a conclusion. You may use them if you wish, it is not wrong to use them, but they are redundant, so it is ok if you don't use them.

Now that you have the basic idea, you are ready to see some derivations. Let's start with a very simple example. Imagine a complex conjunction.

1	P & (Q & R)	P
2	P	1 CE

The rule conjunction elimination permits you to take one of the conjuncts out of a conjunction. In this case, I just took out the first conjunct. However, I could have taken out the second conjunct, like this:

1	P & (Q & R)	P
2	Q & R	1, CE

Of course, this conclusion is another conjunction, so if we wanted to, we could use conjunction elimination a second time in order to take out the Q or the R. The whole argument would look like this:

1	P & (Q & R)	P
2	Q & R	1 CE
3	Q	2 CE

Notice that on line 3, the justification cites line 2 and the rule conjunction elimination. It would be incorrect to cite line 1.

1	P & (Q & R)	P
2	Q & R	1 CE
3	Q	???

Yes, there is a "Q" in line 1, but "Q" does not follow validly from line 1. It follows validly from line 2. Conjunction elimination permits you to take out one of two conjuncts. But look closely at line 1 of that last argument and you'll see that Q by itself is not one of the two conjuncts. P by itself is one conjunct, and (Q & R) is the other conjunct. Since Q by itself is not one of the two conjuncts of line 1, you cannot use conjunction elimination to take Q by itself out of line 1. You have to take it in stages. First take out the (Q & R), and then once you have Q by itself as one of the two conjuncts, then you can take it out.

Exactly the same thing goes for disjunction introduction. However, since we are introducing disjunctions, we are building up smaller claims into larger ones rather than breaking larger claims down into smaller ones.

1	P	P
2	P v Q	1 DI
3	(P v Q) v R	2 DI

Again notice that on line 3, the Disjunction Introduction is applied to line 2. Line 2 has the P v Q which is one of the disjuncts on line 3. You could not go from line 1 immediately to line 3, because the rule disjunction introduction wouldn't justify such a move. Why? Because when you use disjunction introduction on P, the result has to have P as one of the disjuncts; but in line 3, P is *not* one of the disjuncts. Remember what you learned about the *main logical operator*. The main logical operator of line 3 is the *second* wedge. That means that one of the disjuncts is R and the other disjunct is (P v Q). So you cannot go immediately from line 1 to line 3. However, you could do this:

1	P	P
2	P v (Q v R)	1 DI

This is perfectly ok because the rule disjunction introduction permits you to add any disjunct you want onto whatever you begin with. Even if the disjunct you add is very long and complex, the rule disjunction introduction will permit you to add it. You could do this, if you wanted:

1	P	P
2	P v Q → (R & (~S ↔ T))	1 DI

In this argument I've added a long, complex disjunct, but disjunction introduction permits it. Make sure you understand the rule: if you are already given P as a premise, then you know that you have *either* P *or* something else.

The same thing goes for conjunction introduction. It doesn't matter how complex the conjuncts are, conjunction introduction will permit you to put together any two claims you have asserted.

1	P v Q	P
2	R & S	P
3	(P v Q) & (R & S)	1,2 CI

Here we have just taken the two claims we have in premises 1 and 2, and we've stuck them together in the conclusion with an ampersand between them.

This same point about complexity of components goes for the conditional rules. Here is a modus ponens argument with a complex conditional claim.

1	P → (Q v R)	P
2	P	P
3	Q v R	1,2 MP

The main logical operator of the claim in premise 1 is the arrow, which means that the antecedent is simply P and the consequent is (Q v R). So when we affirm the antecedent in premise 2, modus ponens gives us the right to affirm the consequent in 3. We can do the same thing with a modus tollens argument.

1	P → (Q v R)	P
2	~(Q v R)	P
3	~P	1,2 MT

In the second premise we have negated the consequent of the conditional in premise 1, and this gives us the right to negate the antecedent of the conditional claim, no matter how complex either the antecedent or the consequent happens to be.

Section 2: Performing Derivations.

Derivations are just arguments. Here is a simple modus ponens argument, or to put the same thing in other words, here is a simple derivation which uses modus ponens.

1	P	P
2	P → Q	P
3	Q	1,2 MP

If you look at this as a derivation, then you are thinking of it as a conclusion that is derived by a certain rule from a set of two premises. Here is the way we express this as a derivation.

$\{P, P \rightarrow Q\} \vdash Q$

The new symbol in that expression (the ⊢) is called the "turnstile." The curly braces on the left indicate that I am giving you a complete list of the premises you can use to derive the claim on the right. The turnstile indicates that the thing on the right *can be derived from* the set of premises on the left. So you could say that the turnstile means "from this you can derive that." Here is how a modus tollens would look.

$\{\sim Q, P \rightarrow Q\} \vdash \sim P$

This says that using the set of premises that includes only ~Q and P → Q, you can derive ~P. This is how I will give you derivations to do. Here is a sample problem.

Problem: $\{P \rightarrow Q, \sim Q\} \vdash \sim P$
You would solve this problem like this:

1	~Q	P
2	P → Q	P
3	~P	1,2 MT

Notice that I didn't take the premises out in the same order in which they were given. You know that the order of the premises doesn't matter as long as the conclusion comes last. Here is another simple example.

Problem: $\{P \& Q\} \vdash Q$
Solution

1	P & Q	P
2	Q	1 CE

Again, the curly braces on the left gives you a complete list of premises you can use to try to derive the claim listed on the right of the turnstile. Now here is a problem that is a little more tricky.

Problem: $\{P \rightarrow Q, \sim Q\} \vdash \sim P \lor R$

CHAPTER 6: SIMPLE DERIVATIONS

My advice to you is that you begin by setting up the derivation. List the premises, and then put the conclusion below them, so that you know what you have to work with (the premises), and what you are trying to derive (the conclusion). You might start like this:

1	P → Q	P
2	~Q	P
3	???	???
?	~P v R	???

Starting with the premises in 1 and 2, how are we going to get the conclusion? There is no single rule that gives you that conclusion from those two premises. There has to be at least one intervening step, some sub-conclusion that you derive from your premises, and then from the sub-conclusion you'll be able to get to the main conclusion. If you can't think of how the derivation is going to work, then just try deriving whatever you can from the premises. Look at those premises. What valid argument pattern might they fit? What valid argument pattern has a conditional claim for one premise, and then the other premise denies the consequent of the conditional? Answer: modus tollens. The conclusion of a modus tollens is the negation of the antecedent of the conditional claim, so plug that into our incomplete derivation.

1	P → Q	P
2	~Q	P
3	~P	1,2 MT
?	~P v R	???

We've made some progress. Now that we have ~P, can you think of a rule that would justify us in deriving the conclusion we are going for? From ~P does ~P v R follow validly? Yes, by disjunction introduction. So here is our completed derivation.

1	P → Q	P
2	~Q	P
3	~P	1,2 MT
4	~P v R	3 DI

Derivations lead from a set of premises to a specific conclusion. You never know in advance how many intermediate steps you'll need to complete the derivation. Often it requires some ingenuity to figure out which sub-conclusions you should go for in order to get ultimately to your main conclusion. Here is another example, this one uses the new rule Bi-conditional Elimination.

Problem: {P ↔ Q, P → R, Q} ⊢ R
Solution

1	P ↔ Q	P
2	Q	P
3	P	1,2 BCoE
4	P → R	P
5	R	3,4 MP

Notice that I didn't use the premises all at once. Some logicians like you to pull out all the premises at the beginning and list them all once. That is a perfectly legitimate way to do derivations. Here is how that same derivation would look if pulled out all the premises to begin with.

1	P ↔ Q	P
2	P → R	P
3	Q	P
4	P	1,3 BCoE
5	R	2,4 MP

Both versions of the solution are equally correct. Remember that the order of the premises doesn't matter as long as the conclusion comes last. Some people find it easier to have a complete list of the premises first, others find it easier to use only what they need when they need it. Feel free to do your derivations either way, but try both ways so that you are comfortable with them.

The strength of listing all the premises first, is that you get a good look at what you have to work with. The down side is that you won't have a good clean look at many of the inferences you will be using. For example, look at the modus ponens conclusion in line 4. The conclusion is separated from the premises, and it is hard to see it as a modus ponens. There is a rule you can use to help you solve this problem. This rule is called "Reiteration" and is abbreviated as "R" and it simply lets you repeat anything at all you have already entered on a line. Here is a simple example.

Problem: {P, P → Q, P → R} ⊢ R
Solution

1	P	P
2	P → Q	P
3	P → R	P
4	P	1 R
5	R	3,4 MP

In this case, a complete list of the premises separates the only two premises I actually use. In order to put the two premises together again, I reiterate the premise I need, and then the modus ponens follows obviously.

Notice also that in this argument, I didn't use all the premises. Sometimes you will have more premises than you need. Here's another example.

Problem: {P v Q, ~P, ~R} ⊢ Q
Solution

1	P v Q	P
2	~P	P
3	~R	P
4	Q	1,2 DE

Notice that I didn't use the third premise at all. I never used ~R. That's ok. It is very frustrating that authors very often appeal to things they don't need. People waste an awful lot of time fighting over premises that turn out to be irrelevant to the main conclusion. Don't waste your time. Just focus on what is absolutely necessary for the conclusion the author is going for. If you want to discuss the irrelevant stuff later, fine. First worry about the validity of the main argument.

It is also possible for you to have too few premises. Here is an example.

Problem: {P, P → (Q v R)} ⊢ R
Solution

1	P	P
2	P → (Q v R)	P
3	Q v R	1,2 MP
4	R	3 invalid

This argument is invalid, but it doesn't fit any invalid argument pattern, so we just say that it is invalid.

Notice that although this argument is invalid, I didn't simply solve the problem by saying "invalid." I used the premises to get as close to the conclusion as possible. This is very helpful. If someone is trying to develop an argument for a conclusion and you can point out to them not only that their argument is invalid, but you can point out to them precisely what they could add to their argument to make it valid, that may help them fix their argument, or realize that they are in fact wrong.

Section 3: Longer Derivations.

So far I've shown you very short derivations. However, by stacking one derivation on top of another, you can create longer derivations. Actually, you've already seen a derivation like this. Recall this derivation.

1	P	P
2	P v Q	1 DI
3	(P v Q) v R	2 DI

This is one disjunction introduction stacked on top of another. If you wanted to, you could continue this process indefinitely, adding more and more disjunctions.

CHAPTER 6: SIMPLE DERIVATIONS

1	P	P
2	P v Q	*1 DI*
3	(P v Q) v R	*2 DI*
4	(P v Q) v R v S	*3 DI*
5	((P v Q) v R) v S v T	*4 DI*
6	(((P v Q) v R) v S) v T v U	*5 DI*

You get the idea. Conditional arguments can also be stacked on top of one another. Here is an example that involves stacking one modus ponens on top of another.

1	P	*P*
2	P → Q	*P*
3	Q	*1,2 MP*
4	Q → R	*P*
5	R	*3,4 MP*

Theoretically there is no limit to the number of premises you can have in an argument. Of course in practice most arguments won't go on for too long, or if they do, authors will break their arguments down into parts and discuss them one chunk at a time.

Notice also that, especially in longer arguments, it is extremely important to keep track of the premise numbers in the right hand column where you identify the rules that make each inference valid. Every single line of an argument has to have some entry in the right hand column. For now, each line must have one of two things:

(1) a capital letter "P" identifying the claim as a premise, or
(2) line numbers identifying the lines from which it follows, and an abbreviation of a rule it follows (if it follows an invalid argument pattern, then you must specify that it is "invalid by" and cite the abbreviation for the fallacy it follows; and if it is invalid but doesn't follow any rule, then just say "invalid").

Later there will be a third possibility.

Here is an example of an argument that has one valid and one invalid inference.

1	P	*P*
2	P → Q	*P*
3	Q	*1,2 MP*
4	Q v R	*P*
5	~R	*3,4 invalid by FAD*

This is an argument that has three premises: 1, 2 and 4. The sub-conclusion in 3 follows validly from premises 1 and 2 by modus ponens, but the main conclusion in 5 does not follow validly from anything that comes before. From Q and Q v R you cannot derive R. Q v R says that at least one of the two is true. We know that is true because we have already derived Q. Maybe R is true also, but maybe it isn't. From all that we have accepted so far, R doesn't follow. Here is an even longer argument, but this one is completely valid.

1	P	*P*
2	P → Q	*P*
3	Q	*1,2 MP*
4	Q → ~R	*P*
5	~R	*3,4 MP*
6	S v R	*P*
7	S	*5,6 DE*

This has four simple claims and a negation. Can you imagine how big the truth table for this valid argument would have to be?

Using derivation rules, you can decide whether a particular conclusion follows validly from a set of premises. Consider this example.

> Paul spilled gasoline all over the floor, and Quincy lit a match. But if Paul spilled gasoline all over the floor, then if Quincy lit a match, then a raging fire will consume the warehouse. So a raging fire will consume the warehouse.

1. Paul spilled gasoline all over the floor.
2. If Paul spilled gasoline all over the floor, then if Quincy lit a match, then a raging fire will consume the warehouse.
So 3. A raging fire will consume the warehouse.

P = Paul spilled gasoline all over the floor
Q = Quincy lit a match
R = A raging fire consumes the warehouse

1	P & Q	P
2	P → (Q → R)	P
3	R	???

The conclusion doesn't follow from the premises by any rule that you know. So you are going to have to try to derive the conclusion from the premises using the derivation rules that you know.

First, think about the argument to see if it seems valid to you. The second premise tells us that if Paul spilled the gasoline all over the floor, then the stage is set for a terrible tragedy. If he has in fact spilled the gasoline, then all it will take is one match to set the whole place on fire. If Paul has spilled the gasoline, then if Quincy lights a match, then the whole place will go up in flames. Here we have one conditional nested within another. Paul's incompetence has set up a further conditional. If Paul hadn't spilled the gasoline, then Quincy could light a match and nothing would happen. But once the gasoline has been spilled, the match will set off the fire. This is where premise 1 comes in. Premise 1 tells us that in fact Paul did spill the gasoline, and in addition, Quincy did light the match. You do the math. Now that you understand what the premises say, you can see what follows: a raging fire will consume the warehouse. In order to demonstrate this logically, let's go through the argument step by step.

The first thing to do is see if you can figure out the logic of the situation. Start by looking at the premises you are given to work with, and then look at the conclusion you are supposed to reach.

Premise 1: P & Q
Premise 2: P → (Q → R)
Conclusion: R

Given those premises, how are you going to derive R? The first thing to notice is that the conclusion you are trying to get is already there in premise 2. Basically what you are trying to do is use the various derivation rules to get the R out of the second premise. Think about the rules you know, and how you could use them to pull the R out of premise 2.

The first problem is that the R in premise 2 is doubly embedded. It is embedded in the (Q → R), which is in turn embedded in the P → (Q → R). Let's take this step by step. First of all, how are we going to get the R out of (Q → R)? Think of it like this:

Q → R
???
R

What could you put in for the question marks to give you a valid argument? Answer: Q. If you can get a Q and put it there for the question marks, then you can use modus ponens to derive R.

Q → R   P
Q   ???
R   MP

The next question is: where are you going to get the Q from? Look back at the premises that you are given for this argument, and you'll see that premise 1 is P & Q. If you can take that Q out, then you can use it with Q → R to derive the R. Is there a rule that will let you take Q out of P & Q? Yes: conjunction elimination, like this:

1	P & Q	P
2	Q	1 CE
3	Q → R	???
4	R	2,3 MP

We have almost solved this problem. The only question left is how to get Q → R. You can't just write down anything you want. Remember that there has to be a solid justification in the right hand column for everything you write down.

CHAPTER 6: SIMPLE DERIVATIONS

Whenever you are stuck like this, always go back to basics: look at the premises you have to work with. Let's re-write the derivation we have using all the premises we have to work with.

1	P & Q	P
2	P → (Q → R)	P
3	Q	1 CE
4	Q → R	???
5	R	3,4 MP

Notice that because I've added the other premise in, I had to change the justification for R in the last line of the derivation: instead of being from lines 2 and 3, it now is from lines 3 and 4.

Everything works out so far in our derivation except for the justification for premise 4. How are we going to get Q → R? Look at the premises and see if there is any way you could get it from them. Fortunately we see that premise 2 has a Q → R in it. Can we get it out of premise 2? Is there some rule you could use to get you from premise 2 to Q → R? Here is what we are asking:

P → (Q → R)
???
Q → R

What could we fill in for the question marks to make this a valid argument? Answer: P.

P → (Q → R)   P
P   ???
Q → R   MP

Now let's put this together with the 5 step derivation above, and see what we have.

1	P & Q	P
2	P → (Q → R)	P
3	Q	1 CE
4	P	???
5	Q → R	2,4 MP
6	R	3,4 MP

Now our final question is what justifies us in putting P down for step 4? Look at the premises and you'll see that P comes from premise 1 by conjunction elimination. So we can complete our derivation.

1	P & Q	P
2	P → (Q → R)	P
3	Q	1 CE
4	P	1 CE
5	Q → R	2,4 MP
6	R	3,4 MP

Using valid rules of derivation, we can show that the conclusion does indeed follow from those premises. This is a valid argument.

Section 4: Replacement Rules.

In the last chapter I introduced the idea of logical equivalence. Now logical equivalence is really going to pay off. Because logically equivalent claims are saying the same thing, you can always replace one with the other. Let's begin with a very simple example. P & Q is obviously logically equivalent to Q & P. But consider this argument.

1	P & Q	P
2	(Q & P) → R	P
3	R	1,2 ???

The second premise tells you that if Q and P are both true, then R follows. From the first premise we know that P and Q are both true, and so the conclusion has to follow. Unfortunately, in logic we must follow the rules strictly, and there is no rule that allows us to infer that conclusion from those premises. This is almost a modus ponens argument, but not exactly. The antecedent must be affirmed precisely. What we need to do is flip the P & Q around:

1	P & Q	P
2	Q & P	???
3	(Q & P) → R	P
4	R	1,2 MP

This derivation works out perfectly, if we can find out what rule justifies step 2. We need a rule which allows us to replace P & Q with Q & P. This is the "replacement rule" called "commutation," and it comes in three varieties.

P & Q ≡ Q & P
P v Q ≡ Q v P
P ↔ Q ≡ Q ↔ P

(Remember from the last chapter that the triple bar "≡" indicated logical equivalence.) At any point in a derivation, you can flip a conjunction or a disjunction, and the justification you write in the right-hand column will be "Com" which is short for "commutation." The replacement rules make many derivations much shorter than they would otherwise be.

Here is a list of the replacement rules you may use (there will be more later). After each law I've also listed the abbreviation you use to cite the rule.

Double Negation (DN)
P ≡ ~~P

Commutation (Com)
P & Q ≡ Q & P
P v Q ≡ Q v P
P ↔ Q ≡ Q ↔ P

DeMorgan's Laws (DeM)
~(P & Q) ≡ ~P v ~Q
~(P v Q) ≡ ~P & ~Q

Implication (Impl)
P → Q ≡ ~P v Q

Contraposition (CP)
P → Q ≡ ~Q → ~P

Association (Assoc)
P & (Q & R) ≡ (P & Q) & R
P v (Q v R) ≡ (P v Q) v R
P ↔ (Q ↔ R) ≡ (P ↔ Q) ↔ R

These are just examples because, as you well know, you can have lots of different antecedents of conditionals, lots of different conjuncts, lots of different disjuncts, and so on. To show you what I mean, here is another example of Double Negation.

Problem: {Q & R} ⊢ ~~~~Q
Solution:

1	Q & R	P
2	Q	1 CE
3	~~Q	2 DN
4	~~~~Q	3 DN

In this derivation I used double negation twice. The first time (in step 3) I added two negations onto Q. Then in step 4 I added another two negations in order to derive what I was supposed to derive. Double negation permits you to add or take away two adjacent negations from the front of any claim, or from the front of any component of a claim.

The one very significant difference you have to be aware of, however, is that double negation is the only rule that you can use *inside* a complex claim. Here is an example of what I mean by using double negation inside a complex claim.

Problem: {Q & (R & ~~P)} ⊢ P
Solution:

1	Q & (R & ~~P)	P
2	Q & (R & P)	1 DN
3	R & P	2 CE
4	P	3 CE

The claim in step 1 is a conjunction and has two components. One component is Q, the other component is the complex claim R & ~~P. You cannot reach inside this one component and change it in any way except for one: you can use double negation. *No other rule can be used inside a component of a claim.*

Also remember that the examples above are just examples. Just because the standard examples above use the capital letter P, that doesn't mean the very same rule won't work for the capital letter Q. P and Q can stand for anything at all, the content doesn't matter. The logical principle works for any claim whatsoever. Here is another example.

Problem: {P v (Q & R)} ⊢ (Q & R) v P
Solution:

| 1 | P v (Q & R) | P |
| 2 | (Q & R) v P | 1 Com |

The standard example of Commutation just uses single letters on each side of the wedge. But the content of the claims doesn't matter. Commutation says that a conjunction or disjunction can be flipped around, no matter what the disjuncts happen to be. The disjuncts can be really long and complicated, but you can still flip them around. Notice that this rule does not apply to the arrow or the double arrow. Here is another example of the usefulness of the Law of Commutation.

Problem: {R → (P & Q), R, (Q & P) → S} ⊢ S
Solution

1	R	P
2	R → (P & Q)	P
3	P & Q	1,2 MP
4	Q & P	3 Com
5	(Q & P) → S	P
6	S	4,5 MP

Look closely at steps 3, 4 and 5. P & Q is not identical to Q & P, although they are equivalent. Logically speaking, it is a separate step to go from the first claim to the second. You must show every logical step when you do derivations. There is a similar moral to the story in the following derivation.

Problem: {P & (Q & R), (P & Q) → S} ⊢ S
Solution

1	P & (Q & R)	P
2	(P & Q) & R	1 Assoc
3	P & Q	2 CE
4	(P & Q) → S	P
5	S	3,4 MP

From P & (Q & R) you cannot immediately pull out P & Q. In symbolic logic, parentheses are very important, you have to respect the groupings that parentheses make. You have to use Association to regroup the conjuncts in such a way that will allow you to pull out the pair you want.

Section 6: *Basic Derivation Strategy.*

Understanding derivations when you see them done for you isn't all that difficult. If you understand how arguments work, then you understand how derivations work. But many students have trouble moving from understanding derivations that someone else has done to actually doing a derivation yourself. In the last brief section of this chapter I want to give you a few tips that might make it easier for you to begin doing derivations yourself.

The first tip is that you should always make sure that you know what the premises are. Make sure that you understand the new notation that I am using to state derivation problems. Remember that with the turnstile, the list of claims on the left are the premises, and the claim on the right is the conclusion you are supposed to derive from the premises on the left.

Problem: {P, P → Q} ⊢ Q

The premises are always separated by a comma. Look for the commas. Sometimes premises can be quite complex and long, and you have to make absolutely certain that you get the whole claim and don't break it up into pieces. For example, notice that the following problem has only two premises.

Problem: {(P v Q) → (R & (P ↔ S)), P} ⊢ S

One of the premises is simply P, and the other premise is everything before the comma. Don't break apart pieces of premises – look for the commas. (By the way, that problem can be done. Try it!)

So the first tip is that you should always make sure that you know what the premises are. The second tip is that you should always make sure that you know what the conclusion is. You would be surprised how many beginners lose sight of the conclusion they are trying to derive. After identifying the premises, identify the conclusion and make sure you are clear about what you are going for in your derivation.

The third tip is something that I have told you before: always start with the end and work backwards. The biggest single mistake you can make when you try to do derivations is to stare at your premises and ask yourself, "What do I do now?" What happens when you fall into that trap is that your next move is to look at all the different derivation rules and all of the replacement rules, and then you start to play the "What if?" game: "What if I try use this rule? What happens then? What if I use this other rule? What do I get then?" Once you start down that path, you may never come back. You are just using trial and error and you may never find the right sequence of rules to use to get the result you want.

Don't work hard, work smart. Focus on your conclusion and think about what you are trying to get, and then look at your premises to see where you might be able to get it. I have some more advice for you on how to work backwards, but let me give it to you through an example.

Problem: {P, Q, (P & Q) → R} ⊢ R

Step #1: Identify the Premises. Here we have two commas, and that means we have three premises. If we had only one comma, there would be two premises. If there were zero commas, then there would be only one premise. How many premises would there be if there were three commas? Answer: four. Get it? The number of premises equals the number of commas plus 1.

Step #2: Identify the Conclusion. Here our conclusion is R. Keep the R in mind; that is what you are going for. Don't lose sight of the point of what you are doing.

Step #3: Work backwards to decide how to get the conclusion out of the premises. Again this is the single most important tip I can give you in working derivations. *Work backwards*. DO NOT begin by thinking about what rules you can use on the premises: if you do that you will get lost very quickly. Now I have a few more tips for you on how to work backwards.

Step 3A: Find the premises (if any) that have the conclusion in them. If there is a premise that has your conclusion in it, then what you need to do is find some way of getting the conclusion out of that premise. In the example I just gave, here is a list of the premises, together with the conclusion we are going for.

Premise #1: P
Premise #2: Q
Premise #3: (P & Q) → R
Conclusion: R

We are going for R, and so we look back at the premises to see if any premise contains R. Sure enough, Premise #3 contains an R. That is the premise we will focus on in order to get our conclusion.

Step 3B: Try the easiest rules first. The two easiest rules are conjunction elimination and disjunction introduction. If you can get your conclusion by just taking it out of a conjunction, or by slapping on a disjunct, then you are done very quickly. For example, if your premise is P, and your conclusion is supposed to be P v Q, you know that you can take your P, slap a disjunct onto it, any disjunct at all, and that is justified by disjunction introduction. Since what you want is P v Q, just slap a Q on there and you're done. Alternatively, if what you want is Q, and one of your premises is P & Q, all you have to do is take the Q out of the P & Q, and you're done. Conjunction elimination lets you take either conjunct out of a conjunction. But in the sample problem I've been using, we can't do either of these. So we have to go to Step 3C.

Step 3C: Work from the Premise that Contains the Conclusion. We are going for R, and the only premise that contains R is this one: (P & Q) → R. Ask yourself, "How am I going to get the R out of there?" To answer the question, ask yourself, "What is the main logical operator?" In this case, the main logical operator is the arrow. This claim is a conditional, and R is the consequent. How do you get a consequent out of a conditional? A conditional is not like a conjunction. With a conjunction, you can simply take either conjunct out. Think of a conditional as a kind of lock that opens only with a key. In order to unlock the conditional and take out the consequent, you have to use the key of the antecedent. If you use modus ponens, you can affirm the antecedent to unlock the conditional, take out the consequent, and affirm the R, the thing we are trying to get. So in order to get the conclusion we are going for, we have to use this conditional claim, and affirm its antecedent. Here is the argument we are thinking of right now:

1	P & Q	???
2	(P & Q) → R	P
3	R	1,2 MP

That will be justified by modus ponens. Now we know where we are going, and how we are going to get there. We just have one last question: can we affirm the antecedent? We need to affirm P & Q, do any of our rules justify doing that? Here again is our list of premises:

Premise #1: P
Premise #2: Q
Premise #3: (P & Q) → R
Conclusion: R

We need to affirm the antecedent of Premise #3, to do that we need to affirm P & Q, but we don't have a P & Q among the premises. Can we construct it? Yes. Just take premises 1 and 2 and slap a conjunction between them and we are home free. So here is the completed derivation.

1	P	P
2	Q	P
3	P & Q	1,2 CI
4	(P & Q) → R	P
5	R	3,4 MP

Problem solved!

Finally, many people find it helpful to do derivations by using what is called a "scope line." Scope lines are not so necessary with relatively short derivations, but when they get more complex, the scope lines help a lot. You should try some derivations using scope lines. Here is an example.

1	J → I	P
2	I → T	P
3	T → M	P
4	J → T	1,2 CA
5	J → M	3,4 CA

A horizontal line separates the premises from what is derived from the premises. This is another reason why you no longer need to use the three dots (∴): everything below the horizontal line is automatically marked off as a sub-conclusion or a main conclusion. The vertical line goes all the way down in order to hold everything together: as far down as the line goes, the derivation is governed by the premises at the top. We say that everything is "within the scope" of the premises at the top, and that's why it's called a "scope" line. Metaphorically, the premises can "see" everything in the derivation because they can be used as premises everywhere in the derivation. Things will get more complicated in the next chapter and the scope lines will help you to keep things clear, so practice them now.

Chapter Conclusion.

In this chapter you learned the basics of a system of derivation or proof. This is the skeleton of a system of symbolic logic. Logical thinking is systematic, rule-governed thinking. Everything else we do from now on will be built upon this skeleton of derivations. The goal is to give you enough tools so that you will be able to analyze the logic of almost any argument you may come across.

Things to memorize from this Chapter:

Memorize all the abbreviations of the derivation rules. Here they are in alphabetical order.

Assoc: Association
BCoE: Bi-conditional Elimination
CA: Chain Argument
CE: Conjunction Elimination
CI: Conjunction Introduction
Com: Commutation
CP: Contraposition
DE: Disjunction Elimination
DeM: DeMorgan's Laws
DI: Disjunction Introduction
DN: Double Negation
Impl: Implication
MP: Modus Ponens
MT: Modus Tollens
R: Reiteration

Memorize all the abbreviations of the fallacies. Here they are in alphabetical order.

FAC: Fallacy of Affirming the Consequent
FAD: Fallacy of Affirming a Disjunct
FDA: Fallacy of Denying the Antecedent
FRC: Fallacy of Reversing a Chain

Memorize the Laws of Logical Equivalence:
Double Negation (DN): $P \equiv \sim\sim P$
Implication (Impl): $P \rightarrow Q \equiv \sim P \vee Q$
Contraposition (CP): $P \rightarrow Q \equiv \sim Q \rightarrow \sim P$
Association (Assoc): $P \& (Q \& R) \equiv (P \& Q) \& R$
$P \vee (Q \vee R) \equiv (P \vee Q) \vee R$
$P \leftrightarrow (Q \leftrightarrow R) \equiv (P \leftrightarrow Q) \leftrightarrow R$
DeMorgan's Laws (DeM): $\sim(P \& Q) \equiv \sim P \vee \sim Q$
$\sim(P \vee Q) \equiv \sim P \& \sim Q$
Commutation (Com): $P \& Q \equiv Q \& P$
$P \vee Q \equiv Q \vee P$
$P \leftrightarrow Q \equiv Q \leftrightarrow P$

Exercises for Chapter 6

Exercise 6.1: Derivation Completions. *Complete the following derivations by filling in what is missing.*

Example 1
Problem:

1	$M \rightarrow N$	P
2	M	???
3	N	1,2 MP

Solution:

1	$M \rightarrow N$	P
2	M	P
3	N	1,2 MP

CHAPTER 6: SIMPLE DERIVATIONS

Example 2
Problem:

1	R v S	P
2	~S	P
3	R	???

Solution:

1	R v S	P
2	~S	P
∴ 3	R	1,2 DE

Notice that you may use the three dots (∴) if you wish

Problem 1

1	P	P
2	P → Q	P
3	Q	???

Problem 2

1	~Q	P
2	P → Q	P
3	~P	???

Problem 3

1	P → Q	P
2	???	???
3	P → R	1,2 CA

Problem 4

1	P v Q	P
2	~Q	P
3	P	???

Problem 5

1	P v Q	P
2	P	P
3	~Q	???

Problem 6

1	~P	P
2	~Q	P
3	~P & ~Q	???
4	~(P v Q)	???

Problem 7

1	~P	P
2	~P v ~Q	???
3	???	2 DeM

Problem 8

1	P & (Q & R)	P
2	???	???
3	(Q & R) → T	P
4	T	???

Problem 9

1	~P → Q	P
2	~Q	P
3	~~P	???
4	P	???

Problem 10

1	(B v R) v ~S	P
2	???	1 Assoc
3	~B	P
4	R v ~S	???

Problem 11

1	(M v ~T) v ~R	P
2	M v (~T v ~R)	???
3	~M	P
4	~T v ~R	???
5	~(T & R)	???

Problem 12

1	P → Q	P
2	~P v Q	???
3	~Q	P
4	~P	???
5	~P v ~R	???
6	~(P & R)	???

Exercise 6.2: Extremely Simple Derivations. *Perform the following derivations. All of these derivations are valid, and each uses only of the following rules: CE, CI, DE, DI, MT, MP. All of these derivations can be done in only two or three steps.*

Example 1
Problem: {A, B} ⊢ A & B
Solution:

1	A	P
2	B	P
3	A & B	1,2 CI

Example 2
Problem: {M → N, M} ⊢ N
Solution:

1	M → N	P
2	M	P
3	N	1,2 MP

1. {P & Q} ⊢ P
2. {P & Q} ⊢ Q
3. {P, Q} ⊢ P & Q
4. {P, Q} ⊢ Q & P
5. {N & Z} ⊢ Z

6. {P} ⊢ P v Q
7. {P} ⊢ P v Z
8. {P v Q, ~Q} ⊢ P
9. {~P, P v Q} ⊢ Q
10. {M v ~Z, Z} ⊢ M

11. {P → Q, P} ⊢ Q
12. {P, P → Q} ⊢ Q

13. {M → ~Z, M} ⊢ ~Z
14. {~M, ~M → Z} ⊢ Z
15. {~P, ~P → ~Q} ⊢ ~Q
16. {P → Q, ~Q} ⊢ ~P
17. {~P, Q → P} ⊢ ~Q
18. {~Z, M → Z} ⊢ ~M
19. {Z → M, ~M} ⊢ ~Z
20. {P & Q, (P & Q) → R} ⊢ R

Exercise 6.3: Longer Simple Derivations. *Perform the following derivations. All of the following derivations are valid, and each uses only the following rules: CE, CI, DE, DI, MT, MP, CA. Some of these derivations require more than two or three steps.*

Example 1
Problem: {A, B} ⊢ (A & B) & A
Solution:

1	A	P
2	B	P
3	A & B	1,2 CI
4	(A & B) & A	1,3 CI

Example 2
Problem: {M → (N & B), M} ⊢ B
Solution:

1	M → (N & B)	P
2	M	P
3	N & B	1,2 MP
4	B	3 CE

1. {P, Q, R} ⊢ (P & Q) & R
2. {P, Q, R} ⊢ P & (Q & R)
3. {P, Q, R} ⊢ (R & P) & Q
4. {P & (Q & R)} ⊢ R
5. {P & Q, R & S} ⊢ Q & S
6. {P → Q, Q → R, R → S} ⊢ P → S
7. {P → Q, Q → R, P} ⊢ R
8. {P → Q, Q → R, ~R} ⊢ ~P
9. {P} ⊢ P v (Q v (R v (S & M)))
10. {P → (Q & R), P} ⊢ R
11. {P v Q, P → R, ~Q} ⊢ R
12. {P, (P v Q) → ~N} ⊢ ~N
13. {P, (P & Q) → ~N, Q, R v N} ⊢ R
14. {P & (Q & ~R), S → R, M → S} ⊢ ~M
15. {P → Q, R → S, M → T, Q → M} ⊢ P → M
16. {P v (Q & R), R → S, ~P} ⊢ S
17. {P → Q, R → S, Q → T, S → M, T → R} ⊢ P → M
18. {~P v Q, S, T, R v P, (S & T) → ~Q} ⊢ R
19. {P → Q, ~Q v (R & S), T, T → ~(R & S)} ⊢ ~P
20. {P → Q, R v N, ~P → ~R, ~Q} ⊢ N

Exercise 6.4: Derivations With Replacement Rules. *Perform the following derivations. All of the following derivations are valid. Use a replacement rule in each derivation.*

Example 1
Problem: {~Q → ~P} ⊢ ~P v Q
Solution:

```
1 | ~Q → ~P    P
2 | P → Q      1 CP
3 | ~P v Q     2 Impl
```

Example 2
Problem: {~(P v Q)} ⊢ ~Q
Solution:

```
1 | ~(P v Q)   P
2 | ~P & ~Q    1 DeM
3 | ~Q         2 CE
```

1. {~(P v Q), ~Q → R} ⊢ R
2. {~(P v Q), P v R, R → S} ⊢ S
3. {~P, ~Q, (P v Q) v R} ⊢ R
4. {~P, S → (P v Q), ~S → R, ~Q} ⊢ R
5. {~S, R → (P v Q), ~P, Q → S} ⊢ ~R

6. {(~P v Q) → S, P → Q} ⊢ S
7. {(P → Q) → R, Q} ⊢ R
8. {P → Q, ~P → R} ⊢ ~Q → R
9. {P → Q, ~P → R} ⊢ ~R → ~~Q
10. {P → Q, ~P → R} ⊢ ~R → Q

11. {~~Q → R, P → Q, P} ⊢ R
12. {(P & Q) → S, P & (Q & R)} ⊢ S
13. {P & (Q & R), R → S} ⊢ S
14. {P, ~(P v Q)} ⊢ R
15. {P → ~Q, ~(P & Q) → R} ⊢ R

16. {(P v Q) v R, ~P} ⊢ Q v R
17. {(P v ~Q) v R, ~P} ⊢ Q → R
18. {P → Q, ~Q} ⊢ ~(P & R)
19. {(P v Q) → R, ~(S v R)} ⊢ ~Q
20. {~~Q → R, ~(P v ~Q)} ⊢ R

Exercise 6.5: Assorted Derivations. *Perform the following derivations.*

1. {~P} ⊢ ~Q → ~P
2. {~P} ⊢ ~~~(P & Q)
3. {P → (Q & ~R), S → R, (M & P) & N} ⊢ ~S
4. {Q → (R & S), ~P v Q, ~(~P v B)} ⊢ ~~S
5. {Q → (R v S), ~~Q} ⊢ S v R

6. {~P, R → (P & Q)} ⊢ ~R
7. {R → (P & S), ~S, R v ~(M v N)} ⊢ ~N v ~T
8. {P → (Q & R), ~P → ~S, S} ⊢ R & Q
9. {~(B v D)} ⊢ D → R
10. {P → (Q → R), ~(M v ~P), Q v M} ⊢ R & ~M

11. {((P & Q) & R) & S, (~P v ~Q) v B} ⊢ B
12. {(P v Q) → (S & (R → T)), P, R} ⊢ T
13. {P → (S → (N & B)), ~(~P v ~S)} ⊢ B
14. {R → (P → Q), S → R, M & (P & S)} ⊢ Q

15. {(~F v ~E) → ~T, E → (T & ~F), E} ⊢ ~T
16. {P v (Q v (R v (S v T))), ~(P v Q)} ⊢ R v (S v T)
17. {~(~Q → ~P) → (M v N), ~M, R & ~N} ⊢ P → Q
18. {P & (Q & (R & S)), (P & Q) → T} ⊢ T
19. {B → (C & R), ~M & ~R} ⊢ ~B v C
20. {~P} ⊢ ~(P & (M ↔ (B v C)))

21. {(R v S) → (T & D), B & (Q & (P & T)), (P & Q) → (R v S)} ⊢ D
22. {((P v Q) v (~R v L)) → (~S & ~N), ~(S v N) → (B & C), ~B} ⊢ R
23. {(Q & M) → (E v K), M & (E v C), Q & ~N} ⊢ E v K
24. {~(P → Q) & ~R v (M & (N → C)), (M v S) → ((P → Q) & R), T → S} ⊢ D v ~T
25. {~P v Q, Q → ~(M & N), (S & P) & (T & N)} ⊢ ~M

26. {~P} ⊢ P → ~((Q & R) v (S → ~R)) ↔ (T → (C v B))
27. {(B & Q) → (R & (S → T)), ~(P v ~B), P v Q, ~S → ~R} ⊢ T
28. {M & (N & (R v (S → T))), R → ~N, (M & ~R) → S} ⊢ T
29. {~D, ~((B v R) v (M → N)), (~S v T) v D, ~T} ⊢ ~(R v S)
30. {(Q → (R v T)) → ((B v S) ↔ (N → C)) v (B & A)} ⊢ ~((B v S) ↔ (N → C)) v (B & A) → ~(Q → (R v T))

Exercise 6.6: More Derivations.
1. {~M v N} ⊢ ~N → ~M
2. {~B → C, ~(B v R), ~(S v ~C)} ⊢ C
3. {~R, ~S v (R & T)} ⊢ ~S
4. {~(A v A), A v P} ⊢ P
5. {(D → C) & (C → D), E → ~(D → C)} ⊢ ~E

6. {F & (G v H), ~F v ~H} ⊢ F & G
7. {(~J v K) → N, ~(M v N)} ⊢ J
8. {(~N v (M & O)} ⊢ ~(M & O) → ~N
9. {P & P, Q → ~P} ⊢ ~Q
10. {~R, (R → S) → T} ⊢ T

11. {~(~U → (X → W)), Z → (~U → (X → W))} ⊢ ~Z
12. {~D} ⊢ C → ~D
13. {F & (G & H), (~H → S) → ((F & G) → M)} ⊢ M
14. {~(J v K) & ~(J & L), M → J} ⊢ ~M
15. {O → N, (~N → ~O) → P} ⊢ P

16. {~~~(R v S), T → ~(R → ~S)} ⊢ ~T
17. {(~A → ~B) → ~D, ~((~A & B) v (~A & C))} ⊢ ~D
18. {~(D v ~E) & ~(F v ~G), (E & ~F) → (G → D)} ⊢ ~D
19. {H & H, H → ~J} ⊢ ~J
20. {Q → P, ~(P v R)} ⊢ ~(P v Q)

21. {~((Z v Y) v (Z v ~W)), Z → ~~U, ~Y → (W → U)} ⊢ U
22. {~(~U v ~P), S → ~B, ~(U & ~S), T v B} ⊢ T
23. {~((Q & R) v (~Q & ~R)), N → (Q & R), E v N} ⊢ E
24. {~H v (G v F), ~F, S → ~(H → G)} ⊢ ~S
25. {~(J & L), (J → ~L) → (~M & ~X), E v (M v X)} ⊢ E

26. {~((L v M) & (L & ~S)), A ↔ ~L, ~(L → S)} ⊢ A
27. {~(~B v (C v ~D)), (D & B) → P} ⊢ P
28. {~((G v S) v (~G v ~T)), ~R → ~G, (R & ~S) → Q} ⊢ R & Q
29. {~X → ~Y, ~P v ~M, B → P, (X v ~Y) → M} ⊢ ~B
30. {(B & C) → D, ~Q → T, B, M → (R → (S v ~Q)), ~(~B v ~C), Q → ~(~C v D)} ⊢ T

31. {L → (P → ~F), (M & (L & J)) → (H & G), ~(R v (S & P)), (H & G) → L} ⊢ (M & (L & J)) → (P → ~F)
32. {~(A v B), ~X v (M & O), (P ↔ R) v (S → (N v B)), (X → (M & O)) → ~M} ⊢ ~M

33. {~(Z & W) → Q, ~Z, (W & ~Q) v ~R, (S & (P & Q)) → R, (B ↔ (R v A)) & (F & (Z & S))} ⊢ ~P v ~Q
34. {A ↔ B, ~~~(A & B), ((P → Q) → (R & S)) & (G & (P & A)), (R ↔ (Q & S)) → B} ⊢ ~(R ↔ (Q & S))
35. {(A v B) & (A v G), M → ~A, ~Q → (~B v ~G), (M & ~Q) → ~(~M v ~A)} ⊢ ~Q → ~M
36. {~(Y v (~N v A)), ~Y v N, (A → Y) → ~~M, ~Y → ~M, (P v Q) → ~N} ⊢ ~Q v (R ↔ (S → T))
37. {~D → J, (M & N) → ~R, ~G → ~F, D → R, ~H → ~F, ~(M & N) → Z, H → Z, J → ~P} ⊢ P → Z
38. {(D & E) v ~(D v E), (H v ~J) → (D v E), ~(D & E), J → ~(R & (S v T)), M → (S ↔ T)} ⊢ ~(S v T) v ~R
39. {~(Z & W) → B, ~K → E, (~E v Z) & (~U & W), ~K → (~Z v ~W), K → U} ⊢ (S & R) → B
40. {M, ~P → R, Q v T, (M & N) → (B v C), N, (R ↔ Z) → (~B & ~C), (R ↔ Z) v ~R, N → ~T} ⊢ P & Q

CHAPTER 7: DERIVATIONS (CONTINUED)

Now that you understand the basic idea of a derivation, it is time to introduce the main complication: sub-derivations. Once you understand sub-derivations, you will know a system of symbolic logic. There are still a few more things to add into this system, but the derivation is the structure of symbolic logic.

Section 1: Introduction to Sub-Derivations.

If you think about the basic rules of derivations, you will see that there is something crucial missing. You know conjunction elimination and conjunction introduction, you know disjunction elimination and disjunction introduction, you know conditional elimination (modus ponens and modus tollens) *but you don't know conditional introduction.*

Introducing a conjunction is simple, because you are just sticking together two things you already know. If you know P *and* you also know Q, then you know P *and* Q. Disjunction introduction is even simpler: if you know that P, then you automatically know that P *or* Q. But what about conditional introduction? If you know that P, do you know that if P, then Q? That doesn't seem logical. If you know that Q, do you know that if P then Q? That also doesn't seem logical. How, then, do you introduce a conditional?

Start with an argument that makes sense. Suppose that Alice and Bert are working on a project together, and their boss says, "If our client likes the results, then Alice and Bert will both get bonuses."

A = Alice gets a bonus
B = Bert gets a bonus
C = The client like the results
C → (A & B)

Alice thinks about this, and creates the following argument:

1	C → (A & B)	P
2	C → A	???

"If the client likes the results then both Alice and Bert will get bonuses" entails that "if the client likes the results, then Alice gets a bonus." That makes perfect sense, and you can tell that it is a valid argument. But how do you prove or derive it? Using only the inference rules I've shown you so far, it is not clear how you would do it.

To understand how to do this derivation, think about how the argument actually works, think about why it really is a valid inference. Alice doesn't know whether or not she will actually get the bonus, because the project isn't finished yet, and so she doesn't know if the client will actually like the results. So at this point she is thinking purely hypothetically. She is imagining one possibility. Assuming that her boss isn't lying just to motivate her and Bert to do a good job on the project, assuming that the boss's claim is actually true, then she imagines what will happen if the client does like the result. In the situation where her boss's claim is really true, then hypothetically, if the client did like the results, then Alice gets a bonus.

Notice the funny complication here is that Alice is making two assumptions. First, she is assuming that her boss was telling the truth. Second, given her first assumption, taking that for granted, she imagines what would happen if the client likes the results. This is an assumption within an assumption, it is an hypothesis within a hypothesis: Assuming we are in a situation where the boss is actually telling the truth, what happens if we add another hypothesis? When you nest one hypothesis within another, you are doing a sub-derivation.

This is very much like an example from the previous chapter. If Paul spilled the gas, then if Quincy lit the match, then the fire burned the warehouse. Under ordinary circumstances, lighting a match is no big deal. However, if the background conditions include lots of spilled gasoline all over the place, then lighting a match can have explosive results. If certain background conditions are given (e.g. spilled gasoline), then a new hypothetical situation (lighting a match) can have spectacular results.

In order to put this into derivation form, we need some way to display visually in a derivation the idea of nesting one assumption within another. We need some way to put our basic guiding assumptions in one place, mark them as our basic guiding assumptions, and then governed by those basic guiding assumptions, we make some additional subordinate assumptions or hypotheses. If you type your derivations on a computer, then you probably use the Tab key when you begin to type a line; so for our sub-derivations, why not just hit the Tab key again? The regular, primary derivation will occur only one Tab stop in, but the sub-derivation will occur two Tab stops in. So we'll start our derivation like this.

```
1 | C → (A & B)    P
2 |    | C         Hypothesis
3 |    |
4 |    |
5 |    |
```

Remember that in the justification column on the right, "P" stands for "Premise." On the first line we have our basic guiding assumption: our premise. That is our "given." That is what we start with. But once we've been given that premise, we can then go on to imagine different things. Given that basic premise, what would happen if C were actually true? Notice that at this point you can imagine anything you want? If you wanted to, you could ask, "Given that premise, what would happen if the client does *not* like the results?" In fact, your extra hypothesis doesn't have to be directly related to the situation at all. You could ask, "Given what the boss said, what would happen if pigs fly?" That's a silly question to ask, but if you want to, you can ask it. Logic doesn't judge the content of your hypotheses.

But in this case, Alice is thinking of something that is directly relevant and makes sense. Assuming what her boss told her is true, accepting the "given," what happens if the client actually does like the results? Look at lines 1 and 2, and you can see that one of the rules you already know applies: modus ponens.

```
1 | C → (A & B)    P
2 |    | C         Hypothesis
3 |    | A & B     1,2 MP
4 |    |
5 |    |
```

Now it is easy to take the next step. Alice is primarily interested in what happens to her if the client likes the results of her work with Bert.

```
1 | C → (A & B)    P
2 |    | C         Hypothesis
3 |    | A & B     1,2 MP
4 |    | A         3 CE
5 |    |
```

At this point, many people are tempted to make a tragic mistake: they are tempted simply to pull back to the main derivation line and write in the conclusion of the sub-derivation. This is a big mistake. Although there is only one Tab stop difference between the main derivation line and the sub-derivation line, the difference between the two is very important, and you must keep the two separate. Blurring the distinction between the two is like being unable to tell the difference between reality and fantasy. The main derivation line is reality; it starts with your premise, your "given." This is your rock solid foundation in reality, something you can't question. When you start a sub-derivation with an hypothesis, you are entering a fantasy world of imagination (of course it is a fantasy world which is governed by the laws of logic, but beyond that, you are free to imagine any possibility you wish). What is true in your fantasy world doesn't necessarily carry over into reality. Keep this in mind; do not blur the distinction between fantasy and reality; do not blur the distinction between what you have in your sub-derivation, and what you can put in your main derivation.

Now look back at the derivation as we have it so far. It says that given our basic premise, if we make a certain hypothesis, we get a certain result. In other words, we get an answer to our hypothetical question: If the boss was telling the truth, then what happens if the client actually does like the results? Answer: Alice gets a bonus. Of course you could also derive that Bert gets a bonus, but for right now Alice is only thinking about the consequences for herself. She can derive the conclusion that she gets a bonus from the hypothesis, given the premise.

But you can't stop your derivation here. You always have to bring your derivations back to earth, back to your given. You are perfectly free to imagine any hypothesis you want, you may introduce any sub-derivations you want, but you always have to bring it back to the main derivation, and show the point or result of all your assumptions. What does that leave you with if you make that extra assumption? Now look at the sub-derivation from 2-4. Think about what it says. It says that from C you can derive A (given the basic premise). In other words, 2-4 says that if you hypothesize C, then A follows. In other words, If C, then A: C → A. That is just what we were trying to derive. Here is how you put that into the derivation.

1	C → (A & B)	P
2	│ C	Hypothesis
3	│ A & B	1,2 MP
4	│ A	3 CE
5	C → A	2-4 CoI

This is Conditional Introduction (abbreviated CoI): If the hypothesis of your sub-derivation is P, and in that sub-derivation you can derive Q, then in the main derivation you may conclude P → Q.

Let me take you through another example of Conditional Introduction so that you start to get the hang of sub-derivations. Remember that the basic idea is not very complicated: given the assumptions, you make some hypothesis to see what follows from that hypothesis. That gives you the justification for introducing a conditional claim into the main derivation. Consider this problem.

Problem: {P v Q} ⊢ ~P → Q

You could use Implication to work this derivation, but instead, let's use a sub-derivation. Remember the steps you learned in the previous chapter. *Step 1* is to be sure you have correctly identified the premises. Here we have only one premise, and it is a simple disjunction: P v Q. *Step 2* is to make sure you have correctly identified the conclusion. Here our conclusion is a conditional claim: ~P → Q. *Step 3* is to work backwards to decide how to derive the conclusion from the premise. Remember that when you do this, begin by finding which premise contains the conclusion, if any. Here no premise contains the conclusion. This tells you that you are going to have to build the conclusion out of the premise somehow. This isn't going to be a simple derivation. Next, always look for a simple solution. For example, if you can just take a conjunct out of a conjunction, or add a disjunct to a claim and get your conclusion, then you are home free. Unfortunately, our conclusion is a conditional claim, so we can't construct it in such an easy way. In fact, right when you notice that the conclusion is a conditional claim, you might immediately think of using conditional introduction. That is not always true, but it is something to think of. If you can't get your conclusion in an easier way, then you can always try conditional introduction to get a conditional conclusion. The final suggestion I gave you in the last chapter is to work from the premise that contains the conclusion, but you don't have that in this case. This means that the only possible remaining alternative is to try conditional introduction.

Conditional Introduction is actually a pretty easy rule to use, because once you think you have to use it, you already know a lot of what your derivation is going to look like. You have to have a main derivation with the premises of the argument, and then you are going to have to set up a sub-derivation which begins with the antecedent of the conditional claim you want to build. Here's what we have in this case:

1	P v Q	P
2	│ ~P	Hypothesis
3	│	
4	│	

Line 1 gives us our premise, and line 2 begins our sub-derivation. We know it has to begin with ~P because the conclusion we are trying to reach is ~P → Q. We need to prove that given our premises, we can derive Q from ~P. That is our next job. Think about it. Is there any way for you to derive Q from the premise and ~P? Answer: yes there is. Our premise is a disjunction; it says that either P is true, or Q is true. But now we are asking, "Hypothetically, what would happen if P were false?" Answer: given that we are assuming P v Q, then if P is false, the only remaining alternative has to be Q. Now our derivation looks like this.

1	P v Q	P
2	│ ~P	Hypothesis
3	│ Q	1,2 DE
4	│	

We have a simple disjunction elimination here. Premise 1 gives us only two alternatives, the hypothesis imagines what happens if the first alternative is false, and the answer to the hypothetical question is that in that situation, the other alternative would have to be true. Now to complete our derivation, we have to go back to the main derivation line and sum up what we just proved. What we proved is that if you start with ~P, then you can reach Q. In other words, what you just proved is that if ~P, then Q: ~P → Q.

```
1 | P v Q      P
2 |    | ~P       Hypothesis
3 |    | Q        1,2 DE
4 | ~P → Q    3-4, 5-6 BCoI
```

Lines 2 through 3 prove that from the hypothesis in 2 you can derive the conclusion in 3. Just stick an arrow in between the hypothesis and the conclusion, put the result in the main derivation and you are done!

Section 2: New Rules.

Now that you have a basic understanding of sub-derivations, there are a couple of more important rules you can use. Think again about what is missing in the list of rules you know. You know introduction and elimination rules for conjunctions, disjunctions, and conditionals. What is missing? Answer: bi-conditionals and negations. You need introduction and elimination rules for bi-conditionals and negations. Since you already understand conditional introduction, I'll begin with bi-conditional introduction.

Remember that a bi-conditional is a two-way conditional. P ↔ Q means that if P, then Q, and if Q, then P. Let me give you the simplest possible bi-conditional introduction derivation.

Problem: $\{P \rightarrow Q, Q \rightarrow P\} \vdash P \leftrightarrow Q$

You know that this has to be a valid argument because the conclusion is just another way of saying what the premises say. The conclusion says in one claim what the premises say in two claims.

Think about how to solve this before we solve it. Step 1 is to make sure you know what the premises are. Step 2 is to make sure that you know what the conclusion is. Step 3 is to work backwards from the conclusion to the premises to see how to get the conclusion out of the premises. Look for the easiest solution. Can you simply take out a conjunct or add a disjunct to get the conclusion? No. You notice that the conclusion has a bi-conditional and so you immediately are thinking that perhaps you'll have to use bi-conditional introduction. It won't always be true that when the conclusion has a bi-conditional in it, you have to use bi-conditional introduction, but it is something to have in mind in case you can't find an easier way to construct the conclusion. And in fact there doesn't seem to be any other way to get the conclusion from those premises. So let's try a bi-conditional introduction.

A bi-conditional introduction works almost exactly like a conditional introduction, it is just that a bi-conditional introduction has to go both ways, instead of just one way. A conditional introduction has to show only that from P you can get to Q. A bi-conditional has to show that from P you can get to Q, and also that from Q you can get to P. This means that to do a bi-conditional introduction, *you must have two sub-derivations*. The first sub-derivation starts with the first condition and concludes with the second condition; the second sub-derivation starts with the second condition and concludes with the first condition. Here's how:

```
1 | P → Q    P
2 | Q → P    P
3 |    | P       Hypothesis
4 |    | Q       1,3 MP

5 |    | Q       Hypothesis
6 |    | P       2,5 MP

7 | P ↔ Q    3-4, 5-6 BCoI
```

There are several important things going on here that you need to notice. First of all, notice how the rule Bi-Conditional Introduction is labeled. Its abbreviation is BCoI. It is just the abbreviation of Conditional Introduction with a "B" stuck on the beginning. Next, when you cite the line numbers, you need to cite the line numbers of both sub-derivations. Cite the line numbers of the sub-derivation where you proved the conditional connection going one way, and then put a comma, then put the line numbers of the sub-derivation where you proved the conditional connection going the other way.

Remember I asked you at the end of the previous chapter to practice using scope lines in your derivations. With short and simple derivations you really don't need them, but now that we have sub-derivations, they are really going to come in handy. Here is how that last derivation would look with scope lines.

```
1 | P → Q        P
2 | Q → P        P
3 |    | P       Hypothesis
4 |    | Q       1,3 MP

5 |    | Q       Hypothesis
6 |    | P       2,5 MP

7 | P ↔ Q        3-4,5-6 BCoI
```

Notice that the vertical line to the left of the premises goes all the way down. Remember that the premises may be used everywhere in the derivation, and so we say that the entire derivation is "governed" by the premises, and so metaphorically the premises can "see" absolutely everything in the derivation. So the scope line of the premises goes all the way down. But look at the scope lines of the sub-derivations. Obviously the horizontal scope lines separate the hypotheses from the inferences: all the inferences go below the scope lines of the premises and hypotheses that are used in deriving them. Notice that the vertical scope lines of the sub-derivations are very short. This is because the hypothesis on line 3 is used to derive Q on line 4 – and that's it, nothing else. P on line 3 is used for one and only one inference: Q on line 4. Since it is used for that and only for that, we stop the scope line and end the sub-derivation. Keep this in mind: once a sub-derivation is stopped, everything inside it is permanently off limits for the rest of the derivation. That's because everything inside the sub-derivation makes sense only because of the hypothesis; once you've stopped using that hypothesis, the things that follow from it don't necessarily follow from anything else. The only things you may do with a sub-derivation once it is finished are all defined precisely by the sub-derivation rules, so remember this: once a sub-derivation is finished, it is closed permanently and may never be used again by anything other than the rules governing sub-derivations.

For practice with scope lines, here is another derivation that uses bi-conditional introduction. This one is a little more complex than the first.

Problem: $\{J \to I, I \to T, T \to J,\} \vdash I \leftrightarrow J$
Solution:
```
1 | J → I        P
2 | I → T        P
3 | T → J        P

4 |    | I       Hypothesis
5 |    | T       2,4 MP
6 |    | J       3,5 MP

7 |    | J       Hypothesis
8 |    | I       1,7 MP

9 | I ↔ J        4-6,7-8 BCoI
```

Many people find that the lines make things much easier to keep track of. Now that you will be doing more and more complex (and longer) derivations, you might find it handy to use this new method of representing derivations.

Bi-conditional elimination is much easier than bi-conditional introduction. Here is a simple example.

Problem: $\{P \leftrightarrow Q, Q\} \vdash P$
Solution:
```
1 | P ↔ Q        P
2 | Q            P
3 | P            1,2 BCoE
```

Notice that this rule does not require a sub-derivation. Since a bi-conditional works just like a two-way conditional, it is a lock which opens in either direction. The bi-conditional locks the P and the Q together, but you can unlock the Q by affirming the P, or you can unlock the P by affirming the Q.

Now on to the last two basic rules. You need to learn negation introduction and negation elimination. These two rules are at the heart of the experimental scientific method. Suppose that a scientist has a theory, and wants to test it scientifically. For example, suppose that a scientist thinks she has discovered a pill which, if taken before each meal, will decrease cholesterol. To test it, she gets a group of people and tries it out: check their cholesterol the experiment begins, then give them the pill before each meal and when the test is over, check their cholesterol again to see if it is lower. Here is what the scientist thinks.

Hypothesis: This pill lowers cholesterol.
Prediction: The test subjects have lower cholesterol.

The scientist has a hypothesis, and on the basis of that hypothesis has predicted that she will find certain results. But what happens if she checks their cholesterol, and finds that it is *not* lower than before? In fact, what if some of the test subjects have higher cholesterol than before taking the pill? The actual data contradicts what the scientist predicted, and this shows that the hypothesis is false. (In actual scientific tests, it is a bit more complicated than this, but for our purposes, this is roughly how a scientific test works). If your hypothesis entails something that turns out not to be true, then your hypothesis is false, i.e. it is *not* true. That is negation introduction.

Here is an example of negation introduction in logic.

Problem (in words): If Katy is the one who put the poison in Jo's coffee cup, then she would have to have been in two places at one time. (We know she was in Ohio all day Friday, but the poison got into Jo's cup about noon on Friday.) But obviously Katy couldn't be in two places at one time, that's absurd. So we know that Katy didn't poison Jo.

Problem (in symbols): $\{K \rightarrow (N \,\&\, \sim N)\} \vdash \sim K$
Solution:
K = Katy poisoned Jo
N = Katy was in New Jersey

```
1 | K → (N & ~N)      P
2 |   | K             Hypothesis
3 |   | N & ~
      | N
4 | ~K                2-3 NI
```

A contradiction cannot possibly be true, so anything that entails a contradiction cannot possibly be true. If your hypothesis leads to something obviously false, something logically false, i.e. a contradiction, then you know for sure that the hypothesis must be false. The exact same principle works for negation elimination.

Problem: $\{\sim K \rightarrow (N \,\&\, \sim N)\} \vdash K$
Solution:

```
1 | ~K → (N & ~N)     P
2 |   | ~K            Hypothesis
3 |   | N & ~N        1,2 MP
4 | K                 2-3 NE
```

Whatever your hypothesis is, if it entails a contradiction, then you can pull out of your sub-derivation and state that the hypothesis is false. If your hypothesis had no negation in front of it, put one on; if your hypothesis had a negation on it, then take it off. (A third possibility is to use negation introduction on an expression that already has a negation on it. If ~K leads to a contradiction, then instead of taking the ~ off, you could add one on by negation introduction, and end with ~~K).

Section 3: Short Cuts.

Now you have the basic rules for doing derivations. You know introduction and elimination rules for conjunctions, disjunctions, conditionals, bi-conditionals and negations. With these basic rules you can, at least in theory, prove any valid argument. Every valid argument can be derived using only these rules, in various combinations, sometimes with and sometimes without sub-derivations. Some arguments will be longer than others, and some will be harder to figure out than others, but in theory every single valid argument can be derived using just these basic rules.

There are two main difficulties, however, in finding derivations for valid arguments. First, for every valid argument, there are a hundred other arguments that look similar, but are invalid. Sometimes you will be thinking through an argument and you are not sure whether it is valid or not, so you try to do a derivation but you fail. You can't find a way to derive the conclusion from the premises. Does that mean the argument is invalid? Not necessarily. Some derivations are very hard, the fact that *you* have not been able to derive the conclusion from the premises doesn't mean that *no one* can derive the conclusion from the premises. So how do you know when an argument is invalid, so that you don't waste your time trying to derive it? Answer: learn your fallacies.

Many fallacies are easy to spot. Remember the fallacy of affirming the consequent and the fallacy of denying the antecedent. Those two fallacies are almost exactly like modus ponens and modus tollens; the only problem is that the fallacies are unsuccessful mixtures of both modus ponens and modus tollens. The Fallacy of Affirming the Consequent is a kind of mixture of modus ponens and modus tollens. Like modus tollens, the Fallacy of Affirming the Consequent picks on the consequent of the conditional claim, but like modus ponens, it affirms rather than denies the consequent. That is a fallacy. The Fallacy of Denying the Antecedent is a similar mixture. Like Modus ponens, the Fallacy of Denying the Antecedent picks on the antecedent of the conditional claim, but like modus tollens, it denies rather than affirms it. You can spot conjunctive and disjunctive fallacies in the same way.

	VALID	INVALID
Conjunction	1. P & Q ∴ 2. P	1. P ∴ 2. P & Q
Disjunction	1. P ∴ 2. P v Q	1. P v Q ∴ 2. P

Notice that the invalid versions are mixtures of the valid versions. The better you know the valid rules of inference, the easier it will be for you to spot invalid arguments.

That is the first main difficulty in finding derivations for valid arguments. The second main difficulty is that some derivations can be quite long. In theory the basic rules can verify the validity of any valid argument at all, but in practice, many arguments are just too complicated to do using just the basic rules. That is why there are rules of replacement. You already know these six rules:

DeMorgan's Laws (DeM) Implication (Impl)
Double Negation (DN)   Contrapositive (CP)
Commutation (Com)   Association (Assoc)

There are two more rules I want to give you. Here they are with their names and abbreviations.

Exportation (Exp)
$(P \& Q) \rightarrow R \equiv \equiv P \rightarrow (Q \rightarrow R)$

Distribution (Dist)
$P \& (Q \lor R) \equiv (P \& Q) \lor (P \& R)$
$P \lor (Q \& R) \equiv (P \lor Q) \& (P \lor R)$

If you work out the truth tables for any of these claims, you'll see that they are logically equivalent. I'll do a derivation to prove the replacement rule of Exportation, because that will show you a fairly simple example of a derivation that not only has a sub-derivation, it also has a sub-derivation contained within the sub-derivation (or you might call it a "sub-sub-derivation"). There are a number of interesting things about this derivation, but I'll show you first, and then I'll talk about the interesting features.

1		P → (Q → R)	Hypothesis
2		P & Q	Hypothesis
3		P	2 CE
4		Q → R	1,3 MP
5		Q	2 CE
6		R	4,5 MP
7		(P & Q) → R	2-6 CoI
8		(P & Q) → R	Hypothesis
9		P	Hypothesis
10		Q	Hypothesis
11		P & Q	9,10 CI
12		R	8,11 MP
13		Q → R	10-12 CoI
14		P → (Q → R)	9-13 CoI
15	P → (Q → R) ↔ (P & Q) → R		2-7,8-14 BCoI

Notice that the symbol for logical equivalence (≡) amounts to a bi-conditional claim. If one claim is logically equivalent to another, then if one is true, so is the other, and vice versa.

What we have derived here is the replacement rule called "Exportation." When you have a conditional claim with a conjunction for the antecedent, e.g. (P & Q) → R, you may, if you wish, "export" one of the conjunctive conditions, thus: P → (Q → R). Or you can go the other way around; if you have a conditional claim, the consequent of which is itself a conditional claim, then you can "import" the first antecedent into the second conditional claim, and simply conjoin the two antecedents. Each may be replaced with the other because essentially the two claims are saying the same thing. The conditional version says this: "If you have P, then if you also have Q, then you have R." Remember our dynamic duo Paul and Quincy. If Paul spilled the gas, and Quincy strikes a match, then the whole place goes up in flames. You can say this same thing in another way: If Paul spilled the gas, then if Quincy strikes a match, then the whole place goes up in flames.

Next, notice that in the right-hand column of this derivation, where the justifications go, there isn't a single "P" listed. This is a *derivation with no premises*. That is very important. With no premises at all, we can derive something very significant. Whenever you can derive something using absolutely no premises whatsoever, the thing you have derived is a tautology, something that is necessarily true.

Finally, and most importantly, is the issue of accessibility. According to an ancient Chinese story, a man once dreamed he was a butterfly. When he awoke, he was confused and asked, "Am I a man who dreamed he was a butterfly, or am I a butterfly dreaming that he is a man?" The question is pretty deep, if you think about it, but I'm not going to dwell on the implications. I just want to use this story to explain accessibility in sub-derivations. Instead of having the dream loop back on itself, think of the dream getting deeper. Suppose I am a man who is asleep and dreaming that he is a butterfly flying around. I might wake up at anytime and come back to reality, but for now I am asleep, and dreaming that I am governed by the assumption that I am a butterfly.

Keep in mind that dreams are not entirely random. Sigmund Freud is famous for, among other things, proposing that our dreams draw upon the knowledge, experience, beliefs and emotions that we store up from our everyday life. If I am still angry at my father because he spanked me when I was a child, then that remembered experience might show up in different ways in my dreams. Our dreams are not truly random, but are shaped by our real experiences and emotions.

So notice that right away there is an important difference between my real experiences when awake, and my dream experiences as a butterfly. What happens to me in my real life experience can affect my dreams, I take my real experiences into my dream world, and it can affect what happens in there. However, I can't really take things out of my dream world and use them in my ordinary experience. I can't for example, really fly when I wake up after a dream in which I flew. But of course, I might very well be able to learn some lessons while I am asleep, and apply those lessons to my real experience. Many therapists encourage people to keep dream journals, and then analyze the dreams to learn something about yourself. So the first lesson of accessibility is that everything in reality is accessible in the dream, but not everything in the dream is accessible in reality.

Now let's take it to the next level. Imagine that I am a man who is dreaming that he is a butterfly, and then in the dream, the butterfly goes to sleep and dreams that he is a kangaroo. You know what happens next. The kangaroo is going to fall asleep and dream he is some other animal, who then falls asleep and dreams ..., and so on. This can go on forever, or until you wake up. The point is that the same rule that applies between reality and the first dream applies between the first dream and the second dream, the second dream and the third dream and so on. My real life experiences govern the whole thing, and so my real experiences are accessible at all levels. For example, the butterfly might dream he is a kangaroo who dreams he is a Tasmanian devil who dreams he is a chimpanzee who is spanked by my father. My father or mother can enter in, and in fact any part of my real experience can enter into the dream at any point, because the ultimate governing reality applies all the way in. The Tasmanian devil could dream that he his a chimpanzee who is driving a race car because race cars are a part of my reality, and the chimpanzee is part of my dream.

Going the other direction, the truths of the dreams, don't necessarily apply all the way out. The Tasmanian devil may take some lesson away from the dream of being spanked by my father, and then when the kangaroo wakes up, he may take some lesson away from the Tasmanian devil's dream, and so on, but once a dream is over, it is over. The Tasmanian devil cannot swing through the trees like a chimpanzee, the kangaroo cannot scream like a Tasmanian devil, the butterfly cannot hop like a kangaroo, and I cannot fly like a butterfly.

There is one last rule governing accessibility. If last night I dreamed I was a butterfly, who dreamed he was a kangaroo, who dreamed he was a Tasmanian devil, who dreamed he was a chimpanzee spanked by my father, what will I dream tonight? Answer: who knows? I might have the same dream again, but probably not. I might dream that I am the ocean, or that I am fabulously wealthy, or lots of other things. What I dreamed last night might bear no relation to what I dream tonight, except for the fact that both dreams are governed by my real experiences. So the last rule governing accessibility is that nothing from one series of nested dreams (a dream within a dream) applies directly to a separate series of nested dreams.

Now let's drop the talk of dreams and get back to real derivations. There are two ways to think of accessibility: (a) what you *can* do, and (b) what you *cannot* do. What you *cannot* do is (1) travel in time, and (2) use parts of a sub-derivation once it is completed. What you *can* do is anything else.

You cannot travel in time in the sense that you cannot cite a later step on an earlier step. If I am only on line 5 of a derivation, I cannot cite something from line 10. This would be arguing in a circle. I can get line 10 only because I first have line 5, but if in order to get line 5 I need to rely on 10, then I am just going in a circle. Circular reasoning is illogical, and you may not do it.

The second rule governing what you cannot do is important because of the hypothetical nature of sub-derivations. To use the dream analogy again: a new dream is a new reality. This is true of any level. If one night I dream I am a butterfly and then wake up, that particular dream is over. Whatever I dream the next night is a completely separate dream. I cannot reach inside an old dream and use things that happened in it as if they were reality. They weren't reality, they were just a dream, and the dream is over. If you really want to use them, you can set them up as new hypotheses of new sub-derivations, but you may not appeal to the old ones as if they were as rock solid as your premises. Look at this example.

1	P → (Q & R) P	
2		P	Hypothesis
3		Q & R	1,3 MP
4		R	3 CE
5	P → R		2-4 CoI

Once the sub-derivation in lines 2-4 is finished, and I have learned something from that sub-derivation and written the conclusion on the previous derivation line, the sub-derivation is forever closed. However, since the conclusion of the sub-derivation is written on the main derivation line, I can now use P → R anywhere later in my derivation just as if it were a premise of the derivation.

Now let me explain the rules without the dream analogy. Here is a sample derivation that is fairly complex.

1	Xxx			Premise
2		Xxx		Hypothesis
3			Xxx	Hypothesis
4			Xxx	Rule
5		Xxx		Rule
6	Xxx			Rule
7		Xxx		Hypothesis
8			Xxx	Hypothesis
10				Xxx Hypothesis
11				Xxx Rule
12			Xxx	Rule
13			Xxx	Hypothesis
14				Xxx Rule
15			Xxx	Rule
16	Xxx			Rule

Go through this example, and make sure you know what is accessible at each stage. For example, line 1 is accessible everywhere, because it is the premise of the derivation. Line 6 is accessible everywhere below, since it is on the main derivation line, and so has been shown to follow necessarily from the premise. However, once you get to line 6, lines 2-5 are forever locked and may not be used ever again.

Think about line 12. What is and what is not accessible at line 12? First, lines 13-16 are off limits. Next, lines 2-5 are off limits, because that sub-derivation has been completed and is locked forever. Although lines 10 and 11 are inside the same sub-derivation as line 12, lines 10 and 11 form a sub-derivation all their own, and that sub-derivation is now complete. Line 12 can sum up the conclusion of the sub-derivation, it can state the lesson learned from the sub-derivation, but it may not use any part of the sub-derivation. That leaves lines 6-8, and they are all accessible at line 12. By way of summary, here are the two rules governing accessibility in derivations.

Rule #1: Once a sub-derivation has been concluded, nothing inside it may be cited again.
Rule #2: Nothing below a line may be cited on that line.

Section 4: Examples.

You will be doing many different kinds of derivations. I'll give you two more examples to help you develop your ability to see your way through them. Here is the first problem.

Problem: The detectives have been able to rule out any connection between the mob and Joe's former girlfriend. So if the mob put the poison in Joe's cup, then his former girlfriend had nothing to do with it. On a related matter, we have found that Joe's former girlfriend must have been involved somehow. Either she was actually involved in poisoning Joe, or else she can lead us to the hidden bank accounts where Joe put the money he was stealing from the mob. We still don't know who killed Joe, but we do know that if it was the mob, then Joe's former girlfriend can lead us to the hidden bank accounts.

Partial Solution:
1. If the mob poisoned Joe, then Joe's former girlfriend did not poison Joe.
2. Either Joe's former girlfriend poisoned Joe, or she can lead us to Joe's hidden bank accounts.
3. If the mob poisoned Joe, then Joe's former girlfriend can lead us to Joe's hidden bank accounts.
M = the mob poisoned Joe
G = Joe's former girlfriend poisoned Joe
B = Joe's former girlfriend can lead us to Joe's hidden bank accounts
1. M → ~G
2. G v B
3. M → B

Remember your skills at turning English language arguments into symbolic logic. Look for the logical structure of the various claims (e.g. "if ..., then ..."). Make your index and then symbolize the argument. Once you see the structure of the argument, you know you are supposed to derive that conclusion from those premises.

Problem: {M → ~G, G v B} ⊢ M → B

Don't forget what you already know. Step #1 is to make sure you know what the premises are. Step #2 is to make sure you know what the conclusion is. Step #3 is to work backwards from the conclusion to the premises. Look at the conclusion, and you see that it is a conditional claim. The first thought that might pop into your head is that you might have to use Conditional Introduction to derive the conclusion. That is a good thought to have. Whenever you see that you are supposed to derive a conditional claim, the first thought that should pop into your head is to use Conditional Introduction. That won't always be the best way to go, but it is often the best way to go. You should also pause for a moment to see if there is an easier solution, e.g. using Conjunction Elimination or Disjunction Introduction, but there is no simple way to use those rules right away. You might also consider using a replacement rule, and this problem can be worked that way, but I want to use it as an example of a derivation using a sub-derivation.

So if we are going to use Conditional Introduction, you can set up your derivation even before you know how to complete it.

```
1 | M → ~G     P
2 | G v B      P
3 |    | M     Hypothesis
4 |    |
5 |    |
```

We don't know how long this derivation is going to be, so let's just extend our lines a bit beyond what we know. We know that we must start with the premises, and then we know that in order to use Conditional Introduction, we must set up a sub-derivation whose Hypothesis is the antecedent of the conditional we want to derive. Since we want to derive M → B, we need to set up a sub-derivation whose Hypothesis is M. Then we'll see if we can derive B from that Hypothesis, plus the premises. If you now look at the premises plus the Hypothesis, you should be able to see how to get B. Here is the complete derivation.

```
1 | M → ~G     P
2 | G v B      P
3 |    | M     Hypothesis
4 |    | ~G    1,3 MP
5 |    | B     2,4 DE
6 | M → B      3-5 CoI
```

Given our premises, if we hypothesize that M, it would follow that ~G. We know this by modus ponens using lines 1 and 3. But once we have ~G, we can use our other premise from line 2. That gives us B, which is exactly what we wanted! Look at lines 3-5. Those lines are a sub-derivation. What that sub-derivation says is that given the premises, if you hypothesize that M is true, then hypothetically, it would follow that B would also have to be true. In other words, given the premises, if M is true, then so is B. If M, then B. M → B. Problem solved!

New Problem: It is 1pm, I checked the copy machine at noon when I went to lunch, which means that if Roger were the one who caused the paper jam, then he would have to have been using the machine after noon. But Roger doesn't have a key to use this machine, which means that if he is the one who caused the paper jam, then he could not possibly have been using it after noon. So Roger couldn't possibly be guilty.

This argument is a bit confusing, for two different reasons. First of all, it has extra information that you don't really need in order to figure out the argument. This happens quite often. To think logically, you must develop your ability to focus in on just the central logical features of an argument. To do that, focus on the important logical operators like "if ..., then ...." When you do that, you find that there are only three claims with important logical indicators.

    1. If Roger caused the paper jam, then he was using the machine after noon.
    2. If Roger caused the paper jam, then he was not using the machine after noon.
    So 3. Roger did not cause the paper jam.

The other confusing thing about this argument is that it seems to go in a circle. It isn't really a circle, it is a contradiction. Was he or was he not using the machine after noon? Part seems to say he was, but the other part seems to say he was not. This can be confusing, but now that you can think logically, you should find this helpful. Always be on the lookout for contradictions. Anytime you have a contradiction, you know automatically that you can use negation introduction or negation elimination, and you will be able to derive anything you want. Contradictions are like wild cards, and in derivations, they can let you derive absolutely anything.

Before we proceed, we need to turn this argument into symbolic logic. Here is a good index.

R = Roger caused the paper jam
M = Roger was using the machine after noon
1. R → M
2. R → ~M
3. ~R

Problem: {R → M, R → ~M} ⊢ ~R

Again, make sure you know what the premises are, make sure you know what the conclusion is, and always start by working backwards from the conclusion to the premises. Here we want to derive a negation, ~R. Automatically you should think that you might have to use Negation Introduction, since there is a negation in the conclusion. That's not a bad thought to have, although there are lots of ways to derive a negation (e.g. by modus tollens). But let's think of Negation Introduction. This rule requires a sub-derivation, and so even before we know how to complete the derivation, we know how to set it up.

```
1 | R → M      P
2 | R → ~M     P
3 |    | R     Hypothesis
4 |    |
5 |    |
```

We don't know how long the derivation is going to be, so let's just extend our derivation lines a bit beyond what we know for sure. We start with the premises in lines 1 and 2, then we set up our sub-derivation. Our hypothesis is the opposite of what we want to prove. We are going to ask what would happen, given our premises, if R were true, so that we can prove R cannot possibly be true. We want to derive ~R. Now that we have our sub-derivation set up, look at the hypothesis together with our premises. What do you notice? You see the contradiction staring you right in your face. You see the M and the ~M both follow from R. That is a contradiction, and so you know that R cannot be true, since it entails a contradiction. Here is the complete derivation.

```
1 | R → M      P
2 | R → ~M     P
3 |    | R     Hypothesis
4 |    | M     1,3 MP
5 |    | ~M    2,3 MP
6 | ~R         3-5 NI
```

Given our premises, if we hypothesize R, then M follows by modus ponens (using premise 1), but ~M also follows by modus ponens (using premise 2). From R you can get M and also ~M. R entails a contradiction, which means that it cannot possibly be true. So you conclude your sub-derivation once you have the two contradictory claims together, pull back to the main derivation line, and draw your conclusion.

Section 5: Theorems.

There is one final kind of derivation to see, now that you understand sub-derivations. So far, all of the derivations you have seen begin with premises. What would a derivation without any premises look like?

{} ⊢ (~A v B) → (A → B)

At first this looks like a derivation out of thin air, but it isn't. Just because there are no premises it doesn't follow that there are no *rules*. All the rules of logic still apply. A derivation with no premises, therefore, is a derivation from the rules of logic and nothing else.

If it doesn't begin with premises, what does it begin with? The only alternative would be that it begins with a hypothesis. A derivation without any premises at all would have to start in a sub-derivation. Here's an example.

1	~A v B	Hypothesis
2	A	Hypothesis
3	B	1,2 DE
4	A → B	2-3 CoI
5	(~A v B) → (A → B)	1-4 CoI

You should recognize that what this derivation proves is part of the Law of Implication. Notice how the truth table for this claim turns out:

A	B	~A	~A v B	A → B	(~A v B) → (A → B)
T	T	F	T	T	T
T	F	F	F	F	T
F	T	T	T	T	T
F	F	T	T	T	T

(~A v B) → (A → B) is a tautology. You can also see from the truth table that (~A v B) and (A → B) are logically equivalent. They both say exactly the same thing, they just say it in a slightly different form. Some logicians call these things "logical truths" because they are true simply in virtue of their logical form: regardless of whether claims A and B are in fact true, the structure of the claim makes (~A v B) → (A → B) true. As I pointed out in Chapter 5, tautologies are empty. They do not distinguish between the situations that would make them true as opposed to false, because their logical form prevents them from ever being false. Tautologies are true no matter what the non-logical facts are.

This is exactly what is going on when you perform a derivation with no premises whatsoever. A derivation with no premises derives a tautology because it derives from no claims about the way the world it; it follows simply from the laws of logic. Anytime you can derive a claim from absolutely no premises whatsoever, you know that you are no longer dealing with a claim that has to be verified by scientific means or just going out and looking to see how the world is. The fact that a tautology is true

Logicians often refer to these derivations from no premises as "theorems." The word "theorem" derives from the ancient Greek word "*theorēma*," which you should recognize because it is related to the word "theatre." Literally a "theatre" is a place you go to watch a show, to look at a spectacle. That is what "*theorēma*" means: spectacle. The ancient Greeks used the word to refer to festivals and other big productions where you stand around in awe and say, "Golly, would you look at that!" Mathematicians took this word over and used it to refer to items of mental contemplation. A mathematical "spectacle" is a claim you have to think about, e.g. "Golly, that's an interesting claim, I wonder if I can prove that it is true?" A theorem is a kind of thought puzzle.

Here's another thought puzzle, a theorem:

{} ⊢ A → (R → A)

Think about it. How could you derive it? First, it begins with no premises whatsoever, so you have to begin this derivation in a hypothesis. But what hypothesis? Here is where the "spectacle" begins. With theorems, you have to be clever and thoughtful. Think. Look the problem over with your intellect and think it through. First, what type of claim are you trying to derive here? Answer: a conditional claim. The antecedent is A and the consequent is R → A. Ok, so if we are trying to introduce a conditional claim, how about using Conditional Introduction? Let's try it and see. How does Conditional Introduction work? Answer: by a sub-derivation whose hypothesis is the antecedent of the conditional you are trying to derive. The rule itself tells you what your hypothesis has to be

1	A	Hypothesis
2	???	???
3		
4		

Ok, so far so good. Now what are we trying to derive? We are trying to show that if you hypothesize A, you will be able to derive the consequent of the conditional, i.e. R → A. So what we want now is another conditional claim. How do you derive a conditional claim? How about Conditional Introduction? Hypothesize the antecedent of the conditional and show that you can conclude with the consequent of the conditional claim:

```
1  | A                    Hypothesis
2  |   | R                Hypothesis
3  |   | ???              ???
```

Remember, this is a logical "spectacle," so keep in mind what you are trying to derive: A → (R → A). In other words, if you hypothesize A, you will be able to derive that if you hypothesize R, it will be logical to conclude A. What we want is the following:

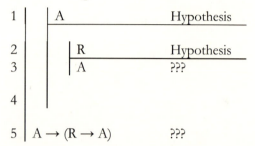

```
1  | A                    Hypothesis
2  |   | R                Hypothesis
3  |   | A                ???
4  |
5  | A → (R → A)          ???
```

Is this logical? Sure. Be careful to follow the scope lines: Line 1 begins in a sub-derivation, and lines 1-4 are all governed by that assumption. Hypothetically, if A were true, then on line 3, A is still true because we have not yet stopped hypothesizing that A is true. We are simply repeating—or Reiterating—the governing hypothesis. So now we have this:

```
1  | A                    Hypothesis
2  |   | R                Hypothesis
3  |   | A                1 R
4  | ???                  ???
5  | A → (R → A)          ???
```

Mentally envision the spectacle here: given A as a hypothesis, we want line 4 to be R → A; that would tell us that with A as a hypothesis, we can derive R → A, i.e. A → (R → A), which is the theorem we are trying to derive. Would it be logical to conclude R → A on line 4? Certainly!

```
1  | A                    Hypothesis
2  |   | R                Hypothesis
3  |   | A                1 R
4  | R → A                2-3 CoI
5  | A → (R → A)          1-4 CoI
```

That is an example of how you derive a theorem from no premises whatsoever, how you derive a claim from nothing other than the laws of logic alone.

Now that you understand theorems, you should have a deeper understanding of the laws of logical equivalence, e.g. DeMorgan's Laws, the Law of Contraposition, the Law of Distribution, the Law of Exportation and so on. What you should understand is that these are all theorems derivable from the ten basic laws that define the system of logic we are developing in this book. Remember that we recognize five logical operators: (1) conjunction, (2) disjunction, (3) conditional, (4) bi-conditional, and (5) negation. There are introduction and elimination rules for each of these five, making ten rules in all that form the foundation of our system of logic; in fact, you might say that these ten rules define the system of logic.

Note for more advanced students: it is an interesting philosophical question whether there are any additional operators. For example, how about references to things that were true in the past, or will be true in the future? "The book is not on the table" involves the logical operator "negation," so should "the book was on the table" involve a logical operator "past"? Some logicians have developed what is called "Temporal Logic." How about possibility: "the book might be on the table"? Should that involve the logical operator "possibly"? Some logicians have developed what is called "Modal Logic" (since "possibly" is a way or "mode" of being true).

CHAPTER 7: DERIVATIONS (CONTINUED)

Because the ten defining rules form the foundation of the system of logic we are developing, every valid rule of inference must either be one of the ten, or must be derivable from the ten. What does this mean for the laws of logical equivalence? All of them must be derivable from the ten basic laws. Sometimes this is easy. Here's an example.

```
1  | A                    Hypothesis
2  |  | ~A                Hypothesis
3  |  | A & ~A            1,2 CI
4  | ~~A                  2-3 NI

5  |  | ~~A               Hypothesis
6  |  |  | ~A             Hypothesis
7  |  |  | ~A & ~~A
8  |  | A                 6-7 NE

9  | A ↔ ~~A              1-4,5-8 BCoI
```

This proves that the Law of Double Negation is a theory of the system; the Law of Double Negation follows from the basic, defining rules of the system with no premises or additional assumptions whatsoever.

"Derive the Law of Implication." This instruction means that you should derive the Law of Implication using only the ten basic, defining laws of the system of logic. Do not use any replacement rules at all. Here's how you do it.

Problem: Derive the Law of Implication.

Step 1. Remember that the Law of Implication is the following: $P \rightarrow Q \equiv \sim P \vee Q$.
Step 2. Interpret the triple bar as the bi-conditional: $(P \rightarrow Q) \leftrightarrow (\sim P \vee Q)$.
Step 3. Think of this as the derivation of a theorem from no premises: $\{\} \vdash (P \rightarrow Q) \leftrightarrow (\sim P \vee Q)$.
Step 4. Work out the derivation, using only the introduction and elimination rules for the five logical operators that define our system of logic.

```
1  | P → Q                           Hypothesis
2  |  | ~(~P v Q)                    Hypothesis
3  |  |  | Q                         Hypothesis
4  |  |  | ~P v Q                    3 DI
5  |  |  | (~P v Q) & ~(~P v Q)      2,4 CI
6  |  | ~Q                           3-5 NI
7  |  | ~P                           1,6 MT
8  |  | ~P v Q                       7 DI
9  |  | (~P v Q) & ~(~P v Q)         2,8 CI
10 |  | ~P v Q                       2-9 NE

11 |  | ~P v Q                       Hypothesis
12 |  |  | P                         Hypothesis
13 |  |  | Q                         11,12 DE
14 |  | P → Q                        12-13 CoI

15 | (P → Q) ↔ (~P v Q)              1-10, 11-14 BCoI
```

Once a law has been derived from the basic, defining laws of the system, it may then be used in ordinary derivations. But every single Law, before it may be used in a derivation, must itself be derived as a theorem using only the basic, defining rules of the system.

DeMorgan's Laws are among the most difficult. Here is a derivation of one part of DeMorgan's Laws.

1	~(P & Q)	Hypothesis
2	~(~P v ~Q)	Hypothesis
3	~P	Hypothesis
4	~P v ~Q	3 DI
5	(~P v ~Q) & ~(~P v ~Q)	2,4 CI
6	P	3-5 NE
7	~Q	H
8	~P v ~Q	7 DI
9	(~P v ~Q) & ~(~P v ~Q)	2,8 CI
10	Q	7-9 NE
11	P & Q	6, 10 CI
12	(P & Q) & ~(P & Q)	1,11 CI
13	~P v ~Q	2-12 NE
14	~P v ~Q	Hypothesis
15	P & Q	Hypothesis
16	P	15 CE
17	~Q	14,16 DE
18	Q	15 CE
19	Q & ~Q	17,18 CI
20	~(P & Q)	15-19 NI
21	~(P & Q) ↔ (~P v ~Q)	1-13, 14-20 BCoI

You should be able to derive all eight laws of logical equivalence in chapter 6 and 7:
Law of Double Negation
Law of Implication
Law of Contraposition
Law of Association
DeMorgan's Laws
Law of Commutation
Law of Distribution
Law of Exportation

Chapter Conclusion.

In this chapter we completed all the basic rules for derivations, including the rules that require using sub-derivations. We also added a couple more replacement rules. Now you know a complete system of derivation, or you could call it a complete system of proof. This is what logic is all about. Now you know in detail how to think logically.

Things to memorize from this Chapter:
Distribution
P & (Q v R) ≡ (P & Q) v (P & R)
P v (Q & R) ≡ (P v Q) & (P v R)
Exportation
(P & Q) → R ≡ P → (Q → R)

Memorize the abbreviations of the derivation rules. Here they are in alphabetical order (new rules in bold).

Assoc: Association
BCoI: Bi-Conditional Introduction
BCoE: Bi-Conditional Elimination
CA: Chain Argument
CE: Conjunction Elimination
CI: Conjunction Introduction
CoI: Conditional Introduction
Com: Commutation
CP: Contraposition
DE: Disjunction Elimination
DeM: DeMorgan's Laws
DI: Disjunction Introduction
Dist: Distribution
DN: Double Negation
Exp: Exportation
Impl: Implication
MP: Modus Ponens
MT: Modus Tollens
NE: Negation Elimination
NI: Negation Introduction
R: Reiteration

New Derivation Rules
Conditional Introduction

```
1 | ???        P
  |
2 |  | P       Hypothesis
3 |  | Q       ???
  |
4 | P → Q      2-3 CoI
```

Bi-Conditional Introduction

```
1 | ???        P
  |
2 |  | P       Hypothesis
3 |  | Q       ???
  |
4 |  | Q       Hypothesis
5 |  | P       ???
  |
6 | P ↔ Q      2-3,4-5 BCoI
```

Bi-Conditional Elimination

1	???	P
2	P ↔ Q	???
3	P	???
4	Q	2,3 BCoE

Negation Introduction

1	???	P
2	P	Hypothesis
3	Q & ~Q	???
4	~P	2-3 NI

Negation Elimination

1	???	P
2	~P	Hypothesis
3	Q & ~Q	???
4	P	2-3 NE

Exercises for Chapter 7.

Exercise 7.1: Extremely Simple Sub-Derivations. *Perform the following derivations. Although it is possible to do some of the following without sub-derivations, make sure that you use one (and only one) sub-derivation in each problem, i.e. use CoI, BCoI, NI, or NE.*

Example 1
Problem: $\{P \to Q, Q \to R\} \vdash P \to R$
Solution:

1	P → Q	P
2	Q → R	P
3	P	Hypothesis
4	Q	1,3 MP
5	R	2,4 MP
6	P → R	3-5 CoI

Example 2
Problem: $\{P \to Q, P \to \sim Q\} \vdash \sim P$
Solution:

1	P → Q	P
2	P → ~Q	P
3	P	Hypothesis
4	Q	1,3 MP
5	~Q	2,3 MP
6	Q & ~Q	4,5 CI
6	~P	3-6 NI

1. $\{M \to N, N \to R\} \vdash M \to R$
2. $\{S \to \sim P, R \to S\} \vdash R \to \sim P$
3. $\{B \to (Q \& \sim Q)\} \vdash \sim B$
4. $\{\sim S \to (R \& \sim R)\} \vdash S$

5. {P → R, P → ~R} ⊢ ~P
6. {L → S, S → M} ⊢ L → M
7. {B → C, A → B} ⊢ A → C
8. {~P → R, R → ~P} ⊢ ~P → ~P
9. {P v Q, R → ~P} ⊢ R → Q
10. {~P → Q, ~P → ~Q} ⊢ P

11. {P → (M & N)} ⊢ P → M
12. {P v Q} ⊢ ~Q → P
13. {P ↔ Q, Q → ~P} ⊢ ~Q
14. {B v C} ⊢ ~B → C
15. {P → ~Q, Q v R} ⊢ P → R

16. {P ↔ R, R ↔ Q} ⊢ P → Q
17. {~P v Q} ⊢ P → Q
18. {(R & Q) ↔ S} ⊢ S → R
19. {T v ~S, M} ⊢ ~T → ~S
20. {D & G} ⊢ D → G

Exercise 7.2: Longer Sub-Derivations. *Perform the following derivations. Use sub-derivations.*
1. {P & ~P} ⊢ R
2. {P → Q} ⊢ P → (Q v R)
3. {(P v ~D) → ~L} ⊢ L → D
4. {P → Q, P → R} ⊢ P → (Q & R)
5. {P ↔ R, P → ~R} ⊢ ~P

6. {P → Q} ⊢ ~(P & ~Q)
7. {P → S, ~P → B, ~S → ~B} ⊢ S
8. {F → C, F v C} ⊢ C
9. {(M v R) & (M v ~R)} ⊢ M
10. {~(B & ~Q) → B} ⊢ B

11. {(P & Q) → (R & S)} ⊢ (Q & P) → (S & R)
12. {B → (M & ~N)} ⊢ (T & B) → ~N
13. {C & ~B, (R & C) → B} ⊢ ~R
14. {~P → Q, ~Q v P} ⊢ P
15. {(~R → F) & (F → ~R)} ⊢ ~R ↔ F

16. {(P v Q) → (P & Q)} ⊢ P ↔ Q
17. {P → Q} ⊢ ~Q → ~P
18. {A ↔ ~A} ⊢ B
19. {P} ⊢ (P → Q) → Q
20. {~P} ⊢ (Q → P) → ~Q

21. {M} ⊢ ~(M & L) → ~L
22. {E → (F → G)} ⊢ (E → F) → (E → G)
23. {~P v (Q & ~R)} ⊢ R → ~P
24. {P v Q, P → R, Q → R} ⊢ R
25. {(A & B) → C} ⊢ A → (B → C)

26. {P → (Q & ~P)} ⊢ ~P
27. {~M ↔ L} ⊢ L → ~M
28. {(L → M) & (M → L)} ⊢ M ↔ L
29. {B → R, (R v Q) → ~B} ⊢ ~B
30. {~R, (P v Q) → R} ⊢ ~P

31. {P & (Q & R), P → ~(T v R)} ⊢ ~B
32. {~(P v Q) v R} ⊢ ~R → ~Q

33. {~(P & Q) v R} ⊢ ~R → (P → ~Q)
34. {P → (~R → Q), P → ~R} ⊢ P → Q
35. {P, ~(P v Q)} ⊢ T

36. {P → R, Q → S} ⊢ (P & Q) → (R & S)
37. {~T v P, P → (M & N), (N v S) ↔ T} ⊢ P ↔ T
38. {P → ~(M v ~N), D & ~(G v N)} ⊢ ~P
39. {B ↔ R, B ↔ (S v N), R → N} ⊢ R ↔ (N v S)
40. {~P & ~Q} ⊢ P ↔ Q

Exercise 7.3: Theorems. *Prove the following theorems.*
Example #1
Problem: {} ⊢ (~Q & (P v Q)) → P
Solution:

1	~Q & (P v Q)	Hypothesis
2	~Q	1 CE
3	P v Q	1CE
4	P	2,3 DE

5   ~Q & (P v Q) → P   1-4 CoI

Example #2
Problem: {} ⊢ P → (P v Q)
Solution:

| 1 | P | Hypothesis |
| 2 | P v Q | 1 DI |

4   P → (P v Q)   2,3 DE

1. {} ⊢ ~(A & ~A)
2. {} ⊢ (P → Q) → ~(P & ~Q)
3. {} ⊢ ~(P & ~Q) → (P → Q)
4. {} ⊢ (P → Q) ↔ ~(P & ~Q)
5. {} ⊢ (P & (P → Q)) → Q

6. {} ⊢ (~Q & (P → Q)) → ~P
7. {} ⊢ ((P v Q) & ~Q) → P
8. {} ⊢ ((P → Q) & (Q → R)) → (P → R)
9. {} ⊢ A → (B → A)
10. {} ⊢ (P ↔ Q) → (P → Q)

11. {} ⊢ P v ~P
12. {} ⊢ A → (B → (A → B))
13. {} ⊢ P → (~P → Q)
14. {} ⊢ R → (D → R)
15. {} ⊢ ~P → (P → Q)

16. {} ⊢ (P → Q) → ((Q → R) → (P → R))
17. {} ⊢ P & (Q & R) ↔ (P & Q) & R
18. {} ⊢ (P v Q) ↔ (Q v P)
19. {} ⊢ ~(P & Q) ↔ (~P v ~Q) *try this without using DeM*
20. {} ⊢ (~P & ~Q) ↔ ~(P v Q) *try this without using DeM*

Exercise 7.4: Assorted Derivations. *Perform the following derivations.*
1. {P → (~N & ~M), ~N → (~M → P)} ⊢ P ↔ (~N & ~M)
2. {~A & ~B} ⊢ A ↔ B
3. {(B → C) → D} ⊢ B → (C → D)
4. {(A & ~B) → (~B & C), C → ~A} ⊢ A → B
5. {~M v (T → B), ~S → (M v B), M → T} ⊢ B v S
6. {~~T v ~R, ~(S v ~R), (T & ~S) → ~Q, W → Q} ⊢ ~W
7. {M v R, M → (R v S), R → (R v S)} ⊢ ~(~R & ~S)
8. {A v B, A → R, B → S} ⊢ R v S
9. {~(C & D), ~C → T, ~D → R} ⊢ T v R
10. {(M & ~P) v (S & B), (~P & M) → A, (S & B) → T} ⊢ A v T

11. {P v (P v P)} ⊢ P
12. {N → M, ~N → ~M} ⊢ N ↔ M
13. {F & ~G} ⊢ ~(F → G)
14. {~(L → C)} ⊢ L & ~C
15. {} ⊢ ~(P → Q) ↔ (P & ~Q)

16. {(S → L) → W, (S → L) v ~W} ⊢ ~W ↔ ~(S → L)
17. {P v ~N, ~P v ~N} ⊢ ~N
18. {A → (Q & B), (~Q ↔ B) & (C → A)} ⊢ (A v B) → ~C
19. {A ↔ B} ⊢ (C ↔ A) ↔ (C ↔ B)
20. {(L → A) v B, (~(L → A) & ~B) ↔ (J → (E & ~F))} ⊢ (J → (E & ~F)) → Z

CHAPTER 8: PREDICATES AND QUANTIFIERS

Now you know a system of symbolic logic. Now you know how to deal with claims and arguments which involve conjunctions, disjunctions, conditionals, bi-conditionals and negations. Although this covers a lot of ground, it leaves out a whole range of terms that are logically very significant: all, some and none. You need to add to your logical repertoire an ability to deal with claims about quantities, i.e. you need to be able to deal with quantifiers.

Section 1: Predicates.

Before you can deal with quantifiers, you first have to learn to deal with predicates. Let's start with something very simple. Consider this argument, and the symbolization you can do now.

1. Either Socrates is Greek or Socrates is Persian.
2. Socrates is not Persian.
∴ 3. Socrates is Greek.
G = Socrates is Greek
P = Socrates is Persian

```
1 | G v P    P
2 | ~P       P
3 | G        1,2 DE
```

This argument is valid by disjunction elimination. So far, this is the best we can do when it comes to translating this argument into symbolic logic.

But notice what we've left out. The first premise says two different things about one person. We are talking about Socrates throughout the argument, but from the symbols, you'd never know that. You could symbolize the following argument in exactly the same way.

1. Either Socrates is Greek or Plato is Persian.
2. Plato is not Persian.
∴ 3. Socrates is Greek.
G = Socrates is Greek

P = Plato is Persian

```
1 | G v P    P
2 | ~P       P
3 | G        1,2 DE
```

Here we have exactly the same symbolization for a somewhat different argument. When you use capital letters to stand for complete statements, you leave out a lot of detail. What we need to do now is to build back in some of that detail. Predicates are the first step.

What you have learned so far is often called "Sentential Logic" because capital letters stand for complete sentences. What you are learning now is often called "Predicate Logic" because capital letters now stand for predicates. Compared to Predicate Logic, Sentential Logic is just too simple to deal with some of the most important logical complexities.

Go back to our disjunctive claim, "Either Socrates is Greek or Socrates is Persian." Here we have two alternatives. One alternative is to say that Socrates is Greek. This is a simple sentence: Socrates is Greek. In English you have a simple subject, " Socrates" and a simple predicate, "is Greek." The other alternative works in exactly the same way, it simply changes predicates. "Socrates" is still the subject of the sentence, but now "is Persian" is the predicate. That is what we want to capture in symbolic notation. We want two expressions that are not totally different. Now we want two claims that show they have the same subject, but emphasize there are two different predicates being attached to one and the same subject. Now instead of standing for an entire sentence, G will simply stand for the predicate "is Greek" and P will stand for the predicate "is Persian."

If capital letters stand for the predicates of sentences, then what shall we use to stand for the subjects of sentences? Why not simply use lower case letters? Capital G will stand for "is Greek" and so little s will stand for "Socrates." So we can translate "Socrates is Greek" like this: Gs.

I apologize for putting the capital G first. G is the predicate, and so really should come after the subject. However, this is the way most logicians symbolize predication, and so you should learn it this way. They did it this way because this way makes logic look more like mathematics and less like a living language. Furthermore, to make logic as much like mathematics as possible, traditional logicians use *variables* or *place holders*, just like in algebra.

Imagine that you are waiting in a line for a long time. You need to go to the bathroom, so you ask someone to hold your place in line for you: you don't want to have to go to the end of the line after waiting so long. They hold your place, and when you come back, they step out of the line and let you take your place again. That's a "place holder," and it's just the sort of thing we can call a "variable." The person standing in line *varies*: first it's you, then it's your placeholder, then it's you again.

Now imagine that this line forms every day, and it's always long. You figure out that you can actually earn some money as a place-holder. You let people know that you'll stand in line for them if they pay you a small amount of money. You might even get in line early, and advertise your spot in line as being for sale. You are a place-holder, but not for anybody in particular: you are just holding the spot, and anyone who pays you can take the spot. Again, that's a *variable*: who gets the spot you are holding can *vary* from day to day.

So now you can distinguish the two different kinds of variables or place-holders. One kind of variable stands in for one particular individual: this is the case where one particular person asked you to hold their place for them. You are standing in for one particular individual—nobody else. The other kind of variable is when you are standing in line and you are willing to sell your spot in line to anybody at all. There is no particular individual who necessarily gets your spot because absolutely anybody could get it as long as you agree to give it up to them.

In logic it makes perfect sense to use variables. After all, it is one thing to say that *Socrates* is Greek, and another thing to say that *Plato* is Greek, and it is still another thing to say that *someone* is Greek. If you want to say that *someone* is Greek, but you don't know who it is, or you don't want to say who it is (to protect the identity of an under cover agent, for example) then you need to have a special letter reserved for just such a case. You need a letter to stand in the place of a subject, but you don't want that letter to refer to anyone in particular. You simply want it to stand for "someone," we're not saying who. Logicians have followed mathematicians and used the last letters of the alphabet (w, x, y, z), lower case, to stand for "variables.".

Actually, this is another apology I have to make for traditional logicians (and mathematicians). The four variables are w, x, y and z. If you need to use more than just four variables, then you have to resort to subscripts to keep the different variables apart. If you've used w, x, y and z and you still need another variable, then you wrap back around to w again, but you start putting numbers with it like w_1, x_1, y_1, z_1, and then wrap back around again and start with 2: w_2, x_2, y_2, z_2 and so on. So you have an unlimited number of variables. But don't worry, we aren't going to need lots of variables. In fact, normally you will only be using just one variable: x. For example, here is how to do an index for our simple argument about how Socrates is Greek.

Index in Sentential Logic:
G = Socrates is Greek
P = Socrates is Persian

1	G v P	P
2	~P	P
3	G	1,2 DE

Index in Predicate Logic:
Gx = x is Greek
Px = x is Persian
s = Socrates

1	Gs v Ps	P
2	~Ps	P
3	Gs	1,2 DE

In Sentential logic, all you have to do is list the capital letters that stand for the different claims, and then you move on to translating the argument using the symbols you know. In Predicate logic, you have to do more work. First, you have to list all the predicates you are going to use, and you have to list them with variables. The predicates can be applied to any individuals, and so you have to put a variable as a place marker, where the individuals will go. After you list the predicates with variables, you need to make a list of "individual constants." They are called "constants" because they are not "variables". The variables can stand for any individual, but the constants always refer to just one individual.

Let's do an example that involves more than one individual constant. Here is a new argument.

Problem: If Socrates is a philosopher, then Plato is a philosophy student. But if Plato is a philosophy student, then Aristotle must be a philosophy student also. Hence, if Socrates is a philosopher, then Aristotle is a philosophy student.

Solution:
1. If Socrates is a philosopher, then Plato is a philosophy student.
2. If Plato is a philosophy student, then Aristotle is a philosophy student.
∴ 3. If Socrates is a philosopher, then Aristotle is a philosophy student.

Px = x is a philosopher
Sx = x is a philosophy student
s = Socrates
p = Plato
a = Aristotle

1	Ps → Sp	P
2	Sp → Sa	P
3	Ps → Sa	1,2 CA

First you list all the predicates with variables, then you list the individual constants, and then you translate the argument using the symbols you already know. All the logical operators work in exactly the same way. In fact, derivations work in exactly the same way too. Things will change a bit when we introduce quantifiers.

So far I have shown you only what are called "one-place predicates." There can be "two-place predicates." For example, here is an argument that involves a two-place predicate.

Problem: John is taller than Sally. If John is taller than Sally, then John is taller than Bert. So John is taller than Bert.
Solution:
1. John is taller than Sally.
2. If John is taller than Sally, then John is taller than Bert.
∴ 3. John is taller than Bert.

Txy = x is taller than y
j = John
s = Sally
b = Bert

1	Tjs	P
2	Tjs → Tjb	P
3	Tjb	1,2 MP

Notice that you have to indicate a two-place predicate in your index. It has to be followed by two variables in the index, and you have to say what the order of the variables means. This is extremely important because the following two say very different things:

John is taller than Bert
Bert is taller than John

Order matters. Tjb says something very different from Tbj. If you have dyslexia to any degree at all, you must use extreme caution when dealing with predicates that have two or more places with it. This notation was created by non-dyslexic logicians who never gave any consideration to people with abilities that were different from their own.

Since there can be two-place predicates, there can also be three-place predicates, four-place predicates and so on. For example, "squealing" is a three-place predicate because it requires someone to do the squealing, someone for them to squeal to, and something for them to squeal about, e.g. "Joe squealed to the cops about the robbery" might end up being: Sjcr (you should be able to figure out what each of those letters means, and why each is upper or lower case).

There is no upper limit here. There can be no zero-place predicates, because then it wouldn't be the predicate of anything. A predicate of nothing is not a predicate. When you define your predicates, use the variables x, y, and z. If you have a four-place predicate, use w, x, y and z. If you have a five place predicate, you have to start wrapping around again and using subscripts. Here is an example of a five-place predicate.

$Mwxyzw_1$ = w is the mother of the quadruplets x, y, z and w_1

Notice that since we are saving w, x, y and z to use as variables, you may not use them to stand for proper names. Even if you have someone named Wayne, Xavier, Yeltsin or Zeno. Pick different letters to stand for these names. For example, you might go to the second letter of the name: let a stand for Xavier and e stand for Yeltsin. But of course then we have to go to n for Zeno, because you cannot use the same letter for two different people

a = Xavier
e = Yeltsin
n = Zeno

When you do your index, each individual constant must refer to only one individual, and each individual must have a single unique letter.

Section 2: The Two Quantifiers.

Now you are ready for quantifiers. Remember that quantifiers specify the quantity of something, but they don't use numbers, like in math. Logic deals with quantity is a much more simplified way. Logic divides all quantities up into two categories: all and some. Of course there are other non-numerical quantities. For example, there is a logic to the concept of most, or more-than-half. There is sometimes a distinction between "some" and "a few." You might also draw a distinction between "a few" and "quite a few," between "several" and "a bunch." You could work out systems of logic using many different quantifiers. Fortunately this is one place where logicians actually make things easy: they use only two quantifiers: all and some.

First take "some." Here is how you symbolize the claim that "some humans exist."

Hx = x is a human being
$(\exists x)$ Hx

Literally, you should read this as saying: *there exists an x such that x is a human being.* Memorize that way of talking; it will help you a great deal when you translate from quantified symbolic logic into English and vice versa. Just to help you with this new expression, here is a list of claims together with their translations.

Hx = x is a human being
Px = x is a philosopher
Gx = x is Greek
Bx = x is blue

$(\exists x)$ Px	There exists an x such that x is a philosopher.
$(\exists x)$ Bx	There exists an x such that x is blue.
$(\exists x)$ Gx & Px	There exists an x such that x is Greek and x is a philosopher.
$(\exists x)$ Hx & Px	There exists an x such that x is human and a philosopher.
$(\exists x)$ Hx & ~Bx	There exists an x such that x is human and x is not blue.

Of course you may come up with smoother translations of these. For example, the fourth one in the above list could be translated as "There is a Greek philosopher" or "some philosopher is Greek." But make sure that you do a literal translation first. A sure way to ruin your chances of learning this stuff is for you to take short cuts too soon. At least in your head, always do the literal translation first, translating the backwards E as "there exists an x such that x is ..." Because of this literal translation, the backwards E is called the "existential quantifier." It is "existential" just in the sense that it says something exists. It means that at least one of the things qualified by the predicate actually does exist.

Now for the other quantifier. Here is a list of claims using the other quantifier together with their proper translations.

Hx = x is a human being
Px = x is a philosopher
Gx = x is Greek
Bx = x is blue

(x) Px	For all x, x is a philosopher.
(x) Gx	For all x, x is Greek.
(x) Bx	For all x, x such that x is blue.
(x) Gx & Px	For all x, x is Greek and x is a philosopher.
(x) Hx & Px	For all x, x is human and a philosopher.
(x) Hx & ~Bx	For all x, x is human and x is not blue.

Instead of being an "existential" quantifier, this is called the "universal quantifier" because it makes the broad, sweeping generalization that absolutely everything is qualified by the predicate that follows. In many systems, the universal quantifier is an upside down A, but I find it simpler and easier to follow the other practice of just putting the universally quantified variable in parentheses.

Again, think of variables as place-holders. Think of the existential quantifier (∃x) like someone who is holding your place in a long line. An existentially quantified variable says, "I'm holding this spot for one person in particular, but I'm not going to tell you." You can't just put anyone in particular in for an existentially quantified variable, because they may not be the person the variable is holding the place for. On the other hand, a universal quantifier (x) is holding the spot for anybody (though maybe you have to pay them for their spot in line). In theory, you can put absolutely anybody in that place for a truly universal quantifier.

So far, quantifiers are not very difficult. The next step is to build up more complex claims with parentheses. Here are a few slightly more complex claims.

Hx = x is a human being
Px = x is a philosopher
Gx = x is Greek
Sx = x is Persian

(x) Px → Gx   For all x, if x is a philosopher, then x is Greek.
(x) Gx ↔ Hx   For all x, x is Greek if and only if x is a human being.
(x) Gx v (Sx & Px)   For all x, either x is Greek or x is both Persian and a philosopher.
(x) Gx → (∃y) Py   If for all x, x is Greek then there exists a y such that y is a philosopher.
(∃x) Hx → (y) Py   If there exists an x such that x is human, then for all y, y is a philosopher.

Again, there are clearer ways of translating these. For example, the first one could be translated as, "whoever is a philosopher is also Greek." Alternatively, that same expression could be translated as "all philosophers are Greek." The next one says that all Greeks are human, and all humans are Greeks. The next one says that everyone is either Greek or a Persian philosopher. The next one says that if everyone is Greek, then someone is a philosopher. The last one says that if someone is human, then everyone is a philosopher. But again I urge you to practice the literal translations first. You will save yourself a lot of confusion and trouble later if you learn the standard translations first.

Now that you understand quantified expressions, there is an extremely important rule you must learn. Let's use the following simple index.

Gx = x is Greek
Sx = x speaks Greek

Given that index, how would we make the general claim that anyone who is Greek speaks Greek? Notice that we are not trying to say that everyone is Greek, or that everyone speaks Greek. We are making a general claim about the connection between being Greek and speaking Greek. We are making the general claim that speaking Greek is conditional upon being Greek, so we are trying to say that "If someone is Greek, then they speak Greek." Since this is a perfectly general claim, it applies to anyone at all, we need to use the general (i.e. universal) quantifier.

(x) Gx → Sx   For all x, if x is Greek, then x speaks Greek

Notice that the variable x occurs twice in this one expression. Since this chapter is about quantity and quantifiers, we should ask the question "how many?" whenever we have a variable. The quantifier always answers the "how many?" question. In this case, how many individuals are we talking about? All of them. Since we have a universal quantifier, this expression is supposed to be true for absolutely every individual.

Now ask a question we first learned to ask back in Chapter 4 (Section 3): what is the *main logical operator* of this expression? In this case, the main logical operator is the universal quantifier (x). Logically speaking, this expression is fundamentally a universal claim about all individuals. It just happens to be universal *conditional* claim, but fundamentally it is a universal claim.

After we have determined that the universal quantifier is the main logical operator of the expression, we can determine the *scope* of the quantifier. The "scope" of a quantifier is simply how far it applies. In this short expression, the quantifier applies to the entire expression, so the scope of the quantifier is the entire expression. This is important because it tells us that every occurrence of the variable x is *within the scope of the universal quantifier*. To help you see this, and why it is important, consider a different example.

Hx = x is a human being
Mx = x is mortal

(x) Hx → (∃y) My   If everyone is human, then someone is mortal.

CHAPTER 8: PREDICATES AND QUANTIFIERS

Look at that expression and determine the scope of the universal quantifier, and the scope of the existential quantifier. Obviously the scope of the universal quantifier (x) is just the antecedent of the conditional; the (x) doesn't range any farther than the antecedent of the conditional. Similarly, the scope of the existential quantifier is just the consequent of the conditional claim. This means that the universal quantifier is not the main logical operator of the entire expression. The universal quantifier is limited in its scope. The main logical operator of this expression is the arrow. Fundamentally, this claim is a conditional claim. It just happens to be a conditional claim whose conditions are quantified, but the quantifiers are logically secondary.

If you want to make the scope of a quantifier absolutely clear, so you don't make any mistake about it, you may use parentheses (just as we did beginning in Chapter 4, Section 3 earlier). For example, you may do this:

((x) Hx) → ((∃y) My)

If you enclose the (x) Hx within a set of parentheses, you mark it out as one logical unit, and you make it absolutely clear that the scope of the universal quantifier is limited: it's scope or its range is limited by the parentheses you just added.

Now that you understand what the scope or range of a quantifier is, you should be able to see that there is something very wrong with the following expression.

((x) Hx) → My: ***Incorrect!!! Never do this!!!***

If we ask the "how many?" question about the x we get a simple answer: all of them. The x in Hx is universally quantified. But when we turn to the y in My and ask "how many?" we get no answer. This is illogical. The whole point of using variables is that they can hold the place for a certain number of individuals, either one or more than one. So when you use a variable in an expression, you are saying, "there is a certain number of these." But if you say that, they logically you must narrow it down: are you claiming that there is at least one, or are you making a claim that applies universally?

The distinction to learn is the difference between a "bound variable" and an "unbound variable." Here are the definitions to learn.

A ***bound variable*** is a variable that is within the scope of a quantifier.
An ***unbound variable*** is a variable that is not within the scope of a quantifier.

It is never permitted to have an unbound variable in an expression. An expression with an unbound variable in it is illogical because it doesn't answer the crucial logical question of "how many?" When you use a variable, you are saying that there is a certain number of something, either one or more, and if you say that there is a certain number, then you are logically obligated to specify which. Notice that we have an unbound variable in the following expression:

((x) Hx) → Mx: ***Incorrect!!! Never do this!!!***

Even though there is a universally quantified x at the beginning of the expression, the variable in the consequent of the conditional is unbound. The reason is that the parentheses shut down the range of the universal quantifier and lock it into the antecedent of the conditional claim. In this expression, the main logical operator is the arrow, not the universal quantifier, so the universal quantifier is limited in scope.

Finally, compare the following two expressions.

(x) Hx → (∃y) My
(x) Hx → Mx

What is the scope of the universal quantifier in both of these expressions? In which expression does the universal quantifier have a larger scope? In the second expression, the universal quantifier ranges over, or has as its scope, the entire expression, but in the first one, the universal quantifier is limited to or restricted to just the antecedent of the conditional claim. We know this because in the first expression, the only x is in the antecedent; since there is no x in the consequent, the universal quantifier doesn't reach that far. But in the second expression, there is an x in the consequent. Furthermore, there are not parentheses to stop the universal quantifier from reaching into the consequent. In general, a quantifier reaches as far as it possibly can, until either the expression ends, or parentheses restrict its scope. Another way to say this is to notice that in the second expression, the universal quantifier is the main logical operator of the entire expression. Since it is the main logical operator of the entire expression, it ranges over, or has as its scope, the entire expression. But in the first expression, there is an x only in the antecedent. So the universal quantifier has a more limited scope. It is not the main logical operator of the entire expression, it is only the main logical operator of the antecedent.

Section 3: Somebody, Anybody, Everybody.

At this point, many students look for shortcuts. As with all shortcuts, by doing this you can get yourself into a lot of trouble and totally confuse yourself. The shortcuts students take most often is to think that "(∃x)" means "someone" and that "(x)" means "everyone." That's not true. Often you will use "someone" to translate the existential quantifier, and often you will use "everyone" to translate the universal quantifier, but that's not always true, and sometimes you will get really messed up if you do that. *So don't do it!*

The universal quantifier is the universal quantifier and the existential quantifier is the existential quantifier. The universal quantifier claims that the quantified expression is true for every member of the group you are talking about. For example, if you are talking about students in this class, I hope that the following is true:

Px = x passes PHIL 221 this semester
(x)Px

Translate this as follows: "for all x, x passes PHIL 221 this semester." Now here is where many students make a mistake: they see "for all x" and they immediately put in "everybody" in its place. If you do that, then perhaps ~(x)Px. In this particular case, "everybody" does work because "(x)Px" can be translated as "everybody passes PHIL 221 this semester." But that translation doesn't always work.

Here's an example. Think of the world of DC comics. In that world, there is an element called "kryptonite," and it has an amazing power: it weakens Superman. This comes in very handy; if you are a criminal mastermind and you worry about Superman showing up to spoil your caper, you might want to keep some kryptonite around to thwart the do-gooder. Kryptonite won't harm your lackeys, minions, thugs and flunkeys, but it will stop Superman. Now consider the following index:

Kx = x is exposed to kryptonite
Wx = x grows weak
s = Superman

The following is true in the world of DC comics: Ks → Ws, i.e. if Superman is exposed to kryptonite, then Superman grows weak. Now here's the tricky part: suppose you wanted to say, "If someone is exposed to kryptonite, then they grow weak." How would you say it? This is actually false because kryptonite doesn't affect anyone except for Superman; but if you did want to say it, how would you do it? If you make the mistake of automatically thinking that "someone" has to be the existential quantifier, then you might do this:

(∃x)(Kx → Wx)

That is *wrong*. Think it through. It says that there exists someone with the conditional property that if they are exposed to kryptonite then they weaken. This statement is actually true in the world of DC comics because in the world of DC comics, Superman is real and if he is exposed to kryptonite, then he weakens. So this statement is true, and obviously that means it cannot be the right translation of "if someone is exposed to kryptonite, then they grow weak" because this second claim is false.

The key is to think through what you are trying to say logically. The false statement that "if someone is exposed to kryptonite, then they grow weak" is a totally general statement – which is precisely why it is false. Kryptonite doesn't affect everybody, only superman. So it is false to say that that in general if someone is exposed to it, they grow weak. Because the false claim is totally general, completely universal, we need to use the universal quantifier, like so:

(x)(Kx → Wx)

There are several different ways you could translate this false universal generalization:

If somebody is exposed to kryptonite, then they grow weak
If anybody is exposed to kryptonite, then they grow weak
Whoever is exposed to kryptonite grows weak

The universal quantifier does not mean "everybody," and the existential quantifier does not mean "somebody." Often those are used in the translation, but not always. Remember to think first, translate second. Make sure that you understand the meaning of what you are translating before you translate it.

There is another place where many students get confused with "everybody." For this example, let's switch from the fictional world of DC comics to the fictional world of the 2003 film Elf, starring Will Ferrell. At the end of the film, Santa's sleigh can't get airborne because there isn't enough Christmas spirit. To lift Christmas spirits, someone starts singing, "Santa Claus is Coming to Town." A few people join in, but it isn't enough. It is not until everyone joins together in singing the song that there is enough Christmas spirit to lift Santa's sleigh. Now, here's the index:

Sx = x sings "Santa Claus is Coming to Town"
Ax = x gets Santa's sleigh airborne

Given this index, how would you say, "if everyone sings 'Santa Claus is Coming to Town,' then they get Santa's sleigh airborne"? The following is what students usually guess first, but it is wrong:

(x)(Sx → Ax)

Students see "everyone" and put in the universal quantifier, then they see "if" and "then" and use the arrow, and then they just put in the two predicates in the right order. But that's no good. Think. *The universal quantifier does not mean "everyone,"* it simply claims that what follows is a universal truth and applies to absolutely every individual we are talking about. In this case, we are talking about everyone in this particular scene of the film, but remember that the first person who sings the song "Santa Claus is coming to Town" is not able to get Santa's sleigh airborne. If it is not true of this person, then it is not true of everybody. Here are various ways you might translate (x)(Sx → Ax):

If someone sings "Santa Claus is Coming to Town," then they get Santa's sleigh airborne
If anybody sings "Santa Claus is Coming to Twon," then they get Santa's sleigh airborne
Whoever sings "Santa Claus is Coming to Town" gets Santa's sleigh airborne

No matter which way you translate it, it is false. One person alone can't do it; to raise Christmas spirits enough, everybody has to sing together.

The problem here is that students sometimes forget what we learned at the very beginning of the semester: identify what type of claim you are working with. (x)(Sx → Ax) is a universally quantified expression, but that's not what we want. We want to say "If everybody sings 'Santa Claus is Coming to Town,' then they get Santa's sleigh airborne." That is an "if ..., then ..." claim, a conditional claim. So we need to have an antecedent that says "everybody sings 'Santa Claus is Coming to Town'," and we need a consequent that says "everybody gets Santa's sleigh airborne." Do it step by step.

(x)Sx (this says "everybody sings 'Santa Claus is Coming to Town'")
(y)Ay (this says "everybody gets Santa's sleigh airborne")

Notice that I added a second variable just to avoid confusion. But now it's easy. We have the antecedent, and we have the consequent, so now all we have to do is put them together with an arrow between them:

(x)Sx → (y)Ay

Here we have just what we want: a conditional claim whose antecedent is the right universally quantified claim, and whose consequent is the right universally quantified claim.

Again, remember that you can't automatically translate either quantifier with the same word or phrase every time you see it. You have to make sure you understand the claim you are translating, and make sure that you translate it into a claim that really does mean the same thing. In other words: *think!*

Section 4: Combining Quantifiers.

And now the next step is to combine quantifiers right next to each other. This is where it will really help if you stick precisely to the way of translating the quantifiers that I have given you. Let's begin by comparing four different but related claims.

Lxy = x loves y
(∃x)(∃y) Lxy   There exists an x such that there exists a y such that x loves y.
(∃x)(y) Lxy   There exists an x such that for all y, x loves y.
(x)(∃y) Lxy   For all x, there exists a y such that x loves y.
(x)(y) Lxy   For all x and for all y, x loves y.

It is easiest to begin with the first and the last of these four claims. The first claim says that someone loves someone. There is some x (at least one person) who loves someone else (at least one person). There is someone who loves someone. This is a very minimal claim, and it is surely true. There is somewhere in this world at least one person who loves someone.

Now compare this to the fourth claim. According to the fourth claim, everyone loves everyone. Wouldn't that be nice? This is a much more sweeping claim. The first claim just makes the very minimal statement that there is at least one person who loves someone; the last one claims that absolutely everyone loves absolutely everyone else.

Now turn to the two claims in the middle. These two claims show you how important it is to make sure that you have things in the proper order. The second claim, (∃x)(y) Lxy, says that there is someone who loves everyone. That means that there is someone who has universal benevolence; she or he loves absolutely every person on the planet. I suppose this is Jesus or Buddha or some saint. The third claim, (x)(∃y) Lxy, says something very different. This claim says that everybody loves somebody. In other words, every single person has someone that they love. Of course it doesn't have to be the same person for each. All this says is that at some point in a person's life, each and every one of us falls in love with someone or other. The order of the quantifiers is absolutely crucial.

But you already know that the order of the individual constants and the variables matters. "John is taller than Bert" is very different from "Bert is taller than John." When you are dealing with variables, the order can matter a great deal. But first, here is an example where the order will not make a big deal of difference.

(x)(y) Lxy: For all x and for all y, x loves y.
(x)(y) Lyx: For all x and for all y, y loves x.

Here the order doesn't really make a big difference. The first one says that everyone *loves* everyone, and the second one says that everyone *is loved by* everyone, which pretty much amounts to the same thing, since everyone ends up loving and being loved. If the expression were more complex than that simple claim, then the order of the x and y might eventually make a difference, but in this short expression it's no big deal. Compare the existential variations.

(∃x)(∃y) Lxy: There exists an x such that there exists a y such that x loves y.
(∃x)(∃y) Lyx: There exists an x such that there exists a y such that y loves x.

Because these are variables, and they could stand for anyone, there isn't really a significant difference between these two expressions. The first one says that someone *loves* someone, and the second says that someone *is loved by* someone. Because the x comes before the y, the x is the focus of each expression. The first one says that there is an x, who loves someone, i.e. someone loves someone. The second expression focuses upon x, but says that there is some y who loves x. So in the second one we are thinking of x as the one who *is loved*, while in the first expression we are thinking of x as the one who is doing the loving. In the end, both of them amount to saying that someone loves and someone is loved. Again, if the expressions were longer, then the order of the variables might end up making a difference, but for this short expression, the difference doesn't matter. How about the cases where the quantifiers are mixed?

(∃x)(y) Lxy: There exists an x such that for all y, x loves y.
(∃x)(y) Lyx: There exists an x such that for all y, y loves x.

Are these two saying anything significantly different? Yes! The first one says that there is someone who *loves* everyone, and the second one is saying that there is someone who *is loved by* everyone. Those are two very different claims. The first claim applies to people like Jesus and Buddha; they are particular individuals who love absolutely everyone. The second claim says that there is some very special individual whom everyone loves. Now finally compare the last two variations.

(x)(∃y) Lxy: For all x there exists a y such that x loves y
(x)(∃y) Lyx: For all x there exists a y such that y loves x.

The first of these says that everyone has someone whom they love. It may be a different person for each. I love someone, you love someone else, the next person loves someone different, but each person has someone or other whom they love. The second one says that everyone has someone who loves them. Isn't that nice? Everyone is loved by someone or other. It may not be the same person for each of us; the person who loves me may be different from the person who loves you, but each of us has someone who loves us. The order of the variables matters, so be careful.

Section 5: *Negating Quantifiers.*

Things are a little more complicated when you negate quantifiers. Here are three claims involving the universal quantifier that will help you to compare different kinds of negations.

Hx = x is human
Mx = x is mortal
(x) Hx → Mx   For all x, if x is human, then x is mortal.
~(x) Hx → Mx   It is not the case that for all x, if x is human, then x is mortal.
(x) ~(Hx → Mx)   For all x, it is not the case that if x is human, then x is mortal.

The first claim is our old friend, "All humans are mortal." The second claim just negates the first claim. The second claim says, basically, "No, not every single human being is mortal." In other words, according to the second claim, there is at least one counter-example; there is at least one human who breaks the general rule; there is at least one human being who is not mortal. The third claim is different. The third claim is a universal generalization and is supposed to hold true for absolutely everyone. The third claim says that for absolutely everyone, it is not true to say that if they are human, then they are mortal. This is very dramatic. It goes way beyond saying that there is one lucky person who avoids death; the third claim says that this is true for all of us: our humanity does not entail mortality. Just because you are human, it doesn't necessarily mean that you have to die, you can find everlasting life. That is the dramatic claim made by the third expression. Where you put the negation makes a huge difference.

Now look at these three claims that use the existential quantifier. I'll do the same thing for the existential quantifier that I just did for the universal quantifier.

Hx = x is human
Mx = x is mortal
(∃x) Hx & Mx   There exists an x such that x is human and x is mortal.
~(∃x) Hx & Mx   It is not the case that there exists an x such that x is human and x is mortal.
(∃x) ~(Hx & Mx)   There exists an x such that it is not the case that x is human and x is mortal.

The first claim is the very modest claim that someone is both human and mortal. There is a mortal human. In other words, some human being has already died or will die. The second claim is very radical. The second claim says that the first claim is false. The second claim says that it is not true to say that some human being has died. In other words, according to the second claim, there is no such thing as a mortal human being. There might be some non-humans (for example, rats) who are mortal, and there might be some humans who are not mortal, but there cannot be someone who is both human and also mortal. That is a very radical claim. The third claim says something a bit less extreme. The third claim says only that there is someone who is not both human and mortal. This can be true in two different ways: it could be true because there is someone who is human but not mortal, or it could be true because there is someone who is mortal but not human (e.g. a rat).

Now let's start to put this all together. Now I'm going to give you a mixture of quantifiers, variables, constants and negations. Also, I'm going to give you the familiar translations of the following expressions, rather than the strict literal translations, as I have been doing above. You should still make sure that you can do the strict literal translations. I'll number these ones to make them easier to refer to. (This is not a derivation or an argument, the numbers are there just for convenience).

Lxy = x loves y
r = Raymond
1. (x) Lrx   Raymond loves everybody.
2. (∃x) Lrx   Raymond loves somebody.
3. (∃x) Lxr   Somebody loves Raymond.
4. (x) Lxr   Everybody loves Raymond.
5. (x) ~Lxr   Nobody loves Raymond.
6. (x) ~Lrx   Raymond does not love anyone.
7. ~(x) Lrx   Raymond does not love everybody.
8. ~(x) Lxr   Not everybody loves Raymond.
9. (∃x) ~Lxr   Someone does not love Raymond.
10. (∃x) ~Lrx   There is someone Raymond does not love.
11. ~(∃x) Lxr   There does not exist anyone who loves Raymond.
12. ~(∃x) Lrx   There does not exist anyone whom Raymond loves.
13. ~(∃x) ~Lxr   There isn't anyone who doesn't love Raymond.
14. ~(∃x) ~Lrx   There isn't anyone whom Raymond doesn't love.
15. ~(x) ~Lxr   Not everyone does not love Raymond.
16. ~(x) ~Lrx   Not everyone is not loved by Raymond.

You need to study this list to make sure that you understand it. You need to be able to go in either direction: you should be able to translate from the symbolic notation into English, or from English into the symbolic notation.

Part of what is going on in these examples is that the order of the r and the x switches. As you know from English, order matters: "Dog bites man" means something very different from "Man bites dog."

However, the more important thing going on here is that you have all the different ways of negating universals. If you look through them, you'll make some important discoveries. First of all, look at the English and compare 4 with 13. What is the difference between saying "everybody loves Raymond" and "there isn't anyone who doesn't love Raymond"? Logically speaking, there is no difference at all. These two are saying the same thing. "Everybody loves Raymond" means that every member of the universe loves Raymond; "there isn't anyone who doesn't love Raymond" means that if you interview every single member of the universe, you won't find a single one who does not love Raymond. But in logic you have only two options: true or false. If you can't find a single one who does not love Raymond, then they all do love Raymond. Logically speaking, these two say the exact same thing; which means that the two symbolic expressions are logically identical. "Not anyone does not" means "everyone does." Here is your first quantifier replacement rule:

$(x) Px \equiv \sim(\exists x) \sim Px$

You can probably start to guess what sort of pattern is going to emerge here.

Now look again at the English and compare lines 3 and 15. What is the difference between saying that somebody loves Raymond, and saying that not everyone does not love Raymond? Again, logically speaking, there is no difference at all. When you say that not everyone does not love Raymond, you are saying that there is an exception to the rule, there is somebody who does not fit into the group of people who do not love Raymond. All those people over there do not love Raymond, but there is someone who is not in that group. Why? Because there is someone who does love Raymond. Remember that we are assuming there are only two groups: either you are for Raymond or you are against him. If you are not in the group of people who do not love Raymond, then you are in the group of people who do love Raymond; in other words, somebody loves Raymond. Here is you next quantifier replacement rule:

$(\exists x) Px \equiv \sim(x) \sim Px$

Notice that this is very much like the previous replacement rule. Each quantifier can be replaced by the other quantifier, as long as you put a negation before and after the replacement quantifier.

Now look again at the English and compare lines 5 and 11. Line 5 says that for all x, x does not love Raymond. Everyone is someone who does not love Raymond, i.e. nobody loves Raymond. Line 11 says that there isn't even a single member of the universe who does loves Raymond, i.e. nobody loves Raymond. Again, logically speaking, these two say exactly the same thing, so here is your next quantifier replacement rule:

$(x) \sim Px \equiv \sim(\exists x) Px$

When you pull the negation out in front of the universal quantifier, you have to change the universal to the existential quantifier. What do you suppose will happen when you pull the negation out in front of the existential quantifier?

Look at the English and compare lines 9 and 8. Line 9 says that there is somebody who does not love Raymond. Line 8 says that not everybody loves Raymond. How could not everybody love Raymond? That could be true only if there is at least one member of the universe who does not love Raymond. Again, these two are saying the same thing, so here is your next quantifier replacement rule:

$(\exists x) \sim Lxr \equiv \sim(x) Lxr$

Just like the last one, you can pull the negation out to the front, but you have to switch the existential to the universal quantifier.

There is even more in these examples that is logically important, but before we move on, let me collect all of the quantifier replacement rules so you can compare them. Also, here are the names of the rules you may use in derivations.

Quantifier Negation (QN): $\sim(\exists x) Px \equiv (x) \sim Px$
Quantifier Negation (QN): $\sim(x) Px \equiv (\exists x) \sim Px$
Quantifier Exchange (QE): $(\exists x) Px \equiv \sim(x) \sim Px$
Quantifier Exchange (QE): $(x) Px \equiv \sim(\exists x) \sim Px$

Quantifier Negation (QN) works in two ways: (a) the negation of an existential is the same as a universal negation, and (b) the negation of a universal is the same as the existential of a negation. Quantifier exchange (QE) works in two ways: (a) an existential affirmation is the same as the negation of a universal negation, and (b) a universal affirmation is the same as the negation of an existential negation.

Now, memorize that last paragraph, and say it 3 times really fast.

CHAPTER 8: PREDICATES AND QUANTIFIERS

Section 6: The Square of Opposition.

Compare (x) Px and (x) ~Px. The first one says that everything is P and the second one says that everything is not P. Those are exact opposites; they both go to opposite extremes. They are both universal generalizations, but they generalize exactly the opposite claim. If P stands for "is pink", then (x) Px says that everything is pink, and (x) ~Px says that everything is not pink, i.e. nothing is pink. This is the all or nothing extreme.

When two expressions go to opposite extremes, logicians say that the two expressions are "contraries." You've probably heard (or been part of) an infantile argument where a disagreement between two immature people escalates beyond all reason.

Bobby: I like strawberry ice cream.
Kenny: Yuk! That stuff is terrible, I hate it.
Bobby: It's not terrible! I like it and so do a lot of other people.
Kenny: They do not! In fact, *nobody* likes strawberry ice cream!
Bobby: Yes they do! *Everybody* likes strawberry ice cream!

Bobby and Kenny are clearly exaggerating; they are going to opposite extremes. You can tell that their opposite claims are extreme because there is a more moderate middle ground. Let me show you the middle ground:

Extreme Claim: Everybody likes strawberry ice cream.
Moderate Claim: Somebody likes strawberry ice cream.
Extreme Claim: Nobody likes strawberry ice cream.

This is the key to the logical concept of "contraries." There is a moderate middle ground between the two extremes, which shows that both of the extreme claims could be false. They could both be wrong because they are going to extremes.

Compare this to a different pair of claims. Look again at the list of Raymond claims and compare 4 and 8. Here they are again:

(x) Lxr   Everybody loves Raymond.
~(x) Lxr   Not everybody loves Raymond.

The opposition here is just like the opposition between lines 3 and 11.

(∃x) Lxr   There is someone who loves Raymond.
~(∃x) Lxr   There is not someone who loves Raymond.

You might imagine our two squabbling little kids having a different sort of argument about strawberry ice cream. Instead of going to opposite extremes, the argument might go like this:

Bobby: I like strawberry ice cream.
Sally: Yuk! That stuff is terrible, I hate it.
Bobby: It's not terrible.
Sally: Yes it is.
Bobby: No its not.
Sally: Yes it is.
Bobby: No its not.

... and on and on. In this case, Bobby and Sally are not going to opposite extremes. You know this because there is no moderate middle ground in between their claims.

Strawberry ice cream is terrible.
Strawberry ice cream is not terrible.

Here there is no middle ground: either it is or it isn't terrible. If Sally had said that strawberry ice cream is terrible, and then Bobby said that strawberry ice cream is terrific, then he would be going to the opposite extreme and there would be a moderate middle ground, i.e. strawberry ice cream is ok, its not terrific but its not terrible. But in the argument I gave you, Bobby doesn't go to the opposite extreme, all he does is *contradict* Sally. Logicians call these two claims "contradictories." Contradictories are like contraries because again, both claims cannot be true. The difference is that with contraries, there is a middle ground, both of the extremes could be false; not so with contradictories. When you have two contradictory claims, both cannot be true, but both cannot be false either, one of them has got to be true.

149

Two Claims are **Logically Contradictory** if and only if, because of their logical form, (a) they cannot both be true simultaneously and (b) they cannot both be false simultaneously.

Two Claims are **Logically Contrary** if and only if, because of their logical form, (a) they cannot both cannot be true simultaneously, but (b) they can both be false simultaneously.

The simple way to remember this is to remember that contradiction is simply saying "no, that's not true" while being contrary is going to the opposite extreme and leaving a more moderate middle ground. Another way to remember the difference is to remember that "all-or-nothing" is contrary, but "all-or-not-all" is contradictory.

Out of the Raymond sentences we have found four logical equivalences, and we have found the difference between contraries and contradictories. There is one more pair of differences you need to see. Before I give you the new pair, think of the pairs I have already given you. I have shown you logical equivalences, and those are two different expressions which are saying exactly the same thing. Then I showed you contradictories and contraries, which are expressions saying the opposite things. The next pair will be pairs of claims which in a way say the same thing, but in a way say something different. In order to see the new pair, I want to show you what I have secretly been working with in this section. Aristotle discovered what has come to be called a "Square of Opposition," and it is from this square that I have been drawing the distinctions I've shown you. You will see the new distinction when you look at the square. Here it is.

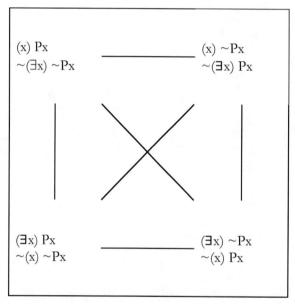

There are important connections in every direction here. First of all, notice that I have listed the logical equivalences in each of the corner boxes. The two expressions in each of the corner boxes are logically equivalent. The two diagonal lines in the center identify contradictories and the horizontal line at the top identifies contraries. What remains is for you to see what the bottom horizontal line identifies, and what the two vertical lines identify.

Start with the bottom horizontal line, and think of the expressions that use the existential quantifier. The lower left box says that there does exist something that is P, while the lower right box says that something exists which is not P. For example, if P stands for "is pink" then the lower left box says that something is pink and the lower right box says that something is not pink. Notice that unlike contraries and contradictories, both of these claims can be simultaneously true. Bobby and Kenny are not arguing if Bobby says that something in the room is pink while Kenny says that something in the room is not pink. They might be playing a game. Kenny says, "I see something which is *not pink*" (a blue ribbon) and then Bobby has to spot something that *is* pink (e.g. a pink ribbon). They might both win this game in the sense that they can both be right. Kenny does see something which is pink, and Bobby sees something which is not pink. In this case, both claims can be true at the same time. (Sometimes these claims are called "subcontraries").

Can they both be wrong? Suppose Bobby looks at the ribbon more closely and sees that it actually isn't pink, it is actually orange. And suppose he looks and looks, and he cannot find anything pink in the room at all. So "something is pink" is false. Could it also be false to say that "something is not pink"? No. If it is not true to say that something is pink, then it has to be true that something is not pink. If you can't find anything that is pink, that automatically means that you've found lots of things that are not pink. Both of these claims cannot be false at the same time. One of them has to be true. Again, they might both be true, but at least one of them must be true.

These two claims are called "Sub-contraries" or "Complements." Notice that the word "Complement" is different from the word "Compliment." A "compliment" is a kind word, while a "complement" completes your claim or gives you the other side. Something is pink, but on the other side, something else is not pink. The scale balances out. Now compare the definitions of contradictories, contraries and complements.

Two Claims are **Logically Contradictory** if and only if, because of their logical form, (a) they cannot both be true simultaneously and (b) they cannot both be false simultaneously.

Two Claims are **Logically Contrary** if and only if, because of their logical form, (a) they cannot both cannot be true simultaneously, but (b) they can both be false simultaneously.

Two claims are **Logically Complementary** if and only if, because of their logical form, (1) they can both be true simultaneously, but (2) they cannot both be false simultaneously.

(x)Px contradicts ~(x)Px because the second one simply negates the first one, and you remember from doing truth tables that P & ~P is a contradiction. If one person says "yes" and the other says "no," then they are simply contradicting one another. But it is equally true that (x)Px contradicts (∃x)~Px: (∃x)~Px is logically equivalent to ~(x)Px, and ~(x)Px is simply the negation of (x)Px. So if one claim is simply the negation of the other, then the two claims are contradictory; but if one of the two claims is logically equivalent to the negation of the other, then in this case also the two claims are contradictory.

Contrary claims do not directly contradict one another. If Al says that "everybody loves cherry ice cream" and Betty says that "nobody loves cherry ice cream" then they are going way beyond simply contradicting one another. Betty isn't simply saying, "no, you are wrong," she is saying to Al "the truth is completely the opposite of what you are saying." Obviously they can't both be saying something true. Fortunately in this case, with such extreme positions, it is easy to put them to the test: pick a sample person and give them some cherry ice cream. Let's use Joe. Al is going to predict that Joe loves cherry ice cream and Betty is going to predict that Joe does not love cherry ice cream.

Lx = x loves cherry ice cream
J = Joe

Given this index, then Al predicts Lj and Betty predicts ~Lj. But Lj and ~Lj are contradictory. So although Al and Betty are not uttering *contradictions*, what they say logically entails contradictory claims, and so they are uttering *contrary* claims.

Complementary claims complete each other; they emphasize two sides of an issue and so they go together naturally. (∃x)Lx means that someone loves cherry ice cream, and (∃x)~Lx means that someone does not love cherry ice cream. That's fair, even, reasonable and balanced. Some do, but on the flip side, some don't. If Al says," some people love cherry ice cream" and Betty says, "Yea, but some people do not love it," then they are not really arguing or disagreeing at all – they are just emphasizing two different, compatible sides of the issue. But notice what happens if we negate both of their claims (i.e. if we imagine what would happen if both were false):

Negate Al's claim: ~(∃x)Lx
Negate Betty's claim: ~(∃x)~Lx

Those two claims do not contradict one another, but they do entail a contradiction, and so they cannot both be true. You can see how to derive a contradiction if you remember Quantifier Negation (QN) and Quantifier Exchange (QE).

Apply QN to the negation of Al's claim: (x)~Lx
Apply QE to the negation of Betty's claim: (x)Lx

Now you can see the contradiction. Both of these are universally quantified expressions, and so both of them apply to everybody. And if they apply to everybody, then they apply to Joe. Now the negation of Al's claim says ~Lj (i.e. Joe does not love cherry ice cream) and the negation of Betty's claim says Lj (i.e. Joe does love cherry ice cream, and Lj & ~Lj is a simple contradiction. Avoid contradictions at all costs, and so if Al and Betty are not arguing, if they are uttering perfectly complementary claims, then do not negate them both or you will end up with a contradiction. Leave complementary claims alone: they can both be true together and so no one is arguing with anyone else, but they cannot both be false, if you negate both of their claims, then you end up with a contradiction.

It is important to notice the "because of their logical form" in the definitions of contradictory, contrary and complement. Here's an example. Suppose Al and Betty got in a huge fight and were throwing cherry ice cream at each other so now they refuse even to be in the same room with one another. In this case, what would we say about the following claims:

A = Al is chatting pleasantly at the dinner table
B = Betty is chatting pleasantly at the dinner table

Given the fact that Al and Betty are so mad at each other right now, we say that both A and B cannot simultaneously be true: if Al were at the dinner table with Betty, they would both be yelling at each other and throwing food; they would not be chatting pleasantly. Given the background information about the status of their relationship, we know that A and B cannot both be true, but that doesn't make A and B *logically contradictory* or *logically contrary*. They are just *factually contradictory* or *factually contrary*. If one is a fact, then given everything else we know, we can reasonable guess that the other must not be a fact. But this is real-world knowledge, not logical deduction. So be careful with these rough characterizations: they can be helpful, but always remind yourself that they are not definitions.

Think about the definitions and you will see that there is one case missing. What sort of claims do you have when (a) both can be true, but (b) both can be false? Those are just two different claims. "Joe is a barber" and "Joe is a mobster" could both be true but they could both be false. Joe could be a mobster barber, but he could be an actor model. There is no special name for pairs of claims which could both be true but could both be false.

Can both be true simultaneously?	Can both be false simultaneously?		
No	No	=	Contradictories
No	Yes	=	Contraries
Yes	No	=	Complements
Yes	Yes	=	*no name*

The final relation you need to see is the relation which holds between the claims at the ends of the two vertical lines. Start with the pair on the left, and just think about the positive versions of each expression:

(x) Px

(∃x) Px

The first one says that everything is P and the second one says that something is P. Notice that this is one of those pairs where both can be true and both can be false. However, there clearly is some relation between the two. The first thing you notice is that the top one is a universal generalization while the bottom one is only an existential claim. The top says that absolutely everything has a certain quality: everything is P (e.g. everything has the quality of being pink). The bottom one makes the much more modest claim that there is at least one thing that has the quality of being P (e.g. there is at least one pink thing). The central difference here is quantity, not quality.

Notice also that if the top one is true, then the bottom one has to be true. If absolutely everything is pink, then there does exist at least one pink thing. Notice that the reverse is not true. It could be true that there is a pink thing without it being true that everything is pink.

These things are also true of the pairs of claims at the ends of the vertical line on the right hand side of the Square of Opposition.

(x) ~Px

(∃x) ~Px

The top one says that everything is non-pink, and the bottom one says that there is something that is non-pink. The top and the bottom differ only in quantity, not quality. Also, if the top one is true, then the bottom one must also be true, but the reverse does not hold: the bottom could be true while the top is false.

In both of these cases, the top expression is called the alternant and the bottom expression is called the subalternate. Perhaps the easiest and best way to give you the idea of the difference between the alternant and the subalternate is to remind you of the difference between genus and species. The scientific name for the polar bear is *Ursus maritimus*, and the scientific name for the grizzly bear is *Ursus arctos*. They are different species in the same genus. *Ursus* is a genus of bears, and there are two different kinds of bears in that genus: polar bears and grizzly bears. If I told you that there is a member of the *Ursus* genus in the next zoo enclosure, you might be able to guess which one: either it is a polar bear, or it is a grizzly bear. You have at least these two alternatives. It might be a polar bear, or alternatively it might be a grizzly bear. The polar bear is one alternate, the grizzly bear is the other alternate. But they are alternates under the genus, so they are subalternates. The altern*ant* is the generic type which gets specified in various alternate ways.

This is why the expressions at the tops of the vertical lines are called the alternants, and why the expressions at the bottoms of the vertical lines are called the subalternates. At the tops we have universal (generic) generalizations: "everything is P" or "everything is not-P." At the bottoms we have existential (specific) claims: "something is P" or "something is not-P." So here is a formal definition.

Two Quantified Claims are **Subalterns** if and only if (1) they differ only in quantity, and (2) the universal claim (the **alternant**) implies, but is not implied by the existential claim (the **subalternate**).

Chapter Conclusion.

In this chapter we plugged a gap in your understanding of symbolic logic. Now you know how to deal logically with claims that involve the words "all," "some" and "none." The only thing that remains is for you to learn how to use these quantifiers in derivations.

Things to memorize from this Chapter:
The four pairs of logical equivalences
Quantifier Negation (QN) $\sim(\exists x) Px \equiv (x) \sim Px$
Quantifier Negation (QN) $\sim(x) Px \equiv (\exists x) \sim Px$
Quantifier Exchange (QE) $(\exists x) Px \equiv \sim(x) \sim Px$
Quantifier Exchange (QE) $(x) Px \equiv \sim(\exists x) \sim Px$

The four types of paired claims

Two Claims are **Logically Contradictory** if and only if, because of their logical form, (a) they cannot both be true simultaneously and (b) they cannot both be false simultaneously.

Two Claims are **Logically Contrary** if and only if, because of their logical form, (a) they cannot both cannot be true simultaneously, but (b) they can both be false simultaneously.

Two claims are **Logically Complementary** if and only if, because of their logical form, (1) they can both be true simultaneously, but (2) they cannot both be false simultaneously.

Two Quantified Claims are ***Subalterns*** if and only if (1) they differ only in quantity, and (2) the universal claim (the ***alternant***) implies, but is not implied by the existential claim (the ***subalternate***).

You should be able to draw the Square of Opposition

Exercises for Chapter 8
Exercise 8.1: Extremely Simple Predicate Translations. *Use the index below to translate the following English sentences into predicate logic (problems 1-10), and the following predicate formulae into English sentences (11-20).*

Predicates
Gx = x is Greek
Rx = x is Roman
Wx = x is wealthy
Px = x is poor

Individuals
p = Plato
s = Socrates
j = Julius
n = Nero

Example 1
Problem: Plato is Greek
Solution: Gp

Example 2
Problem: Rn
Solution: Nero is Roman

1. Socrates is Greek.
2. Julius is Greek.
3. Nero is Greek.
4. Plato is wealthy.
5. Julius is wealthy.

6. Socrates is poor.
7. Julius is poor.
8. Nero is Roman.
9. Nero is poor.
10. Plato is Roman.

11. Rj
12. Wp
13. Pp
14. Gs
15. Ws

16. Rp
17. Rn
18. Wn
19. Pj
20. Ps

Exercise 8.2: Simple Predicate Translations. *Use the index from 8.1 to translate the following English sentences into predicate logic (problems 1-10), and the following predicate formulae into English sentences (11-20).*

Example 1
Problem: Plato is a wealthy Greek
Solution: Wp & Gp

Example 2
Problem: Rn → Wn
Solution: If Nero is Roman, then Nero is wealthy

1. Socrates is a poor Greek.
2. Either Plato is wealthy or Socrates is poor.

3. If Plato is Greek, then Socrates is Greek.
4. Plato is wealthy if and only if Socrates is poor.
5. If Plato is not Greek, then Socrates is not Greek.

6. Nero is wealthy, or Plato is wealthy.
7. If Nero is Roman, then either Julius is Roman or Julius is Greek.
8. Nero is poor and Socrates is poor.
9. Nero and Socrates are both poor.
10. Julius and Plato are both wealthy.

11. Gp v Gs
12. Wp v Ws
13. Gs & Gp
14. Wp & Gp
15. Wj & Wp

16. Rn → Rj
17. Rj → Gp
18. Gp ↔ Gs
19. ~Wj → ~Wp
20. Wp → ~Ws

Exercise 8.3: Predicate Translations. *Use the index from 8.1 to translate the following English sentences into predicate logic (problems 1-10), and the following predicate formulae into English sentences (11-20).*

Example 1
Problem: If Plato is a wealthy Greek, then either Socrates or Nero is poor.
Solution: (Wp & Gp) → (Ps v Pn)

Example 2
Problem: Rn → (Wn v Pn)
Solution: If Nero is Roman, then Nero is either wealthy or poor.

1. Socrates is a poor Greek, or Plato is a poor Greek.
2. If Plato is a poor Greek, then Socrates is a wealthy Greek.
3. If Plato is a wealthy Greek, then Nero is a wealthy Roman.
4. Plato is a wealthy Greek if and only if Socrates is a poor Greek.
5. Plato is wealthy, and he is not Roman.

6. Either Plato is a wealthy Greek, or he is a wealthy Roman.
7. Either Plato is a poor Greek, or he is not a poor Roman.
8. Julius is not poor, but he is Roman.
9. Julius is wealthy only if he is Roman.
10. Plato is a wealthy Greek if and only if Julius is a wealthy Roman.

11. (Gp v Gs) → (Wp v Ws)
12. (Gp v Gs) → (Rj & Rn)
13. (Wp & Gp) ↔ (Ps & Gs)
14. Rj v (Rn → Wn)
15. (Rj & Wj) → Pn

16. ~Wn → ~Rn
17. ~(Wp & Ws)
18. ~(Wp v Ws)
19. ~(Gp → Rs)
20. ~Gp → Rs

Exercise 8.4: Extremely Simple Quantifier Translations. *Use the index below to translate the following English sentences into predicate logic (problems 1-10), and the following quantified formulae into English sentences (11-20).*

Bx = x is beautiful
Sx = x is smart
Txy = x is taller than y
Lxy = x loves y
d = Doug
g = Gilda

Example 1
Problem: Everyone is beautiful.
Solution: (x) Bx

Example 2
Problem: (∃x) Tgx
Solution: Gilda is taller than someone.

1. Someone is beautiful.
2. Someone is smart.
3. Someone is both beautiful and smart.
4. Someone is either beautiful or smart.
5. Everyone is smart.

6. Doug loves someone.
7. Someone loves Doug.
8. Everyone is taller than Gilda
9. Gilda is taller than everyone.
10. Someone is taller than Gilda.

11. (y) By
12. (z) Sy
13. (x) Bx & Sx
14. (∃x) Sx v Bx
15. (∃y) Sy & By

16. (∃y) By
17. (∃x) Sx
18. (w) Lwg
19. (z) Lgz
20. (∃x) Txg

Exercise 8.5: Simple Quantifier Translations. *Use the index from 8.4 to translate the following English sentences into predicate logic (problems 1-10), and the following quantified formulae into English sentences (11-20).*

Example 1
Problem: Whoever is beautiful is also smart.
Solution: (x)(Bx → Sx)

Example 2
Problem: (∃x)(~Sx → ~Bx)
Solution: Someone is not beautiful if they are not smart.

1. Whoever is smart is beautiful.
2. Whoever Gilda loves is loved by Gilda.
3. Gilda loves whoever loves her.
4. Everyone either loves Gilda or is loved by Gilda.
5. Whoever loves Gilda is also loved by Gilda.

6. If anyone is taller than Gilda, then Gilda is not taller than they are.

7. If someone is taller than Gilda, then Gilda is not taller than they are.
8. If everyone is taller than Gilda, then there is someone than whom Gilda is taller.
9. If Gilda is taller than everyone, then Gilda is taller than Doug.
10. If Doug is taller than Gilda, then someone is taller than Gilda.

11. (z) Bz v Sz
12. (x) Bx → Sx
13. (x) Txg → Txd
14. (y) ~Tyg → ~Txd
15. (∃x) Txd & ~Txg

16. (w) Lwg ↔ Lgw
17. (∃x) Sx & Lgx
18. (∃y) ~Bx & Ldx
19. (x) Lxg → Lgx
20. (x) Lgx → Lxg

Exercise 8.6: Quantifier Translations. *Use the following index to translate the following English sentences into predicate logic (problems 1-10), and the following quantified formulae into English sentences (11-20).*

Mx = x is male
Fx = x is female
Pxy = x is a parent of y
Sxy = x is a sibling of y
h = Hunter
j = Jayden

Example 1
Problem: Everyone has a mother.
Solution: (x)(∃y)(Fy & Pyx)

Example 2
Problem: (∃x)(∃y)(Pxy & Pyj)
Solution: Jayden has a grandparent.

1. Hunter has a brother.
2. Jayden has a sister.
3. Hunter has both a brother and a sister.
4. Jayden has both a mother and a father.
5. Jayden has an aunt on her mother's side.
6. Everyone has a grandfather.
7. Whoever has a father also has a mother.
8. By definition, whoever has a sibling is a sibling.
9. By definition, whoever has a brother is a brother.
10. Someone has a grandson or a granddaughter.

11. (∃x) (Mx & Pxj)
12. (∃y) (Fy & Pjy)
13. (∃x)(∃y) [(Mx & Fy) & (Pxj & Pyj)]
14. (z) (Mz & Pzj)
15. (x)(∃y) [(My & Syx) v (Fy & Syx)]
16. (∃x)(y) Fx & Pxy
17. (x) [(∃y)(Mx & Pxy) ↔ (∃z)(Mz & Pzx)]
18. (∃x) (Mx & Sxj) → (∃y) (My & Pyj)
19. (x) (∃y) (∃z) (My & Syz) & Pzx
20. (w) [((∃x)(∃y) (Mx & (Sxy & Pyw)) → [(∃z)(∃w1) Fz & (Szw1 & Pw1w))]

CHAPTER 9: DERIVATIONS WITH QUANTIFIERS

Now that you understand quantifiers, and all the important distinctions that can be made using them, it is time to learn how to use them in derivations. If you look back at Chapter 1, you'll see that we began by considering the difference between an argument that said *most* pigs like to have their bellies rubbed, and one that said *all* pigs like to have their bellies rubbed. The difference made one argument invalid and the other one valid, but it hasn't been until this chapter that you will be able to deal with the difference logically.

Section 1: Preliminary Issues.

Before I introduce the four derivation rules that deal specifically with quantifiers (i.e. introduction and elimination rules for the universal and existential quantifiers), it is important to touch on a couple of preliminary issues. First of all, quantifiers don't necessarily make a significant difference in a derivation. Here is a simple example.

Problem: {(x) Px, (x) Px → (x) Qx} ⊢ (x) Qx
Solution:

1	(x) Px	P
2	(x) Px → (x) Qx	P
3	(x) Qx	1,2 MP

This is just a simple modus ponens argument; the quantifiers are irrelevant. Why? Ask yourself this question: what is the main logical operator of premise 2? What is the primary logical *operator* in premise 2? Answer: the arrow. Premise 2 is just a conditional claim; premise 2 says if antecedent, then consequent. Premise 1 affirms the antecedent, and the conclusion affirms the consequent. That is modus ponens.

The only time you need the special derivation rules for quantifiers is when a quantifier is the primary logical operator of a claim. For example, consider this argument:

Hx = x is human
Mx = x is mortal
s = Socrates

1	(x) (Hx → Mx)	P
2	Hs	P
3	Ms	1,2 ???

This argument says that all humans are mortal, Socrates is human, so Socrates is mortal. That argument is clearly valid, but it is not, as it stands, modus ponens. For modus ponens, you have to have a conditional claim and then affirm the antecedent, but premise 1 is not a conditional claim, it is a universal generalization. Also, in spite of the fact that premise 1 does contain a conditional claim within it, premise 2 does not affirm the antecedent of that conditional. The antecedent of that conditional is Hx, but the second premise doesn't affirm Hx, it affirms Hs, which is different. So you can't do this derivation yet; but soon you will, and you'll see that it is pretty easy to do.

So the first preliminary issue is that just because quantifiers are involved in some of the claims of an argument, that doesn't necessarily mean that the quantifier rules will be used in the derivation. Quantifiers may or may not complicate the derivation. You simply have to make sure that you locate the main logical operator of each claim.

The next preliminary issue has to do with your index when you have quantified claims. A universally quantified claim says that something is true of every member of the universe. For example, given the index above, (x) Hx says that every member of the universe is human. That is a false claim, because, for example, bears are not human, but they are members of the universe. Planets, stars, comets, electrons, desks, countries, kangaroos and so on are all members of the universe, but none of them are human either. But suppose the person who said this meant something a little different. Suppose the author who said "everyone is human" didn't really mean "every member of the known universe is a human being." Suppose the author really meant simply to say that every *person* is human. Implicitly this person had a more restricted "universe" in mind. If you restrict your "universe" to all people, then it may be true to say that "everyone is human." Remember our "Principle of Charity." Try to give others the benefit of the doubt. The way logicians do this when it comes to quantifiers is to specify what they call the "Universe of Discourse." That just means you need to specify what you are talking about, you need to specify the set of things you are talking about. You may be talking about everything in the known, physical universe, but you may have a more limited range of things in mind. Consider this example.

UD: Things
Mx = x is mortal

In this short index, "UD" stands for "Universe of Discourse." In this case, the Universe of Discourse is absolutely everything. So (x) Mx means that everything in the universe is mortal. Compare that index with this one:

UD: Human beings
Mx = x is mortal

Given the previous universe of discourse, (x) Mx meant that everything in the universe is mortal, but given this universe of discourse (x) Mx means that every human being is mortal.

So far I have given you very large universes of discourse. This doesn't have to be true. You can have a very small universe of discourse. For example, someone might say, "Everyone has had to listen to one of the boss's long, boring speeches." Obviously they don't mean that every member of the known universe has had to listen to one of the boss's long, boring speeches; and obviously they don't mean that all human beings have had to listen to one of those speeches. All they mean, probably, is that everyone who works in that office has had to listen to one of those speeches. This might involve only a dozen or so people, if it is a small office. Your universe of discourse can be quite small.

In fact, if you want, you can arbitrarily make up a really small universe of discourse. You can arbitrarily say that Socrates, the planet Mars, and your left shoe make up the universe of discourse.

UD: Socrates, Mars, my left shoe
Hxy = x is heavier than y
Pxy = x is prettier than y
s = Socrates
m = Mars
l = my left shoe

Notice that here I have a complete list of every member of universe of discourse. I have no idea why you would want to set up something like this, but the rules of logic permit it. You can make your universe of discourse anything you want, but you have to make sure that you tell your audience what your universe of discourse is. Many misunderstandings are caused by one person assuming one universe of discourse, but members of the audience assuming a different universe of discourse. If you don't come right out and state what your assumptions are, if you don't specify what your assumed universe of discourse is, you might be completely misunderstood.

Also, when you list individual constants, you *must* list all the ones that will be used in the derivation. You *may* list extra individuals. It is permissible to give too much information; it is not permissible to give too little information.

The third, and final, preliminary issue has to do with the Square of Opposition. I'm going to give you the Square again, but I'm going to include traditional translations to go with each corner.

UD: Human Beings
Mx = x is mortal

```
All humans                    No humans
are mortal.    ——————————    are mortal.
  (x) Mx                       (x) ~Mx
     |                            |
     |                            |
     |                            |
     |                            |
     |                            |
Some humans                   Some humans
are mortal.    ——————————    are not mortal.
  (∃x) Mx                      (∃x) ~Mx
```

This Square of Opposition gives you the basis for translating "all", "some" and "no" or "none" into symbolic logic using quantifiers. As I take you through the various derivation rules for quantifiers, we will develop your ability to translate between English quantifiers and symbolic quantifiers.

Section 2: Universal Elimination & Existential Introduction.

By far the easiest quantifier derivation rule is Universal Elimination (UE). Think about the rule first. With a universal quantifier, something is said to be true about every single member of the universe of discourse. If that is true, then at any point in your derivation, you can plug in an individual constant for the variable in the universally quantified expression. If one of my premises says that every human is mortal, then at any point in my derivation I have every right to say that Socrates is mortal, since Socrates is a human, and my premise says that every human is mortal. So here is a simple derivation using Universal Elimination.

Problem: All humans are mortal. So Socrates is mortal.
Solution:
UD: Human Beings
Mx = x is mortal
s = Socrates

1	(x) Mx	P
2	Ms	1 UE

This is an extremely easy derivation. There is only one premise, but the conclusion follows validly because of the word "all." The premise applies to absolutely every member of the universe of discourse, and that gives us the logical right to plug in for x any name whatsoever.

The reason that derivation was so easy, was that the universe of discourse was human beings. It is just a little bit harder if we change the universe of discourse. Nevertheless, the derivation still isn't very hard.

Problem: All humans are mortal. Socrates is human. So Socrates is mortal.
Solution:
UD: Living beings
Hx = x is human
Mx = x is mortal
s = Socrates

1	(x) (Hx → Mx)	P
2	Hs → Ms	1 UE
3	Hs	P
4	Ms	2,3 MP

Just by changing the universe of discourse, we have changed the derivation from 2 lines to 4 lines. Nevertheless, because of the word "all" the derivation is still pretty easy. Because the first premise says that *all* humans are mortal, the first premise applies to Socrates. It applies to Plato, Aristotle, you and me and any other person you can think of, but the argument just mentioned Socrates, so stick with him. The first premise tells us that for every member of the universe of discourse, if that member is human, then it is mortal. So that goes for Socrates, since he is in the universe of discourse. If Socrates is human, then he is mortal. But our second premise says that Socrates is human, and so by modus ponens it follows that Socrates is mortal.

Universal Elimination (UE): in a universally quantified expression, any individual constant may be substituted for the universally quantified variable, provided that the individual constant is substituted for every occurrence of the variable.

Basically, this is common sense. If it is true that absolutely every single human being is mortal, then you can pick any human being at all—past, present, future, actual, hypothetical, imaginary—and logically infer that the particular human you picked is mortal.

But be careful. A rule of logic can be like a contract: you have to read the "fine print." These derivation rules for quantifiers are logical only if you abide by certain restrictions; they work, only *provided that* you work within the specified restraints. A "provided that" restriction is sometimes called a "*proviso*." Notice that Universal Elimination (UE) has a proviso: "…provided that the individual constant is substituted for *every occurrence* of the variable." If the variable occurs

CHAPTER 9: DERIVATIONS WITH QUANTIFIERS

more than once, then to use UE logically, you have to substitute the individual constant for every single occurrence in just one step. Here's a clear example of why you have to do that.

UD: Living beings
Bx = x is a bachelor
Mx = x is married
a = Al
b = Betty

1 | (x) (Bx → ~Mx)   P
2 | (x) (Ba → ~Mx)   **MISTAKE! MISUSE OF UE!**

Notice that things have gone horribly wrong at this point in the derivation. We start in premise 1 with the perfectly ordinary and true claim that all bachelors are not married. Obviously that is true by the definition of what it is to be a bachelor. But we violated the "proviso" of UE when we brought Al into equation: we substituted Al in for only the first occurrence of the variable. That violates the logic of the rule. What would be logical would be to go from "all bachelors are not married" to "if Al is a bachelor, then Al is not married." That makes perfect sense. But step 2 of that derivation makes no logical sense at all: it says that for all x, if Al is a bachelor, then x is not married—which is crazy. Al's being a bachelor tells us only about Al, it doesn't tell us about anybody else. For example, look at what we could do, if we allowed step 2 to stand.

2 | (x) (Ba → ~Mx)   ?
3 | Ba → Mb   2 UE

If we accept step 2, then we really can use UE again and this time substitute Betty in for the universally quantified variable, because in step 2, the universally quantified variable occurs only once. But then if we do that, look at the nonsense we produce: step 3 claims that if Al is a bachelor, then Betty is not married. That's crazy; that's illogical. Al's being a bachelor has nothing to do with Betty being married or not. Those are two separate cases.

So take this to heart. Whenever you use UE, you must always check to see how many times the universally quantified variable is used in the expression, and make sure that you substitute the individual constant in for absolutely every occurrence of the variable. If you don't, then you are being illogical.

Here is a new index and some examples of Universal Elimination.
UD: Animals in the zoo
Px = x is a penguin
Lx = x is a lion
Tx = x is tame
Fx = x is ferocious
p = Penny the penguin
l = Larry the lion

English Sentence	Symbolic Translation	Sample Universal Elimination
1. All zoo animals are tame.	1. (x) Tx	1. Tp
2. Every zoo animal is ferocious.	2. (x) Fx	2. Fp
3. Every penguin is tame.	3. (x) (Px → Tx)	3. Pl → Tl
4. Every lion is ferocious.	4. (x) (Lx → Fx)	4. Lp → Fp

Notice that the third example is logically ok, but silly. The claim is that every penguin is tame, but when I did my universal elimination, I used "l" for Larry the lion: "If Larry the lion is a penguin, then Larry the lion is tame." Obviously Larry the lion is not a penguin. So why did I put him in? Answer: why not? The claim is a universally quantified claim, and so it is supposed to hold true for absolutely every single member of the universe of discourse. Well, Larry the lion is in the universe of discourse, so the claim must hold true of him. He's actually a lion, but hypothetically, *if he were a penguin*, then he would be tame. That follows logically if you accept that all penguins are tame. That is purely hypothetical, but it is perfectly logical.

Existential Introduction (EI) is almost as easy as Universal Elimination. I'll start with an example.

Problem: Socrates is mortal, so someone is mortal.

Solution:
UD: Human Beings
Mx = x is mortal
s = Socrates

1 | Ms   P
2 | (∃x) Mx   1 EI

Think about Existential Introduction as being almost the reverse of Universal Elimination. Universal Elimination goes from a quantifier to an individual, and Existential Introduction goes from an individual to a quantifier. Of course it is important that you are going to an *existential* quantifier instead of a universal quantifier. If you know that a certain claim is true of one person in particular, then you know that it is true of *someone*, you don't necessarily know that it is true of *everyone*.

Existential Introduction (EI): in an expression containing an individual constant, any instance of the individual constant may be replaced by an existentially quantified variable (you may but are not required to replace every instance of the individual constant with the existentially quantified variable).

The only reason that some people find this rule a little more difficult than Universal Elimination is simply that the inference seems so obvious it is not clear why anyone would ever want to make it. If you know that Socrates is mortal, then of course you know that *someone* is mortal, because you just said *who* is mortal. In real life, this may be true. But this may be important in real life. Our society is quite litigious: people sue other people for lots of reasons, sometimes for poor reasons. This gives us reason to be careful when we say things about other people, even if we are speaking the truth. They might sue you. Even if you win the lawsuit, it is no fun to be sued. Sometimes, even if you know exactly who did something, it might be safer for you to say "somebody did it" rather than to point the finger and say exactly who did it. Also, in criminal investigations, detectives often want to conceal from certain individuals how much they really know. Instead of naming names, they might use Existential Introduction to conceal from a suspect how close they are to proving that he did it. But even aside from its practical uses, Existential Introduction is an important rule, and one that you have to understand, because it helps display the logic of existential quantification. Here is an argument that includes a situation where you would need to use Existential Introduction.

Problem: Someone has managed to break both the pole vault and the high jump records. How do I know that? First of all, Alice broke the pole vault record. But look at that high jump she just made. She's broken that record too!
Solution:
UD: Athletes
Px = x has broken the pole vault record
Jx = x has broken the high jump record
a = Alice

1 | Pa   P
2 | Ja   P
3 | Pa & Ja   1,2 CI
4 | (∃x) (Px & Jx) 3EI

Notice that line 3 contains the individual constant "a" in two places. When you do Existential Introduction, you do not have to replace every single occurrence of the individual constant with a variable. Of course you have to leave everything else alone. Look carefully at this example.

Problem: Alice is taller than Bert, and so someone is taller than Bert.
Solution:
UD: People
Txy = x is taller than y
a = Alice
b = Bert

1 | Tab   P
2 | (∃x) Txb   1 EI

We wanted to conclude that someone is taller than Bert; we wanted the conclusion that there is some x such that x is taller than Bert. We knew that Alice fits the bill; Alice is taller than Bert, so we just did an existential introduction for Alice, and replaced the individual constant "a" with the variable "x." If we had wanted to conclude that Alice is taller than someone, we would have done this instead:

```
1 | Tab        P
2 | (∃x) Tax   1 EI
```

You can substitute the x for any variable you want. But of course you can't substitute one existential quantifier for more than one individual constant. You cannot let "x" stand for two different constants. Look what would happen if you did:

```
1 | Tab        P
2 | (∃x) Txx   Invalid
```

Translate that argument into English. The premise says that Alice is taller than Bert. No problem there. But think about what the conclusion says. The conclusion says that there exists an x such that x is taller than x. In other words, the conclusion says that someone is *taller than herself!* That makes no sense at all. If you want to take both variables out using Existential Introduction, you need a different variable for every constant, and you need to do it one step at a time. Here is an example.

Problem: Alice is taller than Bert, so someone is taller than someone.
Solution:
UD: People
Txy = x is taller than y
a = Alice
b = Bert

```
1 | Tab              P
2 | (∃x) Txb         1 EI
3 | (∃y)(∃x) Txy     2 EI
```

This is the correct way to do it. What we want is the claim that someone is taller than someone, i.e. there exists an x such that there exists a y such that x is taller than y. We built this up one step at a time. We start by replacing one of the individual constants with a variable, and in the next step we take out the next individual constant, making sure to use a different variable than the one we just used.

But even this may not be good enough. Remember that variables can stand for any individual in the entire universe of discourse, so the variable "x" can stand for Alice, but the variable "y" can also stand for Alice. Now, this isn't a big problem, because the existential quantifiers tell us only that somewhere in the universe there does exist an x and there does exist a y which stand in that relation to each other, i.e. the first is taller than the second. It doesn't tell us who x is or who y is. But what if you wanted to make it absolutely clear that when you said "someone is taller than someone" what you meant is that "someone is taller than someone *else*"? If you want to make it explicit that this "taller than" relation holds between two different people and not between someone and herself, then you have to add in a new predicate.

Problem: Alice is taller than Bert, so someone is taller than someone else.
Solution:
UD: People
Txy = x is taller than y
Ixy = x and y are the same person
a = Alice
b = Bert

```
1 | Tab                       P
2 | (∃x) (Txb & ~Ixb)         1 EI
3 | (∃y)(∃x) (Txy & ~Ixy)     2 EI
```

Since we need to specify that someone is taller than someone *else*, and since we are deriving that from the claim about Alice and Bert, we need to specify that Alice and Bert are two different people, and are not just two different names for one and the same person.

There is one more important thing to notice about Existential Introduction. Remember that in the definition of the rule it says that "in an expression with an individual constant, *any* instance of the individual constant may be replaced by an existentially quantified variable that is not already being used." Notice that it says "any" and not "every." If an individual constant appears more than once in an expression, and you want to use Existential Introduction, you do not have to replace every occurrence of the individual constant with a variable. Here is an example.

Problem: Carl is in love with himself, so at least one person loves Carl.
Solution:
UD: People
Lxy = x loves y
c = Carl

1 | Lcc   P
2 | (∃x) Lxc   1 EI

Here I simply replaced the first instance of the individual constant with the variable, and left the other instance alone. This is perfectly permissible. It makes sense for the very same reason that I just gave that last example about there being someone who is taller than someone *else*. A variable could conceivably stand for any of the individuals in the universe of discourse, but since Carl is in the universe of discourse, the variable can stand for Carl. If Carl loves himself, then someone in the universe of discourse loves him, namely, himself.

Section 3: Universal Introduction and Existential Elimination.

Universal Introduction is a bit more difficult. First I'll give you an argument where this rule is used, and then I'll explain the complications.

Problem: Everyone is human, but all humans are mortal. So everyone is mortal.
Solution:
UD: People
Hx = x is human
Mx = x is mortal
s = Socrates

1 | (x) Hx   P
2 | (x) (Hx → Mx)   P
3 | Hs   1 UE
4 | Hs → Ms   2 UE
5 | Ms   3,4 MP
6 | (x) Mx   5 UI

The thing you should notice, and what should worry you, is that we derive the claim in line 6 that everyone is mortal from the claim in line 5 that Socrates is mortal. Just because Socrates is mortal, does that mean we all are mortal? That doesn't make any sense, does it?

Actually, it makes perfect sense. Look again at the derivation, and notice how Socrates got into it at all. He doesn't show up in any of the premises. The premises say nothing at all about Socrates. So how does Socrates get into it? I could have chosen Plato, I could have chosen Aristotle, or any other person at all. The universe of discourse is all people, so the possibilities are almost unlimited. So how did I pick Socrates? Answer: he was chosen purely at random. That is the key to Universal Introduction. The only reason we can go from line 5 to line 6, the only reason we can go from "Socrates is mortal" to "Everyone is mortal" is because Socrates was chosen purely at random. I could have picked absolutely anyone at all, and the same conclusion would have resulted. It didn't matter that I picked Socrates, the same result would have followed if I had chosen any other member of the universe of discourse. The randomness of the choice of Socrates means that for the argument, Socrates is just a generic member of the universe of discourse. There is nothing true about him that isn't also true of every other member of the universe of discourse, so anything I can prove about him, I can prove about any else in the universe of discourse. That is what justifies introducing the universal quantifier.

Universal Introduction (UI): in an expression containing an individual constant, the individual constant may be replaced by a universally quantified variable provided that (a) the individual constant does not appear in any of the premises or governing hypotheses, and (b) every instance of the individual constant is replaced by the universally quantified variable.

Think of a universal quantifier as a kind of short hand. Instead of saying, "Adam was mortal, Eve was mortal, Cain was mortal, Abel was mortal ..." and listing every single human being who has ever lived, or will ever live, we just sum it all up in one short expression: (x) Mx. If we had unlimited resources, we could, at least in theory, list every single person and say of them that they are mortal, but why go to all that trouble when we can just use the quantified expression. That is how Universal Introduction works. In the above derivation, my premises really do entail the claim that every member of the universe of discourse is mortal. The fact that I picked Socrates is irrelevant. Given my premises, I could, at least in theory, go through every single member of the universe of discourse, and prove that each one is mortal. But why do that when I've got the handy short hand? Remember that you can use Universal Introduction only under special circumstances, i.e. when the premises really do entail something about every single member of the universe of discourse, so that your premises really would justify you in going through every single member of the universe of discourse and showing, "Yep, the conclusion is true of that one, and of that one, and of that one ..." Instead of listing every single one, just use the universally quantified expression.

Existential Elimination (EE) is the most difficult rule of all. Well, actually Existential Elimination is so difficult it is impossible. Think about it in comparison with the other three rules. Universal Elimination is easy because it says that something is true of everything in the universe of discourse, so you can eliminate the variable by substituting any individual constant you want. Existential Introduction is easy because you are already told that something is true of this particular individual, all you do is make the claim less definite, you say that it is true of *some* member of the universe of discourse. It is a bit odd that you would want to make some claim less definite rather than more definite, but it is clear that you can do it if you want to. Universal Introduction is a bit harder, but not much. You go from proving that something is true of some arbitrarily chosen generic member of the universe of discourse, and then instead of proving exactly the same thing about every single member, you just sum it up with the universal quantifier. What would Existential Elimination be? Existential Elimination would start with an existentially quantified claim, a claim of the form "there is some individual in the universe of discourse of whom this is true." You then have to pick which one it is true of. How could you possibly do that, especially if the universe of discourse is very large like "all people" or even "all things in the known universe"? I say to you, "I'm thinking of something which is mortal, guess what it is!" I say to you (∃x) Mx, and you have to pick the right individual constant. How do you do that?

The only way you can answer that is by guessing. "Is this what you have in mind? No. Is this it? No. Is this it? Yes? Ok, great!" In other words, there is no logical, principled way to know for sure which individual someone else has in mind unless they tell you. For example, they might do something like this:

1. (∃x) Gx
2. (∃x) Gx → Gs
∴ 3. Gs

They might begin in premise 1 by saying that they have something in mind which is G, and then they might say that if something is G, then Socrates is G. So you know that they have Socrates in mind. But if they don't come right out like this and tell you who they have in mind, then there is no way you can logically be expected to know which individual they have in mind. So if this is what you have in mind by Existential Elimination, then Existential Elimination is impossible, and there cannot be a legitimate derivation rule for it.

Nevertheless, there often is something you can know from just an existentially quantified claim. Here is a simple example.

Problem: Somebody entered the room without setting off the alarm. But it is a general rule that if someone entered the room without setting off the alarm, then the alarm is probably not working properly. Hence, the alarm is probably not working properly.

Solution:
1. Somebody entered the room without setting off the alarm.
2. If someone entered the room without setting off the alarm,
then the alarm is probably not working properly.
∴ 3. The alarm is probably not working properly.

UD: People
Ax = x entered the room without setting off the alarm
W = the alarm is probably not working properly

```
1  │ (∃x) Ax           P
2  │ (x) (Ax → ~W)     P
   ├─────────────────
3  │ │ Ad             H
4  │ │ Ad → ~W        2 UE
5  │ │ ~W             3,4 MP
6  │ ~W               1, 3-5 EE
```

(Notice that you may now abbreviate "Hypothesis" with "H.") Before I take you through this derivation step by step, think about the basic idea. Think like a police detective. The mere fact that *someone* was able enter the room without setting off the alarm tells you something. You don't have to know who it is. Of course, as a detective you might be able to continue this line of investigation further. If you check out the alarm and find that it is in perfect working condition, then you might be able to deduce that if someone was able to enter the room without setting off the alarm, then whoever it was must have had an accomplice who turned the alarm off. In other words, even without knowing who actually entered and left the room, you may be able to deduce that it was an inside job, someone who works at the jewelry store (or whatever it is) must have been helping the person who entered the room. Of course all this depends upon what other premises you have to work with. If all you know is that someone entered the room without setting off the alarm, that isn't enough to go on to deduce much at all. It is only because I also gave you premise 2 that we were able to get anywhere. Even if you never completely solve the case, even if you never find out who actually entered the jewelry store and stole the diamonds, at the very least you might be able to apprehend the accomplice. Sometimes an existentially quantified claim is itself a clue to something else, even if you never figure out which individual the existential is true of.

Now let's go through that derivation step by step. First of all, as usual, I list the two premises. You might wonder about my translation of premise 2. The premise says that if *someone* entered the room without setting off the alarm, then something else is true. "Someone" might sound as if it should be translated by an existential quantifier, not a universal quantifier, because it doesn't say that if *everyone* entered the room without setting off the alarm, then something else is true. It would be very convenient if the existential quantifier was always translated by "someone" and the universal quantifier was always translated by "everyone," but unfortunately it isn't that simple. English is a living language, and so it is not strictly logical. In different contexts, the same word might be used to indicate that a claim applies universally, or to indicate that it applies to at least one. "Someone" is just such a word. "If someone's a bachelor, then they are not married" is a universal truth, and so if you translated this into symbolic logic, you would have to translate the "someone" with the universal quantifier. You can't translate from English into symbolic logic, or the other way around, without thinking about whether or not the claim you are translating is intended to apply universally to all, or to at least one. In this particular case, since the second premise explicitly says that it is a general rule, then we must use a universal quantifier.

Next, in line 3 I start a sub-derivation. This makes sense because we still don't know who it was who entered and left the room. Let's do what the police do and call him "John Doe." Just pick some generic individual at random, and see what follows. So this John Doe comes in and leaves without ever setting off the alarm. How does he do it? Here is where the second premise comes in. Because the second premise is universally quantified, it applies to John Doe, whoever he is. So let's plug him into the universally quantified expression, and out pops what you see in line 4. Next, put 3 and 4 together and you get what you see in line 5. Now comes the important step. Notice that we picked John Doe randomly. John Doe doesn't show up in any of the premises; he is simply a generic member of the universe of discourse. He also doesn't show up in the thing we derive from the hypothesis. That tells us that from our randomly selected hypothesis, we have been able to figure out something definite. Our randomly selected substitute for the existential quantifier has led us to something beyond our random selection. That means this further thing must be true. It doesn't matter who entered and left the room, our second premise tells that whoever did it, the mere fact that someone was able to do it may indicate a problem with our alarm system. That gives us a logical right to assert that as our conclusion.

Existential Elimination (EE): in an existentially quantified expression, any individual constant may be substituted for every instance of the existentially quantified variable with the following provisos: (a) the individual constant must not already appear in any of the premises or governing hypotheses, (b) the substitution must be as the hypothesis of a sub-derivation, (c) this hypothesis must entail an expression which does not contain the individual constant in the hypothesis, and (d) the conclusion of this sub-derivation may be written on the scope line to the left of the line of the hypothesis.

All of these provisos should make sense to you. Proviso (a), that the individual constant must not already appear in any of the premises, is there to insure that you are picking a truly generic member of the universe of discourse. You can't

CHAPTER 9: DERIVATIONS WITH QUANTIFIERS

pick a constant that you know something special about, and then derive something from that, because the one that you know something special about may not be the individual the existential claim is true of. Here is an example.

Problem: Someone just left the coffee area a mess. But yesterday I overheard the boss tell Joe he'll be fired if he leaves the coffee area a mess again. But if Joe will be fired, then Ralph, who shares a cubicle with Joe, is going to have the cubicle all to himself. I'm going to go tell Ralph the good news that he's getting the cubicle all to himself!

Solution:
UD: People who work in the office
Mx = x left the coffee area a mess
Fx = x will be fired
Cx = x will have the cubicle all to himself
j = Joe
r = Ralph

1	(∃x) Mx	P
2	Mj → Cr	P
3	Mj	H
4	Cr	2,3 MP
5	Cr	*1,3-4 EE* **MISTAKE!!! WRONG!!!**

Don't go running off to Ralph to get his hopes up. This is just how rumors are started. Sure, Joe might be the one who left the coffee area a mess, he's done it before and perhaps he did it again. But what ever happened to innocent before proven guilty? If you are trying to used the rule Existential Elimination, you cannot pick an individual constant that is in one of your premises. That is not fair to the one you are picking on; you are just jumping to conclusions. You have to pick someone about whom you don't know anything special; you have to pick someone who is completely generic, so that you are not relying on any special information you have about them in particular. So in this argument, nothing really follows. This argument is invalid, and from these premises, you can't really derive any interesting conclusion.

Proviso (b) should make sense to you because you are just making a preliminary, hypothetical guess. Someone left the coffee area a mess. Who could it be? I don't know. Suppose it was Sally? What would follow then? Well, given the premises we have so far, nothing would follow. So we can't get very far in this derivation. In our previous derivation, it would help us to pick someone at random. If you have another premise that is universally quantifed, then you can use your randomly selected individual and perhaps get somewhere interesting.

Proviso (c), that the hypothesis must entail an expression which does not contain the individual constant which is in the hypothesis, is very important. The individual you are picking on in your hypothesis cannot be a part of the conclusion you reach in your sub-derivation. That wouldn't be fair to the individual you are picking. You don't really know that they are the one who did it, and you are not really trying to blame them. You are picking on them only at random, and only in order to use one of your other premises (probably a universally quantified premise) to get to some other claim which isn't about the individual you selected at random. It's nothing personal, it's not really about them, you are just plugging in their name in order to deduce something that isn't about them.

Finally, proviso (d), that the conclusion of the sub-derivation may be written on the derivation line prior to the hypothesis, really just reminds you of the big picture. Basically all you are doing is setting up a kind of modus ponens. You know that someone made a mess, then you are trying to show that if someone made a mess, it doesn't really matter who, then something else follows. Put those two claims together, use modus ponens and you can conclude with the something else.

Chapter Conclusion.

Now you have a solid grounding in the basics of logic, and you should be able to analyze the logic of most arguments you come across in your daily life, and even most arguments you may come across in a College classroom.

Things to memorize from this Chapter:
Universal Elimination (UE): in a universally quantified expression, any individual constant may be substituted for the universally quantified variable, provided that the individual constant is substituted for every occurrence of the variable.

Existential Introduction (EI): in an expression containing an individual constant, any instance of the individual constant may be replaced by an existentially quantified variable (you may but are not required to replace every instance of the individual constant with the existentially quantified variable).

Universal Introduction (UI): in an expression containing an individual constant, the individual constant may be replaced by a universally quantified variable provided that (a) the individual constant does not appear in any of the premises or governing hypotheses, and (b) every instance of the individual constant is replaced by the universally quantified variable.

Existential Elimination (EE): in an existentially quantified expression, any individual constant may be substituted for every instance of the existentially quantified variable with the following provisos: (a) the individual constant must not already appear in any of the premises or governing hypotheses, (b) the substitution must be as the hypothesis of a sub-derivation, (c) this hypothesis must entail an expression which does not contain the individual constant in the hypothesis, and (d) the conclusion of this sub-derivation may be written on the scope line to the left of the line of the hypothesis.

Exercises for Chapter 9
Exercise 9.1: Extremely Simple Derivations. *Perform the following derivations. The only quantifier rules these derivations use are UE and EI.*

Example 1
Problem: {(x)Gx → Mx, Gd} ⊢ Md
Solution:

1	(x) Gx → Mx	P
2	Gd	P
3	Gd → Md	1 UE
4	Md	2,3 MP

Example 2
Problem: {Gd, Gd → Md} ⊢ (∃x)Mx
Solution:

1	Gd	P
2	Gd → Md	P
3	Md	1,2 MP
4	(∃x) Mx	3 EI

1. {Hp, (x)Hx → Mx} ⊢ Mp
2. {~Mp, (x)Hx v Mx} ⊢ Hp
3. {Hp, (x)Hx ↔ Mx} ⊢ Mp
4. {(x)Px, (x)Dx} ⊢ Pd & Dd
5. {(x)Px, Gd} ⊢ Pd & Gd

6. {Gd} ⊢ (∃x)Gx
7. {Hp, (x)Hx → Mx} ⊢ (∃x)Mx
8. {(x)Dx} ⊢ (∃x)Dx
9. {Dp & Gp} ⊢ (∃x)Gx
10. {Dp, (x)Dx → Hx} ⊢ (∃x)Hx

11. {Hp → Mp, Mp → Gp} ⊢ (∃x)Hx → Gx
12. {Hp → Mp, (x)Mx → Gx} ⊢ (∃x)Hx → Gx
13. {(x)Dx → Gx, (x)Dx} ⊢ (∃x)Gx
14. {Pd & Gd} ⊢ (∃x)Px & Gx
15. {~Gd, (x)Px v Gx} ⊢ (∃x)Px

16. {Bd → Rg, (x)Bx} ⊢ (∃x)Rx
17. {(x)Px ↔ Rx, (x)Rx} ⊢ (∃x)Px
18. {Bd v Pd, (x)~Bx} ⊢ (∃x)Px
19. {(x)Bx, (x)Px} ⊢ (∃x)Bx & Px
20. {(x)Bx} ⊢ (∃x)Bx v Px

Exercise 9.2: Longer Simple Derivations. *Perform the following derivations. In addition to UE and EI, problems 1-10 require using UI and problems 11-20 require using EE.*

Example 1
Problem: {(x)Px} ⊢ (y)Py
Solution:

1	(x) Px	P
2	Pd	1 UE
3	(y) Py	2 UI

Example 2
Problem: {(x)Px → Q, (∃x)Px} ⊢ Q
Solution:

1	(x) Px → Q	P
2	(∃x)Pd	P
3	Ps	H
4	Ps → Q	1 UE
5	Q	3,4 MP
6	Q	2, 3-5 EE

1. {(x)Px, (x)Mx} ⊢ (x)Px & Mx
2. {(x)Px → Qx, (x)Qx → Rx} ⊢ (x)Px → Rx
3. {(x)Px & Qx, (x)Qx & Rx} ⊢ (x)Px & Rx
4. {(x)Px v Qx, (x)~Qx} ⊢ (x)Px
5. {(x)Px ↔ Qx, (x)Px} ⊢ (x)Qx

6. {P & ~P} ⊢ (x)~Qx
7. {(x)Px & Qx} ⊢ (x)Qx v Rx
8. {(x)Px, (y)~Py} ⊢ (x)Qx & Rx
9. {(x)(y)Bxy} ⊢ (x)(y)Byx
10. {(x)(y)Px → Qy, (x)Px} ⊢ (x)Qx

11. {(∃x)Px} ⊢ (∃x)Px v Qx
12. {(∃x)Px, (x)Px → Qx} ⊢ (∃x)Qx
13. {(∃x)Px → Qx, (x)Px} ⊢ (∃x)Qx
14. {(∃x)Px ↔ Qx, (x)Qx} ⊢ (∃x)Px
15. {(∃x)Px & Qx} ⊢ (∃x)Qx

16. {(∃x)Px v Qx, (x)~Qx} ⊢ (∃x)Px v Rx
17. {(∃x)(Px & Qx) → Rx, (x)~Rx, (x)Qx} ⊢ (∃x)~Px
18. {(∃x)Px, (x)Px ↔ Rx} ⊢ (∃x)Rx
19. {(∃x)(y)Bxy} ⊢ (∃x)(∃y)Bxy
20. {(x)(∃y)Bxy} ⊢ (∃x)(∃y)Bxy

Exercise 9.3: Quantifier Derivations. *Perform the following derivations.*
1. {(x)Px, (x)Mx, (∃x)(Px & Mx) → (y)By} ⊢ Bs
2. {(x)Px → Qx, (∃x)Px, (x)Qx → Rx} ⊢ (∃x)Rx
3. {(x)Px & Qx, (x)Qx & Rx} ⊢ (x)Px & Rx
4. {(x)Px v Qx, (∃x)~Qx} ⊢ (∃x)Px
5. {(x)Px ↔ Qx, (x)Px ↔ Rx} ⊢ (x)Qx ↔ Rx

6. {P & ~P} ⊢ (∃x)~Qx
7. {(x)Px & Qx, (∃x)Qx → Tx} ⊢ (∃x)Px & Tx
8. {(x)Px, (∃y)~Py} ⊢ ~(x)Qx & Rx
9. {~((x)Bx v (∃x)Tx), (∃x)Mx → Ts} ⊢ (x)~Mx
10. {(x)Px → ~Qx, (∃x)Px} ⊢ ~(x)Qx

11. {(x)Pxx} ⊢ (z)Pzz
12. {(∃x)Pxx} ⊢ (∃z)Pzz
13. {(x)Gx → Px, Gs} ⊢ (∃y)Py
14. {(x)Mx} ⊢ (x)(~Mx → Mx)
15. {(∃x)Pxxx} ⊢ (∃x)(∃y)(∃z)Pxyz

16. {(x)(Hx & ~Kx) → Ix, (∃y)Hy & Gy, (x)Gx & ~Kx} ⊢ (∃y)Iy & Gy
17. {(x)(y)Cxy} ⊢ (Caa & Cab) & (Cba & Cbb)
18. {(x)(Hx & Fx) → Gx, (y)Fy & ~(z)Kzb} ⊢ (x)Hx → Gx
19. {((∃x)Px) → Pc} ⊢ ((∃x)Px) ↔ Pc
20. {(x)~Ax → Kx, (∃y)~Ky} ⊢ (∃w)Aw v Lwf

21. {(x)(Hx & (Jxx & Mx))} ⊢ (∃x)Jxb & (x)Mx
22. {(x)(~Bx → ~Wx), (∃x)Wx} ⊢ (∃x)Bx
23. {(x)(y)(z)Bxyz} ⊢ (x)(y)(z)Bxyz → Bxyz
24. {(x)(Hx → (y)Rxyb), (x)(z)(Razx → Sxzz)} ⊢ Ha → (∃x)Sxcc
25. {(x)(~Lx v (∃y)Ky)} ⊢ (∃x)Lx → (∃y)Ky

26. {(∃x)(Jxa & Ck), (∃x)Sx & Hxx, (x)((Ck & Sx) → ~Ax)} ⊢ (∃z)~Az & Hzz
27. {(∃x)(Cx v (y)(Wxy → Cy)), (x)(Wxa & ~Ca)} ⊢ (∃x)Cx
28. {(x)(y)Dxy → Cxy, (x)(∃y)Dxy, (x)(y)(Cyx → Dxy)} ⊢ (∃x)(∃y)(Cxy & Cyx)
29. {(x)Px → Qx} ⊢ ((∃x)Px & (∃y)Qy) ↔ (∃z)Pz & Qz
30. {(x)(y)(Ry v Dx) → ~Ky, (x)(∃y)(Ax → ~Ky), (∃x)(Ax v Rx)} ⊢ (∃x)~Kx

Exercise 9.4: Theorems. *Derive the following theorems.*
1. {} ⊢ (x)Px → (∃y)Py
2. {} ⊢ (x)Ax → ~~Ax
3. {} ⊢ ((x)(Ax → Bx)) → ((x)Ax → (x)Bx)
4. {} ⊢ ((∃x)Px & Qx) → ((∃x)Px & (∃x)Qx)
5. {} ⊢ ((x)Ps → Qx) ↔ (Ps → (x)Qx)

6. {} ⊢ ((x)Px → Qs) ↔ ((∃x)Px → Qs))
7. {} ⊢ (x)Px ↔ ~(∃x)~Px
8. {} ⊢ (∃x)Px ↔ ~(x)~Px
9. {} ⊢ ~(x)Px ↔ (∃x)~Px
10. {} ⊢ ~(∃x)Px ↔ (x)~Px

Extra Credit: *work problems 7-10 without using QN or QE*

WHAT'S NEXT?

If you've made it through this book, and you've been able to manage some of the problems from every chapter, then you are smarter than when you began, and you're ready for the next step. But you are at a crossroads, and so your next step can be in many different directions.

More Logic. In this book I tried my best to cut some corners so that beginners wouldn't be put off by logic. If you would like a more formal, systematic and complete study of logic, I suggest you try one of these books.

Bergmann, Merrie, James Moore and Jack Nelson. *The Logic Book*. 3rd ed. New York: McGraw-Hill, 1998.
Kalish, Donald, Richard Montague and Gary Mar. *Logic: Techniques of Formal Reasoning*. Oxford: Oxford University Press, 1980.

Advanced Logic. If you are ready for the next step, and you want to dive into the deeper mysteries of logic, I suggest you try one of these.

Quine, W.V.O. *Mathematical Logic*. Rev. ed. Cambridge, Mass.: Harvard University Press, 1981.
Hunter, Geoffrey. *Metalogic: An Introduction to the Metatheory of First-Order Logic*. Berkeley: University of California Press, 1971.

Alternative Logics. Remember that in truth tables I used only two values in this book: true and false. If you'd like to explore other possibilities than just true and false, consider this book.

Rescher, N. *Many-Valued Logic*. Brookfield, Vt.: Ashgate, 1993.

Modal Logic. Another aspect of logic I skipped is what is called "modal logic" or the "logic of modes." The "modes" are different "ways" of being (the Latin word *modus* means "way" or "manner"). What this means in terms of logic is the difference between possibility and necessity. Modal logic has many extremely interesting applications in philosophy. Try one of these.

Konyndyk, Kenneth. *Introductory Modal Logic*. Notre Dame, Ind.: University of Notre Dame Press, 1986.
Chellas, B. *Modal Logic*. New York: Cambridge University Press, 1980.

History of Logic. If you want to see how logic, and systems of logic developed, try one of these.

Kneale, William, and Martha Kneale. *The Development of Logic*. Oxford: Clarendon Press, 1985.
Nye, Andrea. *Words of Power: A Feminist Reading of the History of Logic*. New York: Routledge, 1990.

Philosophy of Logic. Logic has many interesting philosophical implications. If you'd like to explore this area, try one of these.

Quine, W.V.O. *Philosophy of Logic*. Cambridge, Mass.: Harvard University Press, 1986.
Leblanc, Hugues. *Existence, Truth, and Provability*. Albany, N.Y.: SUNY Press, 1982.

Philosophy. Finally, nearest and dearest to my heart is just philosophy itself. I used Socrates in many of my examples out of respect for tradition, but also because Socrates did play an important role in the history of logic in particular, and in the history of philosophy generally. I think there is no better introduction to philosophy than to read Plato's dialogues, in which he used his teacher, Socrates, as the main character. In my opinion, the very best introduction to Socrates, and the famous "Socratic Method" is to read the following two dialogues.

Plato, "Charmides," and "Laches," in *Collected Dialogues of Plato*, edited by John M. Cooper (Indianapolis, Indiana: Hackett Publishing Company, Inc.) 1997.

SOLUTIONS TO ODD NUMBERED PROBLEMS

Chapter 1: Solutions to Odd Numbered Problems

Exercise 1.1: Identifying Claims.
1. The plate is on the table. *CLAIM*
3. Did you put the forks on the proper side of the plates? *QUESTION*
5. The centerpiece is lovely. *CLAIM*
7. Greed is wrong. *CLAIM*
9. Is capital punishment morally acceptable? *QUESTION*

Exercise 1.2: Identifying Kinds of Claims.
1. SIMPLE CLAIM
3. CONJUNCTION
5. SIMPLE CLAIM
7. CONDITIONAL CLAIM
9. DISJUNCTION
11. SIMPLE CLAIM
13. DISJUNCTION
15. CONDITIONAL CLAIMS (*the consequent is a conjunction*)

Exercise 1.3: Identifying Argument Patterns.

Problem 1:

1	If Socrates is human, then Socrates is mortal.	Premise
2	Socrates is human.	Premise
So 3	Socrates is mortal.	From 1,2, valid by modus ponens

Problem 3:

1	If we've got everything down to a science, then we know everything.	Premise
2	We've got everything down to a science.	Premise
So 3	We know everything.	From 1,2, valid by modus ponens

Problem 5:

1	Socrates is human.	Premise
2	If Socrates is human, then Socrates is mortal.	Premise
So 3	Socrates is mortal.	From 1,2, valid by modus ponens

Problem 7:

1	Socrates is mortal.	Premise
2	Socrates is human or Socrates is mortal.	Premise
So 3	Socrates is not human.	From 1,2, invalid by fallacy of affirming a disjunct

Problem 9:

1	Dogs are smart.	Premise
2	Dogs are obedient.	Premise
So 3	Dogs are smart and dogs are obedient.	From 1,2, valid by conjunction introduction

Problem 11:

1	Dogs are obedient.	Premise
2	If dogs are smart, then dogs are obedient.	Premise
So 3	Dogs are smart.	From 1,2, invalid by fallacy of affirming the consequent

Problem 13:

1	If dogs are obedient, then dogs are smart.	Premise
2	Dogs are obedient.	Premise
So 3	Dogs are smart.	From 1,2, valid by modus ponens

SOLUTIONS TO ODD NUMBERED PROBLEMS

Problem 15:

1	If apples are fruit, then apples are sweet.	Premise
2	Apples are fruit.	Premise
So 3	Apples are sweet.	From 1,2, valid by modus ponens

Problem 17:

1	Either bones are brittle, or bones are durable.	Premise
2	Bones are not durable.	Premise
So 3	Bones are brittle.	From 1,2, valid by disjunction elimination

Problem 19:

1	Rabbits are soft and rabbits are cute.	Premise
So 2	Rabbits are cute.	From 1, valid by conjunction elimination

Problem 21:

1	Cars are fast.	Premise
2	If cars are red, then cars are fast.	Premise
So 3	Cars are red.	From 1,2, invalid by fallacy of affirming the consequent

Problem 23:

1	If justice is a virtue, then cheating is a vice.	Premise
2	Cheating is not a vice.	Premise
So 3	Justice is not a virtue.	From 1,2, valid by modus tollens

Problem 25:

1	Either hope is a virtue, or pride is a virtue.	Premise
2	Pride is not a virtue.	Premise
So 3	Hope is a virtue.	From 1,2, valid by disjunction elimination

Problem 27:

1	If faith is a virtue, then we must seek truth.	Premise
2	Faith is a virtue.	Premise
So 3	We must seek truth.	From 1,2, valid by modus ponens

Problem 29:

1	Either vengeance is a vice, or justice is a vice.	Premise
2	Justice is a not vice.	Premise
So 3	Vengeance is a vice.	From 1,2, valid by disjunction elimination

Problem 31:

1	Cats are mammals.	Premise
So 2	Cats are mammals or dogs are mammals.	From 1, valid by disjunction introduction

Problem 33:

1	Rats have teeth.	Premise
So 2	Either rats have teeth or dogs have teeth.	From 1, valid by disjunction introduction

Problem 35:

1	Either rats are rodents or rats are carnivores.	Premise
2	Rats are not rodents.	Premise
So 3	Rats are carnivores.	From 1,2, valid by disjunction elimination

Problem 37:

1	Marmots are closely related to squirrels.	Premise
So 2	Marmots are closely related to squirrels or marmots are closely related to snakes.	From 1, valid by disjunction introduction

Problem 39:

1	If bugs are crunchy, then cats eat bugs.	Premise
2	Cats eat bugs.	Premise
So 3	Bugs are crunchy.	From 1,2, invalid by fallacy of affirming the consequent

Exercise 1.3: Slightly Trickier Arguments.

Problem 1:

1	If cats are not amphibians, then dogs are not amphibians.	Premise
2	Cats are not amphibians.	Premise
So 3	Dogs are not amphibians.	From 1,2, valid by modus ponens

Problem 3:

1	If each being is what it is composed of, then you can't step into the same river twice.	Premise
2	Each being is what it is composed of.	Premise
So 3	You can't step into the same river twice.	From 1,2, valid by modus ponens

Problem 5:

1	Either God exists or evil does not exist.	Premise
2	God exists.	Premise
So 3	Evil does not exist.	From 1,2 invalid

Chapter 2: Solutions to Odd Numbered Problems

Exercise 2.1: Longer Arguments.

Problem 1

1	Socrates speaks Greek.	Premise
2	If Socrates speaks Greek, then Socrates is Greek.	Premise
∴ 3	Socrates is Greek.	From 1,2 valid by modus ponens
4	If Socrates is Greek, then Socrates is human.	Premise
∴ 5	Socrates is human.	From 3,4 valid by modus ponens

Problem 3

1	If Socrates is Persian, then Socrates speaks Babylonian.	Premise
2	If Socrates speaks Babylonian, then Socrates speaks Assyrian.	Premise
∴ 3	If Socrates is Persian, then Socrates speaks Assyrian.	From 1,2 valid by chain argument
4	If Socrates speaks Assyrian, then Socrates is a polyglot.	Premise
∴ 5	If Socrates is a polyglot, then Socrates speaks Persian.	From 3,4 invalid by fallacy of reversing the chain

Problem 5

1	Socrates is Athenian.	Premise
2	If Socrates is a philosopher, then Socrates is Athenian.	Premise
∴ 3	Socrates is a philosopher.	From 1,2 invalid by fallacy of affirming the consequent
4	Either Socrates is a politician, or Socrates is a philosopher.	Premise
∴ 5	Socrates is not a politician.	From 3,4 invalid by fallacy of affirming a disjunct
6	If Socrates is powerful, then Socrates is a politician.	Premise
∴ 7	Socrates is not powerful.	From 5,6 valid by modus tollens
∴ 8	Socrates is a philosopher and Socrates is not a powerful.	From 3,7 valid by conjunction introduction

Exercise 2.2: Translation.

Problem 1

1	Socrates is Greek.	Premise
2	If Socrates is Greek, then Socrates speaks Greek.	Premise
∴ 3	Socrates speaks Greek.	From 1,2 valid by modus ponens

Problem 3

1	Socrates is not Persian.	Premise
2	Either Socrates is Greek, or Socrates is Persian.	Premise
∴ 3	Socrates is Greek.	From 1,2 valid by disjunction elimination

Problem 5

1	Horses are pretty.	Premise
2	If horses are pretty, then ponies are pretty.	Premise
∴ 3	Ponies are pretty.	From 1,2 valid by modus ponens

SOLUTIONS TO ODD NUMBERED PROBLEMS

Problem 7

1	If horses are pretty, then ponies are pretty.	Premise
2	Ponies are not pretty.	Premise
∴ 3	Horses are not pretty.	From 1,2 valid by modus tollens

Problem 9

1	If horses are pretty, then ponies are pretty.	Premise
2	Horses are not pretty.	Premise
∴ 3	Ponies are not pretty.	From 1,2 invalid by fallacy of denying the antecedent

Problem 11

1	Andy is not a horse.	Premise
2	If Andy is a horse, then Andy is pretty.	Premise
∴ 3	Andy is not pretty.	From 1,2 invalid by fallacy of denying the antecedent

Problem 13

1	Andy is a horse and Andy wears shoes.	Premise
∴ 2	Andy is a horse.	From 1 valid by conjunction elimination

Problem 15

1	Sally is a zebra.	Premise
2	If Sally is a zebra, then Sally has been cloned.	Premise
∴ 3	Sally has been cloned.	From 1,2 valid by modus ponens

Problem 17

1	Betty is a zebra.	Premise
2	If Betty is a zebra, then Betty has an odd number of toes.	Premise
∴ 3	Betty has an odd number of toes.	From 1,2 valid by modus ponens

Problem 19

1	Sally is a zebra.	Premise
∴ 2	Sally is a cow or Sally is a zebra.	From 1 valid by disjunction introduction

Problem 21

1	Carl is a toe-tapping tapir.	Premise
2	Carl is a snappy dresser.	Premise
∴ 3	Carl is a toe-tapping tapir, and Carl is a snappy dresser.	From 1,2 valid by conjunction introduction

Problem 23

1	If you keep spinning, then you will toss your cookies.	Premise
2	If you stay on that ride, then you keep spinning.	Premise
∴ 3	If you toss your cookies, then you stay on that ride.	From 1,2 invalid by fallacy of reversing the chain

Problem 25

1	If Tommy is a tapir, then Tommy has an odd number of toes.	Premise
2	Tommy is a tapir.	Premise
∴ 3	Tommy has an odd number of toes.	From 1,2 valid by modus ponens

Exercise 2.3: Translation of Longer Arguments.

Problem 1

1	Socrates is a philosopher.	Premise
2	If Socrates is a philosopher, then Socrates is human.	Premise
∴ 3	Socrates is human.	From 1,2 valid by modus ponens
4	If Socrates is human, then Socrates is mortal.	Premise
∴ 5	Socrates is mortal.	From 3,4 valid by modus ponens

Problem 3

1	Either Socrates is Persian, or Socrates is Greek.	Premise
2	Socrates is not Greek.	Premise
∴ 3	Socrates is Persian.	From 1,2 valid by disjunction elimination
4	If Socrates is Persian, then Socrates speaks Babylonian.	Premise
∴ 5	Socrates speaks Babylonian.	From 3,4 valid by modus ponens

Problem 5

1	If Socrates is not Persian, then Socrates is Egyptian.	Premise
2	Socrates is not Egyptian.	Premise
∴ 3	Socrates is Persian.	From 1,2 valid by modus tollens
4	If Socrates is Persian, then Socrates speaks Persian.	Premise (Hidden Premise)
∴ 5	Socrates speaks Persian.	From 3,4 valid by modus ponens

Problem 7

1	If Joe is too picky about how his food is prepared, then Joe suffers from a kind of gluttony.	Premise
2	Joe does not suffer from gluttony.	Premise
∴ 3	Joe is not too picky about how his food is prepared.	From 1,2 valid by modus tollens
4	Either Joe is too picky about how his food is prepared, or Joe's brother is too picky about how his food is prepared.	Premise
∴ 5	Joe's brother is too picky about how his food is prepared.	From 1,2 valid by disjunction elimination

Problem 9

1	Sloth is a vice.	Premise
∴ 2	Wrath is a vice, or sloth is a vice.	From 1 valid by disjunction introduction
3	Wrath is a vice.	Premise
∴ 4	Sloth is not a vice.	From 2,3 invalid by fallacy of affirming a disjunct

Problem 11

1	Andy wants to be celebrated for something unworthy.	Premise
2	If Andy wants to be celebrated for something unworthy, then Andy suffers from the vice of vainglory.	Premise (hidden assumption)
∴ 3	Andy suffers from the vice of vainglory.	From 1,2 valid by modus ponens
4	If Andy did not suffer from the vice of vainglory, then Andy is not unhappy.	Premise
∴ 5	Andy is unhappy.	From 3,4 invalid by fallacy of denying the antecedent

Problem 13

1	If patience is a virtue, then courage is a virtue.	Premise
2	If courage is a virtue, then we should never fear death more than dishonor.	Premise
∴ 3	If patience is a virtue, then we should never fear death more than dishonor.	From 1,2 valid by chain argument (hidden assumption)
4	If we should never fear death more than dishonor, then we must never give up hope.	Premise
∴ 5	If patience is a virtue, then we must never give up hope.	From 3,4 valid by chain argument

Problem 15

1	Prudence is a virtue and circumspection is a virtue.	Premise
∴ 2	Circumspection is a virtue.	From 1 valid by conjunction elimination
3	Foresight is a virtue.	Premise
∴ 4	Prudence is a virtue.	From 1 valid by conjunction elimination (hidden assumption)
∴ 5	Prudence is a virtue and foresight is a virtue.	From 3,4 valid by conjunction introduction

Exercise 2.4: More Arguments.

Problem 1

1	Cats are mammals and dogs are mammals.	Premise
∴ 2	Dogs are mammals.	From 1 valid by conjunction elimination (hidden assumption)
3	If dogs are mammals, then wolves are mammals.	Premise
∴ 4	Wolves are mammals.	From 2,3 valid by modus ponens

SOLUTIONS TO ODD NUMBERED PROBLEMS

Problem 3

1	If weasels are rodents, then weasels' incisors grow continuously throughout their lives.	Premise
2	Weasels' incisors do not grow continuously throughout their lives.	Premise
∴ 3	Weasels are not rodents.	From 1,2 valid by modus tollens (hidden assumption)
4	Weasels are rodents or weasels are carnivores.	Premise
∴ 5	Weasels are carnivores.	From 3,4 valid by disjunction elimination

Problem 5

1	If raccoons are closely related to beavers, then raccoons have incisors that keep growing through life.	Premise
2	Raccoons do not have incisors that keep growing through life.	Premise
∴ 3	Raccoons are not closely related to beavers.	From 1,2 valid by modus tollens
4	Raccoons are closely related to beavers, or raccoons are closely related to bears.	Premise
∴ 5	Raccoons are closely related to bears.	From 3,4 valid by disjunction elimination

Problem 7

1	If there are no marsupials outside of Australia, then no animals in South America have a marsupium.	Premise
2	If no animals in South America have a marsupium, then there are no opossums in South America.	Premise
∴ 3	If there are no marsupials outside of Australia, then there are no opossums in South America.	From 1,2 valid by chain argument (hidden assumption)
4	There are opossums in South America.	Premise
∴ 5	There are marsupials outside of Australia.	From 3,4 valid by modus tollens

Problem 9

1	Justice demands equality of exchange.	Premise
2	If justice demands equality of exchange, then charging interest on a monetary loan is unjust.	Premise
∴ 3	Charging interest on a monetary loan is unjust.	From 1,2 valid by modus ponens (hidden assumption)
4	If charging interest on a monetary loan is unjust, then the credit card racket is corrupt.	Premise
∴ 5	The credit card racket is corrupt.	From 3,4 valid by modus ponens
6	If the credit card racket is corrupt, then the banking system is immoral.	Premise
∴ 7	The banking system is immoral.	From 5,6 valid by modus ponens

Problem 11

1	If God exists, then a power of infinite goodness exists.	Premise
2	If a power of infinite goodness exists, then evil does not exist.	Premise
∴ 3	If God exists, then evil does not exist.	From 1,2 valid by chain argument (hidden assumption)
4	Evil does exist.	Premise
∴ 5	God does not exist.	From 3,4 valid by modus tollens

Problem 13

1	Motion exists.	Premise
2	If a First Mover does not exist, then motion does not exist.	Premise
∴ 3	A First Mover exists.	From 1,2 valid by modus tollens
4	If a First Mover exists, then God exists.	Premise
∴ 5	God exists.	From 3,4 valid by modus ponens

Problem 15

1	God could possibly exist.	Premise
2	If God could possibly exist, then God's existence is not impossible.	Premise (hidden assumption)
∴ 3	God's existence is not impossible.	From 1,2 valid by modus ponens
4	Either God's existence is impossible, or God's existence is necessary.	Premise (hidden assumption)
∴ 5	God's existence is necessary.	From 3,4 valid by disjunction elimination
6	If God's existence is necessary, then God exists.	Premise (hidden assumption)
∴ 7	God exists.	From 5,6 valid by modus ponens

Chapter 3: Solutions to Odd Numbered Problems

Exercise 3.1: Using Symbols.

Index for problems 1-10:
T = Toby is a cat
S = Spanky is a cat
M = Magnificat is a cat
F = Fafnir is a cat

1. T & S
3. T v F
5. ~T → ~S
7. M v ~T
9. S ↔ ~M

Index for problems 11-20
A = Alice is a dog
S = Sidney is a dog
W = Winston is a dog
M = Micmac is a dog

11. Alice is a dog and Sidney is a dog.
13. Alice is a dog or Sidney is a dog.
15. If Alice is a dog then Sidney is a dog.
17. Micmac is not a dog.
19. Winston is a dog if and only if Micmac is not a dog.

Exercise 3.2: Symbolizing Arguments.

Index for Problems 1-6:
H = Socrates is human
M = Socrates is mortal
C = Socrates is a cat

Problem 1

1	If Socrates is human, then Socrates is mortal.	Premise
2	Socrates is human.	Premise
∴ 3	Socrates is mortal.	From 1,2 valid by modus ponens

Problem 3

1	Socrates is human or Socrates is a cat.	Premise
2	Socrates is not a cat.	Premise
∴ 3	Socrates is human.	From 1,2 valid by disjunction elimination

Problem 5

1	If Socrates is human, then Socrates is mortal.	Premise
2	Socrates is not mortal.	Premise
∴ 3	Socrates is not human.	From 1,2 valid by modus tollens

Problem 7
E = Socrates is Egyptian
G = Socrates is Greek

1	E v G	Premise
2	~E	Premise
∴ 3	G	From 1,2 valid by disjunction elimination

Problem 9
G = Socrates is Greek
P = Socrates is a philosopher

1	G & P	Premise
∴ 2	G	From 1 valid by conjunction elimination

Problem 11
T = Toby is a cat
S = Spanky is a cat

1	T → S	Premise
2	S	Premise
∴ 3	T	From 1 invalid by fallacy of affirming the consequent

Problem 13
T = Toby is a cat
S = Spanky is a cat

1	T v S	Premise
2	~S	Premise
∴ 3	T	From 1,2 valid by disjunction elimination

Exercise 3.3: Assorted Arguments.

Problem 1
1. Socrates is human.
2. If Socrates is human, then Socrates is mortal.
∴ 3. Socrates is mortal.

H = Socrates is human.
M = Socrates is mortal

1	H	Premise
2	H → M	Premise
∴ 3	M	From 1,2 valid by modus ponens

Problem 3
1. Big Al is getting pizza or Big Al is getting beer.
2. Big Al is not getting beer.
∴ 3. Big Al is getting pizza.

P = Big Al is getting pizza
B = Big Al is getting beer

1	P v B	Premise
2	~B	Premise
∴ 3	P	From 1,2 valid by disjunction elimination

Problem 5
1. If I will love you, then you will plow me an acre of land between the salt water and the sea sand.
2. You will not plow me an acre of land between the salt water and the sea sand.
∴ 3. I will not love you.

L = I will love you
P = You will plow me an acre of land between the salt water and the sea sand.

1	L → P	Premise
2	~P	Premise
∴ 3	~L	From 1,2 valid by modus tollens

Problem 7
1. If Alice gets home, then Alice will be tired.
2. If Alice will be tired, then Alice will take a nap.
∴ 3. If Alice gets home, then Alice will take a nap.
H = Alice gets home
T = Alice will be tired
N = Alice will take a nap

1	H → T	Premise
2	T → N	Premise
∴ 3	H → N	From 1,2 valid by chain argument

Problem 9
1. Miranda bakes brownies.
2. Miranda is a Rudolph Valentino fan.
∴ 3. Miranda bakes brownies and Miranda is a Rudolph Valentino fan.
B = Miranda bakes brownies
R = Miranda is a Rudolph Valentino fan

1	B	Premise
2	R	Premise
∴ 3	B & R	From 1,2 valid by conjunction introduction

Problem 11
1. If Dr. Morbius succeeds, then Robbie the robot keeps a clear head.
2. Robbie the robot does not keep a clear head.
∴ 3. Dr. Morbius does not succeed.
D = Dr. Morbius succeeds
R = Robbie the robot keeps a clear head

1	D → R	Premise
2	~R	Premise
∴ 3	~D	From 1,2 valid by modus tollens

Exercise 3.4: Previous Arguments.
From Exercise 2.2
Problem 1
G = Socrates is Greek
S = Socrates speaks Greek

1	G	Premise
2	G → S	Premise
∴ 3	S	From 1,2 valid by modus ponens

Problem 3
P = Socrates is Persian
G = Socrates is Greek

1	~P	Premise
2	G v P	Premise
∴ 3	G	From 1,2 valid by disjunction elimination

Problem 5
H = Horses are pretty
P = Ponies are pretty

1	H	Premise
2	H → P	Premise
∴ 3	P	From 1,2 valid by modus ponens

Problem 7
H = Horses are pretty
P = Ponies are pretty

1	H → P	Premise
2	~P	Premise
∴ 3	~H	From 1,2 valid by modus tollens

SOLUTIONS TO ODD NUMBERED PROBLEMS

Problem 9
H = Horses are pretty
P = Ponies are pretty

1	H → P	Premise
2	~H	Premise
∴ 3	~P	From 1,2 invalid by fallacy of denying the antecedent

Problem 11
H = Andy is a horse
P = Andy is pretty

1	~H	Premise
2	H → P	Premise
∴ 3	~P	From 1,2 invalid by fallacy of denying the antecedent

Problem 13
H = Andy is a horse
S = Andy wears shoes

1	H & S	Premise
∴ 2	H	From 1 valid by conjunction elimination

Problem 15
Z = Sally is a zebra
C = Sally has been cloned

1	Z	Premise
2	Z → C	Premise
∴ 3	C	From 1,2 valid by modus ponens

Problem 17
Z = Betty is a zebra
T = Betty has an odd number of toes

1	Z	Premise
2	Z → T	Premise
∴ 3	T	From 1,2 valid by modus ponens

Problem 19
Z = Sally is a zebra
C = Sally is a cow

1	Z	Premise
∴ 2	C v Z	From 1 valid by disjunction introduction

Problem 21
T = Carl is a toe-tapping tapir
S = Carl is a snappy dresser

1	T	Premise
2	S	Premise
∴ 3	T & S	From 1,2 valid by conjunction introduction

Problem 23
S = You keep spinning
T = You will toss your cookies
R = You stay on that ride

1	S → T	Premise
2	R → S	Premise
∴ 3	T → R	From 1,2 invalid by fallacy of reversing the chain

Problem 25
T = Tommy is a tapir
O = Tommy has an odd number of toes

1	T → O	Premise
2	T	Premise
∴ 3	O	From 1,2 valid by modus ponens

From Exercise 2.3

Problem 1
P = Socrates is a philosopher
H = Socrates is human
M = Socrates is mortal

1	P	Premise
2	P → H	Premise
∴ 3	H	From 1,2 valid by modus ponens
4	H → M	Premise
∴ 5	M	From 3,4 valid by modus ponens

Problem 3
P = Socrates is Persian
G = Socrates is Greek
B = Socrates speaks Babylonian

1	P v G	Premise
2	~G	Premise
∴ 3	P	From 1,2 valid by disjunction elimination
4	P → B	Premise
∴ 5	B	From 3,4 valid by modus ponens

Problem 5
P = Socrates is Persian
E = Socrates is Egyptian

1	~P → E	Premise
2	~E	Premise
∴ 3	P	From 1,2 valid by modus tollens

Problem 7
P = Joe is too picky about how his food is prepared
G = Joe suffers from a kind of gluttony
B = Joe's brother is too picky about how his food is prepared

1	P → G	Premise
2	~G	Premise
∴ 3	~P	From 1,2 valid by modus tollens
4	P v B	Premise
∴ 5	B	From 1,2 valid by disjunction elimination

Problem 9
S = sloth is a vice
W = Wrath is a vice

1	S	Premise
∴ 2	W v S	From 1 valid by disjunction introduction
3	W	Premise
∴ 4	~S	From 2,3 invalid by fallacy of affirming a disjunct

Problem 11
C = Andy wants to be celebrated for something unworthy
V = Andy suffers from the vice of vainglory
U = Andy is unhappy

1	C	Premise
2	C → V	Premise (hidden assumption)
∴ 3	V	From 1,2 valid by modus ponens
4	~V → ~U	Premise
∴ 5	U	From 3,4 invalid by fallacy of denying the antecedent

SOLUTIONS TO ODD NUMBERED PROBLEMS

Problem 13
P = patience is a virtue
C = courage is a virtue
D = we should never fear death more than dishonor
H = we must never give up hope

1	P → C	Premise
2	C → D	Premise
∴ 3	P → D	From 1,2 valid by chain argument (hidden assumption)
4	D → H	Premise
∴ 5	P → H	From 3,4 valid by chain argument

Problem 15
P = patience is a virtue
C = circumspection is a virtue
F = foresight is a virtue

1	P & C	Premise
∴ 2	C	From 1 valid by conjunction elimination
3	F	Premise
∴ 4	P	From 1 valid by conjunction elimination (hidden assumption)
∴ 5	P & F	From 3,4 valid by conjunction introduction

From Exercise 2.4

Problem 1
C = cats are mammals
D = dogs are mammals
W = wolves are mammals

1	C & D	Premise
∴ 2	D	From 1 valid by conjunction elimination (hidden assumption)
3	D → W	Premise
∴ 4	W	From 1,2 valid by modus ponens

Problem 3
W = weasels are rodents
I = weasels' incisors grow continuously throughout their lives
C = weasels are carnivores

1	W → I	Premise
2	~I	Premise
∴ 3	~W	From 1,2 valid by modus tollens (hidden assumption)
4	W v C	Premise
∴ 5	C	From 3,4 valid by disjunction elimination

Problem 5
R = raccoons are closely related to beavers
I = raccoons have incisors that keep growing through life
B = raccoons are closely related to bears

1	R → I	Premise
2	~I	Premise
∴ 3	~R	From 1,2 valid by modus tollens (hidden assumption)
4	R v B	Premise
∴ 5	B	From 3,4 valid by disjunction elimination

Problem 7
M = there are marsupials outside of Australia
S = there are animals in South America that have a marsupium
O = there are opossums in South America

1	~M → ~S	Premise
2	~S → ~O	Premise
∴ 3	~M → ~O	From 1,2 valid by chain argument (hidden assumption)
4	O	Premise
∴ 5	M	From 3,4 valid by modus tollens

Problem 9
J = justice demands equality of exchange
I = charging interest on a monetary loan is unjust
C = the credit card racket is corrupt
B = the banking system is immoral

1	J	Premise
2	J → I	Premise
∴ 3	I	From 1,2 valid by modus ponens (hidden assumption)
4	I → C	Premise
∴ 5	C	From 3,4 valid by modus ponens
6	C → B	Premise
∴ 7	B	From 5,6 valid by modus ponens

Problem 11
G = God exists
P = a power of infinite goodness exists
E = evil exists

1	G → P	Premise
2	P → ~E	Premise
∴ 3	G → ~E	From 1,2 valid by chain argument (hidden assumption)
4	E	Premise
∴ 5	~G	From 3,4 valid by modus tollens

Problem 13
M = motion exists
F = a First Mover exists
G = God exists

1	M	Premise
2	~F → ~M	Premise
∴ 3	F	From 1,2 valid by modus tollens
4	F → G	Premise
∴ 5	G	From 3,4 valid by modus ponens

Problem 15
P = God could possibly exist
I = God's existence is impossible
N = God's existence is necessary
G = God exists

1	P	Premise
2	P → ~I	Premise (hidden assumption)
∴ 3	~I	From 1,2 valid by modus ponens
4	I v N	Premise (hidden assumption)
∴ 5	N	From 3,4 valid by disjunction elimination
6	N → G	Premise (hidden assumption)
∴ 7	G	From 5,6 valid by modus ponens

Exercise 3.5: Alternative Language.

1. If Al kills a plant to feed it to an animal, then Al uses the plant for its natural purpose. But whenever Al uses a plant for its natural purpose, then Al does not do anything wrong. And so, whenever Al kills a plant to feed it to an animal, Al isn't doing anything wrong.

1.	If Al kills a plant to feed it to an animal, then Al uses the plant for its natural purpose.	Premise
2.	If Al uses a plant for its natural purpose, then Al does not do anything wrong.	Premise
∴ 3.	If Al kills a plant to feed it to an animal, then Al does not do anything wrong.	From 1,2 valid by chain argument

P = Al kills a plant to feed it to an animal
N = Al uses a plant for its natural purpose
W = Al does something wrong

SOLUTIONS TO ODD NUMBERED PROBLEMS

1	P → N	Premise
2	N → ~W	Premise
∴ 3	P → ~W	From 1,2 valid by chain argument

3. Animals are not tools, but being a tool is a necessary condition for being something that it's ok to kill. Hence it's not ok to kill animals.

1.	Animals are not tools.	Premise
2.	If it is ok to kill animals, then animals are tools.	Premise
∴ 3.	It is not ok to kill animals.	From 1,2 valid by modus tollens

T = animals are tools
K = it is ok to kill animals

1	~T	Premise
2	K → T	Premise
∴ 3	~K	From 1,2 valid by modus tollens

5. Doug does not act with charity towards Enid if he kills her. But executing her is sufficient for killing her. Consequently, if Doug executes Enid, then he is not acting with charity. But failing to act with charity is a sufficient condition for acting immorally. That is why executing someone is wrong.

1.	If Doug kills Enid, then Doug does not act with charity towards Enid.	Premise
2.	If Doug executes Enid, then Doug kills Enid.	Premise
∴ 3.	If Doug executes Enid, then Doug does not act with charity towards Enid.	From 1,2 valid by chain argument
4.	If Doug does not act with charity towards Enid, then Doug is acting immorally.	Premise (failing to act with charity is the same as not acting with charity)
∴ 5.	If Doug executes Enid, then Doug is acting immorally.	From 3,4 valid by chain argument (doing wrong is the same as acting immorally)

K = Doug kills Enid
C = Doug acts with charity towards Enid
E = Doug executes Enid
I = Doug acts immorally

1.	K → ~C	Premise
2.	E → K	Premise
∴ 3	E → ~C	From 1,2 valid by chain argument
4.	~C → I	Premise
∴ 5	E → I	From 3,4 valid by chain argument

7. Jesus forbade uprooting the weed in order to spare the wheat (Matthew 13:29-30). This necessarily means that it is wrong to kill the wicked when the good might be killed with them. Hence, capital punishment is wrong.

1.	Jesus forbade uprooting the weed to spare the wheat.	Premise
2.	If Jesus forbade uprooting the weed to spare the wheat, then it is wrong to kill the wicked when the good might be killed with them.	Premise (a necessary condition Is the consequent of a conditional)
∴ 3.	It is wrong to kill the wicked when the good might be killed with them.	From 1,2 valid by modus ponens
4.	If it is wrong to kill the wicked when the good might be killed with them, then capital punishment is wrong.	Premise (hidden assumption)
∴ 5.	Capital punishment is wrong.	From 1,2 valid by modus ponens

W = Jesus forbade uprooting the weed to spare the wheat
K = it is wrong to kill the wicked when the good might be killed with them
C = capital punishment is wrong

1.	W	Premise
2.	W → K	Premise
∴ 3.	K	From 1,2 valid by modus ponens
4.	K → C	Premise
∴ 5	C	From 3,4 valid by modus ponens

9. If it is morally permissible to excise an infection, then necessarily it is morally permissible to commit a lesser evil in order to avoid a greater evil. But suicide can be morally permissible, if we may choose the lesser of two evils. That is how we know that under certain circumstances, suicide is not immoral.

1.	If it is morally permissible to excise an infection, then it is morally permissible to commit a lesser evil to avoid a greater evil.	Premise
2.	If it is morally permissible to commit a lesser evil to avoid a greater evil, then suicide can be morally permissible.	Premise
∴ 3.	If it is morally permissible to excise an infection, then suicide can be morally permissible.	From 1,2 valid by chain argument
4.	It is morally permissible to excise an infection.	Premise (hidden assumption)
∴ 5	Suicide can be morally permissible.	From 3,4 valid by modus ponens

I = it is morally permissible to excise an infection
E = it is morally permissible to commit a lesser evil to avoid a greater evil
S = suicide can be morally permissible

1.	I → E	Premise
2.	E → S	Premise
∴ 3.	I → S	From 1,2 valid by chain argument
4.	I	Premise
5.	S	From 3,4 valid by modus ponens

Chapter 4: Solutions to Odd Numbered Problems
Exercise 4.1: Complex Claims.

Problem 1
1. If apples are fruit and carrots are vegetables, then roses are flowers.
2. Apples are fruit and carrots are vegetables.
∴ 3. Roses are flowers.

A = apples are fruit
C = carrots are vegetables
R = roses are flowers

1	(A & C) → R	Premise
2	A & C	Premise
3	R	From 1,2 valid by modus ponens

Problem 3
1. John is going to the party, and Al is going to the party, and Bert is going to the party.
∴ 2. Bert is going to the party.

J = John is going to the party
A = Al is going to the party
B = Bert is going to the party

1	(J & A) & B	Premise
2	B	From 1, valid by conjunction elimination

Problem 5
1. Either John will go to the party and Sally will go to the party, or Maybelline will go to the party.
2. Maybelline will not go to the party.
∴ 3. John will go to the party and Sally will go to the party.

J = John will go to the party
S = Sally will go to the party
M = Maybelline will go to the party

1	(J & S) v M	Premise
2	~M	Premise
3	J & S	From 1,2 valid by disjunction elimination

SOLUTIONS TO ODD NUMBERED PROBLEMS

Problem 7
1. If I have the salad for lunch and I don't pig out, then I can have a piece of cake for dessert.
2. It is not the case that I have the salad for lunch and I don't pig out.
∴ 3. It is not the case that I can have a piece of cake for dessert.
S = I have the salad for lunch
P = I pig out
C = I can have a piece of cake for dessert

1	(S & ~P) → C	Premise
2	~(S & ~P)	Premise
3	~C	From 1,2 invalid by fallacy of denying the antecedent

Problem 9
1. Either you have the alphabet soup and the crackers, or you have the grilled cheese with slaw.
2. You have the alphabet soup and the crackers.
∴ 3. It is not the case that you have the grilled cheese with slaw.
A = you have the alphabet-soup-and-crackers
G = you have the grilled-cheese-with-slaw

1	A v G	Premise
2	A	Premise
3	~G	From 1,2 invalid by fallacy of affirming a disjunct

Problem 11
1. You are doing some fancy shooting.
∴ 2. Either you are doing some fancy shooting, or you are cheating and we'll tar and feather you.
S = you are doing some fancy shooting
C = you are cheating
T = we will tar you
F = we will feather you

1	S	Premise
2	S v (C & (T & F))	From 1 valid by disjunction introduction

Problem 13
1. If Boston wins, and New York either ties or loses, then Cleveland has a chance.
2. Cleveland doesn't have a chance.
∴ 3. It is not the case that Boston wins and New York either ties or loses.
B = Boston wins
N = New York ties
L = New York loses
C = Cleveland has a chance

1	(B & (N v L)) → C	Premise
2	~C	Premise
3	~(B & (N v L))	From 1,2 valid by modus tollens

Exercise 4.2: Truth Tables.

Problem 1

A	B	A → B
T	T	T
T	F	F
F	T	T
F	F	T

Problem 3

A	B	A v B
T	T	T
T	F	T
F	T	T
F	F	F

Problem 5

A	~A
T	F
F	T

Problem 7

A	B	~B	A & ~B
T	T	F	F
T	F	T	T
F	T	F	F
F	F	T	F

Problem 9

A	B	~B	A ↔ ~B
T	T	F	F
T	F	T	T
F	T	F	T
F	F	T	F

Problem 11

A	B	A & B	~(A & B)
T	T	T	F
T	F	F	T
F	T	F	T
F	F	F	T

Problem 13

A	B	A ↔ B	~(A ↔ B)
T	T	T	F
T	F	F	T
F	T	F	T
F	F	T	F

Problem 15

A	~A	~~A	~~~A	~~~~A
T	F	T	F	T
F	T	F	T	F

Problem 17

A	B	~A	~A & B
T	T	F	F
T	F	F	F
F	T	T	T
F	F	T	F

Problem 19

A	B	~A	~A ↔ B
T	T	F	F
T	F	F	T
F	T	T	T
F	F	T	F

Problem 21

A	B	~A	~B	~A & ~B
T	T	F	F	F
T	F	F	T	F
F	T	T	F	F
F	F	T	T	T

SOLUTIONS TO ODD NUMBERED PROBLEMS

Problem 23

A	B	~A	~B	~A ↔ ~B
T	T	F	F	T
T	F	F	T	F
F	T	T	F	F
F	F	T	T	T

Problem 25

A	B	~A	~A & B	~(~A & B)
T	T	F	F	T
T	F	F	F	T
F	T	T	T	F
F	F	T	F	T

Problem 27

A	B	~A	~A ↔ B	~(~A ↔ B)
T	T	F	F	T
T	F	F	T	F
F	T	T	T	F
F	F	T	F	T

Problem 29

A	B	~A	~B	~A & ~B	~(~A & ~B)
T	T	F	F	F	T
T	F	F	T	F	T
F	T	T	F	F	T
F	F	T	T	T	F

Problem 31

A	B	~A	~B	~A ↔ ~B	~(~A ↔ ~B)
T	T	F	F	T	F
T	F	F	T	F	T
F	T	T	F	F	T
F	F	T	T	T	F

Problem 33

A	B	~B	A & ~B	~(A & ~B)
T	T	F	F	T
T	F	T	T	F
F	T	F	F	T
F	F	T	F	T

Problem 35

A	B	~B	A ↔ ~B	~(A ↔ ~B)
T	T	F	F	T
T	F	T	T	F
F	T	F	T	F
F	F	T	F	T

Problem 37

A	B	C	A & B	(A & B) & C
T	T	T	T	T
T	T	F	T	F
T	F	T	F	F
T	F	F	F	F
F	T	T	F	F
F	T	F	F	F
F	F	T	F	F
F	F	F	F	F

Problem 39

A	B	C	A & B	(A & B) ↔ C
T	T	T	T	T
T	T	F	T	F
T	F	T	F	F
T	F	F	F	T
F	T	T	F	F
F	T	F	F	T
F	F	T	F	F
F	F	F	F	T

Problem 41

A	B	C	B & C	A & (B & C)
T	T	T	T	T
T	T	F	F	F
T	F	T	F	F
T	F	F	F	F
F	T	T	T	F
F	T	F	F	F
F	F	T	F	F
F	F	F	F	F

Problem 43

A	B	C	B ↔ C	A & (B ↔ C)
T	T	T	T	T
T	T	F	F	F
T	F	T	F	F
T	F	F	T	T
F	T	T	T	F
F	T	F	F	F
F	F	T	F	F
F	F	F	T	F

Problem 45

A	B	C	A → B	(A → B) & C
T	T	T	T	T
T	T	F	T	F
T	F	T	F	F
T	F	F	F	F
F	T	T	T	T
F	T	F	T	F
F	F	T	T	T
F	F	F	T	F

Problem 47

A	B	C	A → B	(A → B) ↔ C
T	T	T	T	T
T	T	F	T	F
T	F	T	F	F
T	F	F	F	T
F	T	T	T	T
F	T	F	T	F
F	F	T	T	T
F	F	F	T	F

Problem 49

A	B	C	B & C	A → (B & C)
T	T	T	T	T
T	T	F	F	F
T	F	T	F	F
T	F	F	F	F
F	T	T	T	T
F	T	F	F	T
F	F	T	F	T
F	F	F	F	T

Problem 51

A	B	C	B ↔ C	A → (B ↔ C)
T	T	T	T	T
T	T	F	F	F
T	F	T	F	F
T	F	F	T	T
F	T	T	T	T
F	T	F	F	T
F	F	T	F	T
F	F	F	T	T

Problem 53

A	B	C	A v B	(A v B) & C
T	T	T	T	T
T	T	F	T	F
T	F	T	T	T
T	F	F	T	F
F	T	T	T	T
F	T	F	T	F
F	F	T	F	F
F	F	F	F	F

Problem 55

A	B	C	A v B	(A v B) ↔ C
T	T	T	T	T
T	T	F	T	F
T	F	T	T	T
T	F	F	T	F
F	T	T	T	T
F	T	F	T	F
F	F	T	F	F
F	F	F	F	T

Problem 57

A	B	C	B & C	A v (B & C)
T	T	T	T	T
T	T	F	F	T
T	F	T	F	T
T	F	F	F	T
F	T	T	T	T
F	T	F	F	F
F	F	T	F	F
F	F	F	F	F

Problem 59

A	B	C	B ↔ C	A v (B ↔ C)
T	T	T	T	T
T	T	F	F	T
T	F	T	F	T
T	F	F	T	T
F	T	T	T	T
F	T	F	F	F
F	F	T	F	F
F	F	F	T	T

Problem 61

A	B	C	A ↔ B	(A ↔ B) & C
T	T	T	T	T
T	T	F	T	F
T	F	T	F	F
T	F	F	F	F
F	T	T	F	F
F	T	F	F	F
F	F	T	T	T
F	F	F	T	F

Problem 63

A	B	C	A ↔ B	(A ↔ B) ↔ C
T	T	T	T	T
T	T	F	T	F
T	F	T	F	F
T	F	F	F	T
F	T	T	F	F
F	T	F	F	T
F	F	T	T	T
F	F	F	T	F

Problem 65

A	B	C	B & C	A ↔ (B & C)
T	T	T	T	T
T	T	F	F	F
T	F	T	F	F
T	F	F	F	F
F	T	T	T	F
F	T	F	F	T
F	F	T	F	T
F	F	F	F	T

Problem 67

A	B	C	B ↔ C	A ↔ (B ↔ C)
T	T	T	T	T
T	T	F	F	F
T	F	T	F	F
T	F	F	T	T
F	T	T	T	F
F	T	F	F	T
F	F	T	F	T
F	F	F	T	F

Problem 69

A	B	C	A & B	~(A & B)	~(A & B) → C
T	T	T	T	F	T
T	T	F	T	F	T
T	F	T	F	T	T
T	F	F	F	T	F
F	T	T	F	T	T
F	T	F	F	T	F
F	F	T	F	T	T
F	F	F	F	T	F

Chapter 5: Solutions to Odd Numbered Problems
Exercise 5.1: Truth Conditions.

Problem 1: Tautology

P	P → P
T	T
F	T

Problem 3: Logically Indeterminate

P	~P	~P → P
T	F	T
F	T	F

Problem 5: Contradiction

P	P → P	~(P → P)
T	T	F
F	T	F

Problem 7: Contradiction

P	~P	P & ~P
T	F	F
F	T	F

Problem 9: Contradiction

P	~P	P & ~P
T	F	F
F	T	F

Problem 11: Logically Indeterminate

P	P v P
T	T
F	F

Problem 13: Tautology

P	~P	~P v P
T	F	T
F	T	T

Problem 15: Logically Indeterminate

P	P v P	~(P v P)
T	T	F
F	F	T

Problem 17: Contradiction

P	~P	P ↔ ~P
T	F	F
F	T	F

Problem 19: Tautology

P	~P	~P ↔ ~P
T	F	T
F	T	T

Problem 21: Tautology

P	~P	~~P	~~P → P
T	F	T	T
F	T	F	T

Problem 23: Logically Indeterminate

P	~P	~~P	~~P & P
T	F	T	T
F	T	F	F

Problem 25: Logically Indeterminate

P	~P	~~P	~~P v P
T	F	T	T
F	T	F	F

Problem 27: Tautology

P	~P	~~P	~~P ↔ P
T	F	T	T
F	T	F	T

Problem 29: Logically Indeterminate

P	P & P	~(P & P)	~~(P & P)
T	T	F	T
F	F	T	F

Problem 31: Tautology

P	P → P	~(P → P)	~~(P → P)
T	T	F	T
F	T	F	T

Problem 33: Tautology

P	Q	P → Q	Q → (P → Q)
T	T	T	T
T	F	F	T
F	T	T	T
F	F	T	T

SOLUTIONS TO ODD NUMBERED PROBLEMS

Problem 35: Tautology

P	Q	P → Q	(P → Q) → Q	P → [(P → Q) → Q]
T	T	T	T	T
T	F	F	T	T
F	T	T	T	T
F	F	T	F	T

Problem 37: Tautology

P	Q	~P	~Q	P → ~Q	Q → ~P	(P → ~Q) → (Q → ~P)
T	T	F	F	F	F	T
T	F	F	T	T	T	T
F	T	T	F	T	T	T
F	F	T	T	T	T	T

Problem 39: Tautology

P	Q	~P	~Q	~P → ~Q	Q → P	(~P → ~Q) → (Q → P)
T	T	F	F	T	T	T
T	F	F	T	T	T	T
F	T	T	F	F	F	T
F	F	T	T	T	T	T

Problem 41: Tautology

P	Q	~P	P → Q	~P → (P → Q)
T	T	F	T	T
T	F	F	F	T
F	T	T	T	T
F	F	T	T	T

Problem 43: Logically Indeterminate

P	Q	R	P & Q	(P & Q) v R
T	T	T	T	T
T	T	F	T	T
T	F	T	F	T
T	F	F	F	F
F	T	T	F	T
F	T	F	F	F
F	F	T	F	T
F	F	F	F	F

Problem 45: Logically Indeterminate

P	Q	R	P → Q	(P → Q) & R
T	T	T	T	T
T	T	F	T	F
T	F	T	F	F
T	F	F	F	F
F	T	T	T	T
F	T	F	T	F
F	F	T	T	T
F	F	F	T	F

Problem 47: Logically Indeterminate

P	Q	~P	~Q	P & Q	~Q & ~P	(P & Q) → (~Q & ~P)
T	T	F	F	T	F	F
T	F	F	T	F	F	T
F	T	T	F	F	F	T
F	F	T	T	F	T	T

Problem 49: Contradiction

P	Q	~P	P & ~P	(P & ~P) & Q
T	T	F	F	F
T	F	F	F	F
F	T	T	F	F
F	F	T	F	F

Problem 51: Logically Indeterminate

P	Q	~P	P & ~P	(P & ~P) ↔ Q
T	T	F	F	F
T	F	F	F	T
F	T	T	F	F
F	F	T	F	T

Problem 53: Tautology

P	Q	~P	P & Q	~(P & Q)	~P → ~(P & Q)
T	T	F	T	F	T
T	F	F	F	T	T
F	T	T	F	T	T
F	F	T	F	T	T

Problem 55: Logically Indeterminate

P	Q	~Q	P & Q	~Q → (P & Q)
T	T	F	T	T
T	F	T	F	F
F	T	F	F	T
F	F	T	F	F

Problem 57: Tautology

P	Q	P → Q	Q → P	(P → Q) v (Q → P)
T	T	T	T	T
T	F	F	T	T
F	T	T	F	T
F	F	T	T	T

Problem 59: Tautology

P	Q	~P	~Q	P & Q	~P v ~Q	~(~P v ~Q)	(P & Q) → ~(~P v ~Q)
T	T	F	F	T	F	T	T
T	F	F	T	F	T	F	T
F	T	T	F	F	T	F	T
F	F	T	T	F	T	F	T

Problem 61: Tautology

P	Q	~P	~Q	P v Q	~P & ~Q	~(~P & ~Q)	(P v Q) → ~(~P & ~Q)
T	T	F	F	T	F	T	T
T	F	F	T	T	F	T	T
F	T	T	F	T	F	T	T
F	F	T	T	F	T	F	T

Problem 63: Logically Indeterminate

P	Q	~Q	P & ~Q	P → Q	(P & ~Q) → (P → Q)
T	T	F	F	T	T
T	F	T	T	F	F
F	T	F	F	T	T
F	F	T	F	T	T

SOLUTIONS TO ODD NUMBERED PROBLEMS

Problem 65: Tautology

P	Q	~P	~P & Q	P → Q	(~P & Q) → (P → Q)
T	T	F	F	T	T
T	F	F	F	F	T
F	T	T	T	T	T
F	F	T	F	T	T

Problem 67: Tautology

P	Q	R	P → R	Q → R	P → (Q → R)	Q → (P → R)	[P → (Q → R)] → [Q → (P → R)]
T	T	T	T	T	T	T	T
T	T	F	F	F	F	F	T
T	F	T	T	T	T	T	T
T	F	F	F	T	T	T	T
F	T	T	T	T	T	T	T
F	T	F	T	F	T	T	T
F	F	T	T	T	T	T	T
F	F	F	T	T	T	T	T

Problem 69: Tautology

P	Q	P v Q	P & Q	Q v P	Q & P	(P v Q) → (P & Q)	(Q v P) → (Q & P)	[(P v Q) → (P & Q)] → [(Q v P) → (Q & P)]
T	T	T	T	T	T	T	T	T
T	F	T	F	T	F	F	F	T
F	T	T	F	T	F	F	F	T
F	F	F	F	F	F	T	T	T

Problem 71. Logically indeterminate

P	Q	~P	~P & Q	P → Q	(~P & Q) → (P → Q)
T	T	T	F	T	T
T	T	F	F	F	T
T	F	T			
T	F	F			
F	T	T			
F	T	F			
F	F	T	T	T	T
F	F	F	F	T	T

Problem 73. A → (B & ~C)

A	B	C	~C	B & ~C	A → (B & ~C)
T	T	T	F	F	F
T	T	F	T	T	T
T	F	T	F	F	F
T	F	F	T	F	F
F	T	T	F	F	T
F	T	F	T	T	T
F	F	T	F	F	T
F	F	F	T	F	T

Problem 75. Logically indeterminate

A	B	C	~A	~B	~A & C	(~A & C) v ~B
T	T	T	F	F	F	F
T	T	F	F	F	F	F
T	F	T	F	T	F	F
T	F	F	F	T	F	F
F	T	T	T	F	T	F
F	T	F	T	F	F	F
F	F	T	T	T	T	T
F	F	F	T	T	F	F

Problem 77. Logically indeterminate

H	J	K	~H	~J	H → ~J	K & ~H	(H → ~J) ↔ (K & ~H)
T	T	T	F	F	F	F	T
T	T	F	F	F	F	F	T
T	F	T	F	T	T	F	F
T	F	F	F	T	T	F	F
F	T	T	T	F	T	T	T
F	T	F	T	F	T	F	F
F	F	T	T	T	T	T	T
F	F	F	T	T	T	F	F

Problem 79. Logically indeterminate

P	Q	R	~Q	P v Q	~Q v R	(P v Q) & (~Q v R)
T	T	T	F	T	T	T
T	T	F	F	T	F	F
T	F	T	T	T	T	T
T	F	F	T	T	T	T
F	T	T	F	T	T	T
F	T	F	F	T	F	F
F	F	T	T	F	T	F
F	F	F	T	F	T	F

Exercise 5.2: Logical Consistency and Logical Equivalence

Problem 1. *logically consistent (circle the two T's side-by-side in the final two columns to show that it is possible for both claims to be true simultaneously; not logically equivalent (circle a T and an F side-by-side in the final two columns to show that the two claims do not have the same truth values in all circumstances)*

A	B	A & B	A v B
T	T	T	T
T	F	F	T
F	T	F	T
F	F	F	F

Problem 3. *logically consistent (circle the two T's side-by-side in the final two columns to show that it is possible for both claims to be true simultaneously; not logically equivalent (circle a T and an F side-by-side in the final two columns to show that the two claims do not have the same truth values in all circumstances)*

A	B	A & B	A → B
T	T	T	T
T	F	F	F
F	T	F	T
F	F	F	T

Problem 5. *logically consistent (circle the two T's side-by-side in the final two columns to show that it is possible for both claims to be true simultaneously; not logically equivalent (circle a T and an F side-by-side in the final two columns to show that the two claims do not have the same truth values in all circumstances)*

A	B	A ↔ B	A & B
T	T	T	T
T	F	F	F
F	T	F	F
F	F	T	F

Problem 7. *logically consistent (circle the two T's side-by-side in the final two columns to show that it is possible for both claims to be true simultaneously; not logically equivalent (circle a T and an F side-by-side in the final two columns to show that the two claims do not have the same truth values in all circumstances)*

A	B	~A	~B	~A → B	A ↔ ~B
T	T	F	F	T	F
T	F	F	T	T	T
F	T	T	F	T	T
F	F	T	T	F	F

Problem 9. *logically consistent (circle the two T's side-by-side in the final two columns to show that it is possible for both claims to be true simultaneously; not logically equivalent (circle a T and an F side-by-side in the final two columns to show that the two claims do not have the same truth values in all circumstances)*

A	B	~A	~B	~A v B	A ↔ ~B
T	T	F	F	T	F
T	F	F	T	F	T
F	T	T	F	T	T
F	F	T	T	T	F

Problem 11. *logically consistent (circle the two T's side-by-side in the final two columns to show that it is possible for both claims to be true simultaneously; logically equivalent (circle all four pairs of T's side-by-side in the final two columns to show that the two claims have the same truth values in all circumstances)*

A	B	~A	A & B	A v B	(A & B) → (A v B)	A v ~A
T	T	F	T	T	T	T
T	F	F	F	T	T	T
F	T	T	F	T	T	T
F	F	T	F	F	T	T

Problem 13. *logically consistent (circle the two T's side-by-side in the final two columns to show that it is possible for both claims to be true simultaneously; not logically equivalent (circle a T and an F side-by-side in the final two columns to show that the two claims do not have the same truth values in all circumstances)*

A	B	~B	A v ~B	~B v A	(A v ~B) ↔ (~B v A)	A ↔ B
T	T	F	T	T	T	T
T	F	T	T	T	T	F
F	T	F	F	F	T	F
F	F	T	T	T	T	T

Problem 15. *logically consistent (circle the two T's side-by-side in the final two columns to show that it is possible for both claims to be true simultaneously; not logically equivalent (circle a T and an F side-by-side in the final two columns to show that the two claims do not have the same truth values in all circumstances)*

A	B	~A	~B	A ↔ B	~B ↔ ~A	(A ↔ B) ↔ (~B ↔ ~A)	~A → B
T	T	F	F	T	T	T	T
T	F	F	T	F	F	T	T
F	T	T	F	F	F	T	T
F	F	T	T	T	T	T	F

Problem 17. *logically consistent (circle the two T's side-by-side in the final two columns to show that it is possible for both claims to be true simultaneously; logically equivalent (circle all pairs of truth values side-by-side in the final two columns to show that the two claims have the same truth values in all circumstances)*

E	G	~E	~G	E v G	~(E v G)	~E & ~G
T	T	F	F	T	F	F
T	F	F	T	T	F	F
F	T	T	F	T	F	F
F	F	T	T	F	T	T

Problem 19. *logically consistent (circle the two T's side-by-side in the final two columns to show that it is possible for both claims to be true simultaneously; logically equivalent (circle all pairs of truth values side-by-side in the final two columns to show that the two claims have the same truth values in all circumstances)*

K	L	M	L & M	K & L	K & (L & M)	(K & L) & M
T	T	T	T	T	T	T
T	T	F	F	T	F	F
T	F	T	F	F	F	F
T	F	F	F	F	F	F
F	T	T	T	F	F	F
F	T	F	F	F	F	F
F	F	T	F	F	F	F
F	F	F	F	F	F	F

Exercise 5.3: Validity.
Problem 1: Valid

A	B	A → B	A & (A → B)	A & (A → B) → B
T	T	T	T	T
T	F	F	F	T
F	T	T	F	T
F	F	T	F	T

Problem 3: Invalid

A	B	~A	~B	A → B	(A → B) & ~A	(A → B) & ~A → ~B
T	T	F	F	T	F	T
T	F	F	T	F	F	T
F	T	T	F	T	T	F
F	F	T	T	T	T	T

Problem 5: Invalid

A	B	~A	A → B	(A → B) & ~A	(A → B) & ~A → B
T	T	F	T	F	T
T	F	F	F	F	T
F	T	T	T	T	T
F	F	T	T	T	F

Problem 7: Valid

A	B	A & B	(A & B) → (A & B)
T	T	T	T
T	F	F	T
F	T	F	T
F	F	F	T

Problem 9: Valid

A	B	A v B	A → (A v B)
T	T	T	T
T	F	T	T
F	T	T	T
F	F	F	T

Problem 11: Invalid

P	Q	P v Q	(P v Q) & P	(P v Q) & P → Q
T	T	T	T	T
T	F	T	T	F
F	T	T	F	T
F	F	F	F	T

Problem 13: Valid

P	Q	~P	P v Q	(P v Q) & ~P	(P v Q) & ~P → Q
T	T	F	T	F	T
T	F	F	T	F	T
F	T	T	T	T	T
F	F	T	F	F	T

Chapter 6: Solutions to Odd Numbered Problems
Exercise 6.1: Derivation Completions.

Problem 1
1 | P   P
2 | P → Q   P
3 | Q   1,2 MP

Problem 3
1 | P → Q   P
2 | Q → R   P
3 | P → R   1,2 CA

Problem 5
1 | P v Q   P
2 | P   P
3 | ~Q   1,2 invalid by FAD

Problem 7
1 | ~P   P
2 | ~P v ~Q   1 DI
3 | ~(P & Q)   2 DeM

Problem 9
1 | ~P → Q   P
2 | ~Q   P
3 | ~~P   1,2 MT
4 | P   3 DN

Problem 11
1 | (M v ~T) v ~R   P
2 | ~M   P
3 | M v (~T v ~R)   1 Assoc
4 | ~T v ~R   2,3 DE
5 | ~(T & R)   4 DeM

Exercise 6.2: Extremely Simple Derivations.

Problem 1. {P & Q} ⊢ P
1	P & Q	P
2	P	1 CE

Problem 3. {P, Q} ⊢ P & Q
1	P	P
2	Q	P
3	P & Q	1,2 CI

Problem 5. {N & Z} ⊢ Z
1	N & Z	P
2	Z	1 CE

Problem 7. {P} ⊢ P v Z
1	P	P
2	P v Z	1 DI

Problem 9. {~P, P v Q} ⊢ Q
1	~P	P
2	P v Q	P
3	Q	1,2 DE

Problem 11. {P → Q, P} ⊢ Q
1	P → Q	P
2	P	P
3	Q	1,2 MP

Problem 13. {M → ~Z, M} ⊢ ~Z
1	M → ~Z	P
2	M	P
3	~Z	1,2 MP

Problem 15. {~P, ~P → ~Q} ⊢ ~Q
1	~P	P
2	~P → ~Q	P
3	~Q	1,2 MP

Problem 17. {~P, Q → P} ⊢ ~Q
1	~P	P
2	Q → P	P
3	~Q	1,2 MT

Problem 19. {Z → M, ~M} ⊢ ~Z
1	Z → M	P
2	~M	P
3	~Z	1,2 MT

Exercise 6.3: Longer Simple Derivations.

Problem 1. {P, Q, R} ⊢ (P & Q) & R
1	P	P
2	Q	P
3	R	P
4	P & Q	1,2 CI
5	(P & Q) & R	3,4 CI

Problem 3. {P, Q, R} ⊢ (R & P) & Q
1	P	P
2	Q	P
3	R	P
4	R & P	1,3 CI
5	(R & P) & Q	2,4 CI

SOLUTIONS TO ODD NUMBERED PROBLEMS

Problem 5. {P & Q, R & S} ⊢ Q & S
1 | P & Q   P
2 | R & S   P
3 | Q   1 CE
4 | S   2 CE
5 | Q & S   3,4 CI

Problem 7. {P → Q, Q → R, P} ⊢ R
1 | P → Q   P
2 | Q → R   P
3 | P   P
4 | Q   1,3 MP
5 | R   2,4 MP

Problem 9. {P} ⊢ P v (Q v (R v (S & M)))
1 | P   P
2 | P v (Q v (R v (S & M)))   1 DI

Problem 11. {P v Q, P → R, ~Q} ⊢ R
1 | P v Q   P
2 | P → R   P
3 | ~Q   P
4 | P   1,3 DE
5 | R   2,4 MP

Problem 13. {P, (P & Q) → ~N, Q, R v N} ⊢ R
1 | P   P
2 | (P & Q) → ~N   P
3 | Q   P
4 | R v N   P
5 | P & Q   1,3 CI
6 | ~N   2,5 MP
7 | R   4,6 DE

Problem 15. {P → Q, R → S, M → T, Q → M} ⊢ P → M
1 | P → Q   P
2 | R → S   P
3 | M → T   P
4 | Q → M   P
5 | P → M   1,4 CA

Problem 17. {P → Q, R → S, Q → T, S → M, T → R} ⊢ P → M
1 | P → Q   P
2 | R → S   P
3 | Q → T   P
4 | S → M   P
5 | T → R   P
6 | P → T   1,3 CA
7 | P → R   5,6 CA
8 | P → S   2,7 CA
9 | P → M   4,8 CA

Problem 19. {P → Q, ~Q v (R & S), T, T → ~(R & S)} ⊢ ~P
1 | P → Q   P
2 | ~Q v (R & S)   P
3 | T   P
4 | T → ~(R & S)   P
5 | ~(R & S)   3,4 MP
6 | ~Q   2,5 DE
7 | ~P   1,6 MT

Exercise 6.4: Derivations With Replacement Rules.

Problem 1. {~(P v Q), ~Q → R} ⊢ R
1 | ~(P v Q)   P
2 | ~Q → R   P
3 | ~P & ~Q   1 DeM
4 | ~Q   3 CE
5 | R   2,4 MP

Problem 3. {~P, ~Q, (P v Q) v R} ⊢ R
1 | ~P   P
2 | ~Q   P
3 | (P v Q) v R P
4 | ~P & ~Q   1,2 CI
5 | ~(P v Q)   4 DeM
6 | R   3,5 DE

Problem 5. {~S, R → (P v Q), ~P, Q → S} ⊢ ~R
1 | ~S   P
2 | R → (P v Q) P
3 | ~P   P
4 | Q → S   P
5 | ~Q   1,4 MT
6 | ~P & ~Q   3,5 CI
7 | ~(P v Q)   6 DeM
8 | ~R   2,7 MT

Problem 7. {(P → Q) → R, Q} ⊢ R
1 | (P → Q) → R P
2 | Q   P
3 | ~P v Q   2 DI
4 | P → Q   3 Impl
5 | R   1,4 MP

Problem 9. {P → Q, ~P → R} ⊢ ~R → ~~Q
1 | P → Q   P
2 | ~P → R   P
3 | ~Q → ~P   1 CP
4 | ~Q → R   2,3 CA
5 | ~R → ~~Q   4 CP

Problem 11. {~~Q → R, P → Q, P} ⊢ R
1 | ~~Q → R   P
2 | P → Q   P
3 | P   P
4 | Q   2,3 MP
5 | ~~Q   4 DN
6 | R   1,5 MP

Problem 13. {P & (Q & R), R → S} ⊢ S
1 | P & (Q & R) P
2 | R → S   P
3 | (P & Q) & R 1 Assoc
4 | R   3 CE
5 | S   2,4 MP

Problem 15. {P → ~Q, ~(P & Q) → R} ⊢ R
1 | P → ~Q   P
2 | ~(P & Q) → R P
3 | ~P v ~Q   1 Impl
4 | ~(P & Q)   3 DeM
5 | R   2,4 MP

Problem 17. {(P v ~Q) v R, ~P} ⊢ Q → R

1	(P v ~Q) v R	P
2	~P	P
3	P v (~Q v R)	1 Assoc
4	~Q v R	2,3 DE
5	Q → R	4 Impl

Problem 19. {(P v Q) → R, ~(S v R)} ⊢ ~Q

1	(P v Q) → R	P
2	~(S v R)	P
3	~S & ~R	2 DeM
4	~R	3 CE
5	~(P v Q)	1,4 MT
6	~P & ~Q	5 DeM
7	~Q	6 CE

Exercise 6.5: Assorted Derivations. *Perform the following derivations.*

Problem 1. {~P} ⊢ ~Q → ~P

1	~P	P
2	~P v Q	DI
3	P → Q	2 Impl
4	~Q → ~P	3 CP

Problem 3. {P → (Q & ~R), S → R, (M & P) & N} ⊢ ~S

1	P → (Q & ~R)	P
2	S → R	P
3	(M & P) & N	P
4	M & P	3 CE
5	P	4 CE
6	Q & ~R	1,5 MP
7	~R	6 CE
8	~S	2,7 MT

Problem 5. {Q → (R v S), ~~Q} ⊢ S v R

1	Q → (R v S)	P
2	~~Q	P
3	Q	2 DN
4	R v S	1,3 MP
5	S v R	4 Com

Problem 7. {R → (P & S), ~S, R v ~(M v N)} ⊢ ~N v ~T

1	R → (P & S)	P
2	~S	P
3	R v ~(M v N)	P
4	~S v ~P	2 DI
5	~P v ~S	4 Com
6	~(P & S)	5 DeM
7	~R	1,6 MT
8	~(M v N)	3,7 DE
9	~M & ~N	8 DeM
10	~N	9 CE
11	~N v ~T	10 DI

Problem 9. {~(B v D)} ⊢ D → R

1	~(B v D)	P
2	~B & ~D	1 DeM
3	~D	2 CE
4	~D v R	3 DI
5	D → R	4 Impl

Problem 11. {((P & Q) & R) & S, (~P v ~Q) v B} ⊢ B
1 | ((P & Q) & R) & S   P
2 | (~P v ~Q) v B   P
3 | (P & Q) & R   1 CE
4 | P & Q   3 CE
5 | ~~(P & Q)   4 DN
6 | ~(~P v ~Q)   5 DeM
7 | B   2,6 DE

Problem 13. {P → (S → (N & B)), ~(~P v ~S)} ⊢ B
1 | P → (S → (N & B))   P
2 | ~(~P v ~S)   P
3 | ~~P & ~~S   2 DeM
4 | ~~P   3 CE
5 | P   4 DN
6 | S → (N & B)   1,5 MP
7 | ~~S   3 CE
8 | S   7 DN
9 | N & B   6,8 MP
10 | B   9 CE

Problem 15. {(~F v ~E) → ~T, E → (T & ~F), E} ⊢ ~T
1 | (~F v ~E) → ~T   P
2 | E → (T & ~F)   P
3 | E   P
4 | T & ~F   2,3 MP
5 | ~F   4 CE
6 | ~F v ~E   5 DI
7 | ~T   1,6 MP

Problem 17. {~(~Q → ~P) → (M v N), ~M, R & ~N} ⊢ P → Q
1 | ~(~Q → ~P) → (M v N) P
2 | ~M   P
3 | R & ~N   P
4 | ~N   3 CE
5 | ~M & ~N   2,4 CI
6 | ~(M v N)   5 DeM
7 | ~~(~Q → ~P)   1,6 MT
8 | ~Q → ~P   7 DN
9 | P → Q   8 CP

Problem 19. {B → (C & R), ~M & ~R} ⊢ ~B v C
1 | B → (C & R)   P
2 | ~M & ~R   P
3 | ~R   2 CE
4 | ~C v ~R   3 DI
5 | ~(C & R)   4 DeM
6 | ~B   1,5 MT
7 | ~B v C   6 DI

Problem 21. {(R v S) → (T & D), B & (Q & (P & T)), (P & Q) → (R v S)} ⊢ D
1 | (R v S) → (T & D)   P
2 | B & (Q & (P & T))   P
3 | (P & Q) → (R v S)   P
4 | Q & (P & T)   2 CE
5 | P & T   4 CE
6 | P   5 CE
7 | Q   4 CE
8 | P & Q   6,7 CI
9 | R v S   3,8 MP
10 | T & D   1,9 MP
11 | D   10 CE

Problem 23. {(Q & M) → (E v K), M & (E v C), Q & ~N} ⊢ E v K
1	(Q & M) → (E v K)	P
2	M & (E v C)	P
3	Q & ~N	P
4	Q	3 CE
5	M	2 CE
6	Q & M	4,5 CI
7	E v K	1,6 MP

Problem 25. {~P v Q, Q → ~(M & N), (S & P) & (T & N)} ⊢ ~M
1	~P v Q	P
2	Q → ~(M & N)	P
3	(S & P) & (T & N)	P
4	S & P	3 CE
5	P	4 CE
6	P → Q	1 Impl
7	Q	5,6 MP
8	~(M & N)	2,7 MP
9	~M v ~N	8 DeM
10	T & N	3 CE
11	N	10 CE
12	~~N	11 DN
13	~M	9,12 DE

Problem 27. {(B & Q) → (R & (S → T)), ~(P v ~B), P v Q, ~S → ~R} ⊢ T
1	(B & Q) → (R & (S → T)	P
2	~(P v ~B)	P
3	P v Q	P
4	~S → ~R	P
5	~P & ~~B	2 DeM
6	~~B	5 CE
7	B	6 DN
8	~P	5 CE
9	Q	3,8 DE
10	B & Q	7,9 CI
11	R & (S → T)	1,10 MP
12	R	11 CE
13	R → S	4 CP
14	S	12,13 MP
15	S → T	11 CE
16	T	14,15 MP

Problem 29. {~D, ~((B v R) v (M → N)), (~S v T) v D, ~T} ⊢ ~(R v S)
1	~D	P
2	~((B v R) v (M → N))	P
3	(~S v T) v D	P
4	~T	P
5	~S v T	1,3 DE
6	~S	4,5 DE
7	~(B v R) & ~(M → N)	2 DeM
8	~(B v R)	7 CE
9	~B & ~R	8 DeM
10	~R	9 CE
11	~R & ~S	6,10 CI
12	~(R v S)	11 DeM

Exercise 6.6: More Derivations.

Problem 1. {~M v N) ⊢ ~N → ~M
1	~M v N	P
2	M → N	1 Impl
3	~N → ~M	2 CP

Problem 3. {~R, ~S v (R & T)} ⊢ ~S
1 | ~R   P
2 | ~S v (R & T)   P
3 | ~R v ~T   1 DI
4 | ~(R & T)   3 DeM
5 | ~S   2,4 DE

Problem 5. {(D → C) & (C → D), E → ~(D → C)} ⊢ ~E
1 | (D → C) & (C → D)   P
2 | E → ~(D → C)   P
3 | D → C   1 CE
4 | ~E   2,3 MT

Problem 7. {(~J v K) → N, ~(M v N)} ⊢ J
1 | (~J v K) → N   P
2 | ~(M v N)   P
3 | ~M & ~N   2 DeM
4 | ~N   3 CE
5 | ~(~J v K)   1,4 MT
6 | ~~J & ~K   5 DeM
7 | ~~J   6 CE
8 | J   7 DN

Problem 9. {P & P, Q → ~P} ⊢ ~Q
1 | P & P   P
2 | Q → ~P   P
3 | P   1 CE
4 | ~~P   3 DN
5 | ~Q   2,4 MT

Problem 11. {~(~U → (X → W)), Z → (~U v (X → W))} ⊢ ~Z
1 | ~(~U → (X → W))   P
2 | Z → (~U → (X → W))   P
3 | ~Z   1,2 MT

Problem 13. {F & (G & H), (~H → S) → ((F & G) → M)} ⊢ M
1 | F & (G & H)   P
2 | (~H → S) → ((F & G) → M)   P
3 | (F & G) & H   1 Assoc
4 | H   3 CE
5 | ~~H   4 DN
6 | ~~H v S   5 DI
7 | ~H → S   6 Impl
8 | (F & G) → M   2,7 MP
9 | F & G   3 CE
10 | M   8,9 MP

Problem 15. {O → N, (~N → ~O) → P} ⊢ P
1 | O → N   P
2 | (~N → ~O) → P   P
3 | ~N → ~O   1 CP
4 | P   2,3 MP

Problem 17. {(~A → ~B) → ~D, ~((~A & B) v (~A & C))} ⊢ ~D
1 | (~A → ~B) → ~D   P
2 | ~((~A & B) v (~A & C))   P
3 | ~(~A & B) & ~(~A & C)   2 DeM
4 | ~(~A & B)   3 CE
5 | ~~A v ~B   4 DN
6 | ~A → ~B   5 Impl
7 | ~D   1,6 MP

SOLUTIONS TO ODD NUMBERED PROBLEMS

Problem 19. {H & H, H → ~J} ⊢ ~J
1 | H & H   P
2 | H → ~J   P
3 | H   1 CE
4 | ~J   2,3 MP

Problem 21. {~((Z v Y) v (Z v ~W)), Z → ~~U, ~Y → (W → U)} ⊢ U
1 | ~((Z v Y) v (Z v ~W))   P
2 | Z → ~~U   P
3 | ~Y → (W → U)   P
4 | ~(Z v Y) & ~(Z v ~W)   1 DeM
5 | ~(Z v Y)   4 CE
6 | ~Z & ~Y   5 DeM
7 | ~Y   6 CE
8 | W → U   3,7 MP
9 | ~(Z v ~W)   4 CE
10 | ~Z & ~~W   9 DeM
11 | ~~W   10 CE
12 | W   11 DN
13 | U   8,12 MP

Problem 23. {~((Q & R) v (~Q & ~R)), N → (Q & R), E v N} ⊢ E
1 | ~((Q & R) v (~Q & ~R))   P
2 | N → (Q & R)   P
3 | E v N   P
4 | ~(Q & R) & ~(~Q & ~R)   1 DeM
5 | ~(Q & R)   4 CE
6 | ~N   2,5 MT
7 | E   3,6 DE

Problem 25. {~(J & L), (J → ~L) → (~M & ~X), E v (M v X)} ⊢ E
1 | ~(J & L)   P
2 | (J → ~L) → (~M & ~X)   P
3 | E v (M v X)   P
4 | ~J v ~L   1 DeM
5 | J → ~L   4 Impl
6 | ~M & ~X   2,5 MP
7 | ~(M v X)   6 DeM
8 | E   3,7 DE

Problem 27. {~(~B v (C v ~D)), (D & B) → P} ⊢ P
 | 1. ~(~B v (C v ~D))   P
 | 2. (D & B) → P   P
 | 3. ~~B & ~(C v ~D)   1 DeM
 | 4. ~~B   3 CE
 | 5. B   4 DN
 | 6. ~(C v ~D)   3 CE
 | 7. ~C & ~~D   6 DeM
 | 8. ~~D   7 CE
 | 9. D   8 DN
 | 10. D & B   5,9 CI
 | 11. P   2,10 MP

Problem 29. {~X v ~Y, ~P v ~M, B → P, (X → ~Y) → M} ⊢ ~B
1 | ~X v ~Y   P
2 | ~P v ~M   P
3 | B → P   P
4 | (X → ~Y) → M   P
5 | X → ~Y   1 Impl
6 | M   4,5 MP
7 | ~~M   6 DN
8 | ~P   2,7 DE
9 | ~B   3,8 MT

Problem 31. {L → (P → ~F), (M & (L & J)) → (H & G), ~(R v (S & P)), (H & G) → L} ⊢ (M & (L & J)) → (P → ~F)
1 | L → (P → ~F) | P
2 | (M & (L & J)) → (H & G) | P
3 | ~(R v (S & P)) | P
4 | (H & G) → L | P
5 | (M & (L & J)) → L | 2,4 CA
6 | (M & (L & J) → (P → ~F) | 1,5 CA

Problem 33. {~(Z & W) → Q, ~Z, (W & ~Q) v ~R, (S & (P & Q)) → R, (B ↔ (R v A)) & (F & (Z & S))} ⊢ ~P v ~Q
1. ~(Z & W) → Q | P
2. ~Z | P
3. (W & ~Q) v ~R | P
4. (S & (P & Q)) → R | P
5. (B ↔ (R v A)) & (F & (Z & S)) | P
6. ~Z v ~W | 2 DI
7. ~(Z & W) | 6 DeM
8. Q | 1,7 MP
9. ~~Q | 8 DN
10. ~W v ~~Q | 9 DI
11. ~(W & ~Q) | 10 DeM
12. ~R | 3,11 DE
13. ~(S & (P & Q)) | 4,12 MT
14. ~S v ~(P & Q) | 13 DeM
15. F & (Z & S) | 5 CE
16. Z & S | 15 CE
17. S | 16 CE
18. ~(P & Q) | 14,17 DE
19. ~P v ~Q | 18 DeM

Problem 35. {(A v B) & (A v G), M → ~A, ~Q → (~B v ~G), (M & ~Q) → ~(~M v ~A)} ⊢ ~Q → ~M
1 | (A v B) & (A v G) | P
2 | M → ~A | P
3 | ~Q → (~B v ~G) | P
4 | (M & ~Q) → ~(~M v ~A) | P
5 | ~M v ~A | 2 Impl
6 | ~~(~M v ~A) | 5 DN
7 | ~(M & ~Q) | 4,6 MT
8 | ~M v ~~Q | 7 DeM
9 | M → ~~Q | 8 Impl
10 | ~~~Q → ~M | 9 CP
11 | ~Q → ~M | 10 DN

Problem 37. {~D → J, (M & N) → ~R, ~G → ~F, D → R, ~H → ~F, ~(M & N) → Z, H → Z, J → ~P} ⊢ P → Z
1 | 1. ~D → J | P
2 | 2. (M & N) → ~R | P
3 | 3. ~G → ~F | P
4 | 4. D → R | P
5 | 5. ~H → ~F | P
6 | 6. ~(M & N) → Z | P
7 | 7. H → Z | P
8 | 8. J → ~P | P
9 | 9. ~~P → ~J | 8 CP
10 | 10. P → ~J | 9 DN
11 | 11. ~J → ~~D | 1 CP
12 | 12. ~J → D | 11 DN
13 | 13. P → D | 10,12 CA
14 | 14. P → R | 4,13 CA
15 | 15. ~~R → ~(M & N) | 2 CP
16 | 16. R → ~(M & N) | 15 DN
17 | 17. P → ~(M & N) | 14, 16, CA
18 | 18. P → Z | 6,17 CA

Problem 39. {~(Z & W) → B, ~K → E, (~E v Z) & (~U & W), ~K → (~Z v ~W), K → U} ⊢ (S & R) → B
1 | ~(Z & W) → B | P
2 | ~K → E | P
3 | (~E v Z) & (~U & W) | P
4 | ~K → (~Z v ~W) | P
5 | K → U | P
6 | ~U & W | 3 CE
7 | ~U | 6 CE
8 | ~K | 5,7 MT
9 | ~Z v ~W | 4,8 MP
10 | ~(Z & W) | 9 DeM
11 | B | 1,10 MP
12 | ~(S & R) v B | 11 DI
13 | (S & R) → B | 12 Impl

Chapter 7: Solutions to Odd Numbered Problems
Exercise 7.1: Extremely Simple Sub-Derivations.
Problem 1. {M → N, N → R} ⊢ M → R
1 | M → N   P
2 | N → R   P
3 | | M   H
4 | | N   1,3 MP
5 | | R   2,4 MP
6 | M → R   3-5 CoI

Problem 3. {B → (Q & ~Q)} ⊢ ~B
1 | B → (Q & ~Q)   P
2 | | B   H
3 | | Q & ~Q   1,2 MP
4 | ~B   2-3 NI

Problem 5. {P ↔ R, P → ~R} ⊢ ~P
1 | P → R   P
2 | P → ~R   P
3 | | P   H
4 | | R   1,3 MP
5 | | ~R   2,3 MP
6 | | R & ~R 4,5 CI
7 | ~P   3-6 NI

Problem 7. {B → C, A → B} ⊢ A → C
1 | B → C   P
2 | A → B   P
3 | | A   H
4 | | B   1,2 MP
5 | | C   1,4 MP
6 | A → C   3-5 CoI

Problem 9. {P v Q, R → ~P} ⊢ R → Q
1 | P v Q   P
2 | R → ~P   P
3 | | R   H
4 | | ~P   2,3 MP
5 | | Q   1,4 DE
6 | R → Q   3-5 CoI

Problem 11. {P → (M & N)} ⊢ P → M
1 | P → (M & N)   P
2 | | P   H
3 | | M & N   1,2 MP
4 | | M   3 CE
5 | P → M   2-4 CoI

Problem 13. {P ↔ Q, Q → ~P} ⊢ ~Q
1 | P ↔ Q   P
2 | Q → ~P   P
3 | | Q   H
4 | | P   1,3 BCoE
5 | | ~P   2,3 MP
6 | | P & ~P   4,5 CI
7 | ~Q   3-6 NI

Problem 15. {P → ~Q, Q v R} ⊢ P → R
1 | P → ~Q   P
2 | Q v R   P
3 | | P   H
4 | | ~Q   1,3 MP
5 | | R   2,4 DE
6 | P → R   3-5 CoI

Problem 17. {~P v Q} ⊢ P → Q
1 | ~P v Q   P
2 | | P   H
3 | | Q   1,2 DE
4 | P → Q   2-3 CoI

Problem 19. {T v ~S, M} ⊢ ~T → ~S
1 | T v ~S   P
2 | M   P
3 | | ~T   H
4 | | ~S   1,3 DE
5 | ~T → ~S   3-4 CoI

Exercise 7.2: Longer Sub-Derivations.

Problem 1. {P & ~P} ⊢ R
1 | P & ~P   P
2 | | ~R   H
3 | | P & ~P   R
4 | R   2-3 NE

Problem 3. {(P v ~D) → ~L} ⊢ (L → D)
1 | (P v ~D) → ~L   P
2 | | L   H
3 | | ~(P v ~D)   1,2 MT
4 | | ~P & ~~D   3 DeM
5 | | ~~D   4 CE
6 | | D   5 DN
7 | L → D   2-6 CoI

Problem 5. {P ↔ R, P → ~R} ⊢ ~P
1 | P ↔ R   P
2 | P → ~R   P
3 | | P   H
4 | | R   1,3 BCoE
5 | | ~R   2,3 MP
6 | | R & ~R   4,5 CI
7 | ~P   3-6 NI

Problem 7. {P → S, ~P → B, ~S → ~B} ⊢ S

1	P → S		P
2	~P → B		P
3	~S → ~B		P
4		~S	H
5		~P	1,4 MT
6		B	2,5 MP
7		~B	3,4 MP
8		B & ~B	6,7 CI
9	S		4-8 NE

Problem 9. {(M v R) & (M v ~R)} ⊢ M

1	(M v R) & (M v ~R)		P
2		~M	H
3		M v R	1 CE
4		R	2,3 DE
5		M v ~R	1 CE
6		~R	2,5 DE
7		R & ~R	4,6 CI
8	M		2-7 NE

Problem 11. {(P & Q) → (R & S)} ⊢ (Q & P) → (S & R)

1	(P & Q) → (R & S)		P
2		Q & P	H
3		P & Q	2 Com
4		R & S	1,3 MP
5		S & R	4 Com
6	(Q & P) → (S & R)		2-5 CoI

Problem 13. {C & ~B, (R & C) → B} ⊢ ~R

1	C & ~B		P
2	(R & C) → B		P
3		R	H
4		C	1 CE
5		R & C	3,4 CI
6		B	2,5 MP
7		~B	1 CE
8		B & ~B	6,7 CI
9	~R		3-8 NI

Problem 15. {(~R → F) & (F → ~R)} ⊢ ~R ↔ F

1	(~R → F) & (F → ~R)		P
2		~R	H
3		~R → F	1 CE
4		F	2,3 MP
5		F	H
6		F → ~R	1 CE
7		~R	5,6 MP
8	~R ↔ F		2-4,5-7 BCoI

Problem 17. {P → Q} ⊢ ~Q → ~P

1	P → Q		P
2		~Q	H
3		~P	1,2 MT
4	~Q → ~P		2-3 CoI

Problem 19. {P} ⊢ (P → Q) → Q

1	P		P
2		P → Q	H
3		Q	1,2 MP
4	(P → Q) → Q		2-3 CoI

Problem 21. {M} ⊢ ~(M & L) → ~L
1 | M | P
2 | | ~(M & L) | H
3 | | ~M v ~L | 2 DeM
4 | | ~~M | 1 DN
5 | | ~L | 3,4 DE
6 | ~(M & L) → ~L | 2-5 CoI

Problem 23. {~P v (Q & ~R)} ⊢ R → ~P
1 | ~P v (Q & ~R) | P
2 | | R | H
3 | | (~P v Q) & (~P v ~R) | 1 Dist
4 | | ~P v ~R | 3 CE
5 | | ~~R | 2 DN
6 | | ~P | 4,5 DE
7 | R → ~P | 2-6 CoI

Problem 25. {(A & B) → C} ⊢ A → (B → C)
1 | (A & B) → C | P
2 | | A | H
3 | | B | H
4 | | A & B | 2,3 CI
5 | | C | 1,4 MP
6 | | B → C | 3-5 CoI
7 | A → (B → C) | 2-6 CoI

Problem 27. {~M ↔ L} ⊢ L → ~M
1 | ~M ↔ L | P
2 | | L | H
3 | | ~M | 1,2 BCoE
4 | L → ~M | 2-3 CoI

Problem 29. {B → R, (R v Q) → ~B} ⊢ ~B
1 | B → R | P
2 | (R v Q) → ~B | P
3 | | B | H
4 | | R | 1,3 MP
5 | | R v Q | 4 DI
6 | | ~B | 2,5 MP
7 | | B & ~B | 3,6 CI
8 | ~B | 3-7 NI

Problem 31. {P & (Q & R), P → ~(T v R)} ⊢ ~B
1 | P & (Q & R) | P
2 | P → ~(T v R) | P
3 | | B | Hyp
4 | | P | 1 CE
5 | | ~(T v R) | 2,4 MP
6 | | ~T & ~R | 5 DeM
7 | | ~R | 6 CE
8 | | (P & Q) & R | 1 Assoc
9 | | R | 8 CE
10 | | R & ~R | 7,9 CI
11 | ~B | 3-10 NI

Problem 33. {~(P & Q) v R} ⊢ ~R → (P → ~Q)
1 | ~(P & Q) v R | P
2 | | ~R | H
3 | | ~(P & Q) | 1,2 DE
4 | | ~P v ~Q | 3 DeM
5 | | P → ~Q | 4 Impl
6 | ~R → (P → ~Q) | 2-5 CoI

SOLUTIONS TO ODD NUMBERED PROBLEMS

Problem 35. {P, ~(P v Q)} ⊢ T

1	P	P
2	~(P v Q)	P
3	~T	H
4	~P & ~Q	2 DeM
5	~P	4 CE
6	P	1 R
7	P & ~P	5,6 CI
8	T	3-7 NE

Problem 37. {~T v P, P → (M & N), (N v S) ↔ T, } ⊢ P ↔ T

1	~T v P	P
2	P → (M & N)	P
3	(N v S) ↔ T	P
4	P	H
5	M & N	2, MP
6	N	5 CE
7	N v S	6 DI
8	T	3,7 BCoE
9	T	H
10	P	1,9 DE
11	P ↔ T	4-8, 9-10 BCoI

Problem 39. {B ↔ R, B ↔ (S v N), R → N} ⊢ R ↔ (N v S)

1	B ↔ R	P
2	B ↔ (S v N)	P
3	R → N	P
4	R	H
5	N	3,4 MP
6	N v S	5 DI
7	N v S	H
8	S v N	7 Com
9	B	2,8 BCoE
10	R	1,9 BCoE
11	R ↔ (N v S)	4-6, 7-10 BCoI

Exercise 7.3: Theorems.

Problem 1. ~(A & ~A)

1	A & ~A	H
2	A & ~A	1 R
3	~(A & ~A)	1-2 NI

Problem 3. ~(P & ~Q) → (P → Q)

1	~(P & ~Q)	H
2	~P v ~~Q	1 DeM
3	~P v Q	2 DN
4	P → Q	3 Impl
5	~(P & ~Q) → (P → Q)	1-4 CoI

Problem 5. (P & (P → Q)) → Q

1	P & (P → Q)	H
2	P	1 CE
3	P → Q	1 CE
4	Q	2,3 MP
5	(P & (P → Q)) → Q	1-4 CoI

Problem 7. ((P v Q) & ~Q) → P
1	(P v Q) & ~Q	H
2	P v Q	1 CE
3	~Q	1 CE
4	P	2,3 DE
5	((P v Q) & ~Q) → P	1-4 CoI

Problem 9. A → (B → A)
1	A	H
2	B	H
3	A	1R
4	B → A	2-3 CoI
5	A → (B → A)	1-4 CoI

Problem 11. P v ~P
1	~(P v ~P)	H
2	~P & ~~P	1 DeM
3	~P & P	2 DN
4	P v ~P	1-4 NE

Problem 13. P → (~P → Q)
1	P	H
2	P v Q	1 DI
3	~P → Q	2 Impl
4	P → (~P → Q)	1-3 CoI

Problem 15. ~P → (P → Q)
1	~P	H
2	~P v Q	1 DI
3	P → Q	2 Impl
4	~P → (P → Q)	1-3 CoI

Problem 17. P & (Q & R) ↔ (P & Q) & R
1	P & (Q & R)	H
2	Q & R	1 CE
3	R	2 CE
4	Q	2 CE
5	P	1 CE
6	P & Q	4 CI
7	(P & Q) & R	3,6 CI
8	(P & Q) & R	H
9	P & Q	8 CE
10	P	9 CE
11	Q	9 CE
12	R	8 CE
13	Q & R	11,12 CI
14	P & (Q & R)	10,13 CI
15	P & (Q & R) ↔ (P & Q) & R	1-7, 8-14 BCoI

Problem 19. ~(P & Q) ↔ (~P v ~Q)
1	~(P & Q)	H
2	~P v ~Q	1 DeM
3	~P v ~Q	H
4	~(P & Q)	3 DeM
5	~(P & Q) ↔ ~P v ~Q	1-2, 3-4 BCoI

Exercise 7.4: Assorted Derivations.

Problem 1. {P → (~N & ~M), ~N → (~M → P)} ⊢ P ↔ (~N & ~M)
1. P → (~N & ~M)   P
2. ~N → (~M → P)   P
3.   P   H
4.   ~N & ~M   1,3 MP

5.   ~N & ~M   H
6.   ~N   5 CE
7.   ~M → P   2,6 MP
8.   ~M   5 CE
9.   P   7,8 MP
10. P ↔ (~N & ~M)   3-4,5-9 BCoI

Problem 3. {(B → C) → D} ⊢ B → (C → D)
1. (B → C) → D   P
2.   B   H
3.   C   H
4.   ~B v C   3 DI
5.   B → C   4 Impl
6.   D   1,5 MP
7.   C → D   3-6 CoI
8. B → (C → D)   2-7 CoI

Problem 5. {~M v (T → B), ~S → (M v B), M → T} ⊢ B v S
1. ~M v (T → B)   P
2. ~S → (M v B)   P
3. M → T   P
4.   ~(B v S)   H
5.   ~B & ~S   4 DeM
6.   ~S   5 CE
7.   M v B   2,6 MP
8.   ~B   5 CE
9.   M   7,8 DE
10. T   3,9 MP
11. T → B   1,9 DE
12. B   10,11 MP
13. B & ~B   8,12 CI
14. B v S   4-13 NE

Problem 7. {M v R, M → (R v S), R → (R v S)} ⊢ ~(~R & ~S)
1. M v R   P
2. M → (R v S)   P
3. R → (R v S)   P
4.   ~R & ~S   H
5.   ~(R v S)   4 DeM
6.   ~M   2,5 MT
7.   ~R   3,5 MT
8.   R   1,6 DE
9.   R & ~R   7,8 CI
19. ~(~R & ~S)   4-9 NI

Problem 9. {~(C & D), (~C → T), (~D → R)} ⊢ T v R

1	~(C & D)	P
2	~C → T	P
3	~D → R	P
4	~(T v R)	H
5	~T & ~R	4 DeM
6	~T	5 CE
7	~R	5 CE
8	~~C	2,6 MT
9	C	8 DN
10	~~D	3,7 MT
11	D	10 DN
12	C & D	9,11 CI
13	(C & D) & ~(C & D)	1,12 CI
14	T v R	4-13 NE

Problem 11. {P v (P v P)} ⊢ P

1	P v (P v P)	P
2	~P	H
3	P v P	1,2 DE
4	P	2,3 DE
5	P & ~P	2,4 CI
6	P	2-5 NE

Problem 13. {F & ~G} ⊢ ~(F → G)

1	F & ~G	P
2	F → G	H
3	F	1 CE
4	G	2-3 MP
5	~G	1 CE
6	G & ~G	4,5 CI
7	~(F → G)	2-6 NI

Problem 15. {} ⊢ ~(P → Q) ↔ (P & ~Q)

1	~(P → Q)	H
2	~(P & ~Q)	H
3	~P v ~~Q	2 DeM
4	~P v Q	3 DN
5	P → Q	4 Impl
6	~(P → Q)	1 R
7	(P → Q) & ~(P → Q)	5,6 CI
8	P & ~Q	2-7 NE
9	P & ~Q	H
10	P → Q	H
11	P	9 CE
12	Q	10,11 MP
13	~Q	9 CE
14	Q & ~Q	12, 13 CI
15	~(P → Q)	10-14 NI
16	~(P → Q) ↔ (P & ~Q)	1-8, 9-15 BCoI

Problem 17. {P v ~N, ~P v ~N} ⊢ ~N

1	P v ~N	P
2	~P v ~N	P
3	N	H
4	P	1,3 DE
5	~P	2,3 DE
6	P & ~P	4,5 CI
7	~N	3-6 NI

Problem 19. {A ↔ B} ⊢ (C ↔ A) ↔ (C ↔ B)

1	A ↔ B			P
2		C ↔ A		H
3			C	H
4			A	2,3 BCoE
5			B	1,4 BCoE
6			B	H
7			A	1,6 BCoE
8			C	2,7 BCoE
9		C ↔ B		3-5,6-8 BCoI
10		C ↔ B		H
11			C	H
12			B	10,11 BCoE
13			A	1,12 BCoE
14			A	H
15			B	1,14 BCoE
16			C	10,15 BCoE
17		C ↔ A		11-13,14-16 BCoI
18	(C ↔ A) ↔ (C ↔ B)			2-9,10-17 BCoI

Chapter 8: Solutions to Odd Numbered Problems

Exercise 8.1: Extremely Simple Predicate Translations.

1. Gs
3. Gn
5. Wj
7. Pj
9. Pn
11. Julius is Roman.
13. Plato is poor.
15. Socrates is wealthy.
17. Nero is Roman.
19. Julius is poor.

Exercise 8.2: Simple Predicate Translations.

1. Gs & Ps
3. Gp → Gs
5. ~Gp → ~Gs
7. Rn → (Rj v Gj)
9. Pn & Ps
11. Either Plato is Greek or Socrates is Greek.
13. Socrates and Plato are both Greek.
15. Julius and Plato are both wealthy.
17. If Julius is Roman, then Plato is Greek.
19. If Julius is not wealthy, then Plato is not wealthy.

Exercise 8.3: Predicate Translations.

1. (Ps & Gs) v (Pp & Gs)
3. (Wp & Gp) → (Wn & Rn)
5. Wp & ~Rp
7. (Pp & Gp) v ~(Pp & Rp)
9. Wj → Rj
11. If either Plato or Socrates is Greek, then either Plato or Socrates is wealthy.
13. Plato is a wealthy Greek if and only if Socrates is a poor Greek.
15. If Julius is a wealthy Roman, then Nero is poor.
17. Plato and Socrates are not both wealthy.
19. It is not true that Plato is Greek only if Socrates is Roman.

Exercise 8.4: Extremely Simple Quantifier Translations.

1. (∃x) Bx
3. (∃x) Bx & Sx
5. (x) Sx
7. (∃x) Lxd
9. (x) Tgx
11. (Step 1) For all y, y is beautiful. (Step 2) Everyone is beautiful.
13. (Step 1) For all x, x is beautiful and x is smart. (Step 2) Everyone is beautiful and smart.
15. (Step 1) There exists a y such that y is smart and y is beautiful. (Step 2) Someone is smart and beautiful.
17. (Step 1) There exists a y such that y is smart. (Step 2) Someone is smart.
19. (Step 1) For all z, Gilda loves z. (Step 2) Gilda loves everyone.

Exercise 8.5: Simple Quantifier Translations.

1. (x) Sx → Bx
3. (x) Lxg → Lgx
5. (x) Lxg → Lgx
7. (x) Txg → ~Tgx
9. [(x) Tgx] → Tgd
11. (Step 1) For all z, z is beautiful or z is smart. (Step 2) Everyone is either beautiful or smart.
13. (Step 1) For all x, if x is taller than Gilda, then x is taller than Doug. (Step 2) Whoever is taller than Gilda is taller than Doug.
15. (Step 1) There exists an x such that x is taller than Doug and it is not the case that x is taller than Gilda. (Step 2) Someone is taller than Doug, but not taller than Gilda.
17. (Step 1) There exists an x such that x is smart and Gilda loves x. (Step 2) Gilda loves someone smart.
19. (Step 1) For all x, if x loves Gilda, then Gilda loves x. (Step 2) Gilda loves anyone who loves her.

Exercise 8.6: Quantifier Translations.

Mx = x is male
Fx = x is female
Pxy = x is a parent of y
Sxy = x is a sibling of y
h = Hunter
j = Jayden

Example 1
Problem: Everyone has a mother.
Solution: (x)(∃y)(Fy & Pyx)

Example 2
Problem: (∃x)(∃y)(Pxy & Pyj)
Solution: Jayden has a grandparent.

1. (∃x) Mx & Sxh
3. (∃x)(∃y) [(Mx & Sxh) & (Fy & Syh)]
5. (∃x)(∃y) [(Fx & Sxy) & (Fy & Pyj)]
7. (x) [(∃y) (My & Pyx) → (∃z) (Fz & Pzx)]
9. (x) [(∃y) (My & Syx) ↔ (Mx & (∃z) Sxy)]
11. (Step 1) There exists an x such that x is male and x is a parent of Jayden. (Step 2) Jayden has a father.
13. (Step 1) There exists an x such that there exists a y such that x is male and y is female and x is a parent of Jayden and y is a parent of Jayden. (Step 2) Jayden has both a father and a mother.
15. (Step 1) For all x there exists a y such that either y is male and y is a sibling of x or y is female and y is a sibling of x. (Step 2) Everyone has a brother or a sister.
17. (Step 1) For all x there exists a y such that x is male and x is a parent of y if and only if there exists a z such that z is male and z is a parent of x. (Step 2) By definition, whoever is a father has a father.
19. (Step 1) For all x there exists a y such that there exists a z such that y is male and y is a sibling of z and z is a parent of x. (Step 2) Everyone has an uncle.

Chapter 9: Solutions to Odd Numbered Problems

Exercise 9.1: Extremely Simple Derivations.

Problem 1. {Hp, (x)Hx → Mx} ⊢ Mp
1 | Hp   P
2 | (x)Hx → Mx P
3 | Hp → Mp   2 UE
4 | Mp   1,3 MP

Problem 3. {Hp, (x)Hx ↔ Mx} ⊢ Mp
1 | Hp   P
2 | (x)Hx ↔ Mx P
3 | Hp ↔ Mp   2 UE
4 | Mp   1,3 BCoE

Problem 5. {(x)Px, Gd} ⊢ Pd & Gd
1 | (x)Px   P
2 | Gd   P
3 | Pd   1 UE
4 | Pd & Gd   2,3 CI

Problem 7. {Hp, (x)Hx → Mx} ⊢ (∃x)Mx
1 | Hp   P
2 | (x)Hx → Mx P
3 | Hp → Mp   2 UE
4 | Mp   1,3 MP
5 | (∃x)Mx   4 EI

Problem 9. {Dp & Gp} ⊢ (∃x)Gx
1 | Dp & Gp   P
2 | Gp   1 CE
3 | (∃x)Gx   2 EI

Problem 11. {Hp → Mp, Mp → Gp} ⊢ (∃x)Hx → Gx
1 | Hp → Mp   P
2 | Mp → Gp   P
3 | Hp → Gp   1,2 CA
4 | (∃x)Hx → Gx 3 EI

Problem 13. {(x)Dx → Gx, (x)Dx} ⊢ (∃x)Gx
1 | (x)Dx → Gx P
2 | (x)Dx   P
3 | Dp   2 UE
4 | Dp → Gp   1 UE
5 | Gp   3,4 MP
6 | (∃x)Gx   5 EI

Problem 15. {~Gd, (x)Px v Gx} ⊢ (∃x)Px
1 | ~Gd   P
2 | (x)Px v Gx P
3 | Pd v Gd   2 UE
4 | Pd   1,3 DE
5 | (∃x)Px   4 EI

Problem 17. {(x)Px ↔ Rx, (x)Rx} ⊢ (∃x)Px
1 | (x)Px ↔ Rx P
2 | (x)Rx   P
3 | Pd ↔ Rd   1 UE
4 | Rd   2 UE
5 | Pd   3,4 BCoE
6 | (∃x)Px   5 EI

Problem 19. {(x)Bx, (x)Px} ⊢ (∃x)Bx & Px
1 | (x)Bx | P
2 | (x)Px | P
3 | Bp | 1 UE
4 | Pp | 2 UE
5 | Bp & Pp | 3,4 CI
6 | (∃x)Bx & Px | 5 EI

Exercise 9.2: Longer Simple Derivations.

Problem 1. {(x)Px, (x)Mx} ⊢ (x)Px & Mx
1 | (x)Px | P
2 | (x)Mx | P
3 | Pd | 1 UE
4 | Md | 2 UE
5 | Pd & Md | 3,4 CI
6 | (x)Px & Mx | 5 UI

Problem 3. {(x)Px & Qx, (x)Qx & Rx} ⊢ (x)Px & Rx
1 | (x)Px & Qx | P
2 | (x)Qx & Rx | P
3 | Pd & Qd | 1 UE
4 | Qd & Rd | 2 UE
5 | Pd | 3 CE
6 | Rd | 4 CE
7 | Pd & Rd | 5,6 CI
8 | (x)Px & Rx | 7 UI

Problem 5. {(x)Px ↔ Qx, (x)Px} ⊢ (x)Qx
1 | (x)Px ↔ Qx | P
2 | (x)Px | P
3 | Pd ↔ Qd | 1 UE
4 | Pd | 2 UE
5 | Qd | 3,4 BCoE
6 | (x)Qx | 5 UI

Problem 7. {(x)Px & Qx} ⊢ (x)Qx v Rx
1 | (x)Px & Qx | P
2 | Pd & Qd | P
3 | Qd | 2 CE
4 | Qd v Rd | 3 DI
5 | (x)Qx v Rx | 4 UI

Problem 9. {(x)(y)Bxy} ⊢ (x)(y)Byx
1 | (x)(y)Bxy | P
2 | (y)Bdy | 1 UE
3 | Bdg | 2 UE
4 | (y)Byg | 3 UI
5 | (x)(y)Byx | 4 UI

Problem 11. {(∃x)Px} ⊢ (∃x)Px v Qx
1 | (∃x)Px | P
2 | Pd | H
3 | Pd v Qd | 2 DI
4 | (∃x)Px v Qx | 3 EI
5 | (∃x)Px v Qx | 1,2-4 EE

Problem 13. $\{(\exists x)Px \to Qx, (x)Px\} \vdash (\exists x)Qx$

1	$(\exists x)Px \to Qx$	P
2	$(x)Px$	P
3	$\quad Pd \to Qd$	H
4	$\quad Pd$	2 UE
5	$\quad Qd$	3,4 MP
6	$\quad (\exists x)Qx$	5 EI
7	$(\exists x)Qx$	1,3-6 EE

Problem 15. $\{(\exists x)Px \,\&\, Qx\} \vdash (\exists x)Qx$

1	$(\exists x)Px \,\&\, Qx$	P
2	$\quad Pd \,\&\, Qd$	H
3	$\quad Qd$	2 CE
4	$\quad (\exists x)Qx$	3 EI
5	$(\exists x)Qx$	1,2-4 EE

Problem 17. $\{(\exists x)(Px \,\&\, Qx) \to Rx, (x)\sim Rx, (x)Qx\} \vdash (\exists x)\sim Px$

1	$(\exists x)(Px \,\&\, Qx) \to Rx$	P
2	$(x)\sim Rx$	P
3	$(x)Qx$	P
4	$\quad (Pd \,\&\, Qd) \to Rd$	H
5	$\quad \sim Rd$	2 UE
6	$\quad \sim(Pd \,\&\, Qd)$	4,5 MT
7	$\quad \sim Pd \lor \sim Qd$	6 DeM
8	$\quad Qd$	3 UE
9	$\quad \sim Pd$	7,8 DE
10	$\quad (\exists x)\sim Px$	9 EI
11	$(\exists x)\sim Px$	1,4-10 EE

Problem 19. $\{(\exists x)(y)Bxy\} \vdash (\exists x)(\exists y)Bxy$

1	$(\exists x)(y)Bxy$	P
2	$\quad (y)Bdy$	H
3	$\quad Bdg$	2 UE
4	$\quad (\exists y)Bdy$	3 EI
5	$\quad (\exists x)(\exists y)Bxy$	4 EI
6	$(\exists x)(\exists y)Bxy$	1,2-5 EE

Exercise 9.3: Quantifier Derivations.

Problem 1. $\{(x)Px, (x)Mx, ((\exists x)Px \,\&\, Mx) \to (y)By\} \vdash Bs$

1	$(x)Px$	P
2	$(x)Mx$	P
3	$((\exists x)Px \,\&\, Mx) \to (y)By$	P
4	Ps	1 UE
5	Ms	2 UE
6	$Ps \,\&\, Ms$	4,5 CI
7	$(\exists x)Px \,\&\, Mx$	6 EI
8	$(y)By$	3,7 MP
9	Bs	8 UE

Problem 3. $\{(x)Px \,\&\, Qx, (x)Qx \,\&\, Rx\} \vdash (x)Px \,\&\, Rx$

1	$(x)Px \,\&\, Qx$	P
2	$(x)Qx \,\&\, Rx$	P
3	$Pa \,\&\, Qa$	1 UE
4	$Qa \,\&\, Ra$	2 UE
5	Pa	3 CE
6	Ra	4 CE
7	$Pa \,\&\, Ra$	5,6 CI
8	$(x)Px \,\&\, Rx$	7 UI

Problem 5. $\{(x)Px \leftrightarrow Qx, (x)Px \leftrightarrow Rx\} \vdash (x)Qx \leftrightarrow Rx$

1	$(x)Px \leftrightarrow Qx$	P
2	$(x)Px \leftrightarrow Rx$	P
3	Qa	H
4	Pa $\leftrightarrow$ Qa	1 EU
5	Pa	3,4 BCoE
6	Pa $\leftrightarrow$ Ra	2UE
7	Ra	5,6 BCoE
8	Ra	H
9	Pa $\leftrightarrow$ Ra	2 UE
10	Pa	8,9 BCoE
11	Pa $\leftrightarrow$ Qa	1 UE
12	Qa	10,11 BCoE
13	Qa $\leftrightarrow$ Ra	3-7,8-12 BCoI
14	$(x)Qx \leftrightarrow Rx$	13 UI

Problem 7. $\{(x)Px \& Qx, (\exists x)Qx \rightarrow Tx\} \vdash (\exists x)Px \& Tx$

1	$(x)Px \& Qx$	P
2	$(\exists x)Qx \rightarrow Tx$	P
3	Qa $\rightarrow$ Ta	H
4	Pa & Qa	1 UE
5	Qa	4 CE
6	Ta	3,5 MP
7	Pa	4 CE
8	Pa & Ta	6,7 CI
9	$(\exists x)Px \& Tx$	8 EI
10	$(\exists x)Px \& Tx$	2,3-9 EE

Problem 9. $\{\sim((x)Bx \vee (\exists x)Tx), (\exists x)Mx \rightarrow Ts\} \vdash (x)\sim Mx$

1	$\sim((x)Bx \vee (\exists x)Tx)$	P
2	$(\exists x)Mx \rightarrow Ts$	P
3	$\sim(x)Bx \& \sim(\exists x)Tx$	1 DeM
4	$\sim(\exists x)Tx$	3 CE
5	$(x)\sim Tx$	4 QN
6	$\sim Ts$	5 UE
7	$\sim(\exists x)Mx$	2,6 MT
8	$(x)\sim Mx$	7 QN

Problem 11. $\{(x)Pxx\} \vdash (z)Pzz$

1	$(x)Pxxx$	P
2	Paaa	1 UE
3	$(z)Pzzz$	2 UI

Problem 13. $\{(x)Gx \rightarrow Px, Gs\} \vdash (\exists y)Py$

1	$(x)Gx \rightarrow Px$	P
2	Gs	P
3	Gs $\rightarrow$ Ps	1 UE
4	Ps	2,3 MP
5	$(\exists y)Py$	4 EI

Problem 15. $\{(\exists x)Pxxx\} \vdash (\exists x)(\exists y)(\exists z)Pxyz$

1	$(\exists x)Pxxx$	P
2	Paaa	H
3	$(\exists z)Paaz$	1 EI
4	$(\exists y)(\exists z)Payz$	3 EI
5	$(\exists x)(\exists y)(\exists z)Pxyz$	4 EI
6	$(\exists x)(\exists y)(\exists z)Pxyz$	1,2-5 EE

SOLUTIONS TO ODD NUMBERED PROBLEMS

Problem 17. {(x)(y)Cxy} ⊢ (Caa & Cab) & (Cba & Cbb)

1	(x)(y)Cxy	P
2	(y)Cay	1 UE
3	Caa	2 UE
4	Cab	2 UE
5	(y)Cby	1 UE
6	Cba	5 UE
7	Cbb	5 UE
8	Caa & Cab	3,4 CI
9	Cba & Cbb	6,7 CI
10	(Caa & Cab) & ICba & Cbb)	8,9 CI

Problem 19. {((∃x)Px) → Pc} ⊢ ((∃x)Px) ↔ Pc

1	((∃x)Px) → Pc	P
2	(∃x)Px	H
3	Pc	1,2 MP
4	Pc	H
5	(∃x)Px	4 EI
6	((∃x)Px ↔ Pc	2-3,4-5 BCoI

Problem 21. {(x)(Hx & (Jxx & Mx))} ⊢ (∃x)Jxb & (x)Mx

1	(x)(Hx & (Jxx & Mx))	P
2	Hb & (Jbb & Mb)	1 UE
3	Jbb & Mb	2 CE
4	Jbb	3 CE
5	(∃x)Jxb	4 EI
6	Mb	3 CE
7	(x)Mx	6 UE
8	(∃x)Jxb & (x)Mx	5,7 CI

Problem 23. {(x)(y)(z)Bxyz} ⊢ (x)(y)(z)Bxyz → Bxyz

1	(x)(y)(z)Bxyz	P
2	(y)(z)Bayz	1 UE
3	(z)Babz	2 UE
4	Babc	3 UE
5	~Babc v Babc	4 DI
6	Babc → Babc	5 Impl
7	(z)Babz → Babz	6 UI
8	(y)(z)Bayz → Bayz	7 UI
9	(x)(y)(z)Bxyz → Bxyz	8 UI

Problem 25. {(x)(~Lx v (∃y)Ky)} ⊢ (∃x)Lx → (∃y)Ky

1	(x)(~Lx v (∃y)Ky)	P
2	(∃x)Lx	H
3	La	H
4	~La v (∃y)Ky	1 UE
5	(∃y)Ky	3,4 DE
6	(∃y)Ky	2,3-5 EE
7	(∃x)Lx → (∃y)Ky	2-6 CoI

Problem 27. {(∃x)(Cx v (y)(Wxy → Cy)), (x)(Wxa & ~Ca)} ⊢ (∃x)Cx

1	(∃x)(Cx v (y)(Wxy → Cy))	P
2	(x)(Wxa & ~Ca)	P
3	Cb v (y)(Wby → Cy)	H
4	Wba → Ca	H
5	Wba & ~Ca	2 UE
6	Wba	5 CE
7	Ca	4,6 MP
8	~Ca	5 CE
9	Ca & ~Ca	7,8 CI
10	~(Wba → Ca)	4-9 NI
11	(∃y)~(Wby → Cy)	10 EI
12	~(y)(Wby → Cy)	11 QN
13	Cb	3,12 DE
14	(∃x)Cx	13 EI
15	(∃x)Cx	1,3-14 EE

Problem 29. {(x)Px → Qx} ⊢ ((∃x)Px & (∃y)Qy) ↔ (∃z)Pz & Qz

1	(x)Px → Qx	P
2	(∃x)Px & (∃y)Qy	H
3	(∃x)Px	2 CE
4	Pa	H
5	Pa → Qa	1 UE
6	Qa	4,5 MP
7	Pa & Qa	4,6 CI
8	(∃z)Pz & Qz	7 EI
9	(∃z)Pz & Qz	3,4-8 EE
10	(∃z)Pz & Qz	H
11	Pa & Qa	H
12	Pa	11 CE
13	Qa	11 CE
14	(∃x)Px	12 EI
15	(∃y)Qy	13 EI
16	(∃x)Px & (∃y)Qy	14,15 CI
17	(∃x)Px & (∃y)Qy	10,11-16 EE
18	((∃x)Px & (∃y)Qy) ↔ (∃z)Pz & Qz	2-9,10-17 BCoI

Exercise 9.4: Theorems.

Problem 1. {} ⊢ (x)Px → (∃y)Py

1	(x)Px	H
2	Ps	1 UE
3	(∃y)Py	2 EI
4	(x)Px → (∃y)Py	1-3 CoI

Problem 3. {} ⊢ ((x)(Ax → Bx)) → ((x)Ax → (x)Bx)

1	(x)Ax → Bx	H
2	(x)Ax	H
3	Ad	2 UE
4	Ad → Bd	1 UE
5	Bd	3,4 MP
6	(x)Bx	5 UI
7	(x)Ax → (x)Bx	2-6 CoI
8	((x)Ax → Bx) → ((x)Ax → (x)Bx)	1-7 CoI

SOLUTIONS TO ODD NUMBERED PROBLEMS

Problem 5. $\{\} \vdash ((x)Ps \to Qx) \leftrightarrow (Ps \to (x)Qx))$

1	$(x)Ps \to Qx$	H
2	Ps	H
3	$Ps \to Qd$	1 UE
4	Qd	2,3 MP
5	$(x)Qx$	4 UI
6	$Ps \to (x)Qx$	2-5 CoI

7	$Ps \to (x)Qx$	H
8	Ps	H
9	$(x)Qx$	7,8 MP
10	Qd	9 UE
11	$Ps \to Qd$	8-10 CoI
12	$(x)Ps \to Qx$	11 UI

| 13 | $((x)Ps \to Qx) \leftrightarrow (Ps \to (x)Qx)$ | 1-6, 7-12 BCoI |

Problem 7. $\{\} \vdash (x)Px \leftrightarrow \sim(\exists x)\sim Px$

1	$(x)Px$	H
2	$\sim(\exists x)\sim Px$	1 QE

3	$\sim(\exists x)\sim Px$	H
4	$(x)Px$	3 QE

| 5 | $(x)Px \leftrightarrow \sim(\exists x)\sim Px$ | 1-2,3-4 BCoI |

Problem 9. $\{\} \vdash \sim(x)Px \leftrightarrow (\exists x)\sim Px$

1	$\sim(x)Px$	H
2	$(\exists x)\sim Px$	1QN

3	$(\exists x)\sim Px$	H
4	$\sim(x)Px$	3 QN

| 5 | $\sim(x)Px \leftrightarrow (\exists x)\sim Px$ | 1-2,3-4 BCoI |

Made in United States
North Haven, CT
31 August 2023

40968890R00138